Praise for *Ansv*

A *Financial Times* Bo

A *Daily Express* Book of the Year 2023

'Absorbing. Like all the best football books, *Answered Prayers* is not just about football; it's about hope and despair, friendship and enmity, and the character it takes to handle them' *Guardian* (Book of the Week)

'A magnificent, moving, often funny and deeply researched account . . . Is this just a book for those who know football? Far from it: this is a story of glory and the impermanence of fame' *Sunday Times* (Book of the Week)

'The finest sports book of the year by one of the country's most garlanded sports writers' *Daily Mail*

'Brilliant . . . Hamilton, arguably Britain's greatest sportswriter, tells [Ramsey's] tale with his wonderful panache. He is the master of the vivid phrase . . . Dry humour is never far from the surface in this book's pages' *Daily Express*

'Terrific. As good on post-war Britain as Peter Hennessy. Informed and heart-breaking' Stephen Frears

'An expert observer of different forms of Englishness, he treats sportspeople as three-dimensional humans' *Financial Times*

'Like Alf Ramsey's 1966 team, this book has depth, it has riches and it's a winner – the finest piece of sports writing I have read in ages and a superb piece of contemporary history. Duncan Hamilton's great gift is the blending of character, mood and moment. Even Ramsey might have showed a spasm of emotion were he here to read it' Peter Hennessy

'This may well be one of the best books ever written about football' *Choice Magazine*

DUNCAN HAMILTON has won three William Hill Sports Book of the Year Prizes. He has been nominated on a further four occasions. He has also claimed two British Sports Book Awards and is the first writer to have won the Wisden Cricket Book of the Year on three occasions. He lives at the foot of the Yorkshire Dales.

Also by Duncan Hamilton

Harold Larwood: The Biography
A Last English Summer
The Kings of Summer
A Clear Blue Sky (with Jonny Bairstow)
Wisden on Yorkshire (ed.)
Sweet Summers: The Cricket Writing of J. M. Kilburn
The Great Romantic
One Long and Beautiful Summer

Injury Time

Answered Prayers

England and the 1966 World Cup

Duncan Hamilton

riverrun

First published in Great Britain in 2023
This paperback edition published in 2024 by

riverrun

An imprint of

Quercus Editions Limited
Carmelite House
50 Victoria Embankment
London EC4Y 0DZ

An Hachette UK company

A CIP catalogue record for this book is available
from the British Library.

Paperback 978 1 52942 001 2
Ebook 978 152941 999 3

10 9 8 7 6 5 4 3 2 1

Typeset by Ian Bahrami

Printed and bound in Great Britain by Clays Ltd, Elcograf S.p.A.

Papers used by riverrun are from well-managed forests and other responsible sources.

To Penny. Welcome to the world (cup), beautiful girl.
And, of course, to Sarah and Joe too.

CONTENTS

CONTENTS

Prologue

THE FAR-OFF WORLD OF YESTERDAY

He is waiting for me on a street corner, wedged between two scruffy car parks. The view he gets, the buildings mostly slabby concrete, is so unlovely that even that genius son of Suffolk, John Constable, wouldn't be able to beautify the landscape in oil, on canvas and with a gilt frame.

He's dressed formally: a plain, two-buttoned suit and a collar and tie, the Windsor knot immaculate. His left hand is tucked into his trouser pocket. He's staring into the full brightness of a fat, noonday sun, his expression placidly inscrutable. Behind him, the blossom on a skeletal cherry tree is just beginning to froth – a sign of incipient spring. The sky, cloudless, is the kind of blue you find in a child's paintbox.

It is a little underwhelming – and also wildly incongruous – to be meeting Sir Alf Ramsey here, standing on his lonely plinth.

He is in a slightly dishevelled state. With a lack of respect that can only be deliberate, someone has left the tar-black imprint of the sole of their right boot against the pale stone. Someone else has tried to carve their name with a pocket knife just in front of Ramsey's toes; the gouging-out is crude and indecipherable, as though the perpetrator is still learning his alphabet.

The plinth, it must be said, is suffering from a lack of tender loving care too. The stone is discoloured in places, and Mother Nature has been allowed to wear down and wash away part of the straightforward inscription that tells the don't-knows what Ramsey achieved and when he did it.

This statue, cast in a fetching blue-grey bronze, can't avoid the ignominious fate of every other: it is messily speckled with pigeon shit, the colour of hot cigarette ash; and, when a woman walks in front of me with a muzzled boxer, the dog tries to cock its leg against the plinth, only to be dragged away on a rope lead.

Ramsey has occupied this spot for nearly a quarter of a century. I suppose it is the obvious place to have put him – the junction at which Portman Road and the long stretch of the 'Way' named after him come together beside Ipswich Town's ground, the high stands of which are about to envelop him in shadow. One of the stands is named after Ramsey, but its architecture, like so many modern structures, is blandly workmanlike. Buy a ticket, and you could be sitting anywhere.

I remember standing in the players' tunnel at Wembley, where a hideous bust of Ramsey sits inappropriately on a tall pedestal. It fails not only to restore him to the land of the living – he looks anciently weathered – but also to do him any kind of justice. The facial features, slightly awry, are so grimly morose that the piece reminded me of the poet William Blake's death mask.

Ramsey's statue at least captures his likeness: the high forehead; the unruly eyebrows; the thin lips, which sometimes made even a smile look like a grimace. It quite subtly, even subliminally, captures the essential elements of his character too. There is a certain dignity in the figure. I look at it nonetheless with an amalgam of bafflement and irritation. Is this all there *is* for someone who won a World Cup? Ramsey surely warrants something bolder and more visually striking. I begin comparing the statue with those of his contemporaries: Bill Shankly, his arms aloft in perpetual salute to the worshipping Kop at Liverpool; Brian Clough, who I always imagine is about to take four aggressive strides forward and wag his finger at me (as he so often did); Jock Stein, clutching the European Cup at Celtic Park, as though preparing to present it to the 'fans' without whom, he memorably said, 'football is nothing'; and Sir Matt Busby, in the elegantly romantic pose of the great elder statesman – one hand against his waist, the other resting a ball against his hip, his head turned and his gaze locked on the distant scene around Old Trafford.

Ramsey, though passionate in his own way, was incapable of displaying the frenetic zeal that poured from both Shankly and Clough. He demonstrably lacked what Stein and Busby had in abundance, which was *presence*, a quality difficult to define and even more difficult to describe unless you found yourself in the same room with them and instantly became conscious of it – a charge that disturbed the very air.

Ramsey had other attributes, other virtues.

Intellectually, he travelled light, but he was a scholarly football nerd with a memory so outrageously good as to be almost eidetic. He remembered, almost forever, minor details about matches that those who had played in them forgot ten minutes after climbing out of the communal bath. His commitment was all-consuming, no duty shirked. He tackled management with the devotion, self-sacrifice and conscientiousness of the priesthood. The man was the job, and vice versa.

He was among the motivating spirits of the 1960s, despite being, culturally and socially, entirely out of kilter with them. Amid the tumult of that decade, his manner, his appearance, his attitudes, his accent and his slightly tortured syntax and stiff turn of speech meant he looked and sounded as though he didn't belong, the puritan aghast at an orgy. Everything about Ramsey was buttoned up, held in check. Even on the touchline there were no gurning contortions of the face, no extravagant gestures, no eruptions of anger or celebration. His unwillingness to show or share his feelings was offered as proof that he didn't have any – and also that he didn't possess anything as complicated as a personality.

He didn't particularly rate too many of his rivals either. A quite priceless description of his brusqueness, which was often interpreted as arrogance, came from Stan Cullis, who revolutionised Wolverhampton Wanderers with the silverware he won for them. Cullis's venerable status meant he seldom received nagging tutorials from anyone, but he got several from Ramsey. 'One has the feeling when talking to him,' said Cullis, 'that he is a brilliant mathematics professor explaining a mundane problem to one of his duller students.'

Ramsey was also paranoid about Her Majesty's press. He had a habit of treating questions – often, even the most innocent – like bombs that were about to be detonated. Ramsey had a soft spot for some journalists – often well disguised – but considered most of them, 'dabbling' in what he called 'my profession', to be footballing amateurs masquerading as professionals. They portrayed him as slightly odd: a strange, remote man who was stolid, strictly one-dimensional and lacking any hinterland beyond the game. Some, dwelling on how awkward and uncooperative he could be, ganged up on him to accentuate the negative and harden that stereotype. So, in the beginning, did the ordinary fan, who struggled to make sense of Ramsey, and consequently underrated him.

The full charge sheet against Ramsey would fill both sides of an A4 page – and possibly a third. The list always starts with the following complaints: aloof and coldly stand-offish, intransigent, haughtily superior, broodingly intense, secretive, fiercely demanding, disdainful of interference and also of being contradicted, not always tolerant of dolts, bores and time-wasters, and obsessively and uncompromisingly single-minded in pursuit of what he sought.

If Ramsey hadn't been any of those things, he'd never have done what he did. He would never have prospered after an impoverished, hard-scrabble upbringing. He would never have gone from anonymous Second Division right back at Southampton to briefly become England's captain. He would never have recovered from the sleight, real rather than imagined, that Tottenham delivered, denying him the coaching position he believed was his entitlement. He would never have taken a modest country-town club from the Third Division to the League Championship in seven seasons. When, in 1961–2, Ipswich arrived in the First Division, Ramsey was the short-odds favourite to crash-land, bloody nose first, back where he'd come from, which was near obscurity. That he won the title was – and remains – one of the most extraordinarily improbable successes in the whole history of the competition. And he would certainly never have survived the criticism

– a shower of arrows with poisonous tips – he got as England's boss before 1966. Anyone less resolute would have either broken down or chucked it in.

It's why I've become ever so slightly obsessed with his story and England's. Indeed, it's why I've trekked here to look the old boy in the eye and tell him so. The more I've read about Ramsey, or watched and listened to the interviews he gave and the coverage he got, the more fascinatingly enigmatic he's become to me, like a crossword puzzle with few clues and a lot of blanks.

It is true that even those who thought they knew him reasonably well did not understand him completely. It is also true that attempts to get him to talk about himself – especially if it involved making his private life public – were nearly always doomed. He believed only his work mattered; the rest was gossip.

I think the mistake, committed regularly, is to believe that Ramsey acted the way he did solely out of towering self-regard. He was actually just naturally shy and reserved, and as prone to as much self-doubt as the rest of us. Any requirement to put on a show was a source of horror for him, which is why he didn't try to do it.

Instead, he hid behind the protective shell he built for himself. That shell was tougher than tungsten.

He saw no need to be loved, except by those he loved in return. He also saw no need to be respected, except by his team. If you want to know what player loyalty truly means – as well as what it inspires – evidence comes in two near-identical sentiments about Ramsey, expressed at two different times and in two different places, thus excluding the possibility of collusion.

'On the field, I'd have given my life for Alf Ramsey,' Alan Ball once said.

Nobby Stiles would have done so too: 'I went on to a pitch prepared, if necessary, to die there for him,' he explained.

Ramsey's statue and its surroundings are too unprepossessing for someone held in that kind of awe. If I hadn't been searching for it, I could almost have strolled past without realising it was there. He warrants something finer, grander and terrifically grandiose, even gilded. His chiselled epitaph ought to be made from stirring quotations, or a block of poetry, rather than a collection of bland dates separated by short dashes.

I sense, though, that these days Ramsey is regarded as someone who belongs to yesterday; after all, '66 is a far-off dot now. The World Cup recedes into the past, slowly becoming a memory of a memory, which makes it blithely easy to take Ramsey and his achievement for granted.

In fact, here's my confession: I was guilty of doing exactly that – until something forced me to look harder at him and think longer about him.

* * *

On a Sunday in June 2020, during the trauma of the first pandemic lockdown, I watched England win the World Cup again. The BBC's pictures and Kenneth Wolstenholme's commentary were being broadcast by Channel 4 to raise funds for the National Emergencies Trust, a charitable cause for those whose lives had been affected by Covid.

I can't tell you how many times I've seen the final, either whole or in glittering parts, since the afternoon on which it was played. I stopped counting decades ago. As it always will, the game brought back everything I remember about that mild midsummer's day. My memories are just scraps. I was nearly eight years old, already captivated by football, but not yet compulsively devoted to it.

I see myself sitting on the brown leather sofa in the living room of my maternal grandfather's council house. I am striving to make sense – largely in silence – of what I am watching. I see my grandfather, leaning forward in his chair as though he desperately wants to kick every ball, save every shot, make every sliding tackle. I see my father occupying the chair beside the unlit coal fire. He is mirroring each move and every anguished or elated sound that my grandfather makes. Even my father, a Scot from Stirling, badly wants England to win.

The TV is black and white. The convex screen, set into a walnut case, is the size of a postage stamp. The TV rests on top of a plain, highly polished table two feet high and two feet across (I can be precise about those measurements: that table now belongs to me).

Way beyond my comprehension are both the significance of the occasion and the importance of the result. The magnitude of the triumph entirely escapes me. I have no conception – how could I? – of the swelling pride it generates, the blows it has struck on behalf of the country and the bragging rights it brings.

Caught in the bright glare of the sun, which filters through white net curtains, my grandfather and my father collapse into a half-embrace in the middle of the living room after the final whistle. On TV, the Charlton brothers, born and brought up only 11 miles from my grandfather's front door, are hugging one another too.

To win the World Cup? To beat West Germany? No, I don't get it. Not really. Why is this so special?

I am unaware that cities are still being swept clean of rubble; that parts of towns are still being rebuilt; that grieving, as horrible as slow suffocation, is still gripping those who lost a loved one during a war that ended just 21 years before; and that because 21 years is merely an eye-blink in time, no one has forgotten and very few have forgiven, and a lot, probably most, never will.

I do not understand that the last few crowded hours have epitomised George Orwell's definition of sport as 'war minus the shooting'. I have no idea what my grandfather is talking about when he loudly proclaims that the party to come will be like VE Day all over again. The morning after the night before will be one of hangovers and headaches and misty recollections of someone drinking themselves cross-eyed on beer that costs two shillings a pint before standing on a table to sing 'There'll Always Be an England'.

I know only that *we* have won; that the game has finished 4–2, a score that suggests the result is more emphatic than it actually is (my father says so); that *we* are lifting a trophy with wings that looks very small and modestly un-grand to me; that, outside, the neighbours are rushing into the road, carrying with them beer in brown bottles; that everyone is yelling all at once, like a discordant choir, and banging wooden spoons against pots and pans or waving rattles. Above even that commotion, I hear the blare of a horn from the only car anyone among the two rows of 150 houses possesses. This was an outpouring of euphoria that I had not witnessed before and have seldom seen since.

I'm certain that as the sun went down on that day, I could not have described to you any of the goals (apart from the last) and absolutely none of the pivotal moments around them. I wasn't aware that England were called 'the wingless wonders', seldom a compliment, because of their 4–3–3 formation. With the exception of the Charltons, who, as Geordies, counted as extended members of our family, I knew by sight only Bobby Moore, Gordon Banks (already I had an interest in goalkeepers and the lonely art of goalkeeping) and Nobby Stiles, distinguishable because of the gap where his four front teeth ought to have been. Geoff Hurst, a player about whom I'd previously been ignorant, added himself to the list only when everyone else began sentences that started with his name, singing it like a hallelujah.

If the final had been broadcast in colour, I suppose I would have known about Alan Ball too; his red hair glowed to the extent that you could have tracked his box-to-box running from the moon with a telescope. Within a week, I could reel off the whole team in formation and by number; Ball, Ray Wilson, George Cohen, Martin Peters and Roger Hunt were no longer strangers to me. When I read that Hurst's World Cup breakfast had been beans on toast, I demanded the same meal, which I ate every day for two months.

No game staged in this country – and very few that have been staged elsewhere – has subsequently been picked apart and then put together again so often in an effort to explain definitively what happened and why. So, despite the fact that I sat through it, the way I see and judge the final, and everything I know about how it was played – the teams, the tactics, the drama, the dominant personalities and the peripheral characters – was all learnt second-hand.

My knowledge was accumulated from TV replays and a lifetime of reading a library of books. Ghosted autobiographies pock-marked with clichés. Newspaper reports preserved between hard covers. Contemporary histories written at speed. Oral histories in which a whole cloud of witnesses, who were 50 yards or more from the tunnel end, claim to have seen the ball for England's third goal emphatically cross the line, thus establishing their eyesight as being equal to that of a sparrowhawk gliding over a cornfield. Sober scissor-and-paste jobs, done with the benefit of hindsight but not much insight. Fat albums of photographs on glossy paper that prove how comically different the 1960s were, not only from this century, but also from the 1970s. Scrupulously faithful minute-by-minute accounts of the match in which nothing is left out. Like Charles Darwin, for whom no evolutionary occurrence was trivial, the compilers of these kinds of books record a throw-in near a corner flag or a player retying his laces because the act, however small, impacts in some way upon the bigger pattern of the game.

Memory is such a subjective and temperamental beast, susceptible to benign misrememberings. Childhood memories are particularly erratic and unreliable. I can nevertheless describe, vividly and with as much veracity as the scene in front of me at the final whistle, my grandfather's invitation to me the following morning. He loved newspapers; I think my own love of them began with him. He'd read them from back page to front, and then from front to back, afraid he'd overlooked a paragraph. He'd devour even the six-point type of the small ads and family notices. Early on that Sunday, my grandfather asked me to go with him to the newsagent's. He was scared the shop would be quickly stripped bare of stock. He bought one copy of every paper on the counter, tucking each title beneath his arm. All that newsprint was like a thick roll of carpet. When we got home, he washed the ink from his hands in the kitchen sink. He then took the papers to the dining table and read the headlines to me, savouring the words.

I remember that weekend because of the way the World Cup made my grandfather feel. Because he was happy, I was happy too. That's why something of the final – the important bits – has stayed with me.

There is a coda to this.

At some stage in the very early 1980s – I'm guessing around the fifteenth anniversary of the final – I found myself at Colindale, which was then the dingy home of the British Newspaper Library. After you'd filled in a short form, you'd get in return a colossal bound volume, heavier than a paving slab, or a silver tin containing microfilm. With an hour or two to spare, I decided to scroll through the tabloids and broadsheets from that weekend in 1966: the *Sunday Times* and *Sunday Mirror*, the *Observer* and the *Sunday People*, the *Sunday Express* and the *Sunday Telegraph*. I re-read the headlines:

World Beaters

Glory Boys!

Champions of the World

On Top of the World

Hail to the Masters

I hoped I'd hear my grandfather's voice reading them aloud again. The most astonishing thing happened: I did.

When I began to go through some of the reports, not only from that day but also from the days before and afterwards, I realised at last the full depth and breadth of the emotions the '66 World Cup stirred. In the celebratory prose-poetry, I traced easily the belief that justice had been done and retribution meted out, the result seen as a moral reckoning. Jingoism and gloating amid the joy was seen as perfectly understandable then – and even excusable too – because the suffering was still so raw and the causes and events behind it still so close to those who had lived through them. Their lives, whether awake or asleep, were dominated by thoughts and references to the war. Slim as they were – BBC2 was available to only a sliver of the country – the TV schedules on BBC1 and ITV were stuffed with war films, war dramas, war documentaries and discussion programmes that refought it on a weekly or, occasionally, daily basis, lest we forgot. The war was ever-present, shadowing nearly everything, even when no one talked about it.

As I thought about this, something struck me as profoundly ironic. One word captured the country's mood after that World Cup.

That word is German: *Schadenfreude*.

* * *

We have an awful habit of not seeing properly whatever becomes overfamiliar to us. A place. A building. Even a person. We stop noticing the everyday things, shutting our eyes to them and losing interest. We look properly at them again only when some fundamental change occurs.

The 1966 World Cup falls into that category.

We continued to go through the motions of commemorating that immense summer. We politely ticked off each anniversary and we also summoned up the spirit of it, along with the participants, before every England team set off into Europe, Asia or South America, bidding to imitate the feat of winning the trophy. But, increasingly, it felt to me that all these commemorations resembled everyone's family Christmas – marked with weary set rituals that were done more out of duty, obligation and respect for our elders rather than enthusiasm. Always flashed before us were the same images, which constant repetition had dulled: Wembley dressed for the occasion, the flags aflutter from the Twin Towers; the six goals and Geoff Hurst's 'perfect' hat-trick (header, right foot, left foot); Bobby Moore wiping his sweaty palms on the red–brown velvet of the Royal Box to avoid staining the Queen's white gloves, cut from the smoothest Egyptian cotton;

the spring-heeled lap of honour, on which Nobby Stiles skips along, swinging both his arms like a schoolboy on a seaside holiday. There were hoary stories and recycled jokes, the punchlines arriving with a stagey emphasis crafted through practice. Each of these retellings was sometimes subtly different from the one before, coming with a tiny elaboration or innocent embellishment.

In the end, I didn't know how to tell what was truth, what was half-truth and what was a full-blown fairy tale that stemmed from either a willingness to please an audience or wishful thinking. I saw and heard nothing I hadn't seen or listened to before. So, despite the oceans of time I'd devoted to studying '66, I finally grew bored and yawned in a 'no, not this again' sort of way.

Knowing what was coming next, I moved on or switched over. Disillusion and disinterest set firm in me, like concrete. It belonged to antiquity. I stopped watching and listening. Nor did I care. But Channel 4's decision to show the final in its entirety changed the way I thought about the World Cup, the legacy it left and also the 12 men – 11 players, plus Alf Ramsey – whom that day bound together like climbers tied to the same rope.

I didn't plan to watch the game. Indeed, I intended to avoid it. I thought the programme was designed for chronic nostalgics, eager for another moving meditation on the passing of time and the longed-for music of the past.

I was wrong. For me, it flipped the story of '66 on its head.

* * *

I couldn't find anything else to watch, which is why the match was already ten minutes old before I caught up with it.

The TV coverage of that day was penny-plain. No clock ticked away in the corner beside the scoreline. There were no sophisticated replays, instantly shown from half a dozen different angles. You got a wide view of the play, as though you were watching from a seat in the top tier of the South Stand. There were no garish, whizz-bang graphics that broke down the possession percentages, the number of shots on and off target, the number of corners and those critical areas of the pitch where one team had dominated the other.

It didn't matter.

I can't logically explain what happened. Nor can I quite rationalise how I felt about it afterwards. Perhaps it was because I hadn't seen the BBC's coverage of the final for a while (for over a decade, actually). Perhaps it was Kenneth Wolstenholme's gentle, almost understated but mellifluous commentary ('Here's Ball, running himself daft'). Perhaps melancholy, induced by the pandemic, made me so much more sensitive to the past. Or perhaps, in just wanting to escape the present, I was finding solace in the small mercies of the far-off world of yesterday.

Whatever the reason, I couldn't take my eyes off the screen.

The French phrase *jamais vu* is the opposite of *déjà vu*. The words sum up the most peculiar sensation of looking at something that is well known to you, but experiencing the thing as though seeing it for the first time. Hard though it is to believe, this is how the final appeared to me. I thought I knew the match well, but discovered in fact that I didn't know it at all.

I studied the recording analytically rather than superficially, and everything about it seemed clearer, sharper. It also brought back – and with a flashbulb immediacy – the intimate memories I had of originally watching the game live in my grandfather's living room. I even began to fret about whether England would win in extra time.

It wasn't the major turning points of the match that captivated me. Not the goals, for sure. It was the trivial things, so commonly inconsequential at the time that I didn't notice them.

The way Wembley looked without pitch-side advertising.

The Queen, only 40 years and two months old.

Gordon Banks bouncing the ball from his gloved hands and launching it upfield.

Every player in black boots.

Every player's shirt tucked neatly into his shorts.

Those shirts unsullied by sponsors' logos spread across the chest or a name ironed on to the back.

How no one is caught sending a gob of spit on to the turf.

How no one in the wild chorus of the crowd flicks a V-sign or gives the cameraman the middle finger and screeches, 'Fuck off.'

How the Union Jack, rather than the flag of St George, is prominent around the stadium.

How no player is booked for 'simulation', a fall as fast as a stone's down a well, because no one dares to dive on to his belly in a ludicrous attempt to con the officials.

How sedate some of the build-up seems when compared to the speed of the Premier League, where every counter-attack is a lightning strike.

That there were no substitutes . . . that no one perpetually monstered the referee after he made a contentious decision . . . that no one tried to steal a sneaky five yards with a free kick or a throw-in . . . that no one feigned injury in some pathetic display of amateur dramatics . . . and that even in the last gasps of extra time, when England's lead is still a solitary goal, how no one in a red shirt tossed the ball away, kicked it into the cheap seats or dragged it towards a corner flag, trying to whittle minutes down to seconds.

Channel 4 got an initial audience of 2.5 million for the final, and enough social media attention during it and afterwards to soon garner another quarter of a million downloads. I asked myself how the present generation – some, no doubt, the same age or only a wee bit older than I'd been in '66 – would be reacting to what I supposed could be their first taste of it. Amazed at all the fuss? Unaware, as I had once been, of why everyone was investing so much passion into this game? Asking themselves how, during the dispute about Geoff Hurst's second goal, goal-line technology and the referee's 'special watch' hadn't delivered a definitive judgement?

Nothing was more poignant or more visceral for me than the very end. As Hurst makes a fist with his right hand, raises it and thumps the air. As Jack Charlton sinks to his knees in the D of the German box, both hands smothering his face. As his brother, out of physical and emotional exhaustion, begins to weep, his tears the size of sixpences. As Moore plants a kiss on Ball's cheek. As Ball embraces first Cohen and then Wilson. The camera switches rapidly from one player to the other. In full frame, and very close-up, we see what victory looks like.

But then, and out of nowhere, something occurred to me in a way it had never done before. It started when I heard Wolstenholme describe the achievement as the 'greatest' in 'English sporting history'. He said it just as Moore was about to take the first of those dog-leg 39 steps separating him from the Queen in the Royal Box. I looked at Moore and then from one player to the next. I also looked at Alf Ramsey, who was displaying an Apollonian calm while nimbly sidestepping almost every attempt to push him into the spotlight's glare.

Like most middle-aged men in the '60s, Ramsey, who was only 46, seemed older than he was; in his windcheater-style tracksuit top, he could have passed for someone in his 50s. The average age of his team was a smidgen above 26. It would have been younger still without the 'grey beards': Jack Charlton had turned 31 in early May; Ray Wilson would be 32 in mid-December.

As a boy, I'd queued for the autograph of each member of the England team. As a journalist, I'd either met and/or interviewed all but one of them: Wilson was the only player who'd eluded me; he was like the sticker you can't find to complete an album.

Jack Charlton was the primary focus of my O-level English project, and for a while we became pen pals. I still have the school essay I wrote about him – my teenage handwriting no longer recognisable to me – clipped inside its original green ring binder, chosen to match the colour of a football pitch.

Over a period of six months, Bobby Charlton and I ran into one another frequently, usually when we were competing for one sports-book prize or another. I interviewed Hurst in a bookmaker's, which he had opened, and Moore in the office of the holiday company he owned. I spoke to Peters at Tottenham, Hunt in front of the trophy cabinet at Anfield, Cohen at Wembley and Ball at both Goodison Park and Highbury. Banks came to snip the ribbon on a new five-a-side pitch not far from where I lived. I talked to Stiles about his sending-off in a World Club Championship final, shortly before I set off to cover another of those matches myself.

In '66, we regarded these men as superheroes. We did not think they would succumb to the precariousness of life.

Succumb, though, they did.

We watched them grow older. We noted the lines and the light fissures on their faces. The bagginess beneath the eyes. Their hair thinning or getting greyer. Their puff-boated cheeks. Their stomach thickening to fat.

Five of the team (Moore, Hurst, Cohen, Wilson, Hunt) would never claim another winners' medal.

One (Moore) would die of cancer at 51.

Another (Ball) would die at 61 of a heart attack.

One (Banks) would lose an eye in a car crash, ending both his England and his First Division career at 34, his goalkeeping peak unrealised.

One (Cohen) would be diagnosed with cancer within a decade of collecting his winners' medal.

Six (both the Charlton brothers, Wilson, Stiles, Peters and Ramsey) suffered from dementia, their memories of that July day and every other stolen one by one.

Just two players (Jack Charlton and Ball) would manage a club at the highest level – and only Charlton would go on to manage internationally.

The glory of '66 seemed all too brief a treat to me; and the further you got away from it, the less of a blessing it looked. For someone such as Moore, it seemed the best of times – and with the promise of better times still ahead. But it led him nowhere. It was as though he'd spent all the luck available to him on winning the World Cup. I remembered seeing Moore only a fortnight before his passing. Cadaverously thin, he was silently drinking tea in the press room at Wembley before his shift on Capital Radio. He was so frail, so insubstantial, that he looked like a reflection of a man in water.

And what followed the World Cup final for England – and also for Ramsey – was not a beginning but an end, a decline and fall that happened over seven and a half troubled years.

Defeat against Scotland at Wembley in 1967.

Defeat against Yugoslavia in the semi-finals of the European Championships in 1968.

Defeat against West Germany in the 1970 World Cup.

Defeat – again to the Germans – in the 1972 European Championships.

Defeat against Poland in the World Cup qualifier of 1973.

The sack for Ramsey in 1974.

We live our lives forwards, but we only understand them backwards, after enough time has accrued to bring perspective and order to the jumble of everything. When I mentally stacked up all the evidence, 1966 seemed more like a punishment or the ultimate pyrrhic victory. It made my heart heave that most of these World Cup winners went through a disproportionate number of disappointments and unconscionably tolerated so many snubs – especially from the Football Association. Their lives, too, faded in and out of focus for us, depending on whether or not '66 got forced to the forefront of our minds.

I thought of how, throughout the 1980s and early '90s, I'd witnessed Hurst, Ball, Peters, Stiles and Banks enduring those black-tie banquets usually held in city-centre hotels. The format of these midweek functions soon became depressingly familiar to me: a compère who thought the night was about him; an unfunny comedian; a raffle; an auction; the speech; the Q&A. Whichever player turned up to entertain us, he always seemed a bit perplexed that anyone had paid to eat a plate of rubber chicken and some lukewarm vegetables just to listen to him. Afterwards, blowhard businessmen swilling brandy would slap him on the back to get his attention. These bores would then spout on interminably, as though their ticket allowed them to be a bloody nuisance and damnably rude. Often I'd overhear them, too tipsy to be self-aware, lecturing a World Cup winner about the seminal points of the final, as if the player himself knew the match less intimately than they did. I attended one dinner during which Hurst had to display the patience of a thousand Jobs. A diner asked him repeatedly: 'You're not really convinced, are you, that the ball crossed the line?'

You'd find the World Cup winners signing reproduction shirts, photographs from the final or replicas of the ball. They'd bring out autobiographies. They'd be asked – occasionally – to endorse or sponsor a product. They'd take part in TV programmes about the tournament or the 1960s themselves.

I saw them as benign prisoners of that final, obliged to relive it over and over again because no one wanted to know anything else about them. They were rooted in a single day, which made them rootless in others. The FA was a collaborator in this, careless and uncaring towards them and their manager. Unless it suited their agenda, which usually involved wheeling the players out for another anniversary, the FA treated most of them lousily at best and contemptibly at worst. I felt simultaneously wistful, sad and angry about that.

I began to think about how we treat our heroes, the rewards we give and those we don't. I thought about what happens when those heroes grow old. I thought about the impermanence of fame and the nature of celebrity. I thought about how English football hadn't properly capitalised on the prize Ramsey had handed it; how, indeed, the white heat that the World Cup gave off cooled far too quickly, the promise and optimism it generated unfulfilled.

I thought of how the '60s only looked glamorous to me now through football.

As I followed the celebrations, I had the benefit of knowing what Ramsey and his players possessed no inkling of, which is what came next for them. I knew how, for some of these boys of summer, everything after that day and this shimmering moment was going to be an anticlimax or a setback of one sort or another.

I couldn't bear to sit through it any longer. I switched channels, leaving the World Cup winners on the turf at Wembley, blissfully ignorant of their futures.

* * *

I met Alf Ramsey twice.

I was a 14-year-old autograph hunter, lurking in the car park at Nottingham Forest's City Ground in February 1974. The newspapers had publicised Ramsey's 'scouting trip' there in advance. Unlikely as it seems, he had come to watch a Second Division game between Forest and Middlesbrough. I brought a colour magazine photograph of him, which I clipped on to an inside page of the latest *Topical Times* annual.

I regard it now as one of the better photos ever taken of him. It's a studio portrait in which he cradles the World Cup in his hands. I guess Ramsey, who looks vibrantly healthy, sat for it either in late 1966 or early 1967. He wasn't photogenic, the lens didn't love him, and he always gave the impression of disliking the attention of photographers and regarding the requirement to pose for them as either a chore or a bother. In this one, however, Ramsey looks more relaxed than usual; he's even faintly smiling.

My experience chasing autographs ought to have taught me that the photo was unsuitable for his signature. In it he wears a suit blacker than the boards of the King James Bible. When I handed him my biro, the only place he could possibly sign was across the length of the gold trophy. I remember his gentle apology about there being 'no other option' for him, as though he – rather than I – was to blame for the inconvenience.

Three months later, Ramsey was sacked as England's manager.

Flash-forward to late autumn, 1977.

As the naïvest of know-nothing cub reporters, I tagged along to a press conference he was persuaded to hold, again at the City Ground. He was surrounded in the main corridor, cutting off his possible route of escape, and then manoeuvred against the dimpled windows that ran floor to ceiling. Ramsey shrank into his overcoat, looking so vulnerable that you'd have thought he feared his interrogators with pens and notepads were really torturers who might, if provoked, be prepared to extract information from him by tearing out each of his fingernails. I was struck by the fact that Ramsey spoke while barely moving his lips, staring straight ahead and standing still. He reminded me of a stage ventriloquist who had forgotten to bring his dummy. At one stage, he batted off a question that evidently irritated him by saying: 'I have told you before, gentlemen, that a manager gets too much praise when things go well and too much criticism when things go badly.'

In the days following that Channel 4 programme, I couldn't shake loose those pictures of Ramsey in '66 and also the two close-up views I got of him more than a decade later. During that press conference, he had surely been referring to himself, possibly not so much in relation to the praise but to the bite of criticism.

I finally realised this: we don't fully appreciate *how* England won that World Cup. Or the way in which the team, like travellers arriving from different directions, converged on the same spot in '66. Or, above all, how Ramsey withstood the pressure and the high expectations placed on him. Or the colossal debt still owed to him.

I told his statue all this, very quietly.

The author's autographed magazine photograph of Alf Ramsey, the
signature faint with age

PART ONE

1

DO YOU PLAY FOOTBALL?

The writer W. G. Sebald asked: 'How far must one go back to find the beginning?' Sebald believed beginnings were manifestly more difficult to identify than endings. Where something truly started, and when, is elusive, usually difficult to track definitively because both are surrounded by false dawns, missteps or wrong turns that lead nowhere.

But Alf Ramsey's path towards 1966 can be traced to a specific month and year: August 1949, the moment he began to play for Arthur Rowe.

Rowe was a lean man, his hair flecked with grey. His dark-rimmed eyes, the skin beneath baggy, were beginning to sink into their sockets because of the daily demands of his work and his need for perfection.

Rowe wore flannels and a jacket, often clipping two pens into his top pocket, like a factory foreman. He was a true 'Tottenham Cockney', born – in 1906 – to the sound of club's cockerel mascot rather than the peel of Bow Bells. His home was a mile from White Hart Lane; he could see the rise of the club's stands from his doorstep.

As a player with Spurs, Rowe had been a centre half with a creative streak, winning one cap for England, before a cartilage injury forced him into slightly premature retirement in 1938. After the war, he took charge of Southern League Chelmsford, staying for four years and winning both the League and the Cup. These trophies were sufficient for Spurs, lolling about in the Second Division, to take a risk on him as manager in May 1949.

In that same month, Ramsey, bought on the cheap from Southampton, became Rowe's first signing – though the nuts and bolts of the deal had been fixed and tightened well before he signed his contract and arrived at White Hart Lane.

Rowe, the polite revolutionary, became the first of two men, wildly different from one another, who count as almost hidden figures in Ramsey's life because history has either forgotten them or sorely under-appreciated their contribution. No one was more important to his career than Rowe. He turned Ramsey into a manager by showing him how to act, think, philosophise and problem-solve like one.

In retrospect, it seems as though each was destined to work with the other – and that long, invisible threads pulled them together.

Until the introductions took place at pre-season training, Ramsey would not have recognised Rowe if the pair of them had passed one another on a deserted high street. When Ramsey received his instructions from Spurs, telling him where and when to report, he examined Rowe's signature at the bottom of the letter and admitted: 'It 'meant nothing to me'. He knew only that Rowe was 'a new boy' like him.

When Ramsey began working with Rowe, he immediately recognised him as both a mentor and a role model. He found a visionary, innovative coach unlike any other in the post-war English game. 'We became the closest of friends,' he said. He rated Rowe as a 'very great' man who 'knew what he wanted'.

Theirs was a mutual admiration society comprising only two members. The feeling of compatibility came unbidden and happened instantly. As Rowe confessed, attempting to explain the coming together of minds that thought identically: 'If you can like people on sight, we liked each other.'

Self-improvement constantly motivated Ramsey, who chose his confidantes, such as Rowe, with calculation, seeking out only those whose brains he could profitably pick. Strictly in terms of football, the relationship, which began predictably enough, like a professor tutoring an eager student, became in the end more like a proud father nurturing a nakedly ambitious son.

Rowe drew as much out of the experience as Ramsey did: 'I got a player who I could talk to and who could help me. If I was making a change, I would ask Alf: "What do you think?"' Ramsey had a habit of chewing on the question for a while, before telling Rowe: 'Yes, I think you are probably right,' slowly emphasising the word 'probably', as if italicising it.

Like Ramsey, Rowe would talk about football until his tongue went dry. Like Ramsey, his idea of a roaringly good night out was to go and watch a match – even if it was a kick-about in a park. Like Ramsey, he had an appreciation of the past – the players, the managers, the tactics – because of the conclusions he could draw from it. Also like Ramsey, he read newspapers voraciously to collect information about the opposition.

Rowe had briefly studied in Hungary, where he found an 11-year-old starlet precocious enough to retain possession of the ball as though it were his personal property. No one, said the instantly smitten Rowe, could rob him of that ball. With the audacity of a circus juggler, he could play keepy-up – using his knees, thighs, chest, head and back, as well as his feet – until he got bored with his own brilliance, a process that could take as long as an hour. The boy's name was Ferenc Puskás. Only the outbreak of war dragged Rowe back to England and away from the chance of a lifetime: Hungary had wanted to appoint him as their national coach.

He and Ramsey spent hour upon hour discussing players and systems. Rowe espoused 'definitive and original ideas as to how the game should be played', said Ramsey. Each of these chimed with his own thoughts. He soaked up all the learning Rowe passed on and endlessly asked him supplementary questions. Early on, Rowe discovered that Ramsey was prone to temper tantrums, ignited by frustration, whenever a ploy didn't work or a player failed to follow a pre-set plan. What Rowe said he witnessed from him was 'a volcano of passion, desire and ambition'. Initially shocked by his transformation in character, Rowe came eventually to admire it. Flattered by Ramsey's worship, he looked at him and saw his own reflection. For his part, Ramsey always carried with him what he'd been taught, often slavishly copying without apology or proper acknowledgement. It's said that talent borrows, but genius steals; Ramsey blatantly stole the lot from Rowe, the purloining overt and never resented.

Everything that came later for him he owed to Rowe's patience, tutelage and influence.

* * *

When Alf Ramsey first came into Arthur Rowe's orbit, he was barely a 'name' in his own household – despite possessing a solitary England cap.

His career had already been through one false start. Ramsey was a centre half when Portsmouth, FA Cup winners in 1939, signed him as an amateur. The club then allowed his contract to expire, as though handing it to him in the first place had been an administrative error; Ramsey never kicked a ball for them. With the war under way, he played for the army, including back-to-back games against Southampton, then of Division Two. A Ramsey-led defence ruinously leaked ten goals in the first and another four in the second. Southampton nevertheless saw something in Ramsey that he didn't see in himself. Ramsey briefly became a centre forward before switching to right back. He had no inkling why Southampton thought of him as a natural fit for that position. He made his league debut, against Plymouth Argyle, in October 1946. It took him only another 26 months – in December 1948 – to break into the England team.

Things went so well before his international debut against Switzerland that the setback Ramsey suffered six weeks afterwards – severely strained knee ligaments – seemed inconceivable to him. The player he'd displaced in the Southampton side now displaced him. As if Ramsey didn't have enough to fret about, the club gave him a warning rather than its support. This, coldly delivered, came at a stage when

6

he 'could not even trot around the track'. Ramsey was told he might 'never regain' his shirt. He immediately demanded a transfer, so 'upset' that he subsequently refused all appeals to withdraw it.

Tottenham had tried – and failed – to buy him before the transfer deadline of 1949. Finally, accepting that Ramsey would never change his attitude towards them, Southampton reluctantly agreed to let him go. Rowe's assistant was Jimmy Anderson, a child of Victorian England. He did the grunt work, but dressed flamboyantly in plus-fours, which made him look like a golfer from the 1920s. Spurs were Anderson's whole world. He went from ground-staff boy to would-be player who couldn't cut it, and then on to part-time training and coaching positions. Anderson was constantly given roles because he happened to be there, handy and available whenever Spurs needed someone to fill them.

Anderson, after negotiating the deal, bragged that Ramsey had cost less than £5,000 because he'd flimflammed gullible Southampton. He persuaded them that Eddie Jones, Spurs' Welsh winger, taken in part exchange, was worth as much as £16,000.

Ramsey, wanting to play in London, had believed that Fulham would take him to Craven Cottage. He misread those runes. Fulham, freshly promoted, dismissed him as a bit player, not remotely well known enough for the First Division.

That fact isn't as peculiar as it seems. In 1949, there were five general sports magazines, but apart from the *FA News* and *The Official Journal of the Players' Union*, none was dedicated to football. Only the most prominent players were seen on cinema newsreels or chosen to appear on cigarette cards. Newspapers published few photos, many of those just smudgy headshots.

When Ramsey was chosen for an England squad, he reported to London's Great Western Hotel. He sat in the lounge and watched his new colleagues arrive. Among them were Stanley Matthews, Tommy Lawton, Frank Swift, Wilf Mannion and Tom Finney. None of them recognised him. Nor did one of the England trainers, baffled after

Ramsey shyly went to shake hands with him. Even after his third cap, against Scotland in 1950, two autograph hunters went across to Ramsey, who was 'standing quietly in a corner'. 'Do you play football?' asked one of them. Ramsey gave him a 'friendly smile', shuffling his feet embarrassedly. 'No, son,' he said. 'I don't play football. I only try to.'

The move to Spurs, which Ramsey hadn't wanted, stripped away his anonymity. Within another year, Turf Cigarettes had put his photograph on card number 34.

The series was called '50 Famous Footballers'.

* * *

Just as Tottenham were about to begin what became their League Championship season of 1950–1, the magazine *Illustrated,* competing against *Picture Post*, dispatched its 'star football reporter', Billy Wright, to White Hart Lane to put together a feature titled 'Secrets of Soccer'.

The photographer accompanying Wright arranged Spurs' staff – from players to 'ticket supervisor' – on the training ground. The Spurs players, arms folded, peered up at the camera wearing collared shirts, socks with an immense white turn and shorts so baggy that you could have made bedsheets out of them. Pictures of Arthur Rowe were taken in his oak-panelled office. In one of them Rowe presses his fingers into his temples, as though he can feel a throbbing headache coming on. Group photos of older Spurs teams – some from the 19th century – hang on the wall behind him.

The profile Wright put together concentrated on Rowe, 'the brain that blueprints Spurs' "push and run" strategy', which had just brought them the Second Division title.

Wright did not adequately fill in the background to that story.

Just as Alf Ramsey would learn from Rowe, so Rowe had learnt from Clem Stephenson, a name known nowadays only to those with an encyclopaedic knowledge of Huddersfield Town between the wars, a side Herbert Chapman fashioned out of his own extraordinary

Arthur Rowe, 'the brain that blueprints Spurs' "push and run" strategy'

thinking. Stephenson was an inside right, the motivating force behind Chapman's three consecutive League Championships from 1924 to 1926. Rowe adored Stephenson, who was seldom caught in possession because he received, controlled and passed the ball faster than someone flicking a light switch on and off again. 'He best illustrated the style I wanted my teams to play,' said Rowe.

He was drawn to Stephenson-like characters combining 'entertainment with effectiveness' and who were instinctively one-touch and capable of improvisation. Rowe boiled down his philosophy into nine plain words: 'Make it simple. Make it accurate. Make it quick.'

The average manager in the late 1940s and early 1950s was not as conspicuous on the training pitch as Rowe. Many bosses were figureheads, a chaperone to the team. The approach of Blackpool's Joe Smith was typical. He more or less instructed his side to do nothing more than scatter themselves across the field in likely places and 'get stuck in'. The players were nonplussed when, before a game at Cardiff City, Smith called them together in the dressing room. Expecting an insightful tactical speech, Smith instead gave them this order: 'Don't mess about in the bath afterwards. We want to be away pretty quickly The 5.30 train is the last one with a dining car.'

Rowe was different. Having purchased Ramsey, he gathered together the team he'd inherited and fundamentally changed it. He claimed to have originally outlined 'push and run' with sugar cubes in a train carriage. Spurs were returning to London, 'dead pleased', he said, about collecting a £2 win bonus with a late goal. That goal had comprised 'about seven passes', the first of them struck from their own penalty box. The following week, Rowe took the players into the car park and got them to strike a ball repeatedly against the wall beneath White Hart Lane's grandstand. 'When you do that, the ball comes back to you in an instant. That's what I wanted from them,' he said. 'I took our style back to the streets, the way we played it as kids – off the kerb, off the wall, taking the ball at different angles . . . the kerb [was] a teammate who let you have the ball back immediately after you had played it.'

He brought a small rubber ball to training, substituting it for a full-size football. 'By using a rubber ball . . . [they] are later able to place and use a football more quickly. What some folk do not appear to understand is that time is space in football.'

Spurs, as fluid as water, operated with a smooth swiftness in triangles or squares. Rowe 'wasn't fond' of the 'push and run' label attached to that approach, preferring to say that Spurs' short, rapid and intelligent passing gave the game 'an electric shock'. The electric shock Spurs administered to the Football League was of an exceptionally high voltage; everyone who felt the charge got lit up like one of those cartoon characters whose skeleton becomes suddenly visible after touching a live wire.

Spurs powered through the Second Division, scoring 81 goals and finishing 11 points ahead of Sheffield United. They lost only one of

Alf Ramsey, who originally learnt the craft of defending from Sam Barkas
of Manchester City

their opening 25 matches. Ramsey took mischievous pleasure from the 4–0 thumping of Southampton.

In the post-war period the game boomed, and then boomed again. Unlike nearly everything else – meat, butter, tea, sweets – football was not rationed. The turnstiles spun madly, and the dilapidated grounds, patched up but not significantly improved, nearly buckled and burst. On December 27, 1949, a total of 44 matches produced a record aggregate crowd, the sort of figure you'd expect a Rothschild or a Getty to write on a cheque: 1,272,185. Throughout the First and Second Divisions, thousands upon thousands of men in flat caps, mufflers and overcoats would drift about the streets after being locked out.

Spurs stirred up so much passion that no one in England drew bigger crowds. Their average home attendance topped 54,000 – 5,000 higher than Arsenal's gates in the First Division.

No one gave Rowe a chance of pulling off a repeat performance after promotion. 'Push and run', it was said, wouldn't survive against higher, more rarefied competition.

In their first game Spurs choked, running out of puff against Blackpool, who beat them 4–1. It was a blip. The elite would be just as bamboozled in their search for the ball. Spurs amassed 60 points, the highest total since Arsenal's 59 in 1948, and slammed in 72 goals. Seven came in a hiding Newcastle never forgot. There were six against Stoke, five against both West Bromwich Albion and Portsmouth, the defending champions, and four – twice – against Bolton.

There is little filmed evidence of Rowe's side at or near their zenith, moving from box to box like an exquisite human machine. The Movietone or Pathé News footage, grainy or bleached, that does exist often finds Spurs on winter pitches that resemble ploughed potato fields after a thunderstorm. The mud tenaciously holds the brown leather ball, which almost needs to be dug up with a spade and can't be knocked about without strenuous effort. What you do get is the odd frame or two of the zippy passing – the accuracy, the energy and the speedy movement that Rowe drilled into Spurs so well that these acts

"TURF" CIGARETTES

ALF RAMSEY
TOTTENHAM
HOTSPUR
& ENGLAND

Dux

50 FAMOUS FOOTBALLERS Nº 34

The moment Alf Ramsey truly 'arrived' in the First Division:
the cigarette card produced in his honour

seem to come to them as naturally as breathing. You also see – again, in brief black-and-white flashes – the individuals whom Rowe turned into a team of champions.

The superlatives about Spurs' artistic prowess, written weekly in contemporary match reports, did not flatter them extravagantly, and the anecdotal evidence wasn't hot air either. In his heavy polo-neck jersey, the goalkeeper Ted Ditchburn did fling himself head-first at the pit boots of the opposition number nine, or dived, like an acrobat suspended from a wire, to make clean catches with his long fingers. The tilt of Eddie Baily's nimble body, as he swerved past a tackle, was unforgettable, even though he did it so routinely that you could have become blasé about it. The centre forward with a sharp left parting in his hair, Len Duquemin, did attack a cross so bullishly that anyone who got in his way was likely to end up in the net beside the ball.

No one is over-sold. Not Ron Burgess, the captain, nor Les Medley, the left winger. Not Bill Nicholson, nor Sonny Walters, the top scorer with 15 goals in that championship year. Not Les Bennett, nor the centre half Harry Clarke, nor the left back Arthur Willis. And certainly not Alf Ramsey, whom Rowe credited with giving 'us our momentum from the back'.

Ditchburn claimed his distribution of the ball with his feet was 'awful', which is why he rolled or bowled it to Ramsey. This was a leg-pull, said with a wink. Ditchburn automatically searched out Ramsey. In calling him 'The General', Spurs both acknowledged Ramsey's talent for looking at the pitch in front of him as though it were a battlefield and also his ability to plot a route through it.

At Southampton, while learning the craft of defending, Ramsey had decided to take a short cut. He copied Sam Barkas of Manchester City. There were defenders of that era who looked and behaved as though they broke kneecaps for a living. Barkas, a Geordie, did have the sort of firm jaw that suggested he might be a close relative of Desperate Dan. His play, though, was sublime. He convinced Ramsey that there was 'no such thing as a defender or an attacker' because 'every member of the team should be working together to score a goal'. While playing against Barkas, who was then 36, Ramsey studied his 'astute' use of the ball. He didn't just clear his lines; he found a colleague with precision. Ramsey considered Barkas to be 'an artist'. His positional play was 'brilliant'. He passed with 'confidence and accuracy'. He made 'the other fellow play how *he* wanted him to play'.

Aspiring to be 'just like him', Ramsey became the canniest of campaigners. Before a game against Newcastle at White Hart Lane, he went to inspect a pitch on which sat broad pools of water. Aware he needed an advantage over the winger Bobby Mitchell, Ramsey memorised the 'muddiest spots' and steered Mitchell into them. 'Even the greatest can't be great in the mud,' he said.

There is a second or two of film in which Ramsey, playing for England rather than Spurs, skewers the charge – an ancient joke, really – that 'milk turned faster' than he did. He pirouettes around a winger as though he's wearing ballet slippers. With Spurs, you see Ramsey controlling a ball and beginning an attack, knowing where his pass needs to go and who will be there to receive it. Usually, it is Nicholson. You also see the floating lob-cross, another Ramsey speciality that was struck at an angle from the touchline.

The side Rowe assembled with such imagination played with so much originality, flair and elan because above all he wanted 'things to be fun'. Spurs were also impeccably balanced. On the left were Burgess, Baily and Medley, who sounded like a music hall novelty act. On the right were Ramsey, Nicholson and Walters.

Even those of us who prefer to dwell on the aesthetics of the game rather than its statistics surely mourn the fact that Opta was not about in the 1950s to reveal who commanded most possession, who had the top pass-completion rate, who contributed the highest number of assists . . . and how long the ball belonged to Spurs over 90 minutes.

Some thought – and still think – that Ramsey was the team's headline act. Many favoured the calm and dynamic Burgess. He was a Welsh ex-miner, who had won his place in the last full season before the war, aged only 21. He had hair so thin that you could see his scalp and large, sticky-out ears, but his feet made passes sing. Rowe persuaded Burgess to tweak his style of play, curbing his attacking instincts. Nicholson reckoned he was indisputably 'the greatest player' at Spurs in the post-war era. Others saw Nicholson himself as the first among equals. He was so unselfish because he so obviously cared. His heart seemed to beat purely for the purpose of serving his club. A few championed Duquemin – known as the Duke – because the threat he posed preoccupied defences, who then forgot who else they ought to be marking. Duquemin came from Guernsey. When the Germans invaded the island in 1940, he was 17 days short of his 16th birthday. Catholic monks hid him in a monastery, where he learnt to speak French so fluently that he considered playing in France rather than England.

Most of the crowd's love was willingly given to Baily, described as being 'as cockney as a jellied eel'. He was graceful and artful, and could plant the ball on a half crown from 45 yards. Baily appealed, too, because of his mischievousness. He once hit a corner kick against the back of the referee, knocking him over like a pin in a bowling alley, before snapping up the rebound – illegally, according to the laws – and whipping it over smartly for Duquemin to nod in. His nickname, the Cheeky-Chappie, stemmed as much from what he did off the pitch as on it. His non-stop chatter and persistent banter were reminiscent of the man originally given that sobriquet, the stand-up comedian Max Miller, who escaped the Lord Chamberlain's ire – and his blue pencil – only because he self-censored the raw punchlines of his material, letting the audience reach their own conclusions. One of the staples of Miller's routine was a two-line ditty of pure filth.

> When roses are red, they're right for plucking
> When girls are 16, they're right for . . .

In the dressing room, Baily expertly mimicked Miller's accent and his act.

Ramsey was so dignified and po-faced that it must be true that polar opposites attract. He and the ribaldly irreverent Baily bonded, became friends and roomed together. They did so despite Baily compulsively puffing away, like one of L. S. Lowry's factory chimneys, on Craven 'A' cigarettes, which he was paid to endorse.

After Spurs won the title, awash with cash after pulling in crowds of nearly 55,000 every week, the board's miserly gift to each player was a cigarette lighter. Ramsey, who smoked sparingly, had less need for a lighter than any other member of the side, nearly all of whom could

match Baily fag for fag. He also seldom drank because alcohol went too quickly to his head. Preferring his own company, he built barriers between himself and the rest of the team – even Baily. If he thought someone was prying into his private affairs, however innocently, he would snap, 'It's none of your business,' or refuse to engage in conversation by saying, 'I'm not discussing that with you.'

He would eventually pay for his stand-offish unsociability.

* * *

Most people's favourite subject is themself. Not Alf Ramsey.

He either sidestepped conversations about his roots, his upbringing in Dagenham and his family, or he blustered, obfuscated and evaded such questions. Ramsey once said his family counted as 'good stock', giving the kind of beatific smile that suggested he was remembering a boyhood that was as jolly as a Lionel Bart musical. In being so evasive, however, he succeeded only in making his inquisitors curiouser still, certain a little extra digging would unearth something that Ramsey wanted to stay buried.

It seems inexplicable that Ramsey would, for any reason other than money, publish an autobiography of his early career. It came out in

1952, at a time when the titles of similar books were lame puns, usually variations on a theme, depending on whether the author is a goal-scorer or a goalkeeper:

The World's My Football Pitch (Billy Wright)
Goals Galore (Nat Lofthouse)
Football from the Goalmouth (Frank Swift)

These books are so poor that you mourn the trees pulped to pub-lish them. But even against such weak competition, Ramsey's *Talking Football* is particularly undistinguished. It's only 110 pages long, and the first chapter does not begin until page 11. It is written with a dull, non-controversial politeness and to a set template. The story is told more or less chronologically. Exclamation marks proliferate because the editor, who ought to have plucked them out, forgot to remind the ghost that this superfluous piece of punctuation never rescues a bad joke and doesn't improve a good one.

You discover that Dagenham was then a spot of leafy greenery; that Ramsey liked his mother Florence's meat pies; that his father, Herbert, runs a 'smallholding'; that he has three brothers – Albert, Len and Cyril (and a sister, Joyce); that his love for football, unsur-prisingly, surpassed everything; that his first pair of boots cost four shillings and eleven pence; that he took a 'small ball' with him on his daily four-mile walk to and from his state school; that he left there at 14; that he served an apprenticeship at the Co-op because 'the grocery trade for some unknown reason attracted me'; that after war broke out he was sent to an Infantry Training Unit and became a sergeant; that he liked going to variety shows and listening to the radio; that he read assiduously to expand his vocabulary (though he offers no favourite titles and no authors either); and that he travels among the fans on match days, catching the train from Barking to Tottenham and then back again.

Talking Football isn't *David Copperfield*, but it does reveal Ramsey as just another pro who wasn't living the affluent, bountiful life that his talent ought to have brought him. He got his wage, paid in pounds, shillings and pence, every Friday in a brown packet. He relied on public transport because he couldn't afford a car. He watched what he spent and saved what he could.

As though the welfare and well-being of footballers were a private crusade for them, Pathé News had produced a short documentary highlighting the discrepancy between the big crowds at matches and the lamentably small rewards given to those who entertained them. Pathé packed a lot of controversy into two minutes and a handful of seconds. If you kicked a ball for a living, or aspired to do so, the film was slightly gloomy. The commentary took a stick to the Football League, the Football Association and the fat cat directors in club boardrooms. These men, who had the smell of brandy, cigars and private money about them, got wealthier by inflexibly enforcing the maximum wage. It was a scandal perpetrated by a cartel who relished their privilege and abused their power over players they regarded as no more than hired help – here today, gone tomorrow.

Pathé wasn't afraid to be partisan or to editorialise. The opening lines of the documentary, first shown in 1949, were not the nervous throat-clearings of someone uncertain about the injustice being done or who was responsible for perpetrating it. Pathé went on the attack. It defined the 'stars of the game' as men 'who do so much and by comparison with top earners in other jobs get so little for it'. It spoke with pity about players who 'made the game' but 'seldom make fortunes from it'. It lingered on the brevity of a career – 'the soon to be forgotten men of soccer'.

Just in case the millions in the cinemas who saw and heard all this still doubted whether Pathé's loyalty belonged to the worker rather than the boss, the pay-off line was excoriating. It called for 'an end to the tragedy of good sporting men unsportingly treated', before adding that 'soccer must learn to play the game'.

This was Pathé articulating its anger about the maximum wage, which was then £12 per week. The country's average salary was less than £7, but Pathé conveniently illustrated the rank unfairness of the footballer's lot by showing scene after scene in which grounds with high terracing were so congested that you wondered how anyone, once wedged in there, could ever move or get out afterwards.

At one FA Cup final, the Sousa marching band, hired as pre-match and half-time entertainment, left Wembley with £320, which was £80 more than the players of both teams received.

Babe Ruth, on tour to plug baseball to an English audience, had watched a game between Arsenal and Middlesbrough in front of a crowd of 70,000. Afterwards, he asked the players, 'Hey, how much do you guys earn?' The answer he got produced an instinctively candid reply: 'You are bloody idiots.'

Ruth didn't know the half of it.

There were clubs that issued a rule book, which was a crude means of control. What a player could or couldn't do varied from club to club, dependent on the whims of the board. Some forbade dancing between Wednesday night and Saturday afternoon. Most contained dire warnings about not talking to the press without permission. A player would be told how to dress on match days, when he should report for training, and how and when it was permissible for him to 'leave the club's premises'. One club's rule book ordered players to 'dwell in no place' without its prior approval. The final rule? To carry the rule book 'at all times' and present it before 'all home matches' to 'gain admission'.

A footballer's contract was like a Faustian pact of the soul. Faust, at least, got immortality; footballers got a pittance and a pair of boots.

Pathé lingered on those who had no option but to supplement their football income with other employment. Stanley Matthews was running a hotel. Stan Mortensen had a 'fancy goods' shop. Tom Finney, the plumber, spent his days off unblocking pipes and fixing taps. Ramsey's teammate Ted Ditchburn sat behind a desk in a ticketing agency.

Essentially, Pathé's message was that the game coaxed the players in it down a dead end, abandoning them there once the cheering stopped. Those players living in a club-owned house would be forced to hand over the keys, often before finding another home.

Ramsey seethed about the situation, along with everyone else in the Professional Footballers' Association, but *Talking Football* diplomatically swerved around the issue because directors didn't forget tub-thumping dissent. The book, re-read now, is valuable chiefly for what Ramsey leaves out or dusts over, and, occasionally, the way in which he bends the truth. The reader is left to deduce what he would like to say but is too discreet to disclose.

Ramsey says his family were 'not exactly wealthy', which is his convoluted way of telling us that their income was counted in copper, half-pennies and farthings, rather than silver. The Ramseys' home – 6 Parrish Cottages –was made of wood. It had neither hot running water nor electricity. It did have a tin bath and an outside toilet. Its square footage was small enough to fit five times into the average back garden of most Football League chairmen. His father had an allotment on which he built a pigsty. His main income came from manual labour and an old dustcart that was pulled by an aged horse. He picked up scrap – and whatever else was being given away – in the best tradition of a rag-and-bone man (in the 1921 census, Ramsey's father describes himself as only a 'Hay & Straw Dealer').

It was claimed Ramsey had at least a pint and a half of Romany blood in him, which was damning in those less enlightened, less tolerant times. He acquired the nickname 'Darkie' purely on the basis of that suspicion. Ramsey's forebears were merely peripatetic. When there was no work locally, they walked or biked or hitch-hiked on the back of carts to find it.

Talking Football contained a giant lie, the motive self-protection, which made it forgivable.

In the Golden Age of Hollywood, not long after the talkies made silent pictures antique curios, actors and especially actresses began to shave a year or two off their ages to preserve their longevity as youthful stars. The Oscar-winner Joan Crawford claimed to have been born in 1908. The year of her birth was 1905. Katharine Hepburn, also born that year, instructed her publicists to use 1907. Doris Day chose 1924; she was actually born in 1922.

Ramsey came into the game so late that he thought it prudent to fib about his birth too, believing – rightly – that no one would go to Somerset House to check. He was born in 1920, but pretended to be two years younger in case clubs were wary of taking on or retaining someone nearing 30.

The glaring omission in *Talking Football* is much detail about Ramsey's home life. Questioned about who he thought counted as the 'biggest influence' on Ramsey's career, Arthur Rowe once replied: 'Mrs Ramsey.'

She was the brunette Rita Welch, who had married in 1941 and become Rita Norris. She had a daughter called Tanya.* Soon estranged from her husband, she met Ramsey in Southampton, where she worked as a hairdresser.

Ramsey had a strange verbal tic. When faced with a question he didn't want to tackle, his answer would be suffixed with the words 'I think'. Asked about where his parents lived, Ramsey replied with the ludicrous 'Dagenham, I think,' as though he wasn't sure or seldom went to visit them. Asked about how he met his wife, he said: 'We were introduced by a friend in a club, I think.' His vagueness about his wife continued. Ramsey feigned not to remember how long their engagement lasted, describing it as 'some time' and adding: 'It's not important.' In the index of *Talking Football*, his wife appears only four times. She is named just twice. She is 'interested' in football, he says. They go 'weekly' to the cinema and occasionally to a 'show' too. His adopted daughter is not mentioned at all. He doesn't say, as he will later, that he and his wife 'immediately' had 'what one must call a special relationship . . . I don't know why I had this particular feeling only for her.'

* She was christened Tanaya.

She divorced at the end of 1950. The Ramseys' marriage, held in Southampton's Registry Office, took place at the end of 1951. No one from Tottenham was invited to the wedding, which took place between a 1–0 defeat at Blackpool and a 3–1 win over Middlesbrough. She shed the name Rita, becoming Victoria instead.

Before meeting her, Ramsey had been socially awkward and clumsy in conversation. He found it difficult to make a connection with anyone who didn't like football. But working-class boy and working-class girl were each bent on self-betterment. Victoria – he called her 'Vic' – spoke and dressed well, which is why Ramsey reinvented himself for her, constructing a persona and transforming his accent too.

In the 1950s, your voice could determine your prosperity. A dropped 'h' in received English pronunciation was considered unbearably dirt-common. How you spoke betrayed who you were and where you

When the streets were an imaginary Wembley: where and how post-war boys learnt to kick a ball

came from. The question 'How do you do?', spoken roughly, would condemn a man as an oaf, not worth a light.

Ramsey was falsely accused of attending elocution lessons, but these were prohibitively expensive. The techniques used hadn't changed much anyway since George Bernard Shaw invented Henry Higgins and paired him with Eliza Doolittle in *Pygmalion* in 1913; the rain in Spain still stayed mainly on the plain, and the rascal continued to run around his ragged rock. Wanting to eradicate his cockney twang, Ramsey began to laboriously imitate the voices he heard on the BBC's Home Service. He whittled away the coarseness in his own voice the way you whittle away at wood with a knife, one shaving at a time.

Every BBC newsreader gave the impression of being posher than posh, as though he'd shared a school desk with a senior member of the royal family. The 'r's were nicely rolled and the 'g's came with a crystalline ring. In attempting to be like them, Ramsey sometimes had an awful fight with the English language; he sounded like someone from an amateur dramatic society wrestling with his lines in a Noël Coward play.

Years after Ramsey left Tottenham, Eddie Baily said he was 'astonished' to discover his former teammate had gone from 'cor blimey cockney' to 'all fancy'. A BBC recording, called 'How to Take a Penalty Kick', doesn't support that statement. Ramsey, who took penalties for Southampton, Spurs and England, discussed and demonstrated his technique on a foggy morning at Chelsea's Stamford Bridge. All those hours listening to the Home Service had been worth it. He liked to 'retrieve' the ball himself to 'ensure' it rested 'on a level surface', he said. He isn't a toff, but he doesn't sound like a greengrocer's barrow boy either. Ramsey was already preparing himself for the job he most wanted eventually: to become Tottenham's next manager.

2

THE END AND THE BEGINNING

The wisest man learns as much in defeat as he does from victory. This was true for Alf Ramsey.

Nothing made Ramsey prouder than his England shirt. Nothing made him more embarrassed than losing in it. In his 33-cap career, under Walter Winterbottom, Ramsey was at the epicentre of two catastrophes, each of which profoundly shaped his approach to management and his opinion of the Football Association, which was so low as to be almost subterranean. The first was the single-goal defeat against the amateurs of the United States in the 1950 World Cup. The second was Hungary's nut-and-bolt dismantling of England at Wembley in 1953 – his last international appearance.

As the pre-eminent football writer, Brian Glanville, observed in the *Sunday Times*: 'In no other footballing country in the world could a manager with Winterbottom's results have survived . . .'

Ramsey gradually hardened his attitude towards Winterbottom. He liked him as a person. He didn't especially rate him as a coach.

Winterbottom's CV as a player could be scribbled down in a few lines. Between 1936 and 1939, he'd been a part-timer, still teaching while playing for Manchester United, then a Second Division side. He made only 26 appearances for them – 21 coming in his first season – before a spinal injury shut down his career.

He was inadequate – the wrong man in the wrong place at the wrong time. In Ramsey's eyes, the FA should have replaced him with Arthur Rowe, the most plausible candidate.

Through arrogance and muddled thinking, the FA either refused to acknowledge or were incapable of recognising that England under Winterbottom would never prosper. His personality wasn't big enough for the position. Nor did it expand to meet what England increasingly needed, which was the innovative thinking Rowe would have provided.

Winterbottom's benefactor, the FA secretary Stanley Rous, had appointed him as England's first full-time boss in 1946, combining the role with the post of director of coaching. Winterbottom set up coaching courses for professionals and amateurs alike, developing an orthodoxy on how the game ought be approached, practised and played.

He smoked a pipe and often wore round, dark-framed spectacles, which made him look like a university professor specialising in some obscure branch of chemistry. He often spoke like one, too, adding unnecessary complexity to simple tasks and using a blackboard and chalk to demonstrate them. Winterbottom was responsible for schooling a glut of coaches – a lot of them school teachers who had never played the game. With those who did play it, he failed to communicate on their level.

Len Shackleton scored 127 goals in 384 appearances for Bradford Park Avenue, Newcastle and Sunderland. Dry figures still can't convey the visceral thrill of watching him flit so beautifully around a pitch, never knowing what magician's trick he might pull off next. He was the mercurial entertainer par excellence. Every game was a variety show for the rebellious, comic extrovert. Faced with an open goal, he would flick the ball up with his boot and nod it into the net. In front of the Leazes End at St James's Park, Shackleton once rolled the ball to the goal line, sank down on all fours and headed the thing in. Seldom content to beat a defender once, he sometimes did a U-turn and beat him again for no other reason than that he could. When chasing down the touchline, Shackleton might suddenly stop, put one foot on the ball, fold his arms and jut out his chin, like a Corinthian Casual posing for a Victorian studio portrait. Or he'd beckon a full back towards him with his hands. Or, when very bored, he'd drag the ball off to the corner flag and sit on it.

Shackleton deplored nearly everything about Winterbottom's approach. During one England training session, Winterbottom made him do the sort of drill schoolboys were taught. He was ordered to run down the field, interchanging passes, before slotting the ball into an unguarded goal. Shackleton enquired sarcastically: 'Which side of the goal, Mr Winterbottom?'

He wasn't alone in being appalled – and also a little confused – by Winterbottom's methods. At one get-together, Tommy Lawton said he 'got a migraine' from looking at the diagrams Winterbottom drew. Lawton was sitting beside his friend Stanley Matthews. Exasperated by the jargon, as well as the squiggles and arrows, the two men got up and walked out. Lawton's farewell to Winterbottom was useful tactical advice: 'Look, Walter, let's stop all this guff. It's simple – get the ball on the wing to Stan, get him to cross it and I'll head it in.'

In Winterbottom's early years in charge, England had flair to burn. As well as Shackleton, Lawton and Matthews, he could turn to players with star power: Tom Finney, Jackie Milburn, Stan Mortensen, Wilf Mannion, Raich Carter. You didn't need to coach players of such pedigree; you had only to give them the ball and wait to be amazed. But Winterbottom couldn't curb his instinct to lecture, often very verbosely. He coached the rudimentary – even throw-ins – to expert pros, as though Matthews and his ilk needed the instruction. It was like showing Picasso how to draw a stick-man.

Even Bobby Charlton, hardly known for his outspokenness, subsequently hit the bullseye, identifying a problem the FA didn't believe existed. He said Winterbottom was 'someone who *theoretically* knew everything about coaching . . . at team briefings, you would go through the game from A to Z. He told us a lot we knew already . . . he undoubtedly said a great number of things that didn't need to be said.'

* * *

Alf Ramsey mistrusted the Football Association. He had a particular distaste for those who benefited most from it: the FA councillors, freeloading in their blazers, a badge decorating the top pocket, their ties adorned with the England crest. Players who didn't tug their forelock were either patronised by these pampered bureaucrats – or dropped.

The England team was chosen by committee, which indulged in the worst kind of pork-barrel politics. It embraced jealousy, prejudice, favouritism, selfishness and self-interest, and ignorance. Between nine and 11 'selectors' would go through each position, starting with the goalkeeper, and nominate candidates to fill them. These interminable meetings, which often went on for hours, led to squabbles, bitterness and compromises. One selector might support a colleague over the right half – but only if the colleague supported him over the left winger. Often Walter Winterbottom had to painstakingly explain to them how one player was incompatible with another.

Knowing his place, however, Winterbottom absurdly claimed that the selectors were not a meddlesome bunch but 'largely people of general interest who had played the game and who knew a good deal about it because they were always talking to their managers'. Prominent among these so-called sages were two grocers, a contractor for London Transport, a retired businessman from Wolverhampton and a Huddersfield solicitor with a knighthood. The committee chairman was Arthur Drewry. He was linked with the fishing industry in Grimsby and had experienced the sea: he'd been rescued from a ship torpedoed during the Great War.

As Len Shackleton stressed, his venom traceable: 'All these gentlemen have one thing in common – the striking absence of any soccer-playing background of note.' Of one of the grocers on the panel, he added: 'He should be a better selector of cabbages than footballers.'

The FA reaped £50,000 in receipts from international games at Wembley, but divided only £550 between the eleven players and called in Stanley Matthews and Tommy Lawton to quibble over their expenses. Matthews had charged the FA for a cup of tea and a scone

– total cost, sixpence. Lawton, forced to change trains, overestimated the fare by twopence. He discovered the FA's secretary had gone to the laborious bother of studying the timetables and the ticket prices. Denis Compton tried to claim 'miscellaneous' expenses, but was rebuffed with the put-down that no England player was 'intelligent enough to either spell the word or know what it meant'. According to Matthews, the FA assumed their players were 'always on the make' for an extra shilling. He compared his meeting with the secretary to a scene from a Charles Dickens novel. Your claim would be scratched out in front of you with a blue pencil, and you'd be dismissed with a wave towards the door.

It was common for the FA to hand out third-class train tickets after internationals, which meant the players – even those who were injured – often had to stand in a corridor if the carriages were full. When Shackleton was given complimentary tickets for a match, he began to phone friends and family to arrange for their collection. An FA official rebuked him. 'I hope you've paid for all your phone calls,' he said. Shackleton was once left £5 out of pocket after attending an England training session.

* * *

George Orwell wrote of the 'constant struggle' to see what is in front of your nose. The Football Association didn't even try. Coy and arrogant, it was so preoccupied with England's glorious past that it forgot to make a future. Nothing could shake them out of their preconceived notion that England remained pre-eminent – not even that 1–0 defeat to the United States in Belo Horizonte, Brazil.

No result in England's history – or anybody else's – was as freakish as this shock of all shocks. Even now, picking through the cold wreckage of that match and evaluating every detail, you can't properly rationalise what happened because not a thing about it makes any sense. If there wasn't a thin reel of jumpy film to confirm that England lost 1–0, you'd refuse to believe it and dismiss the story as apocryphal. The United States were 500–1 to win the 1950 World Cup and 100–1 to win the match. Their team, taking advantage of FIFA's residency rules, wasn't purely Uncle Sam's. It contained players who belonged to Haiti, via Belgium, and Scotland.

There is a photograph of Alf Ramsey, wearing a royal-blue shirt, looking incredulous as the ball squirms past his goalkeeper Bert Williams for the United States' winner. Whenever he was asked whether he had played in that humiliation, Ramsey would reply sardonically: 'Most certainly. I was the only one who did.'

England's mitigation was the narrow, rutted pitch, resembling corrugated iron, off which the ball flew at the oddest of angles after striking one of 'thousands' of scattered tiny white stones. The stones had been left behind after builders rushed to finish the 12ft-high perimeter wall that made the ground look like a state prison. The dressing rooms, as dimly lit as the catacombs of a medieval cathedral, were also home to a rat or two, forcing England to arrive in their kit.

The team Walter Winterbottom would have chosen was not the team Arthur Drewry, the selector in Brazil, gave him either. Winterbottom had wanted to rest players, saving them for the final group game against Spain.

England were joint favourites for the World Cup along with the hosts. They were proclaimed, both at home and abroad, as the Kings of Football. Before facing the United States, Winterbottom had lost only four and drawn three of 30 matches, devouring opposition such as Portugal (10–0), the Netherlands (8–0) and Ireland (9–2).

In its complacency and puffed-up sense of entitlement, the FA saw this World Cup – England's first – as a garlanded procession rather than a competition. Stanley Matthews hadn't figured in the first match, a win over Chile, because he'd arrived too late from a pointless FA tour of Canada. Drewry believed Matthews's presence would be superfluous against the United States, and so refused to pick him.

'Our defeat was fated,' said Ramsey.

Walter Winterbottom (in tracksuit, left) struggled to impress the most expressive and individual talents in the England team of the 1950s

England repeatedly rattled the post, twanged the bar and had 90 per cent of the possession. There were extraordinarily inspired saves – with hands, body, face and even his backside – by the American goalkeeper Frank Borghi. The referee rejected two stone-wall penalties, one for a blatant handball, the other for a rugby tackle. He and his linesman also ignored a shot that went a yard over the line. The goal the Americans scored, shortly before half-time, was genuinely bizarre: the centre forward Joe Gaetjens ducked, almost on to all-fours, to avoid a shot that slammed against his right ear, the ricochet taking it into the net.

However much chance and rotten luck were aligned against them, Winterbottom's team ought never to have lost to part-timers who juggled their football between teaching, dishwashing, office work and driving a hearse. As well as Ramsey, England's side included Finney, Mortensen, Wright and Mannion.

There were only eight journalists – and one telephone – on the press benches. When the *New York Times* received the cable from the Reuters reporter, it delayed publication, thinking his dispatch was a hoax.

The *Daily Herald* decided to indulge in black humour. When, a few days later, England lost again – Spain beat them 1–0 – the newspaper printed a small notice inside a funereal border on the front page. It copied the satirical obituary that *The Sporting Times* had published in 1882 after Australia beat England at cricket at the Oval – a result that gave birth to the Ashes. For added impact, the *Herald* set the words in Gothic type:

> In affectionate remembrance of English football, which died at Rio on July 2, 1950. Deeply lamented by a large circle of sorrowing friends and acquaintances. RIP. NB: The body will be cremated and the ashes taken to Spain.

The FA learnt nothing from that World Cup. Nor did Winterbottom.

* * *

He was only 12 years old on November 25, 1953, the afternoon Hungary came to Wembley. As a man, though, he could walk you step-by-step through what had happened.

At five minutes past three, standing in the school playground, he heard someone say, 'England are one down.' He refused to believed it.

The game was televised live, but its Wednesday-afternoon kick-off meant the breaking news that day was principally relayed via radio by Raymond Glendenning. He was a broadcaster fond of expressions such as 'by Jove', 'I say' and 'my word', and he often spoke between taking drags on a cigar that was thicker than a telephone pole. He could talk so rapidly – 300 words per minute – that the waxed tips of his handlebar moustache vibrated. His diction and pronunciation were perfect. He spoke without repetition, banality or cliché. With Glendenning, you got a picture of a scene that was as though Turner had painted the landscape and Holbein had done the portraiture within it.

England equalised, fell behind again, and then conceded another goal.

The boy left school just before four o'clock and caught the train home. He read the stop press in a fellow passenger's evening paper. England were 4–1 down. 'It must be a misprint,' he said to himself.

In the end England lost 6–3, grateful afterwards that the defeat hadn't been heavier.

That night, the boy watched the half-hour-long highlights on the BBC.

'I still didn't believe it,' he said later.

The boy was Bobby Moore.

* * *

You can see more than the future England captain saw merely by clicking on to YouTube. The whole match is there in cloudy black and white. The picture, like England, deteriorates as the game goes on, and the commentary is muffled, as though Kenneth Wolstenholme is broadcasting from the bottom of the ocean.

It was said that Wolstenholme 'should never have been a football commentator' because, 'confronted by odds that made Russian roulette seem comparatively safe, he should have been dead'. During the war, he flew 'exactly 100' RAF missions and was awarded the Distinguished Flying Cross. That service record brought calm perspective to his commentaries about mere sport, but even Wolstenholme was overcome by the Hungarians, who glittered through the murk. Raymond Glendenning had recommended that his listeners park themselves in front of the TV that night to witness 'something quite magical'. Those who did heard, midway through the second half, Wolstenholme exclaim: 'Oh, what football!'

Malcolm Allison, who emerged as Bobby Moore's favourite teacher at West Ham, went to Wembley. He found the Hungarians practising on a patch of tufty grass where the greyhounds were normally tethered before racing around the stadium's cinder track. He watched, mesmerised by all the flicks, back heels and dancing sidesteps. Hungary were like an exhibition team. 'They seemed to have arrived from another planet rather than from behind the Iron Curtain,' he said.

Despite being crowned Olympic champions the year before in Helsinki, the Hungarians were so relatively unknown that their names were originally unpronounceable tongue-twisters: Ferenc Puskás, Nándor Hidegkuti, Zoltán Czibor, László Budai, József Bozsik, Sándor Kocsis.

The *Daily Express* had forecast that England would win the 1950 World Cup and that the United States ought to be given a three-goal head-start to make the match 'interesting'. This time the *Express* predicted that Hungary would be beaten in 'ten minutes'. It argued that England needed only to display the old-fashioned virtues of the long ball and the hard tackle to frighten off such meagre opposition. Hungary were representative of 'Johnny Foreigner', who would faint if we just growled at him. As England walked out of the tunnel, Billy Wright thought so too. He ridiculed their 'strange, lightweight boots', which were 'cut away like slippers under the ankle bone'. He said to Stan Mortensen: 'We should be all right here ... they haven't got the proper kit.' If you weren't aware that science had impacted football fashion, then you were very unlikely to know what else had changed.

Hungary went ahead after 45 seconds. A rising, edge-of-the-box drive from Hidegkuti nailed another canard about the 'continentals', who weren't supposed to be able to shoot accurately from distance.

On that surprisingly warm afternoon, Wembley saw a spectacular celebration of the game. You watch the BBC film unable to take your eyes off the Hungarians. They are fitter, sharper and a yard faster, their passing clicking together as though the player in possession knows, through instinct or telepathy, where everyone is. Seldom does anyone linger over a pass.

Amid the opening razzle-dazzle, Hungary go close with two more shots, miss a sitter and shrug off without complaint a dodgy decision that scrubs out an indisputable goal. You fancy them to score every time England, plodding and brittle, allow an attack to cross the halfway line.

England were level after a quarter of an hour, which seemed like the resumption of normal service, until the Hungarians raced away again, never to be bested: 2–1 ahead after 20 minutes; 3–1 ahead after 24; 4–1 ahead after 27. The marquee moment of this mismatch was something that needs no other label than 'Puskás's goal'. It is so well known that the image of it can be summoned at will. Puskás near the short edge of the six-yard box. Wright hurtling towards him, diving into the tackle. Puskás pulling the ball away from him with the sole of his left boot. The high shot, lashed in between the goalkeeper's dive and the near post. Wright sliding ignominiously into oblivion on his backside. Next morning, in every school playground and on every Football League training pitch, there were a million or more would-be Puskáses.

Everything about Hungary was drama or art. They played in the style Arthur Rowe had introduced there in 1939. Here was Total Football – 20 years before the term slipped into common usage. England looked from Puskás to Czibor and from Budai to Hidegkuti, without knowing when or where or how swiftly any one of them might pop up and punish them.

Winterbottom had watched Hungary, both during the Olympics and in Budapest, but he was caught unawares and showed himself to be hopelessly out of his depth against them. Hungary played 2–3–3–2, a kind of footballing version of three-dimensional chess. England, slavishly sticking to the W–M formation, were stiffly reliant on tactics virtually unchanged since the 1920s and '30s, when Herbert Chapman was successful with them at Huddersfield and Arsenal. Hungary's players were free agents, scissoring across or behind one another and into space. England were utterly confused. The numbers on the Hungarians' cherry-red shirts didn't correspond to the positions the team occupied on the pitch. The usual hidebound rules – that 5 marked 9, that 3 was there to stop 7 – did not apply. Hidegkuti wore the number 9, but he was such a deep-lying centre forward that you almost expected to find him standing on the greyhound track behind his own goal. He was in the D of the Hungarian box one minute; the next he was hugging the ball not far from England's corner flag.

The previous spring, Harry Johnston, a former Footballer of the Year, had captained Blackpool to their FA Cup triumph over Bolton, giving Stanley Matthews his winners' medal at last. His selection at centre half was his seventh international appearance that year, but only his 10th cap since his debut in 1946. Like Ramsey, it would also be his last. The contest between 34-year-old Johnston and Hidegkuti was like watching a shire horse race against a stallion. Johnston didn't know whether to track Hidegkuti, who claimed a hat-trick, or wait for the Hungarian to come to him. He was damned both ways. If he went with him, Hidegkuti flew off. If Johnston followed, Hungary drove through the hole his absence left. The full back, Bill Eckersley of Blackburn, took a beating too. In one clip Eckersley is scrambling on his hands and knees, like a man who has dropped all his loose change, after Zoltán Czibor has jigged past him.

Winterbottom couldn't tell Johnston or Eckersley what to do; he didn't have a clue. The coach with an elaborate theory for everything, who spoke the perfect game fluently, was stuck for words when faced with a practical crisis. Since he hadn't fully appreciated how devastating Hungary could be or the vast range of their play, he hadn't prepared England for them.

Nor did he appreciate that while Hungary made everything seem straightforward, this disguised the effort behind it. Their coach, Gusztáv Sebes, had demanded English-heavy footballs in training. He had also demanded that during warm-up matches the opposition played in an English style. These games were staged on a pitch with the exact dimensions of Wembley. His '12th man' was a theatrical smoke machine, used in case Hungary encountered an infamous London pea-soup fog.

With their appetite sated, Hungary grew bored and eased off. England made it 5–2 but leaked a sixth goal, and were grateful for a penalty, which Ramsey scored, that undeservedly gave the defeat a little faux dignity.

The *Daily Herald* did not publish a second obituary notice, but conceded that Hungary had given England 'the mother and father of a good hiding'. The first continental team to conquer England on English soil might have racked up ten goals. Or eleven. Or a dozen. Or more.

* * *

The Hungarian defeat was the nadir of a wretched seven months for Alf Ramsey.

The previous March, he'd given away the winning goal in the FA Cup semi-final, the worst and most fatuous miscalculation of his playing career. With ten seconds to go, Tottenham were drawing 1–1 against Blackpool at Villa Park. Everyone expected a replay. Everyone also expected Spurs to win it. What was christened 'Ramsey's tragic blunder' came after an innocuous free kick was looped into the Spurs half from Blackpool's. Ramsey should have headed it safely upfield or out for a throw-in. Inexplicably, he tried to chest it down, the ball bobbling away from him. Having made one error, Ramsey then made another. On the half-turn, he tried to sweep a pass back to Ted Ditchburn. He fluffed the kick, which was intercepted.

After the goal, Ditchburn beat his hands savagely against the turf. Then he tore off his gloves and threw them into the net. Ditchburn never liked Ramsey; now he wanted to throttle the life out of him. The whistle went. Ramsey walked back to the dressing room alone, his chin against his chest. He didn't dare look up.

Ramsey didn't travel back to White Hart Lane on the team coach that night. He showered, dressed quickly and drove home with his wife.* A meagre consolation was the fact that only those inside Villa Park witnessed his disgrace.

Hungary was different. Prior to that game few England matches had been televised and only a comparatively small number of people had seen them. In 1950, 400,000 homes owned a TV set; in 1953, the clamour to watch the new Queen being crowned meant that number rose to 1.1 million. You could no longer hide a bad performance. The BBC's coverage of the Hungary game exposed the occasions when Ramsey was drawn into the wrong position or went missing in action. The Hungarians were quick enough to expose how slow, at nearly 34, he'd become. Hands on hips, blowing hard, he looks as though he can't wait for his ordeal to be over.

Ramsey bought a copy of the popular training manual *Learn to Play the Hungarian Way*, which was translated and published only six weeks after the Wembley defeat. He and Arthur Rowe also went to the BBC studios to watch the international, a visit organised by Kenneth Wolstenholme, who was a Spurs fan. Ramsey already believed that 'several of the countries we taught to play' were now 'our masters'. He berated the goalkeeper, Gil Merrick, suggesting England would never have lost if he hadn't been so timid and so ponderous: 'Four of their goals were struck from outside the box,' he moaned. With beautiful concision, though, he also concluded there was 'no choice but change' for England, which sounded like a party political slogan.

Six months later in Budapest, Hungary beat Winterbottom's England again – 7–1. Just four weeks after that, Uruguay outclassed them in the World Cup quarter-finals in Switzerland, winning 4–2.

Still, Winterbottom hung on.

---

* As Ipswich manager, he once walked across Villa Park and stood on the spot where he'd struck the ball towards Ditchburn, still obsessed with the FA Cup final appearance he never made.

After England came home, bruised in body and mind, the newspapers suggested that the Foreign Office should intervene and force the FA to 'drop games against world-beaters such as Hungary' until Winterbottom built a team capable of giving them a fright.

Even the FA had to accept Ramsey's gloomy assessment, but their response to it and the justifiable shouts elsewhere of 'something must be done' was slow, perfunctory and initiated with a flinching distaste. The FA arranged a meeting of Football League managers – a post-mortem held without urgency: it took three and a half months to gather them together. In between the defeat and that preliminary talking shop, the newspapers ran pieces beneath doomsday headlines such as 'English Soccer Style Out of Date', 'Why English Soccer Is in Decline' and 'Is There a Way Back for English Soccer?' The articles asked whether clubs were too 'obsessed' with 'cups and points' and the 'ups and downs' of promotion and relegation to concern themselves with the failings of the England team. They asked whether 'we' had 'invented much in the past 30 years', apart from introducing 'the long throw'. They also asked why 'more time' wasn't devoted to 'ball training' rather than 'stamina building'.

Only two managers – Arthur Rowe and Stan Cullis – thought it would be useful to travel to Hungary and study there in the summer of 1954. The primitive reaction of some clubs, such as Watford, then of the Third Division (south), was to haul in their players every afternoon for extra physical exercise – without a ball.

It took until August before the FA and the Football League managers cobbled together a ramshackle manifesto about being more co-operative over everything from polishing technique to 'talent spotting' for England. 'The mood was confident and happy,' announced Arthur Drewry.

It took a Vienna-born Anglophile, living in London, to diagnose the malaise afflicting Drewry and the FA. Willy Meisl was a columnist for *World Sports* and also the brother of Austrian coach Hugo, who invented 'The Whirl', in which – well before Hungary did it – players interchanged positions. Meisl's book *Soccer Revolution* was a cruel-to-be-kind attack on the English game, designed so that the likes of Winterbottom and Drewry could see themselves as others saw them. Meisl's premise was that England's outlook had narrowed, while everyone else's had expanded, because of its 'superiority complex'. It gave off an air of 'haughtiness, which to an outsider appears unpleasant', and had 'isolated' itself before discovering 'too late that the rest of the world has gained immensely in strength'. Meisl thought the England team, lacking expressive talent, was too negative, too stereotypical, too systemised. 'The player has become a robot – a cog in the machine,' he wrote.

The FA, still believing they were right, refused to take seriously any criticism Meisl levelled at them.

* * *

All things must pass.

Within 18 months of losing his England place, Alf Ramsey was gone from Tottenham too. So was Arthur Rowe. The 1954–5 season proved horrendously life-changing for both of them.

Rowe's Tottenham had been like a comet that blazes fantastically and then dims before it vanishes. The champions succumbed, as every side must do eventually, to the scarring that Old Father Time inflicts. No one – not even Rowe or Ramsey – fully factored in the physical demands of playing the way Spurs did season after season. 'Push and run' sapped the energy from them. Rowe was exceptionally loyal to his players, which is a laudable trait in a man but a fatal one in a manager. Change under him, even when it was unavoidable, arrived on a slow boat. Spurs began falling apart and breaking up not long after failing to cling on to their title in 1952, finishing as runners-up to Manchester United. From then on, wear and tear occurred before the rot set solidly in. Their slide was precipitous: 10th place in Coronation year; 16th in both 1954 and 1955. Rowe couldn't arrest the galloping decay in his pride and joy. The stress of trying wrecked him.

The crucial unravelling for Rowe was a fifth round FA Cup tie against Third Division York City at Bootham Crescent in February 1955. Any referee today would declare the pitch too hard and too treacherous. There was snow everywhere. Snow had settled on the grass in great, wide swathes. Snow covered the tiled rooftops of the houses, visible above the low stands and the shallow terracing. Snow stuck to the ball. And snow fell, often in a blizzard, and turned to slush as the Cup tie went on beneath a sky so dully grey that it was impossible to see even a curl of smoke from the nearby chimneys. But York could have sold every one of the 21,000 tickets at least twice. The game went ahead because of that fact.

Spurs were a goal up so quickly – the 11th minute – that no one anticipated the upset that was coming. York equalised almost on the half-hour and scored again with their next attack. There were ten minutes to go – Spurs had barely threatened in the second half – when the most unlikely giant-killers claimed a third to the disbelief of the crowd, some of whom were pressed behind the kind of quaint white picket fencing you'd find protecting a country garden. The 3–1 defeat devastated Rowe, his nerves already as delicate as a candle flame. Overwork had weakened him before. He'd gone through one break-down 13 months earlier and had returned shakily and too soon, his recovery incomplete. The defeat at York precipitated another collapse. In the 1950s, almost no one talked about – and few understood or were sympathetic towards – matters of mental health, which was stigmatised. Terms like 'nut house' or 'loony bin' were used with a lack of compassion to describe institutions that were Victorian in both attitude and architecture. Psychiatry was a primitive business too: often the 'treatment' was electric shocks delivered to the brain.

Rowe rested in mid-April, on doctor's orders, willingly admitting himself to a sanatorium for 'exhaustion'. He never managed Spurs again. His absence came at the worst possible time for Ramsey and, as far as he was concerned, Jimmy Anderson was the worst possible successor to Rowe. He and Ramsey barely tolerated one another. Ramsey thought of Anderson as a showman who was always his own best advocate. Anderson resented the confidences Ramsey, the teacher's pet, and Rowe traded together, excluding him from the conversation. He mistrusted and disliked him.

Ramsey had expected Spurs to slot him into a coaching role, ideally by moving Anderson sideways to shuffle papers. Shortly afterwards, he would be anointed as Rowe's heir apparent. That calculation contained two critical misjudgements. Ramsey didn't think he needed to flatter his teammates or foster popular support for his candidature. Arrogantly complacent, he also assumed his England caps – three of them as captain – and the club captaincy, which Rowe handed to him at the start of the 1954–5 season, were all the qualifications he needed to overwhelm the competition of his only internal rival, Bill Nicholson.

After retiring as a player nine months before, Nicholson immediately became a coach. Ramsey was unworried, believing that when the time came, Rowe would back him instead, a card to trump all others. But, without Rowe there to play it, Ramsey found himself suddenly marooned, cut adrift from where the decisions were made.

Nicholson was every southerner's idea of a Yorkshireman: blunt, bluff, toughly no-nonsense and no-frills. He had played a cleverer game than Ramsey. He practically lived 'above the shop'. It's only a slight exaggeration to claim that his life-long home, which originally belonged to the club, was close enough to White Hart Lane that a stray shot could have broken his front window. Despite winning just one cap (he was a redundant reserve for 22 internationals), Nicholson steadily ingratiated himself with Walter Winterbottom, the alliance useful for both of them. Soon a disciple, he bought completely into Winterbottom's approach and his beliefs. He passed his FA coaching badge with Winterbottom's encouragement too.

Ramsey had benefited more than Nicholson from Winterbottom's patronage, but he still considered him under-qualified and over-praised, substantially inferior to Rowe. He also didn't believe the FA's coaching badge was necessary for someone of his playing pedigree.

Rowe, he said, had offered him a university education; he didn't need to attend Winterbottom's remedial classes.

When Ramsey arrived at Spurs, Rowe gave him the locker next to Nicholson's, hoping the two of them would form a partnership of like-minded souls. They chose instead to row, most of their confrontations being heard by everyone with a front-row seat. It was said – unkindly and unfairly – that Nicholson did all Ramsey's tackling for him and Eddie Baily did all his running. Nicholson certainly resented how much of his own game he was obliged to sacrifice for Ramsey's. He also resented how the spotlight hung over Ramsey's performances as a consequence. Lastly, he thought Ramsey was ungrateful for all the graft others put in on his behalf.

The wrong word said at the wrong time between them was like tossing a lighted match on to dry straw. Ted Ditchburn's understudy, Ron Reynolds, compared the swapping of insults between them as 'out and out war', the arguments 'enormous' and 'blazing'. He said that Ramsey was 'terrible like that' because he didn't suffer – gladly or otherwise – those he perceived as 'fools'. 'He would quickly chew you out if he disagreed with you,' added Reynolds, speaking from harsh experience.

Tottenham's directors believed he was too touchy, too condescending, too confrontational and sure to split the dressing room. Ramsey was severely critical of others because he was also severely critical of himself. 'I don't too much like to be told I have had a wonderful game. I prefer it when someone points out a fault,' he said.

The main faults with Ramsey were his prickly and irritable personality and his know-all sarcasm, which led to suspicion and mis-understandings. The fact he didn't appear to care who he upset, or even whether or not he was well liked, fractured or broke his relation-ships within the team. As Nicholson said of Ramsey, damning him in the process: 'He was eager to acquire knowledge and you had the impression he was storing it up for when he became a manager. He wasn't the type to share it.'

Ramsey's isolation at Spurs was entirely of his own making. And his struggle for power with Nicholson was lost as soon as Rowe made what turned out to be his last signing.

* * *

A photograph, taken in the Tottenham car park, shows Danny Blanchflower shaking hands with Alf Ramsey, who is supposedly there to welcome him. It is December 1954. Blanchflower, a Belfast 'boy' now aged almost 29, has arrived at Spurs via Glentoran, Barnsley and Aston Villa, who cajoled Arthur Rowe into signing him for as much as £30,000 – only £4,500 below the Football League's record fee.

In the photo, Ramsey's half-smile looks painted on. He seems about as pleased to see Blanchflower as the swimmer is to find a shark in the same water. Blanchflower had a reputation in fusty, know-your-place English boardrooms as a 'troublemaker' for daring to have opinions and being unafraid to voice them – loudly, if necessary. He questioned decisions. He promoted player welfare. He didn't doff his cap. At Barnsley, Blanchflower had the temerity to ask his manager whether the team might practise more with a ball; he didn't want to slog around the perimeter track or do press-ups and stretches. The request produced an exchange, both comic and depressing, that typified the illogical approach to training and preparation in England:

Manager: We think if you don't see the ball from Monday to
Friday, then you'll want it more on a Saturday.
Blanchflower: If I don't see it from Monday to Friday, I might not
recognise it on a Saturday.

One swooning admirer, writing in Charles Buchan's *Football Monthly*, said of Blanchflower: 'If he were a politician, I would vote for him and so would you.' Blanchflower possessed in abundance what Ramsey lacked: charisma. He was dashing, ebullient, loquacious, charming and witty. He was also controversial in his opinions and publicity-savvy. He wrote for newspapers without the need of a ghost to do it for him. He even learnt how to type, fairly quickly, with two fingers. Eventually, when Spurs wanted him to adhere to a Football League dictum that no player should contribute to newspapers or appear on TV or radio without the club's permission, Blanchflower refused to agree a new contract. He relented only when a clause was inserted that allowed him to do whatever media work took his fancy. His first column after signing it – he wrote regularly for London's *Evening News* – attacked the Football League for its bone-headed attempt to strangle free speech. The League, also considering Blanchflower to be a dangerous rabble-rouser, demanded that Spurs punish him. The club, eager to satisfy the request, wanted to fine him £5. To win the argument against them, Blanchflower had to do nothing more than quote the rights and privileges his contract guaranteed him. He was still summoned to the boardroom for a meeting with the Spurs chairman. Blanchflower sat down, producing a notebook and pen. 'What are you doing?' the chairman asked. 'Well, if you say anything interesting, I'm going to quote you,' he said. Spurs backed down, and the Football League lost face.

Ramsey was apprehensive about Blanchflower dropping into the gap at Spurs that Nicholson had left, a vacancy that had never been adequately filled. Ramsey knew he wouldn't do his heavy lifting for him. He also discovered, from day one, that Blanchflower was confident to a degree that disturbed him. Ramsey was being challenged by someone as articulate as a poet; he couldn't compete.

Blanchflower didn't take to Ramsey, regarding him as a 'miserable' man who 'thought too highly of himself and little of anyone else'. Even if Ramsey had been congenial company, Blanchflower still wouldn't have sided with him. His view of the game was incompatible with Ramsey's. It was Blanchflower who laid out a manifesto for football so eloquent and so revered that Spurs still display it at their ground:

The great fallacy is that the game is first and last about winning. It is nothing of the kind. The game is about glory. It is about doing things in style, with a flourish, about going out and beating the other lot, not waiting for them to die of boredom.

Naïvely romantic and wonderfully idealistic as he may have been, Blanchflower believed every word. You only have to read those four sentences to know why he preferred Nicholson to the dispassionate Ramsey, not only as a manager or coach, but also as a character. Blanchflower said he and Nicholson thought alike. 'Our only objective was a higher fulfilment from the game.'

Blanchflower found himself in an invidious position after Rowe's abrupt departure shackled him to Jimmy Anderson. He'd been lured to Spurs to play for someone he respected. He was now playing for a manager he considered to be genial but over-promoted. Anderson shrewdly made Nicholson his assistant for two reasons: it nullified the sole threat to his own survival, and it also placated Blanchflower, who had advocated Nicholson's appointment.

Ramsey saw it as a conspiracy against him. He never forgot it. Nor did he wholly forgive Blanchflower and Nicholson for their collusion. Spurs, the club he considered as family, had stitched him up; and Rowe, gone and ailing, was in no position to rectify a horrible wrong.

Ramsey was livid. The depth of his hurt didn't quite add up – unless you were intimately aware of the club's internal politics – but he was diplomatic enough not to mention Nicholson or Blanchflower. What he did suggest – the words slipped in like small knives – was that Spurs had treated him shabbily. 'I shall be glad to leave White Hart Lane ... My future there is obviously finished.'

Ramsey had once described himself as 'a quiet fellow who never shows emotion'. Well, he was about to show it now.

Woe poured out of the victim. Ramsey had played 35 consecutive matches during the previous season, before sustaining a foot injury, which took more than a month to heal. He came back into a team that lost two games consecutively. Spurs dropped Ramsey before delivering a calculated snub, leaving him at home while the rest of the squad went on an exhibition tour of Hungary in May. He labelled it 'The greatest disappointment of my career . . . it was a blow that I will never forget.' This, from a man who had lost to the United States . . . who had lost to Hungary . . . who had lost an FA Cup semi-final because of his own incompetence.

Included in his sourest of parting shots was another charge levelled against Spurs, intended to prove gratuitous cruelty. Ramsey said he'd agreed to play in a trial game for them to prove both himself and his fitness. 'I said yes . . . I wasn't picked . . . At least that showed me where I stood.'

It seemed preposterous to Ramsey that 'his' club had callously let go of him when he was so devoted to them and possessed such obvious potential as a 'thinking' coach. It would be another seven years before Ramsey realised how fortunate he'd been.

His end at Spurs was his beginning elsewhere.

* * *

In August 1955, Ipswich Town, a club playing in dignified poverty and with a brief, patchwork history behind it, announced that 'Mr Alf Ramsey' had been appointed as their manager.

The start of the new season was less than a fortnight away.

Ramsey replaced Scott Duncan, who had been boss since 1937. Duncan had forsaken Manchester United for Ipswich, then in the Southern League. This seems a lunatic act – until you learn that United had been relegated the previous season while Manchester City imperiously won the League Championship. Ipswich were also paying him a ludicrously high salary: £2,000 per year.

Duncan was described as 'softly spoken' and 'scholarly'. He always wore a suit and tie, and on match days arrived in a black homburg hat and dark coat. Stanley Matthews likened him to 'a bank manager'.

Duncan behaved like one. Born on the north bank of the River Clyde, he also acted as though he wanted to prove that a Scotsman's reputation for frugality was not misplaced, counting every farthing in and every halfpenny out. When one of his players asked him for a penny to buy a cup of tea on the way to a match, Duncan barked at him: 'You pay for your own tea.' He felt no shame after being caught watering down the bottle of whisky that Ipswich left in the referee's room as a gift. He dropped one of his team moments before kick-off because the player had dared to go to the toilet. He refused to allow any of his team to drive a car or own a motorbike. One player would secretly ride his motorbike into the town centre, before catching a bus to Portman Road. Duncan was preposterously superstitious, framing a four-leaf clover and hanging it on his office wall. For some reason, which no one ever resolved, he had a particular dread of hairpins. He couldn't pass one without picking it up from the ground. The players, cottoning on to this peculiarity, would buy hairpins from Woolworths and scatter them wherever Duncan was due to go. He didn't suspect a thing.

After 18 years in charge, Duncan, who was almost 67, had 'agreed' to retire; he nonetheless still hung around and poked his nose into everything.

Recruiting Ramsey was a coup for Ipswich, but an abrupt comedown for him. Ipswich had just been relegated with a bump to the Third Division (south). Their fixture list was about to pit them against unglamorous teams at unappealing grounds. Ramsey was swapping Arsenal's Highbury for Walsall's Fellows Park, Manchester City's Maine Road for Shrewsbury Town's Gay Meadow, Wolves' Molineux for Southend's Roots Hall. A continent, rather than a mere 75 miles and two divisions, seemed to separate White Hart Lane and Portman Road.

It could have been worse.

The first suitor to come along had been Great Yarmouth of the Eastern Counties League. Yarmouth were taking such a wild punt that even the cost of the postage was scarcely worth it. The club must have known that Ramsey would tell them he had no desire to drop out of the Football League.

Coverage of all sport was sparse in those post-war years when paper came at a premium price. The newspapers were predominantly broadsheet, the typography dense and uninviting and the ink so heavy that it rubbed off on your hands, blackening the skin as though you'd been picking up coal. Football's latest news and tittle-tattle was jammed on to half a page at best.

Ramsey's move to Ipswich fitted into a mere paragraph (or two) in most of the morning editions. He was just another ex-player, reduced to the indignity of scrabbling about in the lower divisions, trying to succeed in a profession that came with a high casualty rate. Few gave him a chance of surviving. After only a week at Ipswich, Ramsey didn't think he would survive either.

'I had no plan,' he admitted. 'The first thing I had to do was to forget my set ideas on how football ought to be played. My experience had been in the First Division. I soon found out that what I faced . . . was very different.'

3

GRACE KELLY, THE ALDERMAN
AND THE CHIMPANZEE

He found management awfully awkward. At first, it was like walking around in a pair of shoes that did not quite fit him.

In public, Alf Ramsey declared that Ipswich Town was 'the chance I had been waiting for'. In private, he found himself in turmoil. Less than six months after arriving there, Ramsey had offered – or threatened – to resign so many times that his new employer lost count, refusing on each occasion to let him leave.

He feared that what had initially struck him as an awfully big adventure was about to turn nastily into an awfully big mistake He'd taken over a demoralised club. He'd inherited a ragbag of a squad, mostly unfit for purpose. The first team he picked included five players who were either pushing 30 or already beyond it. The oldest was 35 – a winger-cum-centre forward, Wilf Grant, who had played alongside Ramsey at Southampton.

In his opening league game – against Torquay at Portman Road – nearly 16,000 locals turned up expecting to be dazzled. Instead, the disgusted crowd slow-handclapped the side in the second half, only stopping to indulge in 'ironical cheering' whenever one of their own players mucked up a pass. Ipswich were beaten 2–0. It wasn't that Torquay had done an exemplary demolition job on them, the score failing to reflect Ipswich's constant struggle to complete ordinary tasks.

'We shall play better than this,' said Ramsey afterwards, a statement the *Daily Mail* ridiculed with a sneer: 'This is certainly likely . . . it would be practically impossible to play worse.'

If it had been a theatrical review, rather than a match report, the verdict in the *Eastern Daily Times* would have closed the show immediately, the season over. 'In four years of reporting football,' lamented that newspaper's correspondent, 'one cannot recall anything even approximating this display of dissatisfaction and frustration on the part of the spectators.'

Ramsey wasn't even sure he could fulfil the modest promise he had offered the *Mail*.

Four days after the debacle, also at Portman Road, Ipswich somehow roused themselves to beat Southampton 4–2, but the ghastliness of the defeat to Torquay meant 4,000 fewer fans bothered to watch it. Next, Ramsey lost 2–1 at Newport. After again facing Southampton – a 2–2 draw at The Dell – Ipswich were 18th in the table. The novelty of chronicling a former England captain during his nascent days as a novice manager was quickly wearing off for newspapers that had originally sent reporters to cover the man, not the club. Neither seemed likely to bring glory to the other.

In these very early days, a chain of error and doubt, Ramsey became maudlin and introspective, the sudden drop in his status still more difficult to accept. For the extra pay – and because of his urge for 'total control' – he'd insisted on becoming both manager *and* secretary. He was technically over-qualified for the first post and completely under-qualified for the second.

Ipswich had originally wanted Ramsey as player–manager. He rejected the idea, telling them it was impossible to contemplate coaching players who would also be his teammates. In his first season, however, it might have been useful: Ramsey could have shown the others how to play.

* * *

Think of the early-to-mid-1950s, and what instantly comes to mind is an England, despite its new Queen, so bereft of colour and sparkle that nearly everything seems cast in a sombre monochrome light. The country had accepted for so long the deprivations of rationing, restrictions and shortages. It continued to make do and mend, obliged to carry on regardless, even after the last coupons for food or furniture, sweets, soap and petrol were torn up.

Throughout the decade one survey after another revealed that two-thirds of the population considered themselves to be 'working class'. For many, truly bumping along at the bottom, their homes were so unsanitary that the 'bathroom' was the kitchen sink and an outside lavatory. The rooms, upstairs and down, were so cramped that families fell over one another. A local politician in the north, winning the top prize for insensitivity, called for these homes to be made bigger. 'A man should have privacy to tell his wife off,' he said. The good times were about to roll – a house-building programme was already under way and consumerism would follow – but the change to come remained barely detectable to the ordinary man and woman, who struggled on with little inkling that the age of austerity was about to be transformed into the age of 'You've never had it so good' affluence. As a town, Ipswich then was like every other on the map – desperately in need of a renaissance that would lead to a recovery. Alf Ramsey found that the dust of the war still clung to it. The centre was grey and dingy, the shops entirely lacking kerb appeal. Shrapnel left by the bombs the Luftwaffe had dropped littered the docks, as well as the land around them.

Ramsey was no dandy, but he cut a dapper figure against a dowdy background. In 1955, even a First Division player didn't dress much differently from most of those who paid to see him. Clothes rationing had ended in 1949, but there were plenty of men who still considered a demob suit to be their Sunday best. Keen to appear prosperous, Ramsey had sharpened himself up sartorially while at Tottenham. Wanting to look like a boss rather than a worker, he'd invested in mohair suits, usually tucking a white handkerchief into his top pocket, as well as sober ties and shoes that he polished to a mirrored shine.

At Ipswich, he looked like someone who'd taken a wrong turning on his way to a cocktail reception.

You'd have thought nothing much had changed at Portman Road since the day Ipswich had joined the Football League 17 years earlier. It could have passed for a slum awaiting the bulldozers. Near a lean bend of the River Orwell, the ground sat opposite a cattle market, where Suffolk's farmers gathered every Tuesday to haggle over livestock. One of the stands was named after Churchman's cigarette factory, which stood behind it and produced about a million fags per day for consumers who, despite the first published research into the carcinogenic effects of smoking, didn't know or didn't care or feigned indifference about the fact that their habit might kill them.

Ramsey occupied an office beside the dressing rooms. It was cold, inhospitably bleak and as spartan as a monk's cell. The office was a square prefabricated hut rather than a room, and it did not have a view – the only window overlooked bland concrete. Ramsey's telephone was fastened, at stomach height, to the wall behind his leather-topped desk. The roof occasionally leaked, forcing him to go in search of tin buckets in which to catch the drips. The dressing rooms, housed in a 'pavilion' built in 1907, were even worse. A player in bare feet might get a splinter from the wooden floor or catch his flesh on a nail poking out of the slightly warped boards. The enamel tiles on and around the postage-stamp-sized communal bath were cracked and a little grimy. The boiler to heat the water was a filthy coke-fired contraption that frequently broke down. The boardroom was no better. The table was so big that the sides of it almost touched each wall. The carpet – an odd, lightish shade of pink – was pockmarked, the ingrained stains caused by carelessly spilt alcohol, cigarette ash and crumbs of food that had been crushed underfoot.

No wonder Ramsey wanted to be anywhere else.

* * *

Like the country, English football in the 1950s was in constant transition, unsure about where exactly it was going or what it wanted to be. In the month that Alf Ramsey took over at Ipswich, *Picture Post* magazine ran an interview with the Football League's secretary, Fred Howarth. It appeared below the headline:

Big Changes Are Coming

If true, Howarth came across as the least likely administrator to implement them, the kind of man who only pretended to have the game's best interests at heart. He wanted to get his own way and was outlandish in his stubbornness and dislike of almost anything other than the status quo. Howarth ran the League like the local corner shop. He had enough clout to introduce his own 'accounting system'. The other committee members signed blank cheques, allowing him to pay the bills.

Howarth was born in 1888, the year the League formed. He'd become assistant secretary in 1921, conveniently appointed by his father-in-law. The blatant nepotism worked: Howarth succeeded him a dozen years later. He worked from a desk in what had once been the front bedroom of a Victorian terrace in Preston. The League eschewed London, not wanting to betray its provincial roots. Howarth was convinced that geography would preserve the League's separate identity from what he saw as the threat of the overbearing Football Association.

Gates at League matches were as high as 39.6 million in 1950–1, but had fallen to 34.1 million by 1954–5. According to *Picture Post*, the 'big changes' Howarth envisaged to counter the decline were based on a 'probable reduction in clubs', but he blustered unspecifically about the future – except when it came to those things about which he was either dubious or opposed.

It was a long list.

He was unsure about floodlights. He insisted that 'attractive' midweek friendlies under them would 'reduce attendances' on Saturdays. He was against televising matches, describing bids to show them from both the BBC and its newly launched commercial rival ITV as a 'headache' (for the time being, he'd decided to put the question of TV to 'one side', as though the 'idiot box' was a fad).

There were those who thought Howarth was pro-Europe – supporting the recently formed European Cup – but his words and deeds hid much of his supposed rah-rah enthusiasm for it. The League succeeded in pressurising the champions, Chelsea, to withdraw from the 1955–6 competition after the draw for the opening round was made.

Howarth imprinted his dour personality on the League the way a fossil imprints itself on rock.

He was against the Professional Footballers' Association and also against abolishing the maximum wage. He raged against the possibility of an open market, occasionally getting so worked up that those who heard him thought he might spontaneously combust. He believed it would kill the League. He was perfectly satisfied that footballers – after adding in bonuses and benefits – were 'well paid' in relation to the hours 'they put in'.

The amount workers took home climbed steadily in the 1950s, but not enough to push them into prosperity. Their weekly plan of escape – their hope of scaling the social ladder in a single stroke – was the football pools, which (often after spending money the household couldn't afford) were checked every Saturday tea-time, even by those who couldn't identify Arsenal from Arbroath. As a Methodist, Howarth despised gambling as much as the prospect of footballers being paid a wage commensurate with the takings at the turnstiles. Under him, the League raked in nothing from the pools because it refused to accept the money. He seemed to think, however, that players' salaries were like a weekly pools win. He supplied *Picture Post* with figures to support his claim. In 1954–5, 187 players earned more than £800; 623 earned between £700 and £800; 1,620 earned over £500.

No one at Ipswich, including Ramsey, ever expected to get rich.

* * *

Since Alf Ramsey couldn't inspire himself, he turned to a familiar source to do it for him. He went to Arthur Rowe, who was still coping with troubles of his own.

Ramsey, experiencing a crisis, wanted to see a friendly face, someone with whom he could talk openly, complain, theorise and – most of all – unburden himself about what he'd found at Ipswich. He knew that Rowe wouldn't flannel him.

Rowe had an abundance of time to spare for Ramsey. He'd refused to consider the blandishments of other League clubs who wanted to hire him. He needed a break and was about to start travelling, like a superior salesman, to promote a pair of boots he'd designed and endorsed.

In slow recovery, physically he was a silhouette of his former self: gaunt, frail, downcast. Despite this, he summoned the strength to console Ramsey and restore some of the confidence the opening months of management had drained from him.

At Tottenham, Rowe had been the sort of boss who had an open-door policy. Cups of tea and sympathy were dispensed for those who needed them. He was never the kind of manager who shouted, as though wanting to be heard in a debating chamber. Meetings in his office were not dissimilar to the talks he gave on the training pitch. He was gently patient, quiet rather than shrill, emollient rather than tetchy. Catechism was a favoured technique: 'Have you ever thought of that . . .?' 'What if you did this . . .?' 'How about this idea . . .?' As Rowe said: 'I never told anyone how to play. I just made impressions on playing patterns, put up ideas. I'd ask players if they had ever tried a certain move, talk it over with them, get them to discuss it between themselves . . . then we'd try it out.' In this way, he coaxed a player into thinking he had solved his own problem.

With Ramsey, he did nothing more than plough old ground, giving him a pep talk and a refresher on the principles of management. Ramsey went back to Ipswich to start again, aware from his experience under Rowe that success seldom comes without some suffering and a lot of strife. He remembered that Rowe's ripping success at Spurs, perceived as having come practically overnight, had been prefaced by those seasons of relatively obscure slog at Chelmsford. He hunkered down for the long haul.

His reliance on Rowe became so obvious that any Ipswich player who found Ramsey on the phone in his office – especially on a Monday morning – knew who would be on the other end. 'He would be . . . talking football and picking his brains,' said one player after overhearing those conversations.

* * *

Near the close of that same season, *Picture Post* attempted to promote the idea that winter was the worst possible time to play the game in England. Summer, it argued, was the only sensible option to 'save football' from itself. 'Unless something is done . . . it is doomed,' said the magazine.

The photograph it used as proof was of an unidentified match played on a mud heap. The pitch was covered in sheets of water. A high bank of terracing and the houses behind it were wreathed in thick mist. The players were just dark shapes, as though photographed at midnight. The two closest to the camera were sloshing towards the ball, one of them throwing up a spray of wet dirt that reached the top of his calves. Here, *Picture Post* declared, was a quintessential scene. It asked: 'Who wants to queue, pay and stand for this?'

It was different at Ipswich Town.

Portman Road was an architectural dump, but the stands sheltered a trimmed pitch that looked like paradise when Alf Ramsey first saw it. It was so smooth that you could have played snooker on it. The lovely grass would have been perfect for Tottenham's 'push and run' team, who would surely have flourished there. For Ipswich's far less able combatants, the five-star surface initially exposed two-star passing. Ramsey had wanted to play like Spurs but accepted that practicality should get the edge over art.

What Ramsey did was taken directly from 'the book of Arthur Rowe', in which 'everything, no matter how trivial, seemed important'. Rowe's approach at Spurs had been so basic that it made every other style seem overwrought. 'Football's a simple game. It's the players who make it difficult,' he'd say. Simplicity was always Ramsey's style too. He agreed with Rowe's assessment that 'It's just a case of doing the obvious.'

Rowe broke his beliefs down into bitesize quotes that Ramsey would repeat:

A good player runs to the ball. A bad player runs after it.
Put good football before results. Do it, and the results will come.
You do not ask the players to do the things they cannot do.
It's a team game. Everybody has to come into it.
Don't worry about the opposition. Let them worry about you.

Ramsey took control of players who were not his own. Scott Duncan had brought in Billy Reed, a former milkman who became a Welsh international winger; the forward Tom Garneys, a centre forward at Notts County, until Tommy Lawton seized his shirt; Tommy Parker, a goal-scorer recruited from the navy who had a penchant for cricket; and John Elsworthy, a wing half given his own boots by Ipswich but forced to buy his own laces by skinflint Duncan.

The most significant figure was Jimmy Leadbetter, a winger who'd been bought during the summer Ramsey took over. He was nick-named 'Sticks' because he looked nothing like an athlete; he was more like a stray who'd been taken in on a particularly wet day. His body and limbs resembled a collection of broom handles tied together. Just 27, he was so scrawny that you'd have thought a decent gust off the North Sea would have not only blown him over, but also inside out. He had a long, lined face that was sunken around the mouth because of the number of teeth his dentist had already extracted. He smoked Woodbines, often accepting a lit one from the Ipswich trainer. When he arrived at the club from Brighton for £1,750, Leadbetter went to the newsagent's to buy a paper and heard another customer, canvassed for his verdict on the 'new arrival', remark: 'I hear they've signed another has-been.' A fellow new recruit saw Leadbetter smoking at the back of stand and asked innocently: 'Who's that old fellow?'

'That's our star player,' he was told.

When Rowe went to White Hart Lane, barely knowing anyone, he'd pledged to give each player 'a chance'. Those had been Ramsey's opening words at Ipswich too, and his players began to reward his faith in them. Ipswich ran up 11 goals in their next two matches – 6–2 against Swindon and 5–2 against Walsall. Between early September and early May, Ramsey lost only five league games. Emphatic wins piled up: 5–0 and 3–0 against Millwall; 5–1 against Reading; 5–0 against Northampton; and 4–1 against Queen's Park Rangers. Parker hit 30 goals, plus another in the FA Cup.

Ramsey carried Ipswich into third place. Given how soon it was into his tenure, that seems more than satisfactory until you realise how close he came to promotion. Easter proved to be his Becher's Brook. The fixture list was punishing. Forced to play Norwich twice in four days – and Coventry in between those derbies – Ramsey got a win at Portman Road (4–1) but lost at both Carrow Road (3–2) and Highfield Road (3–1). Ipswich had been second in the table on Good Friday, a point ahead of Brighton. By Easter Monday, they were two points behind them. In the end, the Third Division (south) went to a photo finish. The champions, Leyton Orient, ended up one point in front of Brighton, who were a point better off than Ramsey's Ipswich.

You win championships and promotions as much at the beginning of a season as at the end. With a faster start, Ipswich would have gone up straightaway, but what comforted Ramsey was the response from his board. The congratulations he got for making a decent fist of things were genuine. So were the commiserations and the pledge of continued support.

Within another 12 months, Ipswich had won the Third Division (south) title. The passage of time has smudged the fine print of that feat, and also some of the players who achieved it, but what Ramsey did during the 1956–7 season counts as the great resurrection. On September 29, after 13 games, Ipswich were 20th in the table, one point from the bottom and nine from the top. Again, Ramsey went to see Rowe. Again, Rowe dispensed advice like restorative medicine. On May 1, Ipswich were champions on goal average.

The team scored 101 goals – 41 of them coming from Ted Phillips who, at 23, claimed five hat-tricks. He had been sent on loan to Stowmarket before Ramsey, aware his talent was being wasted, rescued him from the obscurity of the Eastern Counties League. 'He made me out of nothing,' admitted Phillips, who described his manager as a 'god'.

Ramsey was on his way . . .

* * *

Alf Ramsey's favourite saying of Arthur Rowe's was: 'Fifty per cent of the people in the game are bluffers.' He had met some of those 'bluffers' in the boardroom at Tottenham, where amateurs pontificated and pretended to know more than professionals. He despised them most for their cruelty and their lack of appreciation towards Rowe.

Ramsey had seen the back-slapping for Rowe turn into back-stabbing. Ungrateful directors, for whom Rowe could do no wrong after winning them the championship, sniped or let him stew in disdainful silence when he couldn't repeat it. Their treatment of him led to his breakdown.

At Ipswich, the job Ramsey did would have been impossible without someone who, like Rowe, championed him.

He was John Cobbold.

A week after Ramsey secured promotion, Cobbold became Ipswich chairman. He was only 29 years old. Ramsey now had what the other 91 League managers craved: a benevolent boss who was uninterested in power, who didn't even have his own desk at Portman Road, who refused to placate trouble-makers, and who believed his primary purpose was to provide backing, both practical and emotional.

The Cavalier and the Roundhead: Alf Ramsey and John Cobbold

Cobbold's character is epitomised in what he did on the night Ipswich got into Division Two. He decided to throw an impromptu party in the team's hotel, bribing the pianist and violinist not to go home after their shift and hauling extra musicians in from the street.

Ramsey drank so much that, during the wee small hours, Cobbold found him spread out on his back beneath a table. He was singing the opening verse of 'Maybe It's Because I'm a Londoner'.

Cobbold, the least censorious of men, loved that.

* * *

Often fiction can't compete with real life.

John Cobbold was such a supreme eccentric that he deserves emblematic status. Even Evelyn Waugh or P. G. Wodehouse, who specialised in creating extraordinarily capricious characters, might have been too timid to wholly invent Cobbold in case their readers refused to believe that such a man could possibly exist.

The rich are different from the rest of us, but very few chaps with money to burn did so as brightly and as extravagantly as Cobbold. A maverick to a surreal degree, he was wonderfully mercurial – bonkers in a compassionate, civilised, patrician sort of a way. Those who met him never forgot him.

These are the simple facts about a manifestly complicated figure.

Cobbold was born in 1927. Privilege guaranteed him the silver-spoon upbringing of a prince. His father was John Murray Cobbold, a colonel in the Scots Guards who was nicknamed 'Ivan' – after Ivan the Terrible – because of his pyrotechnical childhood anger. The sobriquet stuck so rigidly that only strangers called him anything else except 'Colonel'. Cobbold's mother was Lady Blanche Cavendish, the second daughter of the 9th Duke of Devonshire.

The family seat was the red-brick Glemham Hall, a part-Elizabethan, part-Queen Anne mansion rooted amid 2,900 acres of Suffolk's lushly green and pleasant land. *Country Life*, enraptured by the 'full Palladian flavour' of the place, devoted its cover to the Cobbolds, who were pictured wearing tweeds and stout shoes, every square inch of them an advertisement for the rural gentry.

Ivan was such an expert marksman that he frequently out-shot King George VI at Sandringham. *Country Life* also featured his Scottish grouse moors at Millden, comprising 20,000 acres through which the North Esk river ran.

What paid for all this was a fortune soaked in beer. The family firm, the brewery Tolly Cobbold, was created in 1723, a year when Robert Walpole was prime minister and Christopher Wren, after wandering about St Paul's Cathedral without a heavy coat, caught a chill and died.

John Cobbold's future was drawn for him as precisely as the contours on a map. He wanted for nothing. He didn't have to compete for anything. The brewery awaited him. So did a place, aged only 21, on the board of Ipswich Town in 1948. As befits the Cobbolds' unconventional nature, his father had got involved with Ipswich on a mere whim. It happened – improbably – like this.

Ivan was predominantly a racing man. One day in 1935, he went to Hurst Park in Surrey to watch one of his own horses. There he met his friend, the businessman Sir Samuel Hill-Wood, who was a former soldier, a one-time Conservative MP and an ex-County Championship cricketer (he appeared in the *Guinness Book of Records* as the only batsman to score ten runs off a single ball). Hill-Wood's claim to fame in the 1930s was his chairmanship of Arsenal, who were about to win a fourth First Division championship in five seasons.

Ivan and Hill-Wood shared a liquid lunch. Hill-Wood asked him to go to Highbury with him. Ivan, despite being president of the Suffolk County FA, turned him down. 'Not bloody likely. That round-ball thing. Not interested.' Only after being persuaded that his horse was a seaside donkey, likely to trot in last, did Ivan relent. At his first professional game, he marvelled at both the atmosphere and Arsenal's goal-scorers, Cliff Bastin and Ted Drake.

He decided to take over Ipswich, and turned them professional in 1936. The club immediately swapped the Eastern Counties League for the Southern League. In 1938, they squeaked into the Football League by two votes, chiefly because Ivan's wealth promised prosperity, and also because of the influence of Scott Duncan, who got a £1,000 bonus for successfully lobbying on their behalf.

Ivan never saw his investment in Ipswich draw a sumptuous dividend. He was killed by a V1 'doodlebug' in June 1944 during a Sunday service at the Guards Chapel in Wellington Barracks, held to commemorate the D-Day landings. He and Lady Blanche had married there 25 years before.

The son, like the father, was not really a football man, and so had to turn himself into one. He'd been taken to his first match aged eight, but admitted, even after joining the board: 'I know so little about the game that it is criminal.' Decent enough at gun sports, Cobbold was fairly inept at anything to do with a ball, except when playing the Field Game at Eton, a Frankenstein sport combining elements of football and rugby, with an offside rule as complicated as nuclear physics.

Cobbold didn't have the sheen of someone wealthy or important. He had wavy black hair, the colour of oil, which he slicked back, revealing a high forehead and widow's peaks. His face was well creased, the consequence of his louche living. His 'country' jackets were loose-fitting and he frequently wore wool sweaters beneath them, the V of the neck so high that the knot of his tie was almost the only thing visible. Everyone at Ipswich called him 'Mr John', distinguishing him from his younger brother, 'Mr Patrick'.

Even in his late twenties, Cobbold could sometimes look like a pub landlord who was over-fond of his own products. Quotidian life for him was a non-stop binge that saw him referring to alcohol as his 'drinkie-winkies'. One of Cobbold's close friends said it was advisable to get hold of him 'before noon', if you wanted to talk seriously. His bar bills were bigger than the national debt of a small South

American country; fortunately, he could afford to pay them. When he wasn't drinking, Cobbold smoked incessantly. When not doing either of those things, he swore like a navvy. He could have convincingly played one of those posh rakes frequently found in British comedy films during the 1940s and '50s, the kind of scene-stealing rogue it was impossible not to love.

When the alcohol took Cobbold over, he would be guilty of saying things he shouldn't have – some of them grossly coarse – and doing things that counted as disgracefully unbecoming behaviour. But he could also be kind, scrupulously conscientious and stupidly generous too, paying the club's bills or bailing out players who were experiencing hardship.

Like *The Arabian Nights*, there were a thousand and one tales told about him. At least 95 per cent were true and came without the garnish of poetic licence.

When meeting someone, he did grab their tie and pretend to blow his nose on it.

At a football dinner, where he was supposed to speak, Cobbold did get so drunk that he stood up and immediately vanished beneath the table. He did catch hold of the white tablecloth on his slow descent and take the glasses and side plates with him. He was removed from the room feet-first, like a corpse in a coffin.

He did own a London flat that overlooked Sloane Square, from where he'd shoot pigeons with an air rifle or take aim at milk bottles and TV aerials.

He did instruct the parents of one of Ipswich's most promising players to immediately go to bed 'and get cracking' on the sex, telling the father it was the couple's duty to produce another son capable of 'playing as well as your lad'.

He did – plagiarising and adapting a Winston Churchill quote – once stun a stranger at the Savoy. Cobbold used the urinal, and then began to walk towards the door. The stranger said: 'At Harrow, we were taught to wash our hands afterwards.' Cobbold, without breaking stride, replied tartly: 'At Eton, we were taught not to piss on them.'

He did tell house guests of whom he tired: 'I'm fucking off to bed, but help yourself to the wine.' He often did return to greet them again by sliding down the bannisters in his pyjamas.

He did, while stationed with the army in the Middle East, go out to barter for eggs and end up buying two sheep.

He did shut out his mother and any other woman from the board-room because he didn't want them 'jabbering away' while he told 'dirty stories'.

He did occasionally greet people with a cheery 'Hello, old bean', as if he were still living in the jazz age.

He did buy a chimpanzee for 10s 6d, take the animal with him into the boardroom and introduce it as 'my new director' (the chimpan-zee stole a plate of sandwiches and then escaped through a window, knocking over half-full wine glasses in its break for freedom).

In another boardroom, semi-drunk, he did stumble over the edge of a carpet, performing two somersaults, before stylishly regaining his balance, brushing down the front of his suit and nonchalantly adjust-ing the knot of his tie, as though the pratfall – and his performance afterwards – had been scripted.

He did snub a Suffolk alderman who arrived at a match in his bowler hat. The chain of his watch looped from one waistcoat pocket to the other. After being offered a drink and a cigar, the alderman rather piously refused by saying 'no drop' of alcohol had ever passed his lips and that smoking was 'for chimneys'. Cobbold did as a consequence turn his back on him after delivering a scalding rebuke: 'In which case, sir,' he said, 'we have nothing in common. I bid you good day.'

He did write his name on his shirt cuffs in case he became so inebri-ated on a bender that he couldn't find his way home.

He did, if bored during a meal, chuck bread rolls or flick butter at whomever else was sitting at his table.

He did, while checking on a transfer target during a holiday in Scotland, get drunk on whisky. Afterwards, he did write a lengthy scouting report, without realising the player he'd been sent to watch hadn't appeared in the match at all.

He did once meet a glamorous blonde on the Cresta Run at St Moritz. He and a friend, both entranced by her charm, did invite her to lunch. When it began to snow, he did suggest going to the resort's cinema, where Alfred Hitchcock's *Rear Window* was showing. This is how he took Grace Kelly to watch the film she was starring in.

He did pull a chair away when his younger brother Patrick tried to sit down after making an after-dinner speech.

He did, after being asked about his sex life (Cobbold was believed to be homosexual), reply: 'There's always the dogs,' or 'There's always the donkeys.' He owned a pair of donkeys, allowing them to roam around his house like pet cats. He did, after introducing a prospective signing to them, ask the player: 'Have you ever fucked a donkey?' The deal, unsurprisingly, collapsed in that moment.

And he did say 'fuck' on television, three years before the theatre critic Kenneth Tynan supposedly became the first to do so in 1965. On local TV, Cobbold was asked a damn fool question in a live interview:

Interviewer: Can you tell me what you do at Ipswich Town?
Cobbold: Fuck all.

When Tynan said 'fuck', he whipped up the indignation of 133 Labour and Conservative backbenchers, who signed four separate parliamentary motions. The morality campaigner Mary Whitehouse dragged the Queen into the debate by writing to her. The BBC was forced into making a formal apology, stopping a yard short of promising that Tynan would publicly wash out his mouth with carbolic soap.

Cobbold escaped without censure.

As the nephew of Harold Macmillan, the future prime minister, Cobbold was adopted into the Conservative party but lost twice as a parliamentary candidate. It was just as well. He was more suited to the boardrooms of the brewery and the football club than the House of Commons. 'In no way was I anywhere close to being properly qualified for the job,' he confessed.

He was always very quotable. Anyone who knew nothing about his personality would have assumed he spoke with his tongue firmly pressed into his cheek. It wasn't so. Pretending to be on the periphery of events at Portman Road, he called the decision to make him chairman 'misguided'. His 'efforts for the club', he said, were 'purely social . . . I am there to take care of the hospitality.' He added that he tried to 'give visiting clubs a good time', without needing to explain that 'a good time' came in the form of a vat of wine and a barrel of whisky. Cobbold said he particularly liked football because 'you can have a drink before and afterwards . . . if my health suffers, it is a sacrifice I gladly make for the good of the game'.

His casualness towards what happened on the pitch camouflaged his foresight off it. He wanted to create all-seater stadiums beneath vast roofs. He wanted to play matches on a Sunday. He wanted to provide 'real' attractions before kick-off rather than employ 'some half-wit' blasting out 'canned music' over a loudspeaker.

Cobbold was not behind Ipswich's decision to seek out Ramsey. Another director, Nat Shaw, had known Ramsey for more than a decade. Shaw, a Jewish businessman from London's East End, specialised in two things: greyhounds and the rag trade. Between the wars, he intended to focus his retail empire on Norwich. When the train taking him there stopped at Ipswich, he got out to tour the streets and discovered a gap in the market: the town lacked a suitable dress shop. He'd met Ramsey through their shared passion for greyhounds – Shaw owned dogs, as well as the tracks they ran on, winning two Waterloo Cups – and was initially responsible for Ramsey's wardrobe, making sure the smart suits, shirts, ties and coats he bought came at a generous discount.

From the start, though, Cobbold considered Ramsey to be 'a wonderful man' and sought him out as much as Shaw did. He admired his determination, his industry, his sincerity and the stable influence he soon brought to Portman Road. He was impressed, too, that Ramsey

– while building a side – had passed the two accountancy exams that were imperative to his role as secretary.

The Cavalier Cobbold, who possessed a Corinthian heart, rubbed along well with a Roundhead such as Ramsey. His name for him was 'old stoneface', an insult meant to be endearing, but the secret of their relationship was that each knew how far the other could be pushed. Ramsey was demanding, but also aware of the limitations of working at Ipswich. If he ever went too far, Cobbold would wave his hand at him and say: 'Don't be a silly bugger, Alf.' Otherwise, he didn't get in Ramsey's way and never attempted to impose his will on tactics or selection. 'Football is the game I know least about,' he said. 'I don't talk football with Alf. He doesn't talk about running a brewery with me. No manager should be given advice from anyone in the board-room as to how a team should play. I am someone who has never kicked a ball in his life . . . and I have never argued with him about the team or tactics because he wouldn't stand for it.'

Just one club attempted seriously to take Ramsey away from Ipswich. In September 1956, after sacking Jimmy Seed, First Division Charlton Athletic asked Ramsey to replace him. Seed, boss there for 23 years, had won Charlton the FA Cup nine years before, but after he lost the open-ing five matches of the 1956–7 season, the directors fired him. Fearing a hostile response to the loss of a club legend, they asked Seed to say he had resigned through ill health. Seed dug in indignantly and refused. Ramsey, though flattered by the approach, smelt only decay and duplic-ity at The Valley. Eight months later, Charlton were relegated.

Ipswich was a paterfamilias, concerned for the welfare of the work-ers. If they won, Cobbold drank one bottle of champagne. If they lost, he drank two and would be phlegmatic about the result, however inept. He'd simply remark: 'It wasn't meant to be for us today, but at least we've allowed the other side to experience the sweet pleasure of winning.'

Cobbold was patient. He was aware progress could only come in stages for a club such as Ipswich. Other chairmen, having reached the

Second Division, would have demanded the manager took them into the First instantly. Prepared to wait for that, and seeing the potential in Ramsey, Cobbold allowed him to consolidate and get Ipswich ready for their next promotion. He did not interfere. He did not apply pressure. A vote of confidence from Cobbold was the rarest thing in football: absolutely sincere, a solemn promise on which he wouldn't renege. 'Our manager's name is not written on a chalkboard with a wet sponge nailed beside it,' he once said.

Ramsey already possessed the knowledge to be a manager at the top level, but he had to gain the wisdom to go with it. He was also forceful, but not yet powerful. Like everyone, he stumbled and sometimes made poor choices, but Cobbold gave him the precious gift of time and space to learn his new trade.

After he'd achieved success, Ramsey would look back on his appointment at Ipswich and say: 'I don't think there was anyone better off than me. Not financially, but in freedom . . . They seemed to me to be the ideal club . . . if I failed it would not have been the end of the world.'

He was being disingenuous. If Ramsey had failed, there would barely have been anywhere else for him to go.

4

TALK SLOW AND DON'T SAY TOO MUCH

Alf Ramsey gave the impression of wanting to disprove the poet's claim that no man is an island. He once conceded: 'They say I'm remote. Difficult to get to know. I think this is fair.' The description is actually more than fair; it counts as an understatement.

Ramsey, a knot of Gordian complexity, compartmentalised his life into two parts – home and football – and seldom allowed them to overlap. He made sure that even those who worked closely with him, such as John Cobbold, knew only the bare minimum about him. He invited few people to his home. He neither sought confidences nor offered them. He traded small talk sparingly because he didn't have any, riding out the awkward silences. Smokers, like drinkers, always fib about their consumption, and Ramsey even made lame attempts to cover up his minor nicotine habit, which amounted to only about five cigarettes per day. He puffed away in his office when he thought he wouldn't be interrupted, wafting the blue-grey fumes through his small window. When caught, he became embarrassed and flustered, stubbing out the fag in an ashtray tucked inside his desk drawer.

Cobbold said that Ramsey 'always seemed to find it difficult to make friends', but the truth was he seldom went looking for them. Ramsey was the quintessential example of what the writer Arthur Hopcraft termed 'the football man'. The game consumed him; he spoke of nothing else. On away trips with Ipswich, he wandered from one railway carriage to the next, discussing some aspect of the game with his players. He'd either exhaust or bore them. You could escape, said one player, only if you were able to change the topic abruptly to something else. Ramsey would lose interest and slope off.

With strangers he could be kindly, convivial and likeable – but mostly on his terms and usually for a limited period. If obliged to go to a social event, whether a black-tie ball or pie-and-pea supper at a working man's club, Ramsey did so warily, afraid the questions would be among those he most dreaded – about his past, his personal life or any topic about which he was ignorant. Nervy and over-sensitive about the possibility of that happening, Ramsey could appear an idiosyncratically peculiar figure, even an uncaring one sometimes. But the measured distance he maintained from people for the sake of his own dignity, often mistaken for disdain, was merely the armour he wore. For hidden behind the shy exterior was a shy interior. He kept himself in one of those hard-to-reach places purely for self-protection.

Ramsey was an introvert in an extrovert's job. He was often abrupt, stilted or silent; not to be purposefully rude, but because his conversation was so limited. He had the accent of a gentleman's gentleman. But while knowing how he wanted to sound – and also what he wanted to say – he wasn't polished enough to always carry things off with aplomb. It was said of him: 'The written and spoken word hold for him something close to mortal terror.'

He had a self-conscious concern about the rolling of his vowels and the narrowness of his vocabulary. His sentences were bolted together with the awkwardness of someone assembling flat-pack furniture. If stressed – especially in front of a TV camera – he could get himself into an awful tangle by trying to be something that he clearly wasn't, which was smoothly articulate. He always seemed to be waiting for the English language to stick out a foot and trip him. Often, it did. Spoonerisms, malapropisms or mispronunciations were not unknown. Ramsey tended to choose the wrong word in his struggle to find the right one:

There is great harmonium in our dressing room.
In the second half, we were pushing at an open jar.
It's so hot the compensation is running down the walls.
I may have to make altercations to the side.

Or, when rushing, he would drop his 'h's and 'g's, the anxiety in his voice detectable. His facial expressions would also stiffen, and his gaze, beneath those caterpillar eyebrows, become glassy, a consequence of concentrating so uncomfortably hard. He often found it impossible to relax in front of anyone he didn't know or who wasn't connected with the game. In their company, his speech became clipped and tersely minimalist, which was another coping mechanism.

It was a different matter in the dressing room.

* * *

There was one thing everybody at Portman Road knew about Alf Ramsey because he never tried to hide it: his abiding love for westerns.

Every fortnight, the evening before a Saturday away game, Ramsey took his team to watch a film. No matter where Ipswich went, there was nearly always more than one cinema with more than one screen, but he wanted to see whichever western was being shown there. He was so enthusiastic about westerns that he could not only tell you about the B-list actors in them, but also name their horses. Cowboy films were considered to be low-brow entertainment in which everything was a trope or a stereotype, but Ramsey, relishing their enormous escapist appeal, saw the moral element in them amid the gun smoke. The plots were usually about journeys of discovery leading to revenge or redemption and changed lives, nearly always after an exchange of bullets. Ramsey, who had only ever seen the American West on film, liked the dusty landscapes, the single-street wooden towns and the saloon bar, where a baddie would get thrown through the swing doors. From *Fort Apache* to *Red River*, from *The Searchers* to *She Wore a Yellow Ribbon*, Ramsey would go anywhere to watch John Wayne saddle up. Wayne, always the good guy, demonstrated an insouciant boldness that appealed to him.

But one of Wayne's movies that resonated with Ramsey doesn't find the actor wearing a Stetson or carrying a Colt revolver. It was a black-and-white film from 1953, now rarely seen, even on those channels that specialise in vintage Hollywood. *Trouble Along the Way* is about the beauty of second chances and a display of backbone. Wayne plays a divorced former American football coach called Steve Williams, currently in his cups, who is enticed to an impecunious Catholic college on the precipice of closure. He goes there to revive its gridiron fortunes in the belief that sporting glory will guarantee the college's survival. Of course, he inherits a troop of unruly misfits. Of course, Wayne's character, proud of his own rough edges, transforms them, while being as flexible with the rules and regulations as a circus contortionist. Of course, you can guess the rest.

Ramsey would never have indulged in chicanery, but he liked the spirit of *Trouble Along the Way* and saw broad parallels in it, and in the part Wayne had played, with his own position at Portman Road. He even mentioned the film in one of his early team talks. He recruited the kind of players no one else rated or wanted – especially their former clubs, who couldn't sell them quickly enough in case Ramsey changed his mind. To the squad that won the Third Division (south) title he added Ray Crawford, a left-sided attacker with a skilful right foot, from Portsmouth for £5,000 in 1958; the centre half Andy Nelson, who cost £8,500 from West Ham nine months later; Roy Stephenson, an outside right, who arrived from Leicester City for next to nothing in the summer of 1960; and two wing halves – John Compton, a £2,000 buy from Chelsea, and Bill Baxter from the amateurs of Broxburn Athletic, a team from West Lothian.

Ramsey's sixth sense was to see not only what no one else saw in a player, but also how the new signing would slot into his big plan.

When Jimmy Leadbetter joined Ipswich as an inside forward, Ramsey transformed his career with a question: 'How do you fancy playing outside left?' A perplexed Leadbetter replied: 'Well, the last time I played that position, I was at school.' He expressed the fear he'd be 'too slow'.

'It's not how fast you go,' Ramsey reassured him. 'It's how fast the ball goes.'

Just as he knew Leadbetter was the right player in the wrong role, he also knew that Crawford and Ted Phillips would slot together like a dovetail joint. Crawford was a poacher, claiming the six-yard box as his own and seizing on whatever a goalkeeper spilled. Those opportunities came often to him because his partner had a shot fiercer than Bobby Charlton's. Even in the 1960s, when calculating such things was a cruder business, Phillips could propel a ball at 87mph.

Ramsey also turned Compton into a left back and Baxter into a defender. Leadbetter explained his manager's perceptiveness like this: 'If someone had never played in goal, but he said to them, "You can be goalkeeper," they'd have become one – and been good at it. He knew where everyone should play.'

After his unpleasantly sour exit from Tottenham, Ramsey learnt to be more accommodating and less adversarial. He looked after his players the way Arthur Rowe had looked after him. Disliking the term 'gaffer' – it was too redolent of the building site – he insisted on being called 'Alf'.

Leadbetter thought that 'Alf' was successful because he 'never asked anyone to do something that was beyond them'. The other primary factors, he said, were that he 'never lost his rag', never patronised anyone and never criticised, publicly or privately, one player in front of another. There was a code of loyalty and fairness enshrined in Ramsey, which he took from Rowe. 'He would never put anyone in an awkward position,' said Leadbetter. 'If he had anything to say, he would just have a wee blether in the corner.' Leadbetter was a grateful beneficiary of Ramsey's progressive attitude towards man management. 'He treated me like a man and not a wee daft laddie.' Again, this stemmed directly from Rowe.

Ramsey was a resolutely modern coach, open to new ideas, but with old-fashioned virtues. His work togs were a tracksuit and boots, at a time when a lot of managers – even in the First Division – went to training sessions wearing a suit and an overcoat and stood on the touchline. Ramsey believed it was imperative to 'get out there and get involved' because 'any method of play demands complete under-standing of what you, as a manager, are trying to do and what they, the players, will have to do to make it work'.

It meant getting muddy rather than reaching for the chalk. Even after his 40th birthday, Ramsey would take part in the practice matches, never reacting when someone barged him over into the dirt. He talked to players, never lecturing to them, and recoiled from long dossiers and ring binders. His attention to detail was 'astonishing', said Leadbetter.

When Ramsey went shopping, his wife had to write down a list of what she wanted. Otherwise, she said, 'he comes back with only half the order'. His football brain was different. His mind was a capacious filing cabinet in which everything was stored both thematically and alphabetically and could be retrieved in an eye-blink. He could recall not only the scores of games he'd seen twenty or more years before, but also specific moves – how many passes it had taken to score a goal, the position of each player on the pitch, a space someone ought to have run into but didn't, even the width of the gap a goalkeeper had left at his near post. He was hotly obsessed about the ploys used at cor-ners and free kicks, reeling them off when Ipswich trained and honing each routine until it could be performed like a piece of choreography. Through intricate planning came instinctive understanding.

'He was so organised,' said Phillips, 'he could think of free-kick routines in his sleep.' He added that Ramsey was 'so thorough' that he 'could make a team talk last a couple of hours'. The skill in these briefings was the way in which the conclusions Ramsey reached were still sharp and uncomplicated. 'He made everything simple for us,' said Phillips.

His simplicity embraced two of Rowe's mantras: 'It's a straight-forward game when you learn to pass to a fella wearing the same coloured shirt . . . and don't try to kick the cover off the ball.' A third was 'Don't use jargon'. When the term 'peripheral vision' first crept into the game, Rowe was asked what he thought it meant. He replied unpretentiously: 'It means seeing out of your arse.' The ability to strip away the cant and reduce everything to a punchline was yet another quality Rowe possessed and that Ramsey took from him, as if bor-rowing someone's homework. He was rigorously specific about what he wanted from Ipswich – and equally specific about how things must be done.

While Ramsey shared so many of Rowe's traits, he was completely unlike him in one important regard: he was tougher, more resolute and far less conciliatory. Rowe was self-effacing and extremely self-critical, a hand-wringer who was always worried that his best wasn't good enough – even when it brought him silverware. 'One of the things I dislike is giving orders,' he admitted. Ramsey could ruminate over a decision for a few days or even a week, but he didn't flinch when the moment came to make it – irrespective of whether the consequences wounded.

With those staring eyes – boring through you like drill bits – Ramsey didn't have to speak to express his disapproval, but he was surprisingly tolerant of mild breaches of discipline or bursts of temper. When one player hurled a boot across the dressing room, aiming at someone else, Ramsey swayed his head to dodge it, turning the cheek the boot had almost scarred. He pretended not to notice when a handful of players sloped off into the darkness of the dressing-room toilets – the cubicles were unlit – for a smoke. Before a Saturday game, he allowed them to drink alcohol up until Wednesday, which was always the night the team went to a pub to play darts, sup pints and talk to the fans who paid their wages. Unlike other managers, who employed someone to discreetly watch their players, Ramsey trusted them to behave and not let him down. He didn't need a spy; news travelled through Ipswich – its population was a little over 100,000 – faster than a lit fuse.

The prankster in the team was Phillips, who often thought and acted like a schoolboy in a *Just William* or *Billy Bunter* story. He was nicknamed 'Tearaway' for what he did on the field, but it also applied to some of the things he did off it. He'd tie shoelaces together. He'd unthread buttons from jackets. He'd slip stones, cutlery or a bar of melting chocolate into someone's bag or jacket pocket. He'd hide socks and shoes or a pair of trousers. In a congested Tube carriage, he imitated a guard, shouting, 'All change here,' the passengers obediently filing on to the platform. He ran out before one match in a ginger wig; some supporters were fooled into thinking Ipswich had signed a new player. As a cricketer, a fast bowler good enough to play for Suffolk, he opened the bowling with a red apple (the unimpressed umpires reported him to the MCC). He once conned the Ipswich trainer into climbing on to a train and taking the kit with him. The train was going to Preston on a day when Ipswich were playing at Stoke. The trainer and the kit arrived at the Victoria Ground with '20 minutes to spare'.

Not even Ramsey escaped. Phillips dropped a plastic cockroach into his soup just before it was served to him in a hotel. He filled a bucket with iced water and tipped it into the toilet cubicle that Ramsey was occupying. He nearly went too far, playfully turning a hose on him after training was over and soaking his suit. With immaculate sangfroid, Ramsey gave Phillips the blankest of looks, took off his tie and drove away in his car. When Phillips once kicked the door of his locker open, busting it open, Ramsey said nothing more to him than: 'You're a fool. You might have got hurt.'

During those sessions in which Ramsey insisted that Ipswich work without a ball, Phillips always retrieved one of the many he had previously hidden – burying it among the heaps of coke used to heat the dressing-room boiler – and started to shoot at goal, his palms as black as a miner's. 'It sent him mad,' said Phillips, 'because he could never find out where those balls came from.' Ramsey allowed Phillips to contravene his strict rules about alcohol, letting him have a pre-match pint on a Saturday.

Ramsey's willingness to cut Phillips some very extravagant slack, dismissing whatever was done as insignificant, strengthened the bond between him and the team. During a horribly barren patch for Phillips, parched for goals, Ramsey was asked how long he would wait before dropping him. 'Oh,' he said, very casually, 'another three months.'

He could forgive transgressions in behaviour but not a slapdash attitude. Assumptions of familiarity – especially taking his loyalty for granted – were breaks with protocol that Ramsey punished. He could be deadly. Each Thursday, he would hold one-to-one meetings. Crawford said: 'He would run through what I had done wrong – and right – in the previous game and be meticulous and very precise about it. He wouldn't order, only suggest, but I always had the feeling that if I didn't take his advice, I'd be out. He would do absolutely anything for you, but in return you did what he told you to do. It was like getting one of those Mafia offers you couldn't refuse . . . Mind you, he was right 99 per cent of the time.'

* * *

Where newspapers were concerned, Alf Ramsey adopted one of John Wayne's favourite pieces of advice as his own: 'Talk slow and don't say too much.'

As the least meretricious of managers, Ramsey worked so unobtrusively at Ipswich that he barely had a profile. His hard, creative labour was done almost by stealth. His workaholic drive and his punctilious approach went almost unnoticed – even after he began piling up the wins, pushing not only for promotion but also the Second Division title in 1961. Newspapers were reluctant to acknowledge Ipswich as contenders, regarding them as rustic bumpkins chewing on blades of straw. Between the lines of so many match reports during that season were knowing winks that predicted the next game – or the one after it – was sure to signal Ramsey's downfall.

Ipswich were competing against big-city teams – among them Sunderland, Sheffield United and Bill Shankly's Liverpool – that had the clout of history behind them. The *Daily Telegraph*, thinking of them as humbly nondescript, pointed out that Ipswich were still 'thought of as little more than a Third Division club somewhere down the old Great Eastern Railway line'.

Ramsey admitted it was 'a bit embarrassing' when the 'great clubs' with 'fine grounds and huge staffs' rolled up at Portman Road, looked around and asked themselves: 'Are we in the right place?' But Sunderland, who came sixth that season, were thumped 4–0 there. Liverpool, who finished third, lost 1–0. Among their nearest rivals only Sheffield United, the runners-up, beat them at home.

Ipswich were promoted with three games left; the title came 48 hours later.

Ramsey said the prospect of facing First Division opposition 'frightened' him. He made it seem as though the fixture list was one of those medieval maps in which unexplored land was marked with the menacing phrase 'Here Be Dragons'. Ramsey piled on the mock trepidation, as though depressing self-doubt had descended upon him. He claimed to have asked himself: 'What have I done to deserve this?' Ramsey was more optimistic than he ever let on. 'I think we shall show some people we are quite a team,' he said to those he trusted.

His ambitions were nonetheless modest, never stretching much beyond finishing in the table's top half and tweaking the nose of Bill Nicholson, perhaps by pinching a point from him at Portman Road. His resentment of Tottenham's rejection of him – and what he saw as Nicholson's active but surreptitious participation in it – had not gone away. It had subsequently been compounded by envy too. As he was always supposed to do, Nicholson became Spurs' boss in 1958, replacing Jimmy Anderson, whose reign was twice as long as it should have been and sagged into a noticeable decline. When Nicholson took over, Spurs were sixth from bottom.

Often it was hard to tell whether Ramsey was being icy towards someone because he didn't care for them or because he just found a particular situation awkward. But towards both his former club and his former teammate Ramsey was only cordial. He gave Nicholson the same sort of loose handshake and wan smile that he had given Danny Blanchflower on his arrival at White Hart Lane.

Ramsey still saw himself as unfairly wronged.

* * *

Alf Ramsey had watched Bill Nicholson snatch the high ground from him for a second time. While Ipswich were winning the Second Division, Tottenham were carrying off the Double.

At the start of that season, Danny Blanchflower had promised Spurs' chairman 'both the League and the FA Cup', but the prospect of fulfilling the prediction seemed as unlikely as man putting a toe on the moon. The Double was seen as an unconquerable peak. As soon as Spurs proved it wasn't – beating Sheffield Wednesday by eight points in the League and Leicester City at Wembley – punters blind to any other outcome piled in and backed them to repeat it. The smart money said Spurs had too much depth to be deposed. As well as Blanchflower, their organising grandee, there was Dave Mackay, who considered even a 40–60 ball in his opponent's favour as a fair contest. There was Bobby Smith, a bulldozer of a centre forward. There was John White, his stylishness so much like a form of dance that you would have paid to watch him warm up. When Nicholson signed Jimmy Greaves as well, spending £99,990 to bring him back from well-paid purgatory at AC Milan, anyone who had wagered against them turned their betting slips into confetti.

In August, no one was talking about Ramsey or Ipswich – except to predict their certain relegation, well before the first daffodils appeared in March. Compared with Nicholson's riches, Ramsey had only a scattering of loose change to spend. He went to Scotland again and came back with Doug Moran from Falkirk. An inside right, Moran cost Ipswich £12,500, a small fortune for a club that otherwise shopped cheaply. He'd scored the winning goal in the 1957 Scottish Cup final. Ramsey, valuing Moran at £30,000, believed he'd 'stolen' him.

Ipswich's threadbare finances were put into context six weeks after Ramsey launched them into the First Division. He gave each of his players £18 to buy a new pair of boots from a sports shop in the town. The pair Ray Crawford wanted were Italian-made, costing £30.

'Can I have them?' he asked.

'Of course you can . . . if you pay the surplus yourself,' said Ramsey. 'We're on a budget, you know.'

Crawford invested in those boots. He scored 33 goals in them.

Ipswich's early performances assuaged none of the critics. The fuel for their promotion had come from a 10-game unbeaten run from late August to mid-October, and another of 13 matches from mid-December to mid-March. You wouldn't have guessed it from the new season's opening week. Their record was: played 3, won 0, lost 2, drawn 1.

Ipswich were 20th in the table. 'What is this team doing in the First Division?' asked the *Daily Herald*, curling its top lip.

Ramsey spent the next eight and a half months making fools of the prophets before dumbfounding them. He began by outclassing Burnley 6–2 at Portman Road, a result that was revelatory. Champions only two seasons before – and also European Cup quarter-finalists – Burnley were a team for the connoisseur. They played beguilingly, the ball swished about at pace, often between the two Jimmys: inside forward McIlroy and wing half Adamson, the captain. Claiming their scalp, a statement of intent from Ipswich, was flippantly written off on the back pages as an aberration of no importance.

The early-to-mid-1960s, a period when many teams played a 3–2–5 formation, were stuffed with goals (on Boxing Day, 1963, 65 were scored in 10 First Division matches). If you examined some of

Roy Bailey and Larry Carberry – and the bar – defy Burnley at Turf Moor
during Ipswich's championship season

Ramsey's bruising defeats, without knowing the prevailing attitudes
of that age, you would never think that Ipswich possessed the credentials to become champions. They lost 4–2 to Manchester City at
Portman Road, and 3–0 to them at Maine Road; 5–2 at Everton; 5–0 at
Manchester United; 3–0 at Aston Villa; and 3–1 at Birmingham City.
But, as well as beating Burnley, there were firework wins for Ramsey
over Sheffield Wednesday (4–1), Sheffield United (4–0), Chelsea
(5–2) and West Ham (4–2), and even those sides who had slaugh-
tered him, such as Birmingham City (4–1) and Everton (4–0).

Ipswich hit 93 goals, finishing as second-highest scorers, behind Burnley's blistering total of 101. It makes Arthur Hopcraft's assessment of them seem not only wrong, but also somewhat mean-spirited. Hopcraft, a purist, gave Ipswich a compliment that Ramsey relished. Ipswich were 'a machine', he said. But he diluted the praise considerably by adding that only 'a crushing overall solidarity of method' sent it clanking into gear. His pay-off line was a slap across the face for Ramsey: 'Perhaps there has never been a duller championship side.'

Film of Ipswich during that momentous season does not validate the slur. *Match of the Day* was still only a glint in the BBC's eye, while Pathé and Movietone dispatched their cameramen to gala occasions alone, so the glimpse you get of Ipswich is as narrow as peeking through a keyhole. It's enough to impress nonetheless. You see the fabulous power of Ted Phillips, scorer of 28 goals, charging at defences. You see the cleverness of Ray Crawford, patiently lurking before a loose ball falls at his feet and is stabbed in. You see Andy Nelson, the captain, in command of the airspace around him. You see Jimmy Leadbetter too ...

First Division crowds, packed behind the low perimeter wall, looked on aghast at Leadbetter, so comical in appearance that he seemed to have mistakenly wandered in from a park pitch. 'Come on, grandad' was the most common insult he heard – until the winger wiggled those skinny hips and rolled his foot over the ball. In his hooped socks, the scrawniness of his long neck accentuated by the low-cut V of his shirt, grandad suddenly became the grandmaster.

Despite the goals Crawford and Phillips scored with the appetite of gluttons, Leadbetter was the reason why Ipswich won the title. He was to Ramsey what Sonny Walters had been to Arthur Rowe at Tottenham. Rowe had asked Walters whether he was 'prepared to work harder by coming back more into his own half', an uncommon role then. He told Ramsey to stroke 15- or 25-yard balls to the withdrawn winger. Rowe gauged – correctly – that the marking full back wouldn't follow Walters into the Spurs half, which left him adrift in 'no man's land'. Walters would consequently have 'the vital gift of space', said Rowe, and he could also trade passes with Ramsey, who was given more room to attack. At Ipswich, Leadbetter – plus Roy Stephenson – played the role of Walters; Larry Carberry and John Compton played the role of Ramsey. Leadbetter collected the ball while standing parallel with Doug Moran, the unconventional approach confusing the bejesus out of defenders who were unsure about whether to stick or twist against him. Ipswich sat back, absorbed pressure and then counter-attacked lethally.

In his early days at Fulham, George Cohen had played against Ramsey's side in the Second Division. Confronting them in the First was a far more disorientating experience for him. Early in the season, Fulham had beaten Ipswich 4–2 at Portman Road. Five months later, Cohen was rushing around like a man chasing his hat in a gale. Ipswich won 2–1. Fulham were pulled 'all over the pitch . . . we didn't know where to go'. Cohen, unable to believe the transformation, bleakly told Bobby Charlton that teams could 'dominate' Ipswich 'for 89 minutes and still lose'.

He wasn't alone in making that point.

* * *

March 14, 1962. Alf Ramsey ringed that date, referring to it as one of the 'most satisfying' moments of his managerial career.

Inside, he was gloating.

He had waited nearly seven years to go back to Tottenham. The match, the fulfilment of everything that drove Ramsey on, brought him much more than vindication and revenge. He identified the result – both then and later – as the accelerant that blazed Ipswich towards the most unlikely League Championship in the post-war English game. The hectic plot of the season unfolded like this:

Ipswich were 12th at the start of September and sixth at the end of it. October saw them go fourth. November's results moved them into second place. At New Year, after the odd misstep, Burnley, Tottenham and Everton were above them. When February was over, Ipswich were third and Everton had faded away.

Ramsey had already beaten Bill Nicholson. In mid-autumn – when Ipswich were three places and two points behind them – Spurs came to Portman Road and, like so many before and afterwards, got themselves into a muddle about how to contain Roy Stephenson and Jimmy Leadbetter. Nicholson had wanted to chain them down. He decided his midfield players should do so, believing his full backs could then 'move inside' and nullify Ray Crawford and Ted Phillips.

George Bernard Shaw once said that it was 'easy – terribly easy' to shake a man's belief in himself. For all the authority and gravitas Nicholson exuded, he could sometimes be talked out of things, his belief shaken. His plan to shackle Stephenson and Leadbetter – despite Danny Blanchflower's backing – didn't convince the more combative Dave Mackay, who pointed out that Spurs had won three consecutive matches 'playing the way we wanted to play' and not bothering about the opposition. Nicholson buckled. 'It was one of the few times I bowed to the players' wishes,' he admitted. The price for making that decision was high: Ipswich, twice coming from behind, won 3–2.

On that March night in North London, when Spurs were supposed to get even, Ramsey was in second place on 40 points, three better off than Nicholson in third. Burnley, chasing the FA Cup as well as the championship, were top on 42 points and possessed the comfort blanket of matches in hand (then two, but soon to become four). Jimmy Adamson, at 32 years old, was as fundamental to Burnley as Blanchflower had been to Spurs during their Double season. Born in that football factory called Ashington – where the names Milburn and Charlton were spoken with the respect afforded only to blue bloods – Adamson was in his pomp, pushing Burnley on with his deceptively languid approach. Fleet Street correspondents, who dealt in logic rather than romance, looked on them as champions designate.

What Ipswich did so scintillatingly at White Hart Lane becomes more astonishing than ever when you discover how the team got there.

Every aspect of football in 1961–2 seems just tangentially connected to football now. If you doubt it, you need only watch a 26-minute fly-on-the-wall documentary called *The Saturday Men*, made and released during that season. The film, about West Bromwich Albion, depicts football as common industry and footballers as ordinary working men who live in homes with net curtains at the window and flying ceramic ducks on the wall. There is nothing flashy or fabulously affluent about them. After training, they drink tea out of chipped mugs. They get out of the shower and stand on folded newspapers while drying themselves off with a frayed towel. The team sheet is pinned on a baize-covered noticeboard. The boardroom is a mausoleum made of oak. The manager chivvies his team along in clichés: 'Fight to the last kick' . . . The points are 'absolutely vital' . . . 'Give 100 per cent for 90 minutes.'

If the director of *The Saturday Men* had gone to Ipswich and followed them to Spurs, he'd have come away with the sort of footage that today's audiences would believe had been concocted for dramatic effect. You'd have thought Ipswich's preparation for a floodlit game in which so much was personally at stake for Ramsey, meeting his past again, would look a little less like a cheap works outing. On that Wednesday, Ipswich sent their kit and boots ahead of them in a wicker hamper. The kick off was at 7.30pm. Ramsey and his suited players gathered at the town's railway station at 3.30pm to catch the four o'clock departure to Liverpool Street, arriving as the rush hour got under way. For games in London, the players usually queued for Tube tickets, paying their own fares and later claiming back the amount on expenses. The team would ride with the fans and walk with them to the entrance of a ground. No one thought this was unusual or unprofessional.

But Ramsey didn't want to arrive at White Hart Lane on foot like a motley collection of tradesmen. He organised a coach to take them from Liverpool Street to White Hart Lane.

There are players who give the impression that it's a privilege to play for their club and their manager, but who would eagerly move on and serve another master if the price was right. Ipswich had become a family, which made the club different. Its players, aware this match was everything to Ramsey, played for him first and themselves second. 'Alf left us in no doubt as to the importance of the game. We could all tell it would mean a lot to him if we won it,' said Ted Phillips.

Circumstance turned a league fixture into a cup final, played in a colosseum-like atmosphere that Ipswich had never fully experienced before. Though it was very late in the season, Ipswich still hadn't been to either Highbury or Old Trafford. The 51,000 inside White Hart Lane was the largest crowd Ramsey's side had ever seen. The noise, constantly rolling off the terraces, the blaze of the lights and the fact that Spurs were champions would have intimidated and diminished some; Ipswich, who came to life in those surroundings, were energised by it all.

It was almost a perfect performance.

Again, Nicholson – as if he'd learnt nothing – adopted the same tactics against them.

Again, Ipswich embarrassed him.

As Ray Crawford was walking off the pitch at Portman Road five months before, Spurs' centre half Maurice Norman had stood shoulder-to-shoulder with him and said: 'Wait until you get to our place. I'm going to kick you all over the field.' Now, Norman barely got close enough to blow on Crawford, who gave Ipswich the lead in the ninth minute. When Jimmy Greaves equalised, slipping in a 30-yard through ball from Danny Blanchflower, Spurs expected Ramsey's side to capitulate. Ipswich, as though galvanised, got stronger.

Phillips had scored only twice in his previous 12 league games. In one of them he heard a fan shout from the Churchman's Stand: 'Wake yourself up, Phillips.' He peeled off his shirt, gripping it in a balled fist, and went across to him. 'Here you go, mate,' he said, presenting the shirt to him. 'See if you can do any better.'

At White Hart Lane, Phillips found his form again. He claimed his first goal three minutes before half-time, rising to meet a chipped cross from Roy Stephenson and banging it past Bill Brown with his

The poise. The grace. The cheek. Jimmy Greaves, about to claim another goal
for Tottenham

head. His second – in the 71st minute – came after a typically rum-
bustious 40-yard run. 'There was no way anyone was going to catch
me,' he said. Faced with Phillips pelting towards him, the ball at his
feet, Brown looked petrified, like a pedestrian about to be squashed
by an articulated lorry. The goalkeeper came off his line, stopped
abruptly and began back-tracking. Phillips shot from the edge of the
box; Brown dived the wrong way. Arriving in the box after the ball was
already in the net, Blanchflower berated Brown with a burst of shop-
floor language and accused him of being a coward.

Spurs, 3–1 behind, could not recover. Near the end, as Spurs died
slowly, Phillips rattled the angle of post and bar, denied a hat-trick by
the barest of margins.

Then the whistle went.

Ramsey didn't refer to personal score-settling, preferring to call the
win 'the best in the club's history', but his body language gave him away.
He was more ecstatically animated and spontaneously passionate than

anyone had ever seen him. He waited for his players outside the dressing-room door, honouring each with a slap on the back. He clapped his hands. He rubbed them together. He gave everyone a rictus smile. This was the closest Ramsey ever came to a display of naked triumphalism. He looked 'as though he had won the pools', said Phillips.

In contrast, half an hour later, Crawford gazed into Spurs' dressing room, the door ajar. He found Blanchflower, still in his kit, sitting on a bench with his head between his knees. When he briefly looked up, Crawford saw fatigue and anguish on his face. Blanchflower looked as though he was about to cry.

The same coach had been booked to take Ipswich back to Liverpool Street. Unimaginable as it seems, John Cobbold marched the players – and Ramsey – into the Corner Pin, a pub just outside the ground that was jammed with Spurs' dejected supporters. He bought the first round of drinks too. 'We'd have stayed there all night if we could have done,' said Phillips. Afraid of missing the last train home, Ramsey had to 'drag' his players out of the lounge just before closing time. 'I remember Alf standing there, shouting, "Come on, lads,"' said Philips, who refused to go. 'Not likely, I've still got a pint here,' he replied.

'Imagine that happening now,' added Phillips. 'Well, it wouldn't, would it?'

* * *

The friction between Alf Ramsey and Tottenham, which was bad enough, paled beside the raw animosity of the relationship John Cobbold had with Burnley's chairman, Bob Lord.

It was said that you might as well hate Lord at first sight because it would save you time later on. He was an abominable figure who had a way of being kind when it proved useful. In appearance, he had slightly scrunched-up features, which made him look like an ugly sister in a pantomime. In behaviour, he was infamously manipulative, exploitative and vindictive.

Lord, born in 1908, was a self-made monster, not unlike the unscrupulous northern businessmen who crop up in J. B. Priestley's novels. Aged 19, he bought the butcher's shop in which he worked and built a chain of others around it. A Burnley director by 1951 and the club's chairman four years later, he overhauled Turf Moor, as well as the team, which was entirely to his credit.

Lord would merely have been a bizarre character if he hadn't also become a morally repulsive one. Like many chairmen of his era, he picked a turnstile at Turf Moor and raked the money from it into his own bank account. He so disliked criticism, even in its mildest form, that he regularly refused newspapers entry to the press box. Correspondents retaliated by wearing ties that declared: 'Banned by Burnley'. He regarded the clamour to put matches on television as 'a move to get soccer on the cheap by the Jews who run TV', exposing his anti-Semitism.

From the moment he met him, Cobbold couldn't stand being in the same room as Lord, whom he christened 'bollock chops'. He summed up his revulsion for him in five words: 'I hate racists and snobs.' When Cobbold heard Lord belittle the directors at Leeds for being Jewish, he complained in writing to the Football League. Unfortunately, the man who slit open Cobbold's letter at the League's headquarters was Lord, who told a minion to 'chuck it away'. Cobbold once snubbed him gloriously. Lord was chauffeur-driven to Portman Road and gave his business card to the doorman, telling him to deliver it to the boardroom. 'Put it down the lavatory,' said Cobbold, refusing to let him in.

It is a moot point whether Ipswich won the title or Burnley lost it. Cobbold didn't care, wallowing in what he knew would be Lord's discomfort when Burnley, who ought to have taken the championship, limped feebly to the finishing line. The burden of pursuing the League and the Cup proved too weighty for them. Adamson also lost his stride after Walter Winterbottom perplexingly chose him as his assistant for the World Cup in Chile, beginning in June. Winterbottom did so solely, it appeared, on the basis that Adamson was 'a fully qualified FA coach' who had 'been on very many of our courses'.

Ipswich didn't go top until the last day of March, lost the lead in early April, regained it three days later and lost it once more with a fortnight to go. But Burnley's form was so erratic – they won only two of their last 13 games and drew seven – that Ipswich were always biting into them.

On the season's last Saturday afternoon, facing Aston Villa at Portman Road, Ramsey needed to win as much as Burnley did against already-relegated Chelsea. Burnley were two points behind, but their goal average of 1.61 was superior to Ipswich's by 0.25. They also had a game to spare.

With 18 minutes of the season left, Ipswich were drawing 0–0. Burnley were being held 1–1.

Then, in a great, wonderful kerfuffle lasting four minutes, Ray Crawford knocked the ball in after it came to him off the bar and scored again following a breakaway. News of those back-to-back goals travelled 255 miles to Turf Moor, taking the last of the stuffing out of Burnley, who were unable to find a winner of their own.

Ipswich, a rum concoction of players put together by a manager almost no one rated, were champions.

Ramsey had used only 16 players. Five of them – Phillips, Leadbetter, John Elsworthy, Larry Carberry and Roy Bailey – now owned a unique set of winners' medals: champions of the Third, Second and First Divisions in less than six years. No one had achieved the feat before. No one has done it since.

Everything had happened so suddenly, it was difficult to make a full estimation of their triumph or put it into perspective. The unbylined report in *The Times* at least tried. It described Ipswich, rather like their manager, as a 'fascinating enigma' who brought a 'special character' to the season because 'no one outside Suffolk was quite able to believe in or explain their persistent success'. It also observed that the club seemed 'embarrassed' by all the attention. 'They are not used to excitement and are almost apologetic and self-conscious about it.' It concluded with a detail no one else had noticed: a grandfather clock that stood not far from the boardroom, its hands stopped at ten minutes past eleven. *The Times* used the clock as a symbol to illustrate the peculiarity of the new, unlikely champions and the incongruity of their success.

'It was a day, indeed, when time stood still and when old-fashioned virtues came into their own,' said the newspaper.

* * *

Four days after Ipswich's win at Tottenham, the *Sunday Telegraph* published a Q&A with Alf Ramsey. He said almost nothing worth repeating. Even the question 'When did you first think you could win the championship?' was met with a typically Ramsey-esque reply: 'I never have,' considering such a thing as 'presumptuous'.

The only interesting line was the last one:

What might he do for England if Mr Winterbottom resigns?

It was the first time anyone had so obviously tipped Ramsey to be England's next manager.

PART TWO

5

THE IMPROBABLE BACK-PAGE PROPHET

Success arrived with impeccable timing for Alf Ramsey, creating an air of destiny around what happened next for him.

Everything – even his setbacks – struck him as necessary preparation for what he was about to face, a kind of proof that big events are made from an accumulation of smaller ones. Any novelist would have risked a charge of implausibility with the plot of Ramsey's rise: the way in which he and Arthur Rowe became kindred spirits . . . how Tottenham got rid of him . . . how Ipswich were searching for a manager at precisely the same time . . . how the benign John Cobbold became his boss, letting him learn the trade at his own pace . . . how his sequence of promotions lifted him into the First Division at the perfect point . . . how Walter Winterbottom, following England's fourth World Cup failure in Chile, could not possibly go on.

It was as if a man had come to meet his moment, one that he'd not known had been waiting for him all along. If the England job had fallen vacant in the late summer of 1961, Ramsey would have been only a fringe candidate. If the Football Association had been looking for Winterbottom's replacement in 1963 – when Ipswich were at the bottom of the First Division – he would have been politely considered but ultimately overlooked, his League Championship dismissed as lucky, a break of outrageously good fortune never to be repeated.

But in the autumn of 1962, Ramsey became one of the obvious choices – to everyone, it seemed, except for the FA. As flounderingly inept as ever, it was slow to register the magnitude of what Ramsey had pulled off at Ipswich, and slower still to appreciate that his gifts might outrank those of his rivals.

Winterbottom had believed that England would be 'stronger' than ever before in Chile. He was like a man whistling in the dark to make himself less nervous. The opposition there was too sophisticated for England. After finishing second to Hungary in their group, they were again finessed out of the competition in the quarter-finals. Brazil, shackled in a goalless first half, pushed the ball attractively around and through them in the second to win 3–1. Winterbottom came home to some howling criticism; 'outclassed' and 'wretchedly mediocre' count among the kinder comments. After 16 unsuccessful years, the conclusion was that the next four wouldn't be 'much different' under him either.

In February of that World Cup year, knowing the clock was ticking, Winterbottom had tried to become secretary of the FA. He planned to succeed Sir Stanley Rous, who was about to become president of FIFA, the post for which he had been campaigning, both overtly and covertly, since the end of the Second World War. Winterbottom ought to have been proposed and elected unopposed, but he found himself undone by the machinations of Sir Harold Thompson. Every age has unpleasant men in it, but English football in the 1950s and '60s had an unusually high quota of them. Thompson, an expert in molecular spectroscopy, was a fellow of St John's College, Oxford; he taught Margaret Thatcher there in the 1940s. Thompson was a ghastly figure. He had the eyes of a dead fish, and his breath and clothes reeked from the smoke of too many cigars. He was the kind of snob who looked down his stubby, patrician nose at anyone who didn't possess either a title or a fortune. His opening words to strangers were often: 'What is it that you do exactly?'

No one questioned his remarkable scientific credentials – he was a bona fide boffin – but Thompson's colossal self-regard and ardent self-promotion meant his shoulders were never quite wide enough for the size of his head. He expected colleagues to bow before him – even when they were sitting down.

In 1941, aged only 33, he became an FA councillor. By the early 1950s, he was chairing the International Committee. He also established Pegasus, the combined Oxford and Cambridge team that twice won the FA Amateur Cup in front of a sold-out Wembley. *The Times* chronicled those finals in reports lengthy enough to be classified as novellas.

He was never popular. The words 'bastard', 'shit' and one other – the clue is that it rhymes with 'runt' – were frequently used in reference to Thompson, who was otherwise called 'Tommy'. He was a dagger-wielding lover of intrigue, the sort of bellicose man who needed victims. Machiavelli would have ducked the offer to break bread with him. He was also a lecherous bottom-pincher and toucher-up of women; those who knew of his appalling reputation avoided being in a lift, bar, corridor or room with him.*

Thompson took malicious glee in others' misfortunes, many of which he instigated. With Pegasus, he claimed to have made a 'realistic assessment' of the team's chances before every match. The players suspected Thompson was a great charlatan who merely took a piece of paper to each game with the forecast of defeat written on it. 'If we won,' said one player, 'it stayed in his pocket. If we lost, he would flourish it around, saying, "I knew you'd lose this one."' Thompson's right-hand man at the club, so infuriated with his spiteful antics, once punched him across the chops.

Pitting Winterbottom against Thompson was not a contest.

Thompson backed Denis Follows, a bespectacled, plump-jowelled administrator who had been a minor FA councillor for 14 years and the secretary of the British Pilots Association. Thompson and his supporters, some of whom he bullied, surreptitiously let it be known that the FA councillors did not want another authoritarian in the Rous

---

* I thought Thompson had the same air about him as Hank Quinlan, the character Orson Welles plays in *A Touch of Evil*. British European Airways complained – formally – about his behaviour towards a stewardess.

mould to wield power over them. That line, laughably implying that Winterbottom might become tyrannical, was a convenient smokescreen. Thompson was just being vindictive about the injustices Rous had inflicted on him. Winterbottom, who was blameless, would pay for those.

On the Sunday before the vote, the *Observer* published a piece that was overwhelmingly supportive of Winterbottom's candidature. Before the vote, Thompson waved the paper about, performing like Chamberlain after Munich, but without the wide smile. He lifted his usual flat, expressionless voice in a rage to ask: 'Do we want a newspaper to influence us?'

Winterbottom wasn't so much beaten as embarrassed. He lost 50–20. If he hadn't been, Ramsey would never have become England's manager.

* * *

Aware his position at the Football Association was finally becoming untenable, Walter Winterbottom went for – and seized – a consolation prize. Even before he left for Chile, chivvied along by Sir Stanley Rous, he made a clandestine move to become the next general secretary of the Central Council of Physical Recreation. Not many mourned his departure. Winterbottom, an under-achiever, was stale and bereft of new ideas; he'd already spent a decade too long in Lancaster Gate and wouldn't cast a daunting shadow over his successor. His legacy was a national coaching scheme that worked splendidly, but a national team which didn't.

The country hosting the 1966 World Cup needed a manager capable of winning it for the nation.

The FA chairman, Graham Doggart, was in charge of finding Winterbottom's replacement. He headed a six-strong committee so preposterous and farcically incompetent that you wonder how each member on it managed to climb into his trousers every morning without falling over. Doggart, then 65 years old, was a veteran of the Great War who had been wounded during the Battle of Arras. Since 1932, he had been an FA councillor, representing Cambridge University, where he won a double blue. He had also been an 'FA selector' for eight years. He was shy, quiet and quite diffident, but wealthy enough to keep rooms at the Dorchester and well liked because of his scrupulous fairness and sportsmanship, which befitted a former Corinthian Casual. He scored 160 goals in 170 matches for them and won one amateur international cap.

The appointment should have been straightforward, clean and efficiently crisp. Doggart, as though chairman of the Procrastination Society, over-thought his responsibilities and turned the process into something that was half pig's ear and half dog's dinner. Instead of choosing a candidate and then flattering him with money and promises, Doggart and his committee decided to be very egalitarian about things. In mid-August, the FA advertised the post in the 'Appointments and Situations' columns of the 'posh' newspapers. In *The Times*, the FA's unassuming ad – only 43 words long – was sandwiched between a position for a 'Woman Secretary', aged 23 to 40, at the Medical Research Council and a City firm's search for a qualified accountant.

From the best possible intentions came the worst possible consequences. Among the 59 replies Doggart received, none was suitable and a dozen were written by cranks on cheap notepaper in green ink. None of the credible figures at the top of the First Division – including Alf Ramsey – had bothered to apply, regarding the request to do so as an insult.

In a fluster, afraid his committee would look more idiotic than ever, Doggart compounded his original error. He asked Jimmy Adamson, Winterbottom's assistant in Chile, to take over. The fact Adamson had never managed a club was immaterial to the FA.

When Winterbottom considered his appointment as FA secretary as tantamount to a fait accompli, he 'quietly' asked Ron Greenwood, who was in charge of England's under-23 team, whether he would like to take over from him. Without hesitation, Greenwood said yes, but later admitted that Ramsey's appointment was 'a blessing in disguise' for him. 'The job demanded experience,' he explained. 'I was not ready for it.'

After the World Cup, Winterbottom leant towards Adamson for reasons of 'continuity', he said. Not unsurprisingly, Winterbottom insisted there was no difference between being a club manager and being England boss. Like Adamson, he had never managed a club.

The previous season, despite his team finishing second to Ipswich in the league and losing to Tottenham in the FA Cup final, Adamson had been named as Footballer of the Year. This angered Ramsey, who thought – with great justification – that the honour and the silver statuette should have gone to either Ray Crawford or Jimmy Leadbetter.

Only the FA's track record of consistently making bad choices can explain why Doggart and his committee chased Adamson. Winterbottom hadn't rated Adamson sufficiently highly as a player to cap him; he picked him only the once – for the England B team.

The FA's officials had nonetheless seen enough in Chile to think Adamson could lead England. Adamson, however, had also seen enough of them. He'd watched Winterbottom indulge, out of necessity, in tiptoeing deference, genuflection and diplomatic niceties towards his employers, even carrying the odd bag for them. Adamson didn't want to bow and scrape and ingratiate himself with them. He knew the FA's committee expected the England manager to treat them like royalty while they treated the manager like an equerry. Adamson made his excuses, a couple of which were little white lies that cost nothing. He didn't want to move to London. He didn't want to give up playing for Burnley just yet. Above all, Adamson, like Greenwood, thought he was too inexperienced to take on a role that could only get tougher the closer England got to 1966.

With Adamson out, the matter dragged on, speculation filling the gap where hard news ought to have been. Scan the tabloid press – and also a few of the broadsheets – in the six weeks between September and mid-October 1962 and you'll find a total of 29 names involved in a swirl of rumour. There was going to be a part-time manager . . . The Brazilian coaches Vicente Feola, a winner of the 1958 World Cup, and Aymoré Moreira, who had retained it that summer, were both interested in coming to England . . . Billy Wright, who had taken over at Arsenal the previous May, was on the brink of being approached . . . Tom Finney 'could be' a candidate . . . Others who might be tapped on the shoulder, as if knighted, included Don Revie, Jackie Milburn, Vic Buckingham, Billy Slater and Andy Beattie. There was even a suggestion that Gyula Mándi, assistant to Gusztáv Sebes when Hungary humbled England, had already signed a contract with the FA. This piece of whimsy teased out such an ignorant response from Doggart that you ask yourself whether he was the best person to be conducting the search. 'Mándi who?' he enquired. 'Never heard of him.'

In complete disarray, Doggart admitted that 'there is not a glimmer of light . . . it may well be we shall have to ask a league club to help us out by loaning their manager to take charge of the side for the weekend when we are playing a match'.

* * *

In the 13th century, it once took almost three years to elect a Pope. Between the first vote and the last, three cardinals died and one resigned. In the late summer and early autumn of 1962, it looked as though the Football Association might match that papal conclave for indecision, prevarication and squabbling. As a cheeky marketing ploy, a bookmaker offered odds on the FA failing to make a decision before the Queen snipped the ribbon to open the 1966 World Cup.

The days went by, and then weeks turned into months, without a wisp of white smoke. The FA dithered, as though the prime candidates were strangers to them. It wasn't as if Lancaster Gate was considering a cast of thousands either. The field was minute. England wasn't ready for an overseas manager – certainly not before hosting a World Cup. You could take out anyone who wasn't already in the First Division. After Walter Winterbottom, the average man on the terrace wanted someone prominent who had won a trophy or two as boss and preferably owned a few England caps as a player too.

Four names appeared and reappeared in nearly every article, writers and readers alike baffled about why the FA wasn't arm-twisting one of them into putting country before club.

They were Bill Nicholson, Stan Cullis, Joe Mercer and Alf Ramsey.

Nicholson was entrenched at Tottenham, so devoted to them that on the allotments behind his home he could be found planting or pulling up vegetables while wearing a pair of Spurs shorts and a baggy Spurs shirt.

In the hard currency of trophies won, Cullis was better qualified. He'd become boss of Wolves in 1948, aged only 31. He'd taken them to three League Championships and two FA Cups. He knew the whole game the way a sea captain knows his ship, from engine room to top deck. He'd pioneered floodlit midweek friendlies against continental opposition in the 1950s.

As a player for Everton and Arsenal, Mercer had a mantelpiece festooned with winners' medals and five England caps. As a manager at Aston Villa, he'd claimed the inaugural League Cup in 1961.

The FA had niggles about each of these managers. Nicholson's marriage to Spurs was so strong that a divorce, even for the good of England, would be messy and possibly never finalised. He might also be a little too forthright for them. While Ipswich were winning the title, Wolves were lolling fifth from bottom of the table. Cullis looked physically worn down and his strategies seemed worn out. The FA didn't think he had the energy for another great burst of work, his peak already over. Mercer, being jovial, wasn't considered 'serious' enough.

Graham Doggart's committee also wouldn't countenance an approach to a manager on their own doorstep, whose international pedigree was indisputable. George Raynor had struggled throughout his playing career, a jobbing journeyman who had moved between the sort of clubs that were seldom mentioned except in Saturday's classi-fied results: Mansfield Town, Rochdale, Bury, Aldershot. As a lifelong student of tactics and teamwork, Raynor, a self-confessed 'son of toil', was always preparing himself to be a coach. He wasn't even on the bottom rung of the ladder, organising Aldershot's reserves, when Sir Stanley Rous recommended him to the Swedish FA. The game in Sweden then barred professionals. Raynor was hired to prepare their amateurs for the 1948 Olympics in London. He won the gold medal.

He was a rugged man with oversized ears and a prominent nose. To combat the Swedish cold, he often arrived for training in a huge polo-neck sweater that made him look like a seafarer advertising Fisherman's Friends. His players said of him what Ipswich's said of Ramsey: he was a 'father figure' to them.

A mockumentary, screened in 2002, tried to hoax Swedish viewers into thinking the 1958 World Cup was never staged there. *Conspiracy 58* pretended that the tournament took place in America, a Cold War stunt to test the persuasive power television held over an audience. Plenty of people were gullible enough to believe the film. In fact, the competition was far-fetched enough. Raynor guided Sweden, now professionals, to the final, where they lost 5–2 to the Brazil of Didi, Garrincha and the precocious 17-year-old Pelé.

You'd have thought First Division chairmen would have been form-ing an orderly queue for Raynor. No one of any calibre approached him. Within six weeks of the World Cup, Raynor signed a £10-per-week contract with Skegness Town of the Midland League. 'We can just afford him,' said a club official. Even 13 months later, after Raynor contributed a little something towards Sweden's 3–2 win against England to Wembley – he was credited with identifying a tactical weakness in Walter Winterbottom's team – no prospective employers of substance thumped on the door of his three-bedroom bungalow on the Lincolnshire coast.

The FA continued to pretend it didn't know how to find Raynor, who had hardly gone into hiding.

The *Sunday People*, fed up of waiting for the FA, contacted each of the 92 league managers, asking them the obvious question and promising anonymity once they supplied an answer. Only five among this elite electorate refused to take part; a sixth even wanted Winterbottom to carry on.

Cullis won most votes – 34 – followed by Nicholson (18) and Mercer (16).

Fourth place went to Ramsey, who didn't get into double figures. He won the support of only nine of his contemporaries.

* * *

It looked as though nobody worthy of the job wanted the thing, but Alf Ramsey had been waiting for the Football Association to call on him.

The common misconception is that Ramsey hadn't seen himself as England manager until the FA asked him to take over. But he wasn't as reluctant and coy as he seemed to be when it came to being courted. He'd sensed that Walter Winterbottom would go after the World Cup, calculating that it was impossible for him to stay. Ramsey was also encouraged by the FA's decision to appoint a director of coaching,* splitting Winterbottom's duties; the new manager wouldn't waste weeks supervising courses, sometimes for amateurs.

Within a week of Winterbottom's resignation, Ramsey had topped a quite different poll from the one that appeared in the *People*. The *Daily Express* went directly to its readers. As there were almost four

---

* The FA made Allen Wade director of coaching. Barely anyone had heard of him. Asked to comment on his appointment, even Arthur Rowe was slightly impolite. 'I can't,' he replied. 'I don't know who he is.' Wade was a 35-year-old lecturer at Loughborough College who had coached at Lilleshall since the mid-1950s.

million of them, the result was a toe-in-the-water test of opinion from the terraces, which gave it both validity and heft. Ramsey came first – though his 17.5 per cent would never have given him a working majority. Second was Billy Wright (16.5 per cent). Joint third were Bill Nicholson and Stan Cullis (15 per cent). The rest – apart from Stanley Matthews (5 per cent) – came nowhere. While this was an eye-catching headline for the *Express*, it also indicated, however superficially, that Ramsey had a chance.

Ipswich, despite their gleaming championship, remained a small club in a small town. No riches followed the title for them. Since there was no bonus scheme at Portman Road, John Cobbold gave every player a pay rise of £10. The Football League stipulated that the prize money, amounting to £1,500, should be distributed among the squad strictly on the basis of the number of games played. John Elsworthy, who had figured in 41 of them, earned £2.12s for each appearance – before tax. With that small windfall, he bought his wife a washing machine. When the players arranged a celebration dance, hoping to divide the profits, many of the tickets were left unsold.

Ramsey still refused to take the credit for the transformation he had wrought, as though someone else had been responsible for it. 'I have been lucky in the type of players I found at Ipswich,' he said. But, ever realistic, he doubted whether the side, a season older and the mystery surrounding them gone, could go any further or even finish in the top six again. He couldn't consistently deliver miracles there.

Tottenham beat them 5–1 in the Charity Shield. Ramsey's opening dozen league games in defence of the title brought him only two wins. Already, the team had begun to rust, and Ramsey lacked the resources to improve it.

He thought of what he'd say and do – and how he'd present himself – if the FA came calling.

If possible, Ramsey would do anything to avoid talking to the press. He once hid under a blanket on the back seat of his car to dodge a journalist who was wandering about Portman Road. If the phone rang, he'd sometimes refuse to answer it. On other occasions, he'd insist the line was crackling so badly that he couldn't hear the caller. A national reporter who came to interview Ramsey discovered he had removed the other chairs in his office – a ploy to make him ask his questions standing up.

He rarely gave one-on-one interviews, avoiding newspapers, radio and television as much as possible. Quotes, especially for the tabloids, are the golden nuggets of journalism, but what Ramsey said seldom glinted off the page. The innocuous paragraph or two he supplied were usually stuck on the bottom of a story, where a subeditor could cut them. As one reporter said of Ramsey: 'You had to make up your own quotes – you wouldn't get any from him.'

Ramsey seldom spoke until he had something to say. So it was no coincidence when the master of the stony silence gave an exclusive story – in two parts – to the *Daily Mail* in mid-September. The premise of these articles was explained long-windedly as 'ways in which club football as well as the national team can be brought to a new peak of success before the 1966 World Cup'. Ramsey used them for brazen self-promotion, staking his claim unequivocally.

When Greta Garbo switched from silent movies to the talkies, MGM promoted her first such film with the tag line 'GARBO SPEAKS', aware that the sound of her voice alone guaranteed a box-office bonanza for them. The *Mail* could have promoted their scoop with the same brevity. 'Ramsey Speaks' was enough to sell a paper to anyone who had tried – and failed – to encourage him to be garrulous before. It was worth letting your breakfast go cold to read his thoughts.

These Q&A pieces are more revealing now than anyone imagined back then. Ramsey, the improbable back-page prophet, outlined his ideas and philosophy. Here was the Ramsey manifesto for England – the very blueprint he would use over the next four years.

The first piece was headlined 'Players Come First – Not Plans'. He spoke about how his tactics had evolved at Ipswich. 'It was never a question of imposing a plan on players, but rather developing the idea *with* them,' he said. He constructed a 'well-organised defence' in a team capable of swift counter-attacks – preferably involving only 'three' passes from one box to the other. If he went to manage elsewhere, he would 'study the players he'd got and try to create another method'. The word 'method' was doubly underlined, as if to suggest Walter Winterbottom had been working without one. 'No method' could possibly work unless the players were 'happy with it', was Ramsey's fundamental message – another sly dig at Winterbottom.

He wanted to demonstrate his thoroughness to the FA. He'd looked at other countries with the intensity of a pathologist examining a bloodstain. 'While they may have talent, they have not got such a rigid plan [as us] . . . I am sure it is because we have a better understanding and have made more use of perhaps our more limited capabilities.' Even the FA, dumb as it was, couldn't fail to detect the subliminal message in the text: yes, I can take an average First Division player and make him into something.

All this was merely a warm-up. In the second piece – 'Let One Man Pick Our Team' – Ramsey talked more directly than before to Graham Doggart and his committee. He mixed pragmatism with optimism, noted problems but presented probable solutions, and positioned himself as a patriot who believed the English game should be superior but sadly wasn't.

The opening question was a free hit.

He was asked how much of what he'd achieved at club level would prove valuable internationally. Ramsey answered with three sharp words: 'A great deal.' As if the FA might have forgotten his own England career, he harked back to the defeats against Hungary and the USA, stressing that the need to 'change' and 'adapt' to 'foreign teams' was paramount. When discussing how England could become a 'success' – a euphemism for winning the World Cup – he returned to his theme of 'method' and a 'rigid plan'. It was more condemnation of Winterbottom. 'I have heard it said that England once had great players – Matthews, Finney and Carter and so on – and they never needed a plan,' said Ramsey. 'Well, I played with many of these players and I would say England's team was good then, but it would have been many times better if we had also had a rigid plan. Remember, many of those great players were in England's 1950 team, but the fact is even then they couldn't score against the United States . . . and football has become more advanced and complicated [since then]'.

He believed England had 'plenty of talent', implying that Winterbottom hadn't recognised it, picked it or played it in the correct formation. 'Understanding', said Ramsey, was a necessity. 'By that I mean the ability to play together to a set method . . . I think an England manager must make up his mind what players he has and then find a rigid method for them to play to.' In the next sentence Ramsey signalled what was to come. 'If any player, no matter how clever or individual, is not prepared to accept the discipline of the team's method, then I see no advantage in selecting him.'

On Ramsey went . . .

He wanted the FA and the Football League to become closer, clearing dates in the calendar so the England manager could prepare his squad. 'Under the present system, I am certain it must mean either a poor England team or poor club teams . . . I feel the League should employ – and I emphasise the word employ – a man or committee to work out how the system should be changed. If we don't find a way to cut down the League programme and make room for more competition against European teams, I don't see how club and country can work together . . . Perhaps we could shorten the season to give the England party time to work together and be rested before the World Cup really starts.'

Did Ramsey see 'any hope' for England in 1966?

Of course he did.

'We won't have to travel or get used to foreign food or suffer heat we are not used to. This must count for a lot.' If clubs and country could 'work out something', Ramsey concluded, 'I think we can win.'

Winterbottom still had two England matches to play, but Ramsey's cogent analysis had already consigned references about him to the past tense. Ramsey also advised the FA: 'England should appoint a manager on exactly the same basis as a club appoints a manager. He must be carefully chosen and then he must be allowed to pick his team alone and to decide how players will play. And, like a club manager, if he fails he must be replaced.'

Graham Doggart got the message.

According to John Cobbold, the Ipswich board approved the FA's approach in a discussion that lasted less than 'two and a half minutes'. It did take almost two and a half weeks, however, to hold that meeting. Doggart, ever the stickler, had decided to write to Cobbold – perhaps with a quill pen – rather than telephone him at Capel Hall, his home near Felixstowe. His letter went unanswered for a week because Cobbold knew nothing about it; he was rough shooting in Scotland. Doggart finally rang Cobbold's home and spoke to his butler, who passed along a message.

Ramsey was not a good actor. All he had in his repertoire was the kind of poker face that –with the right cards – could have broken the bank in Monte Carlo. Anyone who had read the *Daily Mail* saw clean through Ramsey's 'surprise' at getting what he'd publicly lobbied for. 'I never, for a moment, imagined the FA would offer me the job,' he protested. 'I have never seriously considered what ought to be done.'

Ramsey had a 'great ambition', which he outlined to the FA, and later to everyone else. It grew out of 1953. It was: 'To knock down and destroy the image of that Hungarian team. I want it replaced by an image of an even greater England team.'

* * *

Walter Winterbottom was about to take charge of his farewell game – his 139th. Of the previous 138, he'd won 77, but 32 of those had come against the home nations. Six of his 28 defeats had also been inflicted on him when it truly mattered, during the World Cup finals, which meant his record was only superficially good.

Fairness demands that Winterbottom's results in Sweden in 1958, when England didn't even climb out of the group, be accompanied by an asterisk to denote the fact that several players were not part of it because of the numbing tragedy of the Munich air disaster four months before. The very mention of it instinctively sets all those reels upon reels of grainy news footage spooling in your mind again. Slush on the runway; snowy air; plumes of smoke dragged by an easterly wind; Manchester United's BEA 'Elizabethan Class' aircraft, the tail ripped from the body of the plane. Your mind fills in the rest: ice stuck to the wings; two aborted take-offs and then a third; the wheels slipping on the runway; the plane slamming through a fence, careering across a road and into a house; the noise, like an eruption, and then the silence. You also see the last team photograph of Matt Busby's Babes. It was taken in Belgrade's Army Stadium, where United – edging Red Star 5–4 on aggregate – reached the European Cup semi-finals for a second successive season on a pitch 'where the last remnants of melting snow produced the effect of an English lawn flecked with daisies'. Eight members of United's team were killed – the average age of the dead was 23 – as well as three of the club's backroom staff, eight football writers, the co-pilot of the aeroplane, a steward and two other passengers.

The previous Saturday, Winterbottom had watched United against Arsenal at Highbury in one of those games that made anyone who saw it feel grateful forever. Goals were traded like cigarette cards. United, 3–0 ahead at half-time, were hauled back to 3–3, before scoring twice more and winning 5–4. Winterbottom was checking on three players already certain of going to Sweden with him – Roger Byrne, Tommy Taylor and Duncan Edwards – and a fourth, Bobby Charlton, whose England debut was imminent.

Byrne, who had won his 33 caps consecutively, and Taylor, United's centre forward, died instantly at Munich. Edwards, only 21, broke his ribs and his pelvis and fractured his right thigh in multiple places. A piece of metal lanced one of his kidneys. One of his lungs collapsed. He fought for 15 days, before dying on the fourth floor of the Rechts der Isar hospital. Wearing his tweed jacket, Edwards used to ride his Raleigh bicycle the two miles from his digs to Old Trafford, tying it to a drainpipe with knotted string. In his red shirt, he used to ride over the opposition too. Edwards was irreplaceable, proof that genius acts unconsciously; he could do anything because he possessed everything, making him a near-perfect player more than half a dozen years before reaching what would have been his peak.

Would Winterbottom have won the World Cup if Edwards and the others had lived? Probably not; Brazil wouldn't have let them. England, though, might have reached the semi-finals or even the final. One thing is certain: Winterbottom's 1962 team would have been assembled around Edwards, who would surely have been the captain by then.

Nothing excuses the fact that, from one World Cup to the next, Winterbottom was a poor judge of players who could have made a substantial difference to his fortunes. He had a particular blind spot when it came to goal-scorers who were in form. For example, in 1950 and 1954, the five top scorers in the First Division were English; on each occasion, Winterbottom took only one of them to the World Cup. Worse, he had a pronounced tendency to hide the fault behind the spurious collective responsibility of the 'selection system'. The great fallacy, which Winterbottom perpetuated, was that in matters of selection he was a marionette; the FA committee picked his team.

In reality, it had become a one-man show. By 1958, Winterbottom had been in the post long enough that the FA trusted his judgement and let his selections pass, mostly without argument or prolonged debate. According to one unnamed FA 'selector', Winterbottom was only 'a half per cent' short of total control over the side. In the four years before his resignation, he was overruled in the committee room just once.

He made two grave miscalculations before Sweden. He didn't take Nat Lofthouse, scorer of two goals when Bolton beat a patchwork Manchester United in the FA Cup final. He did take – but didn't play – Charlton.

Charlton's physical injuries at Munich were minor: a cut head, some bruising, shock. The emotional damage, however, was cavernously deep. When the fatalities were read out to him, Charlton said he felt 'my life was being taken away from me piece by piece'. He had to 'persuade' himself that 'football could once again occupy the core of my being'.

Two months after Munich, Charlton got his first cap – and first goal – against Scotland. He claimed two more goals in his second appearance against Portugal. Winterbottom still wasn't convinced. Shortly before England got to Sweden, and after Yugoslavia had swept them away 5–0 in a friendly, he pulled Charlton aside. Winterbottom said the 'selectors' had decided to drop him. Charlton was advised to 'think more deeply' about his 'contribution to the team' and to 'do a lot more running'. He accepted the advice, which was really a rebuke, without appreciating that the other 'selectors' had nothing to do with his axing. Winterbottom consulted no one other than his captain, Billy Wright; he just wasn't brave or honest enough to own up to it. When Winterbottom arrived home from Sweden, his family was waiting for him at Heathrow. The first thing his nine-year-old son said to him was: 'Daddy, why didn't you pick Bobby Charlton?'

* * *

The Football Association thought it would need to pay only around £3,250 to £3,500 a year to get another England manager. It was a top wage in 1962. A manual worker earned less than £800. A doctor employed by the National Health Service took home £2,300. Not even Members of Parliament were raking in small fortunes, but at least the £1,000 they got for sitting on Westminster's green leather benches was supplemented with expenses of up to £750.

Ramsey cost the FA £4,500, but he still took a pay cut: the sum was £500 less than Ipswich were giving him. The FA's promise of an annual increase of £500 until 1967 wasn't an attractive inducement to anyone craving riches rather than status. Ramsey obliquely referred to it when he said: 'The challenge of the job, not the money, made me accept.'

What also made him accept were the words of Arthur Rowe. Ramsey had gone, as ever, to visit Rowe, for once seeking reassurance rather than guidance. 'I told him to take it,' said Rowe. 'He'd have his pick of the country's best players.' Time and tide were in Ramsey's favour, added Rowe. If he didn't take the chance, it might not come again. He was better equipped than Walter Winterbottom had ever been. Ramsey considered one other factor: where else would he go? Not back to Tottenham. Not to Arsenal, where Billy Wright was so new he was still unsure about where to hang his coat. And certainly not somewhere in the north, which was like another country to a committed southerner such as Ramsey, who had lived and worked nowhere else.

Ramsey already knew all this, but he needed someone – especially Rowe – to say it out loud to him.

He claimed to have wrestled with England's offer. 'One of the most difficult decisions of my life,' he called it. The statement was true – but only up to a point.

When Ramsey was named England boss, he was three weeks away from facing AC Milan in the second round of the European Cup. Ipswich were 18th in the table, only one point off the bottom.* He felt honour-bound to carry them through the whole season before going to Lancaster Gate. He didn't want to be seen like a cruel parent abandoning his children. That concession was won without a squabble, the FA acquiescing because it no longer had anything with which to bargain. Through its own dithering, the FA had cornered itself. If, at

---

* Ipswich finished 17th, four points better off than Manchester City, who were relegated with Leyton Orient.

the last minute, Ramsey backed away, the FA could hardly have then chased after others with conviction. No one wanted to be seen as the desperate third choice.

Ramsey pinned down one finicky detail in the contract. The 'half per cent' influence that the selection committee retained was wiped out. He then adopted the simplest of plans.

Whatever Winterbottom had done, he would do the opposite.

6

TEN GUINEAS FOR THE REVOLUTION

On January 2, 1963, while some revellers were still shaking off a New Year's hangover, Alf Ramsey got up early and travelled 91 miles from Ipswich to the BBC studios in London.

In the circumstances, it was an extraordinary journey. It also counted as a noble sacrifice, made only because of Ramsey's abiding sense of obligation and duty. The country, hit by fog and pelted with blizzards three days before Christmas, was now smothered in ever-thickening snow and ice, the severity of which hadn't been seen since 1740 during the reign of George II.

That morning, the Met Office grimly warned that what was to come would make what was already there look as insignificant as sprinkles of decorative cake-frosting. The forecasters were right. Over the following nine weeks, Mother Nature got nastier. Snow piled into monstrous drifts, some as high as 25ft. Temperatures fell as low as −20°C. Icicles hung from trees, as well as guttering, like the blades of medieval swords. The sea froze at Whitstable (boats and ships were imprisoned in the harbour). The Thames froze at Oxford (where a motorist drove his Austin Seven across it). A milkman died from hypothermia at the wheel of his float. A railway signalman died not far from the refuge of his signal box. Factories, offices, shops and schools were shut. Villages were marooned, many becoming islands in weather-made archipelagos. Food ran short. Power was cut off. Telephone lines snapped. Pipes burst, the water from them freezing in mid-flow. Mail and coal went undelivered. Dogs were not walked. Trains did not run. Aeroplanes did not fly. Roads were closed.

All you could do was hunker down and wait for the great thaw to come.

Football went into suspended animation. The third round of the FA Cup, which began on January 5, wasn't completed until March 11. A tie between Lincoln and Coventry was postponed 15 times. In Scotland, it was even worse: Stranraer v. Airdrie was called off 33 times. One club, Norwich, hired a flame-thrower to attack the snow. Another, Halifax Town, surrendered to it, turning their pitch into an ice rink to make money. The Pools Panel was created to cope with the disruption, its deliberations as hush-hush secret as a jury's before the verdict is read. The backlog of fixtures was horrendous. Manchester United had to play three games in four days – and then a fourth only 48 hours later.

On the day Ramsey set off for the BBC as intrepidly as a polar explorer, the AA announced only 200 snow ploughs had been deployed to clear 200,000 miles of road. On some routes, cars were abandoned in hedgerows.

Ramsey was fulfilling a promise he had made a month before to someone he respected. Peter Dimmock was the BBC's most influential sports broadcaster. The midweek programme *Sportsview* was his baby, but his influence spread throughout the corridors of the corporation. He was a presence on the screen and a power behind it. A decade before, Dimmock had organised coverage of the Coronation.

Dimmock asked Ramsey to be the headline act on *Sportsview*'s opening programme of the new year. A profile of his career would be followed by a set-piece interview, recorded on the day of transmission. Ramsey saw it as his chance to speak directly to the nation, his words unfiltered.

Sportsview was deftly positioned in the BBC schedules. The planners slotted it in between the police drama *Z Cars*, which at its zenith pulled in 14 million viewers, and the late-evening news. Dimmock was also the kind of man Ramsey aspired to be – urbane, suave, with brushed-back hair, a clipped moustache and a public-school upbringing. He wore ties that were said to be 'the most neatly knotted ever beheld'. Harry Carpenter, known even then for his boxing commentaries, was

Ramsey's inquisitor. Like his *Sportsview* boss, Carpenter thought a fireside-like chat was more likely to coax revelations out of Ramsey than a beady-eyed confrontation. He guessed correctly.

He asked Ramsey whether England would win the World Cup . . .

Hardly caught off guard, Ramsey could have offered a few pre-prepared platitudes or got Carpenter entangled in one of those slow, preambular conversations that were always on the brink of going somewhere but never did. Instead, Ramsey said: 'Most certainly, I think with all sincerity that we will win the World Cup.' In case he hadn't been emphatic enough, Ramsey even repeated the prediction for Carpenter later on: 'England will win the World Cup in London in 1966.'

Dropping London and also the year into that sentence was inelegant, but it made the message unambiguous. When, ten weeks before, the Football Association had appointed him as manager, Ramsey had merely said that England 'had a wonderful chance to win'. Now there were no 'mights' or 'maybes', no qualifying remarks or disclaimers, like the small print in a contract, that would allow him to disown his statement.

The most circumspect and deliberate of managers had been uncharacteristically careless. If a new England manager made a promise of that magnitude nowadays, the newspapers would go into convulsions. The news would be trailed across the top of the front page – the blurb accompanied by his head-and-shoulders photograph – as well as splashed all over the back. Inside, the remark would be an excuse for analysis and opinion pieces.

The strangest thing happened after Ramsey's boldness: almost no one reported what he had said.

It took four days for the silence to be broken. In devoting just a single paragraph to the story, the *Sunday Mirror* under-played things, but at least recognised both the rarity of what Ramsey had said and the bravery behind it. The paper remarked on the 'most courageous TV forecast of the week', pointing out that Ramsey was normally 'the most careful word-chooser'.

He quickly came to regret his rashness. One of the propaganda posters from the Second World War, seen everywhere, had proclaimed: 'Loose Lips Sink Ships'. Ramsey's loose lips almost sank him. For the next three years, his promise to 'win the World Cup' dragged behind him like a great, clanking ball and chain. The quote was run beside every dip in England's form, every small change that Ramsey introduced without success. 'It was my fault,' he said, calling it 'the most reckless thing I did'. The prediction 'created more pressure for me than any other in my career', he added.

Having insisted that England would become the next World Champions, Ramsey had no option but to stick with it. Over the next nine months he did so on four more occasions. 'I always had to repeat myself,' he said, also admitting how 'embarrassing' this became. Ramsey had to explain why he thought so too. 'We have the ability. We have the determination. We have strength. I believe in England and Englishmen, as well as in English football.' The patriotic flourish at the end, appealing to the heart, gave the impression that Ramsey walked into work each morning humming 'Jerusalem', the flag of St George fluttering at his back.

He scared the living daylights out of the FA's top brass, who felt compelled to back him while nervously conceding among themselves that the public's expectations might already be too high. Only two host nations – Uruguay in 1930 and Italy in 1934 – had won the World Cup. Ramsey had immediately divided the nation into those who thought him mad and those who thought him 'possibly right' but still mad to say so.

Ramsey was forced to defend himself from not just sceptics, who doubted England could ever fulfil his promise, but also those who regarded his words as a noose that he had unnecessarily made for himself. Accused by one journalist of 'sticking [his] neck out a bit', Ramsey bridled and snapped back: 'It is what I believe. I couldn't have taken the job if I didn't think we could win.'

It was a bluff.

He confessed later: 'I don't think I really meant it when I said it. The pressures at that time were enormous. It was probably a case of saying the first thing that came into my mind, something I don't normally do.'

* * *

Walter Winterbottom's final game, against Wales, was played in front of a crowd so thin that anyone who had paid for a seat almost got a whole row to themselves. As the team coach travelled towards Wembley, Jimmy Greaves turned to Winterbottom and said in amazement: 'There's no one here.'

Only 27,500 bothered to turn up on that late-November afternoon, which was indicative of the apathy and disillusionment towards Winterbottom's over-long era. You'd have thought England was preparing to hold a wake rather than the World Cup.

Alongside the parish churches of other grounds, Wembley, nearly 40 years old, was still a cathedral, but the fabric of the place urgently needed a restorative facelift. Scattered around the stadium that day were skeletal cranes, scaffolding, paving slabs, girders and dusty bricks. They were symbolic of the rebuilding required in the team too. England were in a state of shabby disrepair. If Winterbottom's side had been a house, the rising damp would have been rampant, and you'd have been able to see the sky through the holes in the roof. It was said, only half in jest, that you wouldn't volunteer to watch them unless one of your relatives was playing – and only then if he'd given you a complimentary ticket. Against Wales, the spivs and touts were selling at below half price. A band outside Wembley, belting out tunes for tips, gave up half an hour before kick-off, knowing there would be no late rush for the turnstiles.

Winterbottom didn't leave much for Alf Ramsey to inherit, but it suited the new manager to take a shell of a thing and rebuild from scratch. He wasn't tied to any tactic – or any player.

So much in life is about the luck of timing. Ramsey – yet again – was the beneficiary of it. English football's industrial revolution, arriving with a bang in January, 1961, was integral to his own prosperity.

Clown Prince of Soccer – the autobiography of Len Shackleton – was the antithesis of the fluff in Ramsey's *Talking Football*. Published in 1955, it contained the most infamous page in the game's literature and also a tart note of explanation: 'This chapter has deliberately been left blank in accordance with the author's wishes.' The blank in question, on page 78, appeared beneath the title of chapter nine. It was called: 'What the Average Director Knows about Football'. Shackleton believed mockery of that kind would garner publicity. He was right. Reviews of the book led with the provocative snub.

Shackleton sent paper and ink into battle against the maximum wage and the grossly iniquitous retain-and-transfer system, which allowed a club to hold on to a player – and to pay him less than he had earned before – even after his contract expired. You didn't have to be an expert in employment law to sniff out the inherent injustice in that arrangement. For Shackleton, a footballer's contract was 'an evil document' that made players 'no better than professional puppets, dancing on the end of elastic . . .' But, however much Shackleton kicked against it, the game's antediluvian, upstairs-downstairs world of masters and servants still seemed unlikely to be dismantled any time soon. Over the next half-dozen seasons, though, everything changed because of the pressure he and others applied. A struggle that had lasted more than 50 years was over, the resolution more constructive than destructive. It had taken so long to arrive only because vested interests continued to resist until the last push.

Alan Hardaker had become Fred Howarth's assistant at the Football League in 1955, taking over from him at the beginning of 1957. Like Howarth, he insisted he was 'always the first to implement change', a boast so demonstrably false it wouldn't have withstood two minutes of casual examination. Hardaker controlled the League's headquarters as though presiding over his personal fiefdom. He did it even more forcibly than his vainglorious predecessor. 'The League will do as it is told, as long as it is broadly what it wants to do,' said *Football Monthly*, offering a commentary on Hardaker's method of working and his disdain for diplomacy (unless a little oil or soft-soaping suited his agenda). It's Hardaker's own fault that history remembers him, if at all, as the kind of insular, intransigent Yorkshireman that Monty Python came to satirise so well. He was actually much worse than that: a pompous, egotistical, table-thumping bully with a saggy, craggy face and a pipe, the stem of which he would point like a bayonet at anyone who disagreed with him. He regarded his sobriquet, the Great Dictator, as a compliment, but preferred not to hear the substitute his critics used, which was the Great Dick. He did admit that 'there are many people in football who do not like me'. If a queue had formed to endorse that opinion, it would have covered at least half the 245 miles that separated the League's new headquarters in Lytham St Anne's from Lancaster Gate.

Hardaker went unarmed into any battle of wits against Jimmy Hill, the Professional Footballers' Association's spokesman. Hill, about to become a household name as a TV pundit, was unstoppably voluble. Hardaker's siege mentality, as well as his efforts to portray the PFA as insolent insurrectionists and economically ignorant, resisted the end of the maximum wage until the point at which the line couldn't possibly hold.

When Shackleton's *Clown Prince of Soccer* went into bookshops, the salary cap was £15 per week. By 1958, it was still only £20 per week. By the 1960–1 season, the PFA, believing money and principles were inextricably linked, moved to the brink of a strike to get more. A ballot among players totalled 690 in favour and only 18 against. The figure mocked those league chairmen who, criticising their own players for 'wanting the moon', talked about sacking anyone who refused to pull on his boots. The PFA had the backing of the Ministry of Labour, as well as popular support. The fans saw Hardaker's reaction as the victimisation and the demonisation of players. His outrage came across as meanness and petulance.

The abolition of the maximum wage was the transformative leap forward that Hill and the PFA had always said it would be. For the first time, the professional footballer began to dress differently from the men who went to watch him, live in a different house and drive a car rather than cadge a lift or take the bus. Everyone knows that Johnny Haynes became the country's first £100-per-week footballer at Fulham. Few are aware that his teammate George Cohen asked for £50, received £40 – 'a staggering amount of money', he said – and then bought a £4,000 house on a £3,000 mortgage; he called it his 'suburban castle'. Blackpool gave Jimmy Armfield, then the England captain, half of Haynes's salary, after initially offering him only £30. Blackpool were stingy. When Stanley Matthews moved from there back to Stoke City, swapping the First for the Second Division, he doubled his £25-a-week basic wage – and got a further £25 for every appearance he made. Matthews signed his contract – live on Peter Dimmock's *Sportsview* – while regretting he hadn't demanded a flat £100 per week. At Manchester United, Bobby Charlton went from £20 to £35. At West Ham, Bobby Moore earned £30 – but only after a stand-off akin to trench warfare with much sniping. At Tottenham, without the hassle and the bad feeling, Jimmy Greaves picked up £60, which was classified as a fortune when you consider that a pint of beer cost 2s 6d and a pint of milk eight and a half pence. You could buy a Ford Cortina for £597, and the petrol to put in it was only 4s 11d a gallon.

Not everyone could fling money about. Larry Carberry's benefit game, marking his five years at Ipswich, brought him only £750, as well as the coppers the crowd threw into a blanket, which was carried around the ground at half-time. In the summer – even after Ipswich had won the championship – Carberry worked on Liverpool's docks.

Ramsey had always supported the PFA. On the very day he became England manager, he quietly sent them the ten-guinea fee he had earned for doing an interview with BBC news.

By the time he became England manager, the contracts of those at the top were beginning to influence the ones given to those at the bottom. Football's trickle-down economy was working – more or less. The pay increases given to the players were a boon to Ramsey, enabling them to train and play with an element of financial security behind them.

He saw the end of the maximum wage as 'integral' to England's success.

* * *

Alf Ramsey made a clever political move.

Though he wouldn't officially become England's manager until May 1, 1963, he insisted on taking 'unofficial' charge for the internationals before that date. The first was against France in Paris at the end of February, the second leg of a European Championship tie.

Ramsey was juggling tasks, answering questions about England while Ipswich scrapped for their First Division lives. Ostensibly because of his dual responsibilities, but also because so few matches had been played in that malign winter, Ramsey asked the Football Association's selection committee to reconvene and 'advise' him on the team to face the French. As a courtesy, Ramsey had agreed to tell the FA in advance the names of those players he'd picked and explain his reasons for picking them. This did more than preserve the councillors' sense of self-esteem; importantly, it also protected their entitlement to take full advantage of the FA's free hospitality – drinks, meals, a hotel room.

By letting them recommend players while he listened to the debate, Ramsey also got an insight into the men he neither trusted nor respected, and with whom he felt no empathy. He weighed up the strength of the friendly fire he might have to dodge later on and observed who was likely to possess most of the ammunition.

Ramsey's reign began ignominiously. In the Parc des Princes, a cold wind numbing the bones, England fell behind after two minutes and were quickly 3–0 down. There was a second-half revival during which

Bobby Moore, always the graceful stylist, does in training what he seldom did in
matches – the rarest of headers

England scored twice, but the comeback flickered and then faded out when France, who had not won for 11 matches, claimed two more goals, winning the match 5–2 and the tie 6–3 on aggregate.

So much for winning the next World Cup . . .

England hadn't conceded five goals since those two debacles against Hungary. Ramsey was criticised for the absence of a plan, which is ironic, because later he would be castigated for adhering too slavishly to one. And England were lambasted for lacking anyone who could graft, scheme or play inside forward. Sheffield Wednesday's goalkeeper, Ron Springett, got locked in the stocks and pilloried too, blamed for three mistakes.

Ramsey took the blow inflicted on him philosophically. 'Do we always defend like that?' he asked his captain Jimmy Armfield. In truth, the European Championships were something to be got through for Ramsey, who was unable to experiment freely. 'I dare say we will lose a few matches,' he said. 'I don't think we need to be afraid of that.'

* * *

Alf Ramsey was adamant that he needed 'three world-class players' to win a World Cup. Already, he thought England had found two of them: Bobby Moore and Bobby Charlton. His next four matches, which included a Wembley defeat to Scotland and a scratchy draw against a weary Brazil without Pelé, showcased the potential of two more: Gordon Banks and Ray Wilson.

Charlton and Moore were automatic picks. 'I knew, even years before the World Cup, that he would have the number nine on his back,' Ramsey said of Charlton.

Charlton had won 39 caps and scored 29 goals, including three hat-tricks, before Ramsey took over. He was a pin-up idol, receiving 'hundreds of letters' each week that demanded his autograph, contained an invitation or included a question to be answered from an inquisitive fan. His first ghost-writer, Kenneth Wheeler, watched

Charlton stuff the correspondence in his boot-locker at Old Trafford, not knowing what to do with it. Wheeler saw him as a 'little boy lost' who couldn't 'cope' with the 'hero-worship he inspired'. *Book of Soccer*, which he produced for him, was only 82 pages long. Wheeler calculated that Charlton produced so few words for it that his contribution would hardly have filled 'the back of a postage stamp'. Odd, since in the introduction Charlton claims to have wanted to become 'a writer' one day.

Everyone knew that Moore lacked pace; he could barely out-run a chicken. Everyone also knew that it made no difference, never diminishing his performance. He turned as sharply as a cat coming around a corner. And the warp speed of his brain enabled him to anticipate the shape of an attack at least a full minute before it was launched. Moore read a game with a kind of extrasensory perception. He registered danger before the opposition had even thought about creating it. Patience, waiting like a predator for its prey, was another Moore attribute that seemed other-worldly to Ramsey. He seldom rushed in or lunged. He headed the ball only when it couldn't be avoided, preferring to take a high pass on his chest. His movements were so precisely timed that he counted them in micro-seconds. To tackle scruffily, scrambling for possession, was also an affront to Moore. He was elegant, almost poetic, in his grace, satisfying the eye. He was nerveless, too, exuding an immense strength. It gave him poise and serenity on the ball. If a bomb had gone off, ripping up the turf in front of him, Moore would have nonchalantly stepped over or around it, before passing to whomever was unmarked.

He was immaculate in appearance as well, sartorially splendid both on and off the pitch. Moore travelled with his own iron to smooth away the wrinkles from his shirts and suits, which would then be carefully placed, rather than slung, on wooden hangers. His shoes had the sheen of new glass. Before matches, he would walk around the dressing room without his shorts on – partly through superstition, partly because he didn't want to crease them. He'd even iron the laces of his boots.

The greatest 'save': not even a dog, running at full pelt, could escape Gordon Banks

Even those with only a rudimentary knowledge of art appreciate a Rembrandt or a Vermeer at first sight. Those with only a rudimentary knowledge of football could similarly have appreciated Moore from the off. He didn't just stand out; he looked as though he'd just stepped out of the sun.

After the defeat in Paris, Ramsey had deliberately sat beside Moore on the coach taking them away from the ground. Moore said he began to ask him 'a million things about the way things had been done' under Walter Winterbottom. Moore had won only 11 caps – just three of them under Ramsey – when he became England's captain temporarily (Jimmy Armfield had stubbed his toe so badly it looked as though someone had hit him with a builder's mallet). Six internationals later, the job was his permanently. He was only 22 years old. Ramsey saw him as 'an extension of myself on the field'.

* * *

It is always trickier to assess goalkeepers, who can showboat with diving saves when others would have caught the ball with a sidestep. But Ramsey knew right away what Gordon Banks could become. Banks was only 25 when he played for England – and lost – against Scotland at Wembley in 1963. Six weeks later, he played – and lost again – in the FA Cup final for Leicester City, who were beaten by Manchester United.

He was entirely self-taught. There were no specialist goalkeeping coaches and not much in the way of specialist training manuals to be bought or borrowed. He began to learn on a dingy recreation ground. The goals had no nets. The touchline was fringed with a row of terraced houses. When it rained, he said, the pitch was a 'quagmire'. When it was cold, he added, the surface became 'so icy that the teams had trouble turning around at half-time'. His first club was Chesterfield, where he got used to conceding goals alongside the stiffs. One game was lost 7–0; without Banks, it would have been 14–0. He arrived at Leicester unaware there were five other goalkeepers there and that the club considered him sixth choice.

Goalkeeping was seen as a romantic art for masochists, and goalkeepers were thought of as outsiders with a few loose screws. Banks sought to change all that. As well as the compulsory training he did with his club in the morning, he worked on his game every weekday afternoon as well as on Sundays. He relied on the benevolence of his friends, who aimed long-range shots at him, tested his reactions from close range and launched crosses, corners and free kicks into the box. Banks even practised making saves while running backwards. He did it all with ungloved hands, his fingers sore and raw and dirty. Whenever he could, Banks went to watch other goalkeepers. He realised positioning, adjusting the stance and cutting down the angles, crucially separated the great from the merely competent; he was a Pythagoras between the sticks.

Ramsey had a high opinion of himself as a full back. His opinion of Ray Wilson was higher still. He was quicker, more mobile and surpassed Ramsey in terms of distributing the ball accurately. Wilson was also so undemonstrative that a winger hardly knew he was there – until he thieved possession from him.

He was christened Ramon. His mother was besotted with the Hollywood actor Ramón Novarro, a Mexican American who appeared in both the original *Ben-Hur* and beside Greta Garbo in *Mata Hari*. Novarro was a screen heart-throb who masked his homosexuality. He was brutally murdered by two men he'd invited to his house for sex. The phrase 'legend has it' guarantees the story that follows it is almost always false; Navarro, despite the salacious rumours, was not found by police with a dildo in his mouth.

On the mean streets of the mining village of Shirebrook, where he grew up, Ramon Wilson became Ray to avoid ridicule and bullying. His mother left the family home when Wilson was six years old, returning three years later to raise him with her new husband. Without a school qualification, he became a railwayman, cleaning locomotives at night and playing as an amateur inside forward or wing half at weekends. Huddersfield rescued Wilson, converting him into an overlapping full back. He matured in the era when being an apprentice meant spending every Monday forking the pitch, every Tuesday sweeping the terraces, and every day scrubbing boots. 'We didn't start training until about 4pm,' he said. He was 25 before England capped him.

Wilson was determined to leave Huddersfield, then in the Second Division. They were equally determined not to sell him. He complained of the 'ghosts' there, the triple championship-winning team of the 1920s against which the current side was being compared. He also complained about the crowd's distaste for him, criminalising his efforts to leave for another club. 'Big Head' was the name the fans gave him. 'They're shocking like that . . . They don't really like me,' he said.

Ramsey did like Wilson. With him, plus Banks, Moore and Charlton, a third of the England side picked itself. There should have been a fifth name to add to those, but even during his early months in charge, Ramsey scratched a question mark beside Jimmy Greaves's. Not because of his lack of ability – Greaves had a boundless talent for self-expression – but because of what Ramsey considered to be a basic lack of application.

* * *

After taking over, Alf Ramsey admitted he knew 'nothing at all' about being an international manager. He explained that, at Ipswich, he'd always looked at every other club's players simply 'as an opponent' and thought 'only about how to stop' them. He used Jimmy Greaves as an example. Now, Ramsey added, he had to decide 'where best to deploy him'.

He never did so satisfactorily.

There were imperatives each player had to meet to win Ramsey's favour. He looked for three qualities: 'technique, supreme physical fitness and adaptability', the latter being defined as 'fitting in alongside everyone else'. Ramsey wanted commitment, as evidenced by glistening beads of sweat. 'There were some very talented players who I preferred to ignore because there was a selfish, egotistical edge to their game. Give me a team player any time ahead of the exhibitionist,' he said, leaving everyone to make obvious guesses about who fell into that category.

Greaves was gregarious, impetuous, full of himself and popular without discernible effort. These were virtues that sometimes Ramsey considered to be vices. He poached big goals in small spaces. He could go on short, rapid, sinewy runs. He made the best of defenders, struggling to stop him, look so uncoordinated that you thought their legs had been screwed on backwards.

Ramsey never disputed Greaves's abundant skill. He did damn his work rate, which was lackadaisical even in training. After one game, Ramsey, incensed with Greaves's laissez-faire attitude, said privately that he needed 'fuckin' stranglin'' for insubordination.

Anyone who met Greaves never doubted his friendly, welcoming nature, his self-deprecating charm and his wit, which was sharp without ever being acidly cruel.* Ramsey perceived a militant edge to it and also a need to draw attention to himself, pilfering the limelight. He also thought Greaves, even in his mid-20s, had yet to grow up and was too easily distracted. He was also too larky and adolescent-like for him.

With the kind of understatement that makes your jaw drop, Greaves said that he and Ramsey 'had something of a clash of personalities'.

Not much.

During Ramsey's first tour with England, Greaves had asked whether 'a few of us' might go off for a drink. Ramsey responded with: 'If some of you [he meant Greaves] want a fucking beer, you can come back to the hotel to have it.' Greaves insisted that Ramsey –'when he dropped the mask' – was 'a different person altogether', but also admitted 'there were occasions when I stretched his charm and affability to the limit'.

Too often for Ramsey's liking, Greaves was at the bull's eye of some escapade that led to either disruption or trouble. He was concerned, too, that Greaves errantly led astray his room-mate, Bobby Moore. When Greaves and Moore broke curfew, sneaking out of the Waldorf Astoria on New York's Park Lane to hear Ella Fitzgerald perform in a plush club near Times Square, Ramsey blamed the most likely suspect. He didn't know that Moore had instigated the escapade (nor had he heard of Fitzgerald, a multiple Grammy award-winner by then).

'You two,' he said, 'will take the piss once too often.'

As he had at Ipswich, Ramsey would accept some leg-pulling, or even fragments of mild dissent, and he didn't object to a player chucking his three-pennies' worth into a debate at team meetings. 'Only a fool turns down constructive ideas – or ignores constructive criticism,'

* In the 1980s, Greaves and Ian St John would visit Nottingham Forest's City Ground when filming either there or in the vicinity. I was fortunate enough to witness a few two-man 'shows' they gave in the Chairman's Room to entertain Brian Clough.

he said. What he despised was 'complacency', the assumption that a player could do one thing when he had specifically ordered them to do another.

Even as he kept on picking him, Ramsey came to the conclusion that he could twist Greaves's arm behind his back as far as it would go without ever changing him. He was also sure of this: if he didn't build a team specifically around Greaves, he would eventually be the one piece in it which didn't quite fit.

* * *

On October 15, 1963, a damp Tuesday, Alf Ramsey met the Football Association's councillors again at Lancaster Gate. He presented the England side he'd chosen for the FA's Centenary Match against FIFA's Rest of the World Select XI, which was to be staged the following week at Wembley. It was an exhibition match with an edge. The Rest of the World were bringing with them Lev Yashin, Eusébio, Raymond Kopa, Denis Law, Jim Baxter, Alfredo di Stéfano and Ferenc Puskás.

But the date on which Ramsey read out his team sheet was important for another reason: there were exactly 1,000 days to go before the start of the 1966 World Cup. In their previous four matches, England had scored 18 goals (eight of them smashed past Switzerland). Consequently, the mood since the loss to France had changed, becoming a little rose-tinted. The idea of England as World Champions was no longer seen as 'a foolish dream', said Ramsey, who nonetheless stressed the obstacle to be overcome.

'I have to create a team,' he said.

The *Playfair Football Annual* of 1963–4 is an unlikely totemic book. Between pages 89 and 105 is its roll call of First Division players. The 22 clubs had 601 professionals between them. Quote that figure and you'd assume that Ramsey was spoilt for choice, the talent pool almost limitless. That pool was actually much narrower and shallower, as evidenced by *Playfair*'s decision about who to use as the poster boy for the season to come. It put Stanley Matthews on the cover (he's about to cross the ball from near a corner flag). If Matthews had been born in the mid-1930s, Ramsey would have selected him. But when *Playfair* was published, he was six months shy of his 49th birthday.

The book highlights Ramsey's dilemma.

Take away those who are either too old, such as Matthews, or too young. Take away those born in Scotland, Ireland or Wales. Take away those who had been called up by England and then allowed to drift back into the ranks. Take away those who occupy positions that are already filled or over-subscribed. And, finally, take away those Ramsey had seen and discounted for their lack of international quality.

Ramsey was left with 81 names.

It would have been 82, but two months before Ramsey became manager, Johnny Haynes was involved in a freak accident. A red MG sports car, in which he was a passenger, got stuck in tramlines. A wicked whip of wind then blew it across Blackpool's Queen's Promenade. The car flew into the path of an oncoming vehicle, through a low wall and into the front of a house. A policeman attending the accident naïvely said to Haynes: 'Don't worry. You've only broken your leg.' Haynes's injuries, which included ripping a cruciate ligament, were so severe that he never played for England again.

Players were always being flung at Ramsey from the back pages of the newspapers. Possession of two legs and a birth certificate, confirming you were under 30, seemed to be the only qualifications required. None of these pieces championed three of the players Ramsey had noticed, almost out of the corner of his eye.

* * *

The first player was a centre half in the Second Division – but about to burst into the First – known as 'The Big Bastard', a 6ft 2in stick of bone with a goose-neck. When he jumped, it was like watching a man ascend on stilts.

Before the 1960s died, Leeds United under Don Revie would infamously begin establishing themselves as the Damned United. When Ramsey originally went to watch Jack Charlton, most of that team was already established at Elland Road: Billy Bremner, Johnny Giles, Gary Sprake, Norman Hunter, Peter Lorimer, Paul Reaney and Paul Madeley. Charlton was widely considered to be not much more than an ungainly, awkwardly stiff centre half, deficient in everything but height – someone who couldn't play himself but was eminently capable of preventing others from doing so, not necessarily while adhering to the nobility of the Queensberry Rules. He was an awkward bugger too, a non-conformist and dressing-room shop steward who regularly let either his rhetoric or his actions run ahead of his judgement. In his early days, Charlton was so obstreperous and undisciplined that he could have picked a fight on the moon. If criticised, he had a habit of tearing off his shirt and throwing it away like an oily rag. He threatened to punch one of his own coaches. As a player at Leeds, Revie told Charlton flatly: 'You piss around too much.' As manager, he transfer-listed him. Charlton defended his own cussedness by criticising others for being 'too weak and too spineless' to speak up.

Off the pitch, where he was less quarrelsome, there was an entrepreneurial zeal about Charlton. He was soon opening menswear shops – he couldn't bring himself to call them boutiques – and on the morning of home matches attempted to sell the opposition bolts of cloth for bespoke suits, unloaded from the back of his car, before kicking them to pieces an hour or so later.

In demeanour, temperament, behaviour and interests he was so different from his brother Bobby, who was 18 months younger. You almost convince yourself that one of them must have been adopted. When documentaries were eventually made comparing the disparate Charltons, it was like finding out that Lord Snooty and Dennis the Menace had once shared the same house.

Their mother Cissie allowed her sons to use the legs of her Queen Anne sideboard as goalposts, ignoring the chipped polish and the

Cissie Charlton, the most prominent woman in football during the 1950s and '60s

splinters of wood. Born into football aristocracy – she was a Milburn – her four brothers each played for league clubs. She coached her sons, joined in their backyard games, washed kit and also cut oranges and baked stotty cakes for the school team. 'I don't think there's much I don't know about the game. It's been my life,' she said.

Cissie explained the difference between her boys this way: 'One's an angel. The other's a devil.' Bobby was 'always so quiet and so good'. As for Jack . . . 'I gave him more hidings than half-pennies.' The contrast in their personalities continued into adulthood. Everything Bobby did was understated and mannered. He wore V-neck sweaters, cosy cardigans and suede driving gloves. In a collar and tie he chipped golf balls across his back lawn. When he left home, his family waving him off from the driveway, his mackintosh was spotlessly beige.

Jack was livelier and unpredictable, which made him more interesting too. In his flat cap and wellington boots he gunned for rabbits in the fields or went bird-nesting around Ashington, a village that continued to produce coal and footballers. He bet on whippets who raced on a home-made grassy track. He lifted his father's pigeons out of their coop. In the 1930s and 1940s, his family ate the birds that flew too slowly. He fished like Huckleberry Finn, casting his line and then going to sleep. He talked proudly about a boyhood catch, a one-pound grayling, as though he'd landed a blue whale. He had a pint in The Welfare. He listened to brass bands and sang 'The Blaydon Races' out of tune. He walked around Ashington, pointing out the 'million' windows he had broken and reminiscing about his child-hood home. It had no running hot water, no central hearing, no bathroom; his father, a miner, sat in a tin bath in front of the fire and scrubbed the coal off his back. In Ashington, Jack said, you couldn't leave a baby in a pram without a cover; like everything else, it would be covered in coal dust. Briefly, he worked down the pit, folding his lanky body into tunnels only three feet high, like Houdini squashing himself into a trunk.

You could tell that Jack belonged in Ashington, which was home for him. You can also tell that Bobby left it behind long ago. The things that attracted Jack – the place, the people, the inexhaustible memories – repelled Bobby.

When the Charltons were growing up, they'd be asked: 'What's it like to be Jackie Milburn's nephew?' In 1963, Jack was being asked: 'What's it like to be Bobby's brother?' He'd made only a modest name for himself. No one thought he'd be the kind of player or sort of per-sonality to attract Ramsey.

* * *

The second player was a centre forward, the son of a centre half.

The coaching books sensibly advised that a central defender should be 6ft or preferably even taller, like a Swiss pine. Charlie Hurst was only 5ft 8in. He explained to his son, Geoff, the painful method he'd relied on – for Bristol Rovers, Rochdale and Oldham – to stop goal-scorers: 'If I can't get my head to the ball, I can always get my head to the back of his head.' While not a full-blown kamikaze mission, the weekly sac-rifice of thumping his forehead into someone's skull – a different kind of Glasgow kiss – can only mean he spent a goodly part of his weekly salary stocking up on Anadin.

When Geoff Hurst was only six years old, his father moved the family to Chelmsford, which is why Ramsey heard about him as soon as he broke into West Ham's team early in 1958. Arthur Rowe was responsible for signing Charlie Hurst. The Hursts and the Rowes lived on the same street. Beneath the lamp posts, Rowe's son kicked a ball about with Hurst's. In these impromptu games, Hurst knocked it so regularly into a neighbour's garden that the local policeman was finally called. Hurst was summoned to court and fined 30 shillings. His father, so convinced of his son's potential, paid it without complaint. Afterwards, the only remark he made about it was: 'Make damn sure you keep the ball out of that bloke's garden.'

Hurst made a false start at West Ham. He was a wing half at a club that could have fielded a full team of them – plus substitutes.

Frequently in life, like one nudged domino initiating a chain reaction to bring down all the others, a row of coincidences startles you. West Ham's manager Ron Greenwood picks Hurst, drops him and then decides to take a risk. Hurst is 'big and strong and not afraid of work', says Greenwood, who suggests he should play inside left. Rowe, now boss of Third Division Crystal Palace, watches him and is impressed. When West Ham want to buy Johnny Byrne from Palace, Rowe tries unsuccessfully to make the boy who used to play in front of his lounge window part of the deal. He sees – well before Greenwood – that Hurst is in the wrong position. In Hurst, who is nearly four inches taller than his father, he recognises something of Tommy Lawton. Lawton was almost the same height and had a similar physique. Rowe tells Ramsey about Hurst.

* * *

Martin Peters, the third player, spent his boyhood swallowing spoonfuls of cod liver oil, which he loathed, because his mother thought

Martin Peters, so versatile he could have played anywhere on the pitch – and often did

he needed thickening out. His father, a Thames lighterman, used his muscles to move flat-bottomed barges and his mind to navigate the current, the eddies and the tides. Peters thought the Thames would be his workplace too. When scouts lined the touchline at his school pitch, he assumed they had come to watch someone else. Peters could – and did – play anywhere; even, once, as an emergency goalkeeper. Ron Greenwood described him as a 'connoisseur's dream' who did 'everything so perfectly he made it look too easy'. He also had a 'delightful' understanding of 'time and space', added Greenwood.

In that terrible winter of 1962–3, after the fixture list went haywire, Ipswich faced West Ham twice in four days over Easter. At Portman Road, West Ham were 2–1 behind with a quarter of an hour to go.

Ramsey would one day burden Peters with the millstone label 'a player ten years ahead of his time'.* Initially, though, he had one reser-

---

* He said it before England faced Scotland in 1968. Jimmy Greaves is supposed to have asked Ramsey: 'If Martin is ten years ahead of his time, Alf, why is he playing now?'

vation about his abilities: he thought Peters was a weak header of the ball.

In this match, Peters proved him wrong. When a corner was swung over, he checked away from his marker and nodded in West Ham's equaliser.

Ramsey then saw what Rowe had already spotted in Geoff Hurst.

An angled ball was played in from the left. For two years – ever since watching Real Madrid beat Eintracht Frankfurt 7–3 at Hampden Park – Hurst had been working on the touches that make one forward superior to another in a crowded box. That European Cup final had awakened him to a standard of the game that 'I hadn't known to exist'. Hurst had previously gone 'along with the myth' that 'foreign teams were fancy' but lightweight. After the final, he constantly talked about Real and the 'growing wonder' he felt while following Di Stéfano and Puskás. Hurst supposed he must have 'bored stiff' anyone who hadn't watched them.

At Ipswich, the graft he put in on the West Ham training ground was manifest in his goal. He was seven yards out. The ball came to him shin high. He lifted his right boot, turned it slightly to meet the flight of the cross and grazed the shot, very gently, into the net for West Ham's winner.

Hurst was just 21 years old. West Ham had yet to win a trophy, and only those closest to the club referred to Upton Park as an academy. But as Ramsey once said about someone else: 'One might come across a player who does something only in a flash, but this is enough to alert you to what he might do again. One takes note of that and does not forget.'

Ramsey filed away Hurst's classy flick and Peters's header.

He did not forget them.

7

TEA AND BISCUITS AT ELEVEN O'CLOCK

In his documentary *My Generation*, which explores how the 1960s shook Britain to its staid roots, the actor Michael Caine stares into the Thames while the Kinks sing about the 'dirty old river' and the 'paradise' of a Waterloo sunset. The '60s, Caine declares, were the 'first time' the 'young working class' stood up for themselves and said: 'We are here, this is our society and we are not going away.'

Another clip of film proves it.

Three months after Alf Ramsey had appeared on *Sportsview* to talk about himself and the World Cup, a self-possessed 18-year-old named David Jones turned up on the BBC's current-affairs programme *Tonight*. He was launching a society for men with long hair (he defined 'long' as between 'eight to nine inches'). He retained his composure even when the audience, mostly male and middle-aged (a lot were also bald or balding), began heckling him.

At the time, the programme was largely ignored because it seemed irrelevant. Seen now, it strikes you as the harbinger of several new beginnings.

Soon David Jones changed his name – becoming David Bowie – and barbershops offering only short back and sides and 'something for the weekend, sir' were going slowly broke.

Within another two years the American country singer Roger Miller, half mockingly, was warbling about 'bobbies on bicycles', before insisting that 'England Swings (Like a Pendulum Do)'. Within three, after the step and rhythm of the '60s were already established, *Time* magazine writer Piri Halasz was anointing London as 'the *fin de siècle*' capital of the world, likening its cultural renaissance to 'dreamlike' Vienna under the

Hapsburgs, the 1920s Paris that enraptured Hemingway and Fitzgerald, and Berlin before Hitler shut down the party in the 1930s. Halasz declared London to be 'pulsing' with 'veins of excitement', 'new vitality' and 'indulgence'. Not bad for a country that, less than 15 years before, had looked as though it had lost a war rather than won one. After the rubble was cleared, London began to grow taller on the empty spaces the bulldozers and the wrecking balls created. Office blocks and flats were built by workers who, immune to vertigo, walked confidently along iron girders in ordinary shoes, baggy trousers and woollen jackets, a fag smouldering between their lips. Paint and concrete was also still drying on 11 new English towns – eight of them within a 30-mile radius of the capital.

Since decades never fall into tidy historical bundles, instead spilling into one another, there will forever be a squabble about exactly when the '60s began and ended and also when they properly ignited, accelerating away in a rush from the drabness of what had gone before. No one explained this better than Craig Brown, the critic and humourist. 'By 1963,' he wrote, 'the 1950s had been going on for nearly 13 years.'

When anyone who was famous in the '60s starts to reminisce about those years, you know what is coming, which is a list of other famous people who were there too – some of whom pretended they wanted to die before they got old but never managed that feat. What you always get first is the music, followed by the fashion – either Mary Quant's mini-skirt or the elfin Twiggy on a catwalk in a caftan and a pair of kinky boots. Next come the social landmarks, rising like obelisks: the Lady Chatterley trial; the Pill, said to be 'more explosive than dynamite'; and Philip Larkin's retrospective verse lament about sex, which arrived 'a little too late' for him. As Brown also pointed out about the '60s: 'Sex, which had been strictly formal, was fast becoming casual. Some young people even claimed to be doing it for pleasure.'*

* Actually, in his exceptional book *White Heat: A History of Britain in the Swinging Sixties*, the historian Dominic Sandbrook reports that in 1968 two-thirds of women were still virgins on their wedding night.

The baby-boomers, sassy and non-conformist, sometimes considered themselves wise in the way a drunk always considers himself sober, but the charges against them came mostly from those who were old enough to have survived the Depression and at least one war, and who then had to live with the hard consequences of both. The '60s, which sent everything spinning, were always going to be a disorientating shock to the system for men and women still bound by the strained but polite strictures of class, who dressed as formally as their parents had done, who shared their established social values and who had listened to their first music on shellac 78s. You might regard branding the Beatles and the Rolling Stones as 'moral enemies of the state', as some did, a bit extreme, but resistance to what the '60s stood for – and also what they strived to achieve – was the natural reflex action for anyone unable to comprehend how pomp and pageantry were suddenly being overwhelmed by pop culture and flower power.

Throughout the decade, however, there was a stucco house in London that remained untouched by the hedonism, the colour, the razzle-dazzle. Outside this building, the '60s were coming to the boil. Inside it, you'd have thought nothing much had changed since 1945.

* * *

Alf Ramsey considered the England managership to be a 'curious job'. He said it came with 'this feeling of loneliness', which is why it took him a year to settle into it.

At Ipswich, he had planned for games that were less than a week away. With England, he was adjusting to a fixture list in which months could separate one match from the next. In 1964, England played 12 games. The first of these wasn't staged until mid-April. The next seven were pressed into four hectic weeks straddling early May and early June. Ramsey spent most of his days behind his desk rather than on a training pitch.

This was 'difficult', he admitted. 'I am used to a day-to-day involvement with players and, at first, I missed it.'

Knowing this, John Cobbold tried to tempt Ramsey back to Ipswich in 1964 after sacking Jackie Milburn, the manager he'd appointed to replace him. As unhappy as he was, Ramsey would not countenance the possibility. The loss of face – and the 'I-told-you-so's – would have been too great for him to bear. Cobbold was sanguine about his failure to persuade Ramsey otherwise. 'Alf never did like leaving a job unfinished,' he said.

For Ramsey, the struggle went on.

Cobbold's lack of pomposity and his almost-anything-goes irreverence meant there had been no p's and q's to be careful about at Portman Road. The Football Association, however, was tethered solidly to its traditions and attitudes, some of which seemed to pre-date the Second Boer War. Progress towards modernity meant sideways, crab-like shuffles of reluctant compromise for them.

As a child of the Georgian 1920s, and the son of Victorian parents, Ramsey observed the upheavals of the 1960s without actively participating in them. He would never have been seen – even on the mortuary slab – wearing jeans or a flowery shirt from Carnaby Street. But even as a man of habit, conservative in his tastes, the formality of the FA's office at Lancaster Gate was stifling to him. On occasions, needing to clear his head, he would walk briskly through Kensington Gardens, a circuit that took him around one of the ponds and the bandstand.

Two photographs give you a sense of how Lancaster Gate looked and felt, and how oppressive, intimidating and coldly austere those surroundings could seem to anyone unfamiliar with them. The first marks the end of Walter Winterbottom's tenure as England manager. The second marks the beginning of Ramsey's. Winterbottom is sitting in the committee room. Beside him is the secretary, Denis Follows, and eight members of the selection committee. One of the selectors is wearing a bow tie. He and at least two others seem to be of an age that suggests their first vote in a general election was probably cast for Lloyd George. Ramsey is seen with some of those same men. The table has such a mirrored sheen that you imagine at least a dozen tins of wax polish were rubbed into it. Behind him – hanging on the wall in wide, dark frames – are oil portraits of football's pioneers and of former FA grandees. There is also an oak clock, which first chimed sometime between the wars, and a picture of Queen Elizabeth, pearlescent in her youth. The rest of the interior decor hardly reflected the vibrancy of the '60s. The rooms contained dark wood furniture, original tiled floors, a glass case or two filled with silver trophies, and high ceilings with filigree plaster mouldings.

The weight of history pressed against Alf Ramsey at the Football Association's Lancaster Gate offices

The FA had been there since as long ago as 1929, moving from Russell Square, a building that was reputedly haunted. The architectural historian Nikolaus Pevsner called Lancaster Gate 'tall' and 'well to do', which hardly does it justice. The FA's home was among a Georgian terrace of four-storey properties – each with the bonus of a basement – that were built in the mid-19th century. Formerly a hotel, the FA's headquarters had a Doric porch, cast-iron railings and square-headed windows. A small brass plate beside the door was the only signage. Those who visited Lancaster Gate – and also those who worked there – likened it to a quaintly eccentric gentlemen's club in need of modernisation and younger members.

The FA boastfully described the building as 'the hub of a huge wheel', making it sound as though everything there turned in well-oiled clicks. But there were brigades of committees, subcommittees and associations, which led to layers upon layers of bureaucracy, necessitating countless meetings and creating pyramids of paper. If the FA had been a machine, you'd have concluded that only Heath Robinson could possibly have designed it.

Nothing exemplified the FA's dull traditionalism more than the organisation's 'official journal', a glossy monthly magazine of only 16 pages. It was once said of John Bunyan's *The Pilgrim's Progress* that 'no one ever wished it longer'. That damning critique applies also to the *FA News*, so yawningly dull that reading it had the same effect as taking a sedative. A typical issue would include some dust-dry profile of an FA official, the obituary of another, an account of a meeting at one of the county associations, a brief history of an amateur team or a league ground, and a page of random statistics. Nearly every piece confirmed the FA as being at least a decade behind the present day.

There were only 45 staff at Lancaster Gate. Each of the men had to wear an FA tie, as if attending a public school, and '60s fashions – especially Beatles haircuts – were prohibited. At least everything was very civilised: tea and biscuits were punctually served to Ramsey in his office at 11am.

That office, on the third floor, was 56 steps from the FA's front door. It was described as being 'utterly without character' and like the 'servant's quarters'. The secretary's desk was almost as big as a snooker table, which made it only slightly smaller than the whole space Ramsey occupied. Only 13ft by 8ft in size, his office walls were blank and the furniture was sparse: a desk, a filing cabinet, a telephone, a waste-paper basket and an Adams-style marble fireplace, the mantel often being used as a shelf for books. Here, on myriad blocks of paper, Ramsey plotted his path to the World Cup, considering this to be a matter of organisation. He was fastidious about being neat and tidy. At the end of each day, his notes would be locked away or taken home for safe keeping. You wouldn't have known that his desk belonged to anyone.

Ramsey confided to a friend that he always knew 'history was watching'; that it would remember him as someone who either won the competition or missed his chance to win it. To apply himself to the former task he relied on routine. From Monday to Thursday (he always took Friday off), Ramsey would catch the 8.35am train from Ipswich, occupying a seat in a first-class compartment, and then take the Central Line to Lancaster Gate, arriving at 10am. He always left at 4.30pm. He usually wore a white shirt, dark tie, sober suit and either put on or carried his mackintosh, as though constantly afraid of the threat of rain.

Often, using it as camouflage, he hid behind his copy of the *Daily Mail* – a broadsheet newspaper in those days – to dissuade commuters who might buttonhole him. He was able to look straight through his fellow passengers in silence, never acknowledging their presence, or stare at them in such a way as to signal his displeasure at being interrupted. Only a small percentage failed to get the message.

Today, if there is a Friday-night fixture, the England manager can feasibly watch three games in the top division over the course of a long weekend and a fourth on the Monday. Ramsey had only midweek matches to supplement his Saturday travels. On average, he saw three games per week. If a player interested him, Ramsey made a point of watching him away from home, where the crowd would be partisan and hostile, and the referee possibly less sympathetic to the visitors. 'That is when you see what someone is made of and what he can do,' he said.

Every likely candidate for the England team had his own dossier, which Ramsey, a tireless collector of facts, compiled and constantly updated. He said he amassed 'about 100' of them, also including promising players from the Second and Third Divisions who might one day be bought by First Division clubs. The dossiers contained strictly factual information: a player's match-by-match record and his medical history. Ramsey never wrote down his personal opinions in case the contents were either lost or leaked. 'Their strengths and weaknesses, I keep in my head,' he explained.

Film was scarce and so was little used by managers, but Ramsey had a distinct advantage over everyone else. The FA had an arrangement with the BBC. Reels of 16mm recordings of matches, such as internationals and cup finals from home and abroad, would be dispatched to Lancaster Gate in silver cannisters. As well as England's games, which the FA filmed at Wembley, Ramsey was able to watch European and South American opposition. As befitted a lover of the movies, he liked sitting in the dark, memorising every move. He'd ask the FA's film and photographic department, which actually comprised one teenager who had only recently left school, to produce a compilation of clips from England's matches, particularly the goals and each set piece. In our digital age this can be done in an hour; in the 1960s, it took at least two days – spooling, respooling, cutting, splicing.

Ramsey was a loner, the authentic auteur, but Harold Shepherdson and Les Cocker did the shop-floor work for him – unsung tasks that no one notices until they aren't done.

Shepherdson came from a background more unforgivingly harsh even than Ramsey's own. Born in Middlesbrough, less than a fortnight before the First World War ended, he said he never went hungry, but thought his parents had shared their food among the family to protect them from near starvation. He played for Middlesbrough and Southend before knee trouble pushed him prematurely into coaching and also physiotherapy, during a period when the remedy for everything – except a broken leg – was usually a bucketful of icy water and a sponge.

Cocker was once described by Brian Clough as an 'aggressive, nasty little bugger', which was a half-compliment. A forward, scorer of 91 goals in 295 games for Stockport County and Accrington Stanley, he'd gone into coaching at Luton, before switching to Leeds, his reputation rising as the club rose. Cocker was army-trained; he'd served with the Reconnaissance Regiment in France after D-Day. For someone whose physical fitness regimes could tear the guts out of retching players, unable to cope with them, he seemed the unlikeliest disciple of biomechanics and kinesiology. Cocker studied both, when the science was thought to be so experimentally faddish that even pronouncing 'kinesiology', let alone spelling the word correctly, was beyond most of his peers. He was much more than a thuggish, earthy, sergeant-major type who could shout until you were deaf, but sometimes he played up to that part.

As preposterous as this seems, the FA had never considered it might be sensible to find a doctor to accompany England until Ramsey appointed Alan Bass, the third man of his backroom staff. Before Bass – bluff, convivial, father-like – England's approach to medicine had been hazardously slapdash, amounting to a shopping trip to Boots to stock up on bandages, plasters and iodine. Bass was a consultant on Harley Street and at two London hospitals. He also worked with Arsenal. Few footballers had even bothered to learn about how to care for their feet. Bass taught them, including giving a tutorial about cutting toenails.

Ramsey recognised that Shepherdson, Cocker and Bass were naturally loyal. Solely in charge of his own project, he still did so much in secret. He discussed neither his 'problems' nor his 'teams with anyone', he said, because he liked to 'think them out myself'. This was only half the story. He was even reluctant to share too many of his private thoughts with other managers, preferring to take information from them rather than reciprocate with advice or suggestions of his own.

It was a question of trust.

Despite Bill Nicholson's occasional involvement with England's under-23s, Ramsey's wariness of him remained. Most of his wariness about everyone else stemmed from the concern that someone might accidentally – or deliberately – say too much to a reporter. Ramsey didn't want to wake up to find his opinion of a player had made it into a newspaper from an 'anonymous source'. Consequently, he fostered amiable working relationships, rather than friendships, with Don Revie, Bill Shankly, Joe Mercer and Ron Greenwood. Ramsey did speak regularly – and a little more openly – with Matt Busby, whom he regarded as impeccably discreet.

Again, though, he chiefly spoke with Arthur Rowe. If the FA's phone bill had been itemised in the 1960s, Rowe's number would have appeared there regularly. Rowe didn't seek publicity. He advised Ramsey without recognition, accepting only the occasional lunch or dinner at the FA's expense, often at the Windsor Hotel, which was a few doors down from Lancaster Gate.

After his first tour abroad with England, Ramsey had congratulated everyone for their contribution. His only reference he made to the FA was purposefully barbed: 'I would like to thank the England officials for keeping out of our way,' he said. It had been standard practice for FA councillors to send reports about players to Walter Winterbottom. Ramsey paid no attention to those he received, filing most of them among the rubbish. When he was asked what he did with each report, Ramsey made a twisting action with his hands and a throwing motion over his shoulder. He was careful, however, to make sure he didn't drop the evidence into his own waste-paper basket in case a cleaner raked through it. Most of it was torn up and placed in the public bins dotted along his route to the Tube station or across the railway station concourse.

He was a manager who thought of everything . . .

* * *

Alf Ramsey took over an England side that was broken. He was working for a Football Association that, after being awarded the 1966 World Cup in 1960, didn't properly appreciate until the end of 1962 how much pressure would be placed on it to win the trophy at home. While Walter Winterbottom was in charge, both geography – especially those two World Cups staged in South America – and minimal television coverage had protected the FA from too much scrutiny. Holding the World Cup in its own backyard made it vulnerable because every match would be screened live on television. There'd be armchair critics who, if things went badly, would need to be pacified afterwards.

After some unseemly tantrums – especially from Alan Hardaker, who talked about TV like a hellfire preacher making a speech about sin and damnation – *Match of the Day* was rolled out in August 1964. The military dum-da-da of the programme's theme tune, 'The Drum Majorette', preceded Liverpool v. Arsenal. The viewing figure, hovering around 20,000, was less than half the gate at Anfield, but that paltry figure didn't perturb the BBC, which was committed for the long haul. *Match of the Day* served two purposes. It tapped into a new market, which the BBC was convinced would swell. It also trained cameramen, producers and directors to cover football in preparation for the World Cup. So few games had previously been televised – and fewer still had been live – that the BBC, like England, was getting its 'team' ready.

The FA didn't interfere with Ramsey's plans. He alone decided which opposition England would play. He also chose the timing of arrival and departure, the hotels, the training facilities, the pre-match menus and which cinemas the squad would visit to watch another

John Wayne western. His authority was absolute, his planning as thorough as double-entry bookkeeping; he was specific even about the number of practice balls he needed.

Ramsey's silences could be more eloquent than his words, but he was unexpectedly forthright about how he thought England were perceived at home and abroad. 'Some people say our players don't care about playing for England, that our crowds don't give backing to the international team. As an international player, I was never aware of that . . . but if that feeling of pride in playing for England is not there, we shall have to put it there.' He also spoke about the 'average fan', the fervent club supporter who, he said, tended to regard international matches as 'exhibition stuff'. With the World Cup looming, Ramsey explained he could sense a shift of opinion: 'Only now is it beginning to dawn on [our fans] that [the finals] carry a considerable amount of national prestige and are the yardstick by which the rest of the world judges us as a power.'

While Ramsey didn't declare Walter Winterbottom guilty, or the FA as complicit in that guilt, he pointed a crooked index finger at both of them for being unaware of something that was strikingly obvious to him: 'Football is now a world game. No longer can any country . . . rest on past successes.'

He looked back analytically at England's post-war performances. The wins and the mountainous pile of goals racked up against moderate opposition. The stumbling performances during each World Cup. With one damning sentence, he summed up the discrepancy between England's success in friendlies and their failures in competition: 'No team can improve by gaining easy victories over poor sides.' Ramsey gave Winterbottom another dig in the ribs. He referred to 'bad results' and 'low morale' and the loss of 'prestige' in the 1950s. He couldn't 'develop overnight' the 'type of side' he was certain could become 'the best', because what had gone before had been inferior. 'I believe it will take me up to three years to mould the England team,' he said. He then promised: 'It can be done and it will be done.'

Ramsey announced that 'priority number one' was to foster 'a club spirit', so the players would 'know one another not only as footballers but also as men'. He believed what had worked so spectacularly for him at Ipswich would also work with England. He had always treated his players as individuals, as prone to black moods and bad days as anyone who worked in a factory, shop or office. He had made the same case during his playing days at Tottenham. 'One of the drawbacks in making your mark in football is that too many people seem to forget that you're only human,' he'd said. 'You are just like the fellow who lives next door or maybe catches the same bus as you in the morning.'

No England player had to hop on to a bus any longer, but the kernel of Ramsey's argument influenced his approach. He constantly talked about finding 'the right blend'. He wasn't referring only to the team on the pitch. Ramsey reiterated his suspicion of 'egotists', the overly 'flashy' and those who were 'cynical'. Anyone who fell into one of those categories never survived long in his squads.

Bobby Moore believed there was a message 'sewn in invisible stitching' into every England cap Ramsey awarded. That message was: 'Just remember you are here to play for me . . . and to do what I say.' There was certainly no easy intimacy between Ramsey and his players because he disliked what he described as 'excessive familiarity'. One meeting was sufficient for the squad to suss out the basic differences between Ramsey and Winterbottom. There was a touch of ferocity about Ramsey, who was always explicitly insistent about what he wanted. He was prepared to coax but seldom flattered. His view of players, which sounds a little sinister, was: 'They all need help. They all need encouragement. They all need to be punished by the tongue sometimes.' Whoever played for Ramsey understood that all the things he said about himself were true:

I am a good winner and a bloody bad loser.
I am not a light-hearted man. I take things seriously.
The game is what matters to me.

In the 1960s, the public tended not to be embarrassed by patriotism. Before an international, Ramsey would occasionally resort to near jingoism – especially against Scotland or West Germany – by telling his team: 'This lot don't like the English, you know. So let's go out and show them what real football is about.'

Sometimes striving to be gently avuncular, Ramsey always told newcomers five things. The first four were: 'You're here because you are a good player . . . The fact you have been selected is proof of that . . . You don't have to prove anything . . . Don't worry if you struggle at first because I won't forget you.' The fifth was: 'Play the way you do for your club.'

Four conversations – with Jack and Bobby Charlton, Ray Wilson and Geoff Hurst – highlight the contradictions in Ramsey and also his zealous need for control. Jack Charlton admitted that he found him to be 'a strange bloke . . . I'm never really comfortable chatting to him.' When he rashly questioned Ramsey's methods, he found himself in a brief and brutally uncompromising exchange:

Ramsey: Do it my way or else.
Charlton: What does that mean?
Ramsey: Or you're out.

On another occasion, he blurted out on the training pitch: 'Alf, you're talking shit.' Ramsey folded his arms and cast him the kind of look that James Bond villains cultivate. 'That's as it may be, Jack, but of course you will do as I ask.'

Ramsey was known to be a manager who would always give a player a straight answer – even if that answer was usually no. Charlton said that 'No, Jack' became Ramsey's favourite words. No to letting him go for a walk or buy a pint. No to changing the time of, or venue for, training. No to giving him an extra half-hour to play cards before the lights were turned out. Ramsey did compliment him on his astute defending. Whenever Moore went forward, he automatically occupied the space behind him. 'I like the way you don't trust him,' said Ramsey.

Wilson's first meeting with Ramsey was as inauspiciously awkward as everyone else's. After a few pleasantries, each man calling the other 'Mr', Ramsey asked: 'How do you like to play?' When Wilson gave an unexpected answer, Ramsey's response was the less than friendly 'You will play the way I want you to play.' As Wilson reflected: 'He never let you forget who was in charge.'

Hurst originally thought of Ramsey as 'remote . . . something of a mystery man' and also 'a cold fish'. Stuck in a railway carriage with him, Hurst found himself under interrogation. He remembered it as a 'quiet probing', which was 'quite frightening' and 'hard on the nerves'. The train hadn't pulled out of the station before Ramsey began flinging questions at Hurst. 'What did you think of so-and-so . . . How did they use this player or that . . . How did you manage to stop them?' Hurst called it a 'two-hour quiz'. If he gave an opinion, Ramsey countered it combatively. Hurst was midway through giving his opinion of a player when Ramsey interrupted him. 'That man's a bloody coward,' he said. Hurst saw all this as an extreme form of catechism. In getting him to reveal insights about another professional's abilities, Ramsey discovered whether or not he possessed a serviceable knowledge of the game. 'I was damn glad when the journey ended,' said Hurst. He radically revised his view of Ramsey only after getting to know him. His lack of 'warmth' came from his surfeit of 'resolution', he said. Ramsey believed 'in what he was doing more than any man I have ever met'.

Bobby Charlton's experience was similar to Hurst's. He never forgot his introduction to Ramsey because he was as relieved as Hurst to escape from him. Ramsey encouraged his senior pros to tell him about anything – 'however small' – that might improve England's preparation for 1966. When no one spoke, Charlton did so only because he didn't want Ramsey to think he was 'an idiot without opinions'. The squad always stayed at Hendon Hall, an imposing Georgian-style hotel with a signature pediment and four huge red-brick Corinthian columns. The hall was only five miles from Wembley, but more than

13 separated it from Roehampton, where England trained on the Bank of England's pitches. In heavy traffic, it took an hour to drive there and at least another hour to drive back. Charlton suggested to Ramsey that it might be useful to find either a hotel closer to Roehampton or another training ground closer to the hall. Ramsey could make it seem as though he was carefully considering a matter about which his mind was already made up. He did that now. The pause was 'terrible', said Charlton. Finally, Ramsey said, very slowly and with the slap of condescension: 'Bobby, I've most certainly listened to what you've had to say, but I think we will leave it as it is.' In that moment Charlton knew the type of character he was butting up against. 'When all was said and done and argued, it was he who would always make the decisions,' he said.

Charlton didn't learn from the bite Ramsey gave him. Preparing for a summer tour of Europe, the FA had provided the players with lustrous worsted suits, as heavy as chain mail and unsuitable for temperatures in the mid-30s. Charlton was reluctantly pressed by the team into making an appeal to Ramsey. Could the squad dress 'casually' while travelling, wearing the suits only during official functions? 'I'll think about it,' said Ramsey, who calculatingly waited five seconds as Charlton turned and walked a pace or two away from him. 'I've thought about it,' he said, forcing Charlton to stop and face him again. 'I've decided we'll wear the suits.'

When the tour began, Ramsey startled Charlton again, casting himself in a wholly different and much softer light. In Bratislava, about to play Czechoslovakia, he used the training pitch like a chessboard. He began by telling the players he had picked: 'Go to the positions you would naturally take up once the match starts.'

They did so, a little bemused.

Aware of how long he needed to maintain the suspense to achieve maximum impact, Ramsey walked along the halfway line and let his eye wander from one player to the next, assessing the shape of the team. A full minute ticked by before he said in a flat tone: 'Now I'll tell you where you should be – and what I want you to do when you get there.' It was said that Ramsey had a 'quasi-religious dedication to the game – which, for him, was hardly a game at all'. Charlton had just witnessed it. He called the session 'brilliant' in its 'simplicity', because 'position by position, he explained, very briskly, what he expected from each player'. Charlton added that what Ramsey offered England that day was 'the distillation of all his years in the game' and also an 'attention to detail' that was plainly 'quite fanatical'.

He began to believe England just might win the World Cup.

* * *

Every generation is conceited enough to see itself as unequivocally superior to the previous one. The 1960s made the 1940s and '50s look so anachronistic that both seemed to belong to another century. Now, as the sugar-coated gleam of the decade dims, the '60s themselves appear substantially less glamorous to those who didn't live through them and wonder what the fuss was all about.

The energy of the '60s certainly did not crackle everywhere. The singer Tom Jones said the pubs were awful places where 'men could fart and be vulgar together'. Often sawdust was sprinkled on the floor, and the spittoon in the corner wasn't there for ornamental purposes. 'Ladies' were discouraged from drinking except on designated evenings. A pianist, usually no Chopin, would bash out singalong classics, long before anyone had heard of karaoke. And the pubs were closed for more than half of each day because the licensing laws hadn't changed since 1914.

So much of the country either smelt of smoke and smuts or else a whiff of dampness clung to it. Haute cuisine was a prawn cocktail starter and chicken in a basket. The popular wines were Mateus Rosé and Blue Nun. Hardly any shops, other than the newsagent's, opened on a Sunday. When the '60s began, there were only two TV channels, and the BBC had no reservations about broadcasting *The Black and*

White Minstrel Show, watched by 20 million viewers, or Miss World from the Lyceum Ballroom. On the radio, you tuned in to the Light Programme or the Home Service. And Dr Beeching, the destroyer of railways, was about to make nearly 5,000 miles of track redundant and close more than 2,300 stations – even though a family car counted as an unimaginable luxury for the working class.

When Piri Halasz landed in London to file her breathless report for *Time*, she assumed the rest of the country must look like Soho and Piccadilly Circus. She didn't travel much further north than Hampstead or much further west than Hammersmith Bridge. If Halasz had trekked into the provinces, she'd have discovered towns and cities that were still living in the 1930s. The north, the north-west and the Black Country were so industrialised that you felt you had to wipe your feet before leaving them for London. There was still shipbuilding in Newcastle and Liverpool . . . still silver and silver plate being made in Sheffield . . . still clacking looms producing wool and textiles in Bradford . . . still cars being wheeled out of Coventry . . . and still pitheads and coal-stacks everywhere, guaranteeing that no competent chimney sweep was ever unemployed.

Huge pockets of slum housing – properties that ought to have been condemned and cleared away at least ten years before – were shamefully still standing, further proof of how thinly the sparkle of the '60s had spread. Michael Caine, filming *Get Carter* in and around Newcastle, had an epiphany among the conspicuous poverty he found there. 'I've always gone on about the working-class image I've got,' he said. 'Now I've been to Newcastle, I realise I'm middle class.'

But there is *something* that draws you to the football of the '60s. The game doesn't need romanticising, and you don't have to be lachrymosely sentimental to be attracted to it. For despite the awful pitches, the savagery of the tackle from behind and some of the rickety stands that were no more than sheds, the game back then retains an allure. While it was slower than today's Premier League – how could it not be? – everything was simpler and less wrapped up in the kind of anal micro-tactics that today fill hours upon hours of pre- and post-match TV analysis.

Language can pin down a period, the vocabulary as reliable as carbon dating. There were wing halves and inside forwards, descriptions now as fuddy-duddy as describing something as either 'fab' or 'groovy'. There were two points for a league win. Some teams packed in five forwards. Others, copying Brazil, experimented with 4–2–4. The consistently quotable Bill Shankly liked to repeat that a player shouldn't be on the field if he wasn't 'interfering with the play'. Offside reflected that belief; the flag would go up, punishing those who hadn't touched the ball or were nowhere near it.

At the beginning of each season, you could never be sure who would emerge with a trophy at the end of it. In the '60s, there were eight different winners of both the championship and the FA Cup. Each year the silversmith engraved a new name on the plinth of the three-handled League Cup – including that pair of Third Division giant-killers, Queen's Park Rangers and Swindon, who each scalped First Division clubs at Wembley.

The game was avowedly 'English' – no one bought players from Italy or Spain, France or Germany – but Ramsey's team would have looked so different as to be unrecognisable if some of the players he favoured hadn't been born across the Irish Sea, north of Hadrian's Wall or west of Offa's Dyke.

There were five players that Ramsey regretted had been born in the 'wrong' country.

The quixotic Derek Dougan, from Belfast, would have been his centre forward. Dougan, who was 6ft 3in, had played – and lost – in an FA Cup final with Blackburn, moved to Aston Villa and, for a while, shaved his head bullet-smooth to look more intimidating. When Ipswich faced Villa in the last match of their championship-winning season, Ramsey fixated on stopping him. He liked Dougan's strength, his work rate, his willingness to be bravely fearless. Dougan chose to drop from the First Division into the Third, signing for Peterborough, a switch he regretted and which seems inexplicable until you know that his character could be as combustible as a box of fireworks. He kept falling out with people – especially managers. Leicester City soon took Dougan back to the First Division.

Billy Bremner and Johnny Giles, who gave Leeds their momentum, would have been the axis around which Ramsey's midfield turned. Ramsey told Bremner: 'You're a dirty player.' Bremner, a Scot, bristled aggressively, about to spit back words of four letters, before Ramsey turned the insult into a compliment. 'But you play so very well,' he said. Bremner was the muscle. Giles, of the Republic of Ireland, was the brain. Matt Busby had unaccountably allowed him to drift across the Pennines, swapping the red rose for the white and one United for another. Busby called it the greatest mistake of his managerial career. Ramsey's lament was more straightforward. Of Giles, he said wistfully – and more than once – 'I wish he was English.'

Mike England would have partnered Bobby Moore. England was born in North Wales, captained his country at only 22 years of age and would eventually cost Tottenham £95,000 – then a record fee for a defender – when they signed him from Blackburn. (Bill Nicholson later made an unsuccessful attempt to buy Moore too.)

And then there was George Best . . .

The '60s were the optimum time to be young. Best, contemptuous about 'the good old days of yesteryear', burnt every candle he could find at both ends and made a lovely light. A modern combination of the hedonistic Lord Byron and the dandy Beau Brummell, Best didn't look like any other footballer; he looked like a pop singer or a model, made for fame and so photogenic that the camera swooned over him. Women did so too – in their tens of thousands. A teammate made the mistake of parking his car alongside Best's, returning to find it scratched and dented after Best's female fan club sat on or leant against it while waiting for their heart-throb to appear. Best could have worn a hessian sack and still looked more regal than any man standing next to him in a freshly pressed suit. Like every aspect of his life, football was about pure sensation for Best. Ramsey once went to Old Trafford to watch one player, but his eyes followed Best around the pitch – even when he didn't have the ball. Asked what he thought of him, Ramsey replied in a single word: 'Wonderful.' When questioned how, as a former full back, he might have stopped him, Ramsey candidly confessed: 'I would not . . . I would have hoped someone else had taken the ball off him before he reached me.'

If Best had been born in Birmingham, rather than Belfast, the debate about whether Ramsey liked or loathed wingers would have been nailed in an instant.

Ramsey had quickly tried four of them, searching for what was eluding England: Peter Thompson of Liverpool; Blackburn's Bryan Douglas, a veteran of two World Cups under Walter Winterbottom; Southampton's Terry Paine, once thought to be the heir apparent to both Stanley Matthews and Tom Finney; and also John Connelly. But Ramsey still complained – though often only in private – that England 'don't have anyone who can go past a full back and cross the ball'.

In striving to find his elusive 'blend', Ramsey was like a poet struggling for a rhyme. 'Sometimes,' he said, 'a team comes quickly, sometimes it takes days.'

In his first 14 matches, Ramsey picked 28 different players. He was accused of throwing England caps into the air like 'sweets'. Some of those who caught them included names seldom remembered now. The Liverpool pair of right half Gordon Milne and inside left Jimmy Melia, whose hairline had receded so high up his forehead that he looked to be wearing a clown's skull cap and wig. Bobby Tambling, who assumed the goal-scoring responsibilities at Chelsea after Jimmy Greaves left the club for Italy. Tambling's teammate, the full back Ken Shellito, who was once so dazed after Best led him on a non-stop jig across Stamford Bridge that he left the muddy pitch 'with twisted blood' and his eyes rolling like the symbols of a seaside fruit machine. Another full back, Bobby Thomson of Wolves, who was only a little better than his muck-and-brass contemporaries. The Blackpool goalkeeper Tony Waiters. The Everton forward Fred Pickering, known as 'Boomer', a flattering reflection on the supposedly 'sonic-like' speed of his shots. There was also the tragically stupid left half, Tony Kay, briefly the country's most expensive player – Everton paid Sheffield Wednesday £60,000 for him – before becoming one of the most notorious too. He spent ten weeks in prison, his career over, for his part in the infamous betting scandal that was broken by the *Sunday People* 16 months after the fact. Given favourable odds of 2–1, Kay placed a £50 wager on Wednesday losing at Ramsey's Ipswich, who were then second from bottom of the table. In December 1962, Wednesday were beaten 2–0. The *People* reporter at Portman Road ironically made Kay his team's man of the match.

Ramsey said his strategy was to 'try' every player he thought might be 'worthy of a place' during his first two and a half years in charge. 'I will not worry about results until the World Cup starts.'

But what Ramsey saw as the sensible, orderly creation of a squad – every match an experiment of sorts – got interpreted as the shilly-shallying of a manager lost in a maze of his own making.

8

THIS PRECIOUS JEWEL

Alf Ramsey continued to regard journalists in the same way as a dog regards its fleas: a bloody nuisance, but unavoidable.

Ramsey referred to reporters collectively as 'you people', as if they belonged to another species, almost definitely strange and certainly inferior. Nor did he discriminate between someone with a notebook and pen and someone holding a microphone; he was equally contemptuous of both. He came into press conferences, a job he considered to be a bit grubby, looking as though shooting someone might be on his mind – usually the first man (there were rarely any women) to ask something he considered intrusive or ill-informed. He would tilt his head towards the questioner and squeeze his eyes into slits.

Matt Busby advised would-be managers to treat the press 'just the way you would treat a policeman', which meant being polite and truthful. Bill Nicholson, beneath the bluster, subscribed to the same view, aware that compromise was necessary. 'Even when you don't want to say anything you still have an obligation to say something,' he said. Bill Shankly sought to disarm with his repartee of one-liners. Don Revie wanted newspapermen inside his tent, pissing out; he flattered them, anxious to make everyone part of Elland Road's extended family.

With fans, Ramsey was capable of kindnesses. He would reply to every letter he received, sometimes by hand and even to those who wrote offensively, addressing him as 'Dear Big Head' or 'Dear Stupid'. He took care over trivial matters, such as answering enquiries about tickets or factual information concerning his own career. One correspondent, searching for a decade-old Tottenham match programme, couldn't believe Ramsey went to the bother of tracking it down for him. He was conscientious about giving his autograph too, taking deliberate care to do so legibly rather than dashing off his signature in a scrawl of ink. As he walked into or away from a match, Ramsey said fans tended to talk loudly so he could clearly hear them. 'I knew what people thought of me,' he said. 'They made it so obvious.' Occasionally, believing a shouted point had been well made, he would talk to them, shaking their hand before and afterwards.

With writers, he could be outwardly courteous without disguising his inner contempt. 'If pressed too hard, he becomes rude, frequently profane,' said one reporter.*

Newspapers mattered then – and not only because you could still wrap fish and chips in them, the vinegar soaking ink into your haddock. The press, not TV, was responsible for shaping public opinion. When Ramsey became England boss, there were 17 national titles. From Monday to Saturday, they sold more than 21 million copies per day (the *Daily Mirror* and the *Daily Express* were responsible for nearly 10 million sales between them). On Sunday, the figure was even higher – nearly 25 million. The *News of the World*, infamous for chronicling the misbehaviour of seedy Boy Scout leaders and randy vicars under titillating headlines, shifted almost 6.5 million copies on its own. Journalists, especially the columnists, had the kind of extravagant expense accounts that could effectively double their salary without interference from the Inland Revenue. In football, the friendly, come-and-have-a-pint-on-me relationship between journalists and players changed only when even an average player, who'd previously struggled to stand his own round, got rich enough to buy the pub.

---

* Ramsey usually referred to Hugh McIlvanney as 'the Scotsman'. I once asked Hugh about this. He said it was 'polite' of me to have omitted the expletive that separated those two words.

Ramsey kept journalists at a furlong's distance for a reason. They were 'just too nosy', always 'asking for something' from him, he explained. 'There is nothing I ever want from them.'

Preparing for his marital tellings-off from Queen Victoria, Prince Albert would steel himself for the confrontation, saying over and again: 'Look upon this with patience, as a test which has to be undergone.' Ramsey saw interviews that way too. He was so easy to rile or rub up the wrong way that asking the first question almost got you the George Medal. He wasn't afraid to guillotine a discussion with a scornful 'You've asked too many stupid questions'. Even the most benign of them could produce an acidly sarcastic reply:

Reporter: Everyone fit and well?
Ramsey: If everyone was not fit and well, I wouldn't be doing my job, would I? Are you telling me I'm not doing my job?

When unable to stonewall or sidestep an awkward question, Ramsey would give his inquisitor the kind of look that threatened to melt his bones and then ask: 'How many caps have you won?'

'He stabs you with his eyes,' said one correspondent. Another, who announced he would like Ramsey to 'bare his soul', was rebuked with a question: 'Do you think I am insane? I will not speak to you about my personal life or my beliefs.' He also had a tactic that journalists knew well but were unable to navigate. Ramsey would deliberately leave it as late as possible to emerge from England's dressing room at Wembley, appearing only when the team coach was already parked outside the door with its engine revving. He would toss out a few 'remarks', knowing everyone would soon be coughing up exhaust fumes.

When one of the game's foreign correspondents wanted to know whether Ramsey remembered him, he was sent packing in two short sentences: 'Yes, I do. You're a fucking pest.' At an airport, a journalist asked whether he could have 'a word' with him. Ramsey, hurrying past him, merely replied: 'Goodbye – but I suppose that is not the word you were hoping for.' It wasn't as though journalists demanded grandiloquent speeches from him; the odd quote to furnish a story would have been enough.

Few had Ramsey's home telephone number: Ipswich 52054. Even those who did used it sparingly. In reply to one caller, who rang him on a Sunday morning, Ramsey remained silent for a short while, as though the line had been cut, before telling him: 'I am now going to put down the phone *very* slowly.'

On occasions when he agreed to be profiled at length, Ramsey seldom let the interviewer into his office at the Football Association. He preferred to meet them in either the foyer of Lancaster Gate or in the committee room. Those who got into his office usually remarked on the lack of paperwork on his desk, unaware that Ramsey had hidden every scrap of it in a drawer in case the reporter could read upside down.

To meet Ramsey solo could be daunting. One journalist insisted that his 'shadow hung over every young football reporter's life like some dark angel of Nemesis'. The same journalist had been told by Eddie Baily that, in 1951, Ramsey had been found sitting on the toilet after Tottenham's championship win. He was eating a sausage roll. When faced with Ramsey, especially in one of his most obstinate moods, the journalist tried to imagine the undignified scene to make him a less intimidating figure. It didn't always work. After receiving one 'bollocking' from Ramsey, he tried to mollify him with some easy-going conversation, and promptly got another. 'You'll never get round me, not in a month of fucking Sundays.'

The one-to-one interviews he did were almost always narrow in scope. Ramsey refused to discuss anything except football. 'My life is football,' he'd say. 'It occupies 24 hours a day.'

He claimed to read the *Daily Mail* only because of the *Fred Basset* cartoon strip. He also insisted he seldom picked up any other newspaper or magazine, but always knew what was in them. His near-perfect memory meant Ramsey could quote verbatim someone's opinions and criticisms of both himself and his team – even if the piece had been published years before. A journalist, attempting to flatter him for his selection of a particular player, was embarrassed when Ramsey stopped him: 'But in March 1963, you said he was not of international class because . . .'

He disliked articles in which the writer had interviewed other players and managers. 'If I had my own way, you wouldn't be able to speak to anyone about me,' he said.

Ramsey thought only someone who had played football at a decent level could comment on it expertly. He pointed to the gulf, which he considered unbridgeable, between how an 'amateur' observer judged a game and the way a current or ex-professional perceived it. A journalist, sharing a train carriage with Ramsey, told him how much he'd 'enjoyed' that afternoon's match. Ramsey was incredulous: 'You cannot have enjoyed it. There were so many mistakes, so much unprofessional play.'

Ramsey explained his lack of co-operation like this: 'I appreciate that everyone feels he is a football expert and that everyone feels he has a right to make known his own conclusions. I have the right to keep my own opinions to myself.'

There were journalists whom he did respect. Among them were the *Daily Mail*'s Brian James, Ken Jones of the *Sunday Mirror*, Reg Drury of the *Sunday Citizen* and then the *News of the World*, Peter Lorenzo of the *Daily Herald* and Geoffrey Green of *The Times*.

James, who later wrote one of football's true classic books, *Journey to Wembley*, conducted the interview in which Ramsey had staked his claim to become England boss in 1962. For a while James switched to news reporting because the Aberfan disaster – which killed 116 children and 28 adults – persuaded him that 'Sport was no job for a grown man.'

Jones belonged to a footballing dynasty forged in Wales. His father had played for Everton; his uncle had played for both Wolves and Arsenal; his cousin, Cliff, was a double-winner with Tottenham. Jones had made appearances for Southend and Gravesend, turning to journalism only after snapping his Achilles tendon.

Drury got to know Ramsey as a player, covering Tottenham for the *Enfield Gazette*. A master of gleaning exclusives, he possessed the most enviable contacts book in Fleet Street. His loyalty towards his sources was reciprocated, every friendship kept in constant repair. As well as their past history, Drury had something else in common with Ramsey: his mind was encyclopaedic. He was able to store and pull out facts and figures about even little-known lower-division players.

Ramsey had handed Lorenzo, who later became an accomplished BBC broadcaster, the scoop about his decision to become Ipswich's manager and those quotes about his disenchantment at Tottenham.

Green came from the same mould as John Cobbold. He could also match Cobbold drink for drink, bottle for bottle. Green had originally taught divinity at a prep school, generously giving his pupils the exam questions in advance. He had a bony frame, a ravaged face, a melliflu-ous toff's voice. He dressed shambolically in jumpers and cardigans that moths had feasted upon, shirts that had never come close to an iron and unpressed trousers. He wore an oversized coat that swamped his body, its colour described as 'duck shit' green. Hobbling into a press room with a walking stick – following a hip replacement – Green was told he looked like Long John Silver. He immediately pulled a stuffed parrot out of his pocket and stuck it on his shoulder. He christened his daughter Ti, which is 'It' spelt backwards.

Until 1966, *The Times* printed advertising rather than news on its front page. It eschewed reporters' bylines until 1967. Green was known only as 'Our Association Football Correspondent'. He established himself, nonetheless, as one of the game's greatest poets. 'In football, I see ballet and dancing,' he said. 'In the crowd I hear a symphony of music.' What the reader got from Green was filigree phrase-making. Billy Wright's tearing lunge at Ferenc Puskás at Wembley in 1953 was like watching 'a fire engine going to the wrong fire'. A match report from a stodgy, goalless international evoked Shakespeare: 'If a rose is a rose is a rose, then a goal is a goal is a goal. How much we needed one to enrich Wembley last night.' The effort of shackling Stanley

Matthews, jinking along the touchline, was compared to 'trying to catch a sunbeam in a matchbox'.

Those writers, representing each stratum of the country's newspaper readership, generally saw England's results not in terms of triumph or disaster, but in the sympathetic context of what Ramsey was striving towards. But since Ramsey couldn't work out *why* other newspapers couldn't be patient with him, he was unnecessarily petty towards them. In turn, the newspapers were often too gleefully keen to magnify his follies, his failures and especially his foibles. Ramsey gave up on some journalists. It was 'impossible to please those people who do not wish to be pleased', he said. He also claimed to have developed 'three skins' to cope with the beatings he took from them.

He was about to need a fourth.

* * *

It was one of those insanely congested end-of-season tours for England: seven matches in five different countries, spanning 32 days, totalling 18,500 air miles and ending in Rio and São Paulo, where Brazil and Pelé awaited them. In 1964, the Brazilians organised a four-team tournament – dubbed 'The Little World Cup' – to mark the halfway point between the last competition and the next. As well as the hosts, England faced Argentina – led by Antonio Rattín – and Eusébio's Portugal. Ramsey saw each game as a continuation of a greater work still in progress. Everyone else saw it as a formal laboratory test of his mettle. When it was over, you'd have thought only a lunatic would still be backing England to win in 1966.

England took a squad of only 19 players – Ramsey wanted no one travelling just to carry the bags and send a postcard home – but among them were two players he'd already marked down as 'probables' for the World Cup.

No one was better qualified to know a right back when he saw one. George Cohen was whip-smart positionally and whip-fast out of the blocks. In a sprint he often went into a crouch, like a man who had fastened his braces to a button on his fly. You could have trained him to win the Greyhound Derby. Ramsey admitted wryly: 'I could never have hoped to out-run him in a foot race ... unless he gave me a considerable head start. Perhaps 50 yards ...' Cohen's chance came after Jimmy Armfield wrenched his groin so badly that doctors advised him that his career could be over. The doctors were wrong – Armfield attributed his recovery in part to daily bathes in the sea – but Cohen was four years younger, and his pace gave Ramsey the option of not picking a right winger. George Best considered Cohen, able to attack as well as defend, as the most formidable full back he'd faced in the First Division.

If Ramsey – minus the speed – recognised a little flicker of himself in Cohen, he saw even more of it in Roger Hunt. There's a story – a folklore tale, perhaps – about a church near Anfield that pasted up a poster asking: 'What Would You Do If Jesus Came?' A Merseyside wit scrawled his answer underneath it: 'Play Him alongside Hunt'.*

Just as Ramsey had done during his own career, Hunt prospered through total commitment. He was the archetypical pro's pro. In every game Hunt uncomplainingly completed a marathon in hard-yards sprints for Liverpool. He was a prolific scorer, but never a glamourous one because he gave so much of himself to the team. Had Hunt been more selfish, more self-possessed, his goals would have needed to be weighed, not counted. He didn't move ethereally, like Jimmy Greaves, or score from vast distances, like Bobby Charlton. He ran and chased and covered, a slave in training inside what Liverpool called The Sweat Box – four large sections of board arranged in a square. You had to bang the ball against one of the walls and belt the rebound back first time, usually in sessions lasting a minute and a half. His stamina came from that exercise.

Hunt would pounce in the six-yard box or near the penalty spot. For whole segments of a game, you sometimes thought of him as

---

* The same thing has been said about both Ian St John and Kenny Dalglish.

The poacher's instinct for a goal: Roger Hunt making the six-yard box his own

an unassuming presence, never rapaciously hogging the ball. Out of nothing, or next to nothing, he would claim goals by uncannily knowing where he ought to be. Hunt didn't get enough credit and often received too much criticism. As Bill Shankly sagely said of him: 'Yes, Roger Hunt misses a few, but he gets into the right place to miss them.' Hunt could suddenly transform a game the way the piccolo trumpet solo transforms the Beatles' 'Penny Lane'. As a Second Division player, he had been given his first cap by Walter Winterbottom in 1962. When, two years later, Ramsey took Hunt to Brazil, he had scored 101 goals in his previous three seasons, and Liverpool were League Champions.

* * *

Three and a half weeks before going to the Maracanã, Alf Ramsey watched Brazil, playing 4–2–4, beat West Germany 2–1 in Hamburg. After controlling a short pass and turning sinuously, Pelé had smashed a shot into the top corner. He did it so gracefully that Degas ought to have been alive to paint it. 'I have never seen another player like Pelé,' said Ramsey.

While admiring the World Champions, Ramsey maintained England could beat them. He was almost alone in his belief that Brazil were on the wane and could not win a third successive World Cup. While Pelé would be 25 in 1966, still awaiting his peak, the Brazilians who had retained the trophy in Chile – such as Didi and Zagallo – were spent forces. Zito would also be 33 by then; Santos would be 37; the goalkeeper, Gilmar, would be 35; Garrincha would be 32.

England had already faced Uruguay at Wembley, Portugal in Lisbon, the Republic of Ireland in Dublin and the United States in New York. They were dog-tired and drained before even reaching Rio. The build-up was chaotic, the gamesmanship from Brazil crudely blatant and impolite. A game which ought to have kicked off at 8pm didn't begin until nearly 9pm, leaving England in their kit and shut inside their dressing room for nearly two hours. The Brazilians claimed their team bus, caught up in crowds, had been delayed. Ramsey knew that excuse was feeble, fatuous and false.

It was a cool, wet, starless evening. The pitch, greasy after rain, was as soft as Wembley in winter. The Brazilian fans blew bugles and brandished rolled-up newspapers, setting them alight like flaming torches.

Watching film of the game is like trying to look through a window that you've misted up with your own breath.

England had nine shots. One of them was hacked off the line. Brazil, 1–0 ahead at half-time, got pegged back so quickly after the restart that many in the crowd missed it. Pelé then took control, ripping into England with a fury. Brazil scored four rat-a-tat goals in the last half-hour. Pelé claimed one of them, and was integral in creating three others. Brazil won 5–1. It was England's heaviest defeat for seven years. Bobby Moore described the impossibility of stopping Pelé that night: 'You go into a tackle. You make contact. You think you've got him or the ball. Then you find out you don't have either.'

* * *

At the beginning of September 1965, the *Soccer Review*, the official publication of the Football League, took the unprecedented step of publishing a short front-page *cri de coeur*. It was a 140-word defence of a misunderstood man who, for the last 12 months, had been attacked in print almost ceaselessly. Though he never rose to them, these attacks had punched holes clean through him. The League's unsigned editorial thundered out: 'We have a request to make. Will the critics stop trying to ride on the back of Alf Ramsey.'

There was no question mark at the end of the sentence, but what followed highlighted the personal abuse poured on and over Ramsey since England had come back from South America 14 months before. 'For months now we have been listening to the sneers that England have no chance in the World Cup . . . that the manager must have been mad to say, as he did . . . that we could win the Jules Rimet Trophy. They say the man is looking at our footballers through rose coloured glasses,' said *Soccer Review*.

The League was being rather polite. The *Daily Mirror*, a little over-dramatically perhaps, had decided that England were 'no nearer being a World Cup force than they were 10 years ago' and that Ramsey would need to hire 'an assassin' to take out Pelé before the prospect of beating Brazil could even be dimly contemplated. After losing in Rio, Ramsey had lost again there to Argentina (1–0) and also been held 1–1 by Portugal in São Paulo. Were England 'a match' for the Brazilians, the Argentinians or Europe's best? asked the *Mirror*. 'Forget it,' was the newspaper's view.

The consensus was that Ramsey picked weeds, not flowers. He was urged to choose a team and glue himself to it, but everyone had a different idea about its composition. Some wanted Springett instead of Banks or Armfield instead of Cohen, and they considered Greaves to be 'a luxury', imploring Ramsey to look at Mick Jones at Sheffield United or Arsenal's Joe Baker. Others called for the recall of Johnny Haynes.

Jack Charlton, just a month adrift of his 30th birthday, had made his debut only the previous April against Scotland. He learnt of his call-up on the night Leeds beat Manchester United in an FA Cup semi-final replay. Jack barged maladroitly into the opposition dressing room to tell the news to 'our kid', Bobby. It was like taking party balloons into a mortuary. 'That's very nice for you, Jack – but fuck off,' said more than one defeated United player.* Charlton was performing so well for England that there were suggestions Bobby Moore should be dropped in favour of Norman Hunter, thus bringing together Leeds's central defensive partnership. 'A lot of the press were saying I wasn't good enough,' said Moore.

A familiar critic thought no one was good enough. In the *Sunday Express*, Danny Blanchflower had argued that Ramsey had taken a 'considerable risk' by accepting the Football Association's shilling in the first place. As though deliberately wanting to needle Ramsey, his old adversary, he tipped Scotland to win the World Cup. 'I wonder if England have the resources to win . . . I doubt they will have the spirit,' wrote Blanchflower. From the start, he thought England 'fooled around' too much with selection, playing a kind of 'Ramsey Roulette'.

Between October 1964 and May 1965, England played nine more matches, winning four and drawing five, and Ramsey handed out 10 more new caps. The high tide of the international season was a 1–0 win over West Germany in Nuremberg. Low tides came with each disjointed performance. Seven of England's fixtures pitted them against opposition that would only watch the World Cup unfold on TV. *Soccer Review* questioned whether Ramsey was 'champ or chump?', purely so it could proclaim him 'a champ', an opinion that got belly-laughs for its optimism and presumption.

October was the blackest of months for Ramsey.

---

* The Charltons were the first brothers to play for England since Frank and Fred Forman of Nottingham Forest in 1899.

Against Wales, in a grim, goalless game at Cardiff, England were incoherent. Against Austria came only the third defeat inflicted on them at Wembley, the 3–2 result preposterously bonkers. Austria had finished bottom of their World Cup qualifying group, earning just a point. Only a week and a half before, West Germany had devoured their patched-up team 4–1. Some of the Austrians were barely of Second Division standard. In the closing minutes, England were booed, whistled and slow-handclapped.

Even before England lost to Austria, Brian Glanville had argued in the *Sunday Times* that Ramsey 'remains an enigma, perhaps even to his players'. *World Sports* claimed Ramsey 'still baffled those who dealt with him'. In the *Observer*, Hugh McIlvanney, alluding to Ramsey's prediction about '66, compared him to a racing trainer who, after betting a colossal sum on a horse, was now so nervous about the wager that he could only watch it race 'from a lavatory window'. He added that England were 'saddled with a comparatively modest crop of footballers' and lacked 'the core of class needed to win' the World Cup. McIlvanney didn't expect Ramsey to 'work miracles'. He did want him to stop 'practising a form of positive thinking that may be tarnished with self-delusion'. The feeling that Ramsey was fooling himself in the name of hope was shared elsewhere.

The *Daily Mail* declared that he was 'facing failure' because there was now 'too much' for him to do and 'too little time to do it'. The *Guardian* claimed that on the basis of such an awful defeat against Austria, England would never have qualified for the World Cup without the privilege of staging it. It lamented the 'lack of spirit' in them. The *Daily Telegraph* shook its head sorrowfully at a side that had 'lost its way'. The *Daily Sketch* proclaimed England were 'flat, warm, tasteless beer'. Even Pathé News put the boot in: 'Ramsey, What Now?' was the title it gave to the highlights of the Austria game.

Beneath the bleak headline 'Why the World Cup Will Elude Hosts', the magazine *World Soccer* had concluded two months before: 'While ours is now a precise, professional and honest national approach, we cannot expect to win our way to success with . . . sweat and courage.' It forecast the 'greater panache and fantastic ability of the South Americans' would 'ensure that Saturday, July 30 will *not* be the greatest day in English soccer history'. And, when the French newspaper *L'Équipe* ranked the world's top teams, England came 10th – behind even Scotland, who didn't qualify for the finals.

Here was proof that no one is an expert on the future.

Unbeknown to everyone, Ramsey had a plan, already thought out and practised behind closed doors. He had also decided that two more players would now be part of his World Cup squad.

They would become a double act, rooming together and referring to one another as 'brother'.

* * *

He never forgot the Munich air disaster. When it happened, he was a 17-year-old apprentice. After training, on what he described as a frosty, 'bone cold' day, he had soaked himself in the dressing room's 'big bath'. He was towelling himself down as the news began arriving in bits, incomplete and incoherent. Like his friends, he believed the crash was nothing more than 'an inconvenience, a delay'. He remembered that someone – without remembering precisely who – had joked that, if the Manchester United team was late arriving back, everyone there might 'get a chance to show what we could do' on Saturday.

Perhaps someone had broken a leg, he thought.

He left Old Trafford, as usual catching the number 112 bus. It carried him into Manchester, where he'd get on another bus to his parents' home in Collyhurst, north-east of the city. He bought the first edition of the *Evening Chronicle* and found, staring back at him, the headline:

United Air Disaster – 30 Killed*

---

* The headline was inaccurate: 23 people were killed.

Inside were the faces of the men whose boots he cleaned at Old Trafford.

He went directly to St Patrick's Church, only half a mile from his front door. He was a cradle Catholic. He'd been an altar boy at the church, arriving for 7am Mass amid silence and incense. It became 'part of my life, my identity', he said. He'd marched while holding plaster figurines of saints and virgins. He'd felt the nuns had 'adopted me to a certain extent'. He'd played in the green shirt and gold trim of its football team, which his father – an undertaker – had co-run, also creating the club's pitch out of a waste tip, the lines on it marked with sawdust.

St Patrick's, built from red brick and white stone, was an architectural combination of art deco and Romanesque, its square tower rising above the terraced houses nearby. There, completely alone, he prayed that the *Chronicle* had 'got it all wrong'; that 'some terrible mistake' had been made, which God could review and make right 'with one stroke'. He wept for those he had known.

He sat in the pews trying to comprehend how something so cruel, so suddenly brutal, could have happened and what it truly meant, and whether anyone, including himself, could ever recover from it. He was unable to say how long he contemplated those things – 'an hour or two, I don't really know' – because shock had set in; he had an appreciation of place but not of time.

His father's job had made him familiar with the business of death and grief, and also with the 'paraphernalia' of funerals. As a boy, playing hide and seek, he had come across a dead body lying on wasteland. 'It's not the dead ones you have to worry about,' his mother had said, giving him comfort and life advice.

This was different. 'It was devastation,' he said.

His hero, with a twisted quiff of black hair, was Eddie Colman, called Snakehips because of the swerve that got him beyond tackles. Like Colman, he was a right half. He had tried to copy him, mirroring his gestures and his spurts of pace. Also like Colman, he was relatively miniature in height – only 5ft 7in. Of all the boots he polished, he spent most time shining Colman's, wondering if this 'home-town God' ever knew how much work he put into making them 'brighter' than anyone else's.

'Coly was dead,' he said. 'It kept coming into my head, but it wouldn't stay,' forced out by a refusal to believe that everything had changed.

This was Nobby Stiles.

He thought of himself as 'lost' in the aftermath of the disaster. 'But for Munich there would have been no Nobby Stiles in the Manchester United team . . . I would never have got past Duncan Edwards and Colman.'

Stiles had to wait until 1960 for his United debut, playing 26 games that season in a team still under slow reconstruction. He was unglamorous enough to look like a misfit, whether in kit or in civvies. 'I was weedy,' he said.

A fear of the dentist had rotted his teeth. Stiles began to play without his dentures after they were twice 'knocked out', once during a midweek cup tie, when he spent three-quarters of an hour unsuccessfully hunting for them on the muddy pitch. His eyesight was so poor that he saw shapes that lacked definition. He was like the cartoon character Mr Magoo. In one episode the myopic Magoo mistakes a hat-stand for his dance partner, waltzing it across the ballroom floor. In another, he thinks an escaped zoo lion is the neighbour's pet cat; he pours a saucer of milk for it.

Off the pitch, Stiles's dark-rimmed glasses, which would slide down his nose, were telescopically thick. On the pitch, he wore contact lenses, but only after accepting he had been playing – and living – 'half blind' and 'guessing' when to trap the ball and where to stroke a pass. The lenses were a revelation, like spring after a bad winter, because everything – faces, colours, landscapes – was instantly made clean, bulb-bright and vivid.

He was also as accident-prone as the characters Harold Lloyd and Buster Keaton played in silent films. Stiles could have been Lloyd, dangling from a clockface, or Keaton, unaware the façade of a house has just fallen on him because he's standing in the right place to be saved by an open window. Stiles was capable of tripping or bumping into something – or knocking it over – even in an empty room. He went to open some bedroom curtains, only to pull them on top of himself. He tried to switch on a radio, mounted on to wall, and yanked it from its screwed-on bracket. He tucked a tablecloth beneath his chin, thinking it was a napkin, and scattered wine glasses and cutlery everywhere.

Stiles continued to have his Mr Magoo moments too. He took a seat in a hotel function room, waiting for a football event to begin, before discovering he'd gone through the wrong door and was among a wedding party, waiting for the arrival of the bride and groom. In his first under-23 international, against Scotland at Aberdeen, he forgot the lubricant for his contact lenses. Alf Ramsey asked him to 'sort out' the Chelsea winger Charlie Cooke. Stiles tracked his target, 'shot him up into the air' and left him in a tangled heap. He was satisfied with his work until a teammate ran towards him in agitation. 'You stupid bastard. What the fuck do you think you're doing?' Like the bungling assassin who shoots the wrong man, Stiles had chopped down the red-headed Billy Bremner instead of Cooke.

Sparks flew wherever Stiles went. He was not the sort of player who advanced by making concessions. He competed as though his soul was at stake. He marked some players so tightly that they could hear his heart beat. He left the imprint of his studs on the shins or calves of others.

In 1963, he'd considered quitting the game entirely. Before the FA Cup final, he pulled a hamstring in the Manchester derby. Attempting to prove his fitness in the season's last league game, at Nottingham Forest, his hamstring twanged again in the opening minute. Deprived of a Cup-winners' medal, Stiles was also in and out of the side again the following season, playing only 17 games. He was switched from wing half to inside forward and then half back. He'd begun to feel like 'an errand boy', fetching and carrying for those around him. Desolation

– a 'terrible sense of futility' – washed over Stiles. It was as if 'somebody had turned out all of the lights', he explained. He agonised over a transfer request. He took an hour to complete a letter of a dozen words, filling the waste basket with torn-up failures. 'I was as near to packing the game in as I could be. I couldn't see myself making the top grade. I was very mixed up.' Within 48 hours, after two sleepless nights, he changed his mind about quitting United.

Ramsey was grateful for that.

Stiles won his first cap at the same time as Jack Charlton. 'Your job is to get the ball,' Ramsey told him. 'When you've got it, do something useful with it.'

A month later, against Yugoslavia, Stiles played alongside a debutant. They became the oddest of couples.

* * *

No footballing father ever pushed a son harder than Alan Ball Sr pushed Alan Ball Jr.

In 1952, the father pointed to his seven-year-old son and told a journalist emphatically: 'This boy will play for England.' The journalist admitted later: 'I made the mistake of sniggering . . .'

The father had been a very average inside forward at Southport, Birmingham City, Oldham and Rochdale, making just 53 league appearances and scoring a meagre 11 goals in six seasons immediately after the war. He snatched at his second chance of success, moulding his son into the player he had once aspired to be, reliving his career vicariously through him.

'He was my Svengali,' said Ball adoringly of his father, evidently unaware that the *Shorter Oxford English Dictionary*'s definition of Svengali is to 'mesmerise' for 'sinister purposes'.

The work his father piled on top of him, like house bricks, seems punishingly unsympathetic when it is described, but the motivation behind the regime was tough love. Ball trained with his father, who

A rare quiet, contemplative moment for Alan Ball, for whom
perpetual motion was almost possible

deliberately toe-poked him on the shins to test his tolerance of pain. In
the Ball household, his father's word was legal scripture. Two hours of
solid, uninterrupted graft with a ball every night were enshrined into
it. 'You've got to be better than anyone else,' he was repeatedly told.
Ball spent hour upon hour kicking only with his left foot to make it the
equal of his right (his father tied his right leg to a drainpipe and rolled
the ball towards his left). He spent more hours practising his heading

to eradicate the bad habit of shutting his eyes before impact; the skin on his forehead cracked, occasionally bleeding a little. He would run everywhere – up and down the stairs of the family home, across fields, along roads, around the touchlines of pitches. His father refused to buy him a bike. Delivering newspapers on foot with a heavy bag became an exercise to build strength and speed. At Christmas, when other boys got train sets or toy soldiers, Ball's presents were footballs or boots, football shirts and tracksuits. If this seems controlling – even manipulative and cruel – there is one image that shatters it: Ball sitting at the front window, cradling his football, watching the clock until his father arrives home. He was neither rebellious towards his father nor disillusioned by him.

With his red hair and a constellation of freckles on the palest of skin, Ball described himself as 'a little nobody', a label cloaked in humility. He was a slip of a thing – just 10 stones and 5ft 6in tall. He had a voice so high-pitched that he sounded as though he'd been sucking helium through a pipe. Neither Wolves nor Bolton were prepared to take him on, the clubs unable to see the prize they could have won because the packaging it came in was so plain.

Subterfuge got Ball his big break at Blackpool. Not wanting the club to know the truth, his father was economical with it. 'This lad is Alan James,' he told them, which was both true and untrue – James was Ball's middle name. One of the two statements that followed was a complete whopper: 'I just met him in the stands.' The other was disingenuous in a good cause: 'He looks pretty useful to me.'

In his formative years, Ball hogged the ball, holding on to it too long in an effort to carry it too far. Stanley Matthews liked a pass to come to his feet. In a practice match, Ball delivered it a little ahead of the master, obliging him to chase it. Disgruntled that a whippersnapper-commoner was dictating to royalty, Matthews had Ball substituted for his impudence.

Ball was always trying to prove that perpetual motion was possible. Nor did he ever lose gracefully; it wasn't in his nature. Like a weeping stick of gelignite, he could go off at any moment. This was a time when a blind eye was turned to a lot of butchery. You could tackle someone from behind or throw yourself at him with both feet and get away without even a ticking-off. You almost had to chop off an opponent's leg – or attack them with a pair of scissors – to be cautioned. Ball was still booked *nine* times before his 20th birthday.

But he typified the player Ramsey sought: adaptable and inexhaustible. Work for Ball was both pleasure and obligation.

Ramsey also recognised that Ball and Nobby Stiles were suited to one another, like-minded in their application and approach to the game. Stiles agreed: 'Perhaps, if you live for football like we do, you have to be a little crazy . . . We're both driven . . . We came from the same part of the world, the same part of life.'

Ramsey made sure Ball and Stiles roomed together, which was a masterstroke. Every night Stiles would reassure his friend: 'Don't worry. We're going to win the World Cup.'

Ramsey was increasingly sure of it too.

* * *

Lilleshall Hall, tucked between the folds of Shropshire, looks like one of those country houses where Jeeves might spend a long weekend saving Bertie Wooster from himself. The stately home, though remodelled in 1829, was essentially still a superb specimen of Elizabethan craftsmanship when it became a centre for sport after the Second World War: a port cochère tower, ridge-topped chimney stacks, feature fireplaces, a hammerbeam roof, a grand dog-leg staircase, wood panelling and heraldic shields.

In the 1960s, the accommodation was bare and could be a little cold, the plumbing gurgled as if it had indigestion, and some of the mullion and transom windows needed a decent clean. Alf Ramsey liked taking England there because the estate guaranteed seclusion amid its 30,000 voluptuous acres.

Ramsey swotted up a good deal on the history of the game, which fascinated him. He read Geoffrey Green's 'biography' of the Football Association, his account of the FA Cup's birth and growth, and the four-volume bible *Association Football*. Within those pages he thought there might be an idea, previously overlooked, that he could adapt.

There had always been dribblers, especially on the wing, for England. In 1879, at the Kennington Oval, Charles Bambridge took the ball from his own box, ran past the entire Scotland team and scored. When Ramsey was at Tottenham, the First Division was full of lively wingers; he had played with and against the finest of them. Finally, though, he came to the conclusion that a famine had followed that feast. Ramsey felt no one had the quality or met the criteria he sought, a problem that had proved unsolvable since he'd taken charge. As he couldn't find a winger, he would devise a system to operate without one.

It was the 4–3–3 formation. 'I had to think of *something*,' said Ramsey.

Instead of three midfield players and three attackers, Ramsey would in effect have six forwards, each attempting to create openings for the others.

February 8, 1965, was his eureka moment.

He arranged an hour-long match that pitted the full internationals, operating in a 4–3–3 formation, against the under-23s, who were using 4–2–4. He admitted: 'I played what amounts to a rather cruel trick on the younger players. I gave them no advance warning of the tactics the senior players had been instructed to employ.'

The First Division clubs had been awkward about releasing players for get-togethers. There was no Bobby Moore and no Bobby Charlton at Lilleshall. Ramsey had to play Bryan Douglas, George Eastham and Johnny Byrne in midfield; Jimmy Greaves was up front. The under-23s were left dizzy because conventional tactics no longer applied. They didn't know who was playing where, whether to drop deep or push up, or how to close down and mark players who were constantly switching positions. No one logged the score, but Ramsey said the full internationals 'ran riot against the young lads', who 'didn't know what it was all about'.

The game got only half a dozen lines in the following day's newspapers. No one cottoned on to the significance of it. Ramsey casually said afterwards: 'We shall be trying other ideas . . . I am keen to broaden players' minds.'

Ramsey said he 'protected' his strategies 'until the time we needed them the most'. In the coming months he twice tried 4–3–3 – against West Germany and Sweden – but did so behind the cloak of wingers, substantially weakening the surprise and the sting it carried.

In December 1965, when everybody else was thinking of cards, advent calendars and shopping, England went to Real Madrid's Bernabéu stadium. Spain were the European Champions. England were in the doldrums. There was no official attendance figure, but the crowd was estimated as between 20,000 to 25,000 – low because the temperature was only just above freezing and England were not a box-office draw.

Banks was in goal. The back four were Cohen, Moore, Jack Charlton and Wilson. The midfield was Eastham, Stiles and Bobby Charlton. The front three were Roger Hunt, Alan Ball and Joe Baker, given only his second cap. Ramsey said something vital beforehand, as though needing to defend his abandonment of wingers: 'The numbers these men will wear are nothing more than a means of identifying them for the spectators.' To appreciate what happened you need only to read the reviews. England were hosed in the kind of superlatives that usually appear on theatrical billboards:

> Phenomenal . . . Imaginative . . . Powerful . . . Brilliant . . . Quite beautiful . . . Exceptional and exhilarating . . . The standard for a new era . . . The shape of soccer to come . . . Marvellously unbelievable.

The Spanish newspaper *Arriba* thought it was like watching 'a cat playing with a mouse'.

England won 2–0 – one goal in the first half by Baker, another in the second from Hunt. They could have scored half a dozen times. The *Daily Express* described the result as a 'thrashing of painful humiliation for the Spaniards' and shouted: 'England can win the World Cup next year.'

The players criss-crossed, whirling around Spain or whipping past them. Wilson and Cohen bombed down the touchlines to complement attacks. Ball and Stiles ran incessantly. Eastham found gaps 'visible only to him'. Bobby Charlton played in full, billowing sail. The Spanish defence was spun into a bedraggled state. Their midfield was yanked out of joint. Their attackers were made redundant.

England turned themselves from a minor irrelevance – fumbling to tie their own boot laces – into a major force, bedazzling even the Spanish fans, who celebrated the rapid passing with admiring *olés*, as though it was a bullfight.

There were another six months to go until the World Cup, and England would face another eight matches beforehand. But Ramsey had sent up a flare. 'What do you think of your performance?' he was asked, a question so bland it gave him the scope to say anything. Ramsey paused, pretending to gather his thoughts, before responding with the fantastically deadpan: 'I feel we can play better.'

Brandy or whisky often took the starch out of Ramsey, but, said Geoffrey Green, 'champagne corks popped' in England's hotel during the early hours of the following morning. A giant crystal chandelier 'sparkled like the milky way'. Green calculated that 'every quarter of an hour' Ramsey, a little tipsy, laid a drink aside to murmur one phrase: 'This precious jewel', by which he meant 'a football'. Each time he said it, Green tottered to his feet, raised his goblet and gave a Russian toast: 'Here's to the four corners of the room.' Green was so drunk that he didn't realise the room was circular.

Ramsey awoke, after very little sleep, convinced of one thing: 'The system could win us the World Cup.'

PART THREE

9

WHEN THE LEGEND BECOMES FACT

The 1966 World Cup got lucky. Its chief archivist was an obscure, slightly eccentric Chilean called Octavio Señoret, his hair as silvery as a half crown. He didn't kick a ball, but pointed a whole battalion of cameras at everyone who did. His film, *Goal!*, is indisputably football's first great documentary and arguably still the best of the best, even during a period when others appear at a ludicrously industrial rate.

Señoret's film was inspired by *Tokyo Olympiad*, the poem in celluloid that Kon Ichikawa made about the 1964 Games. He creatively borrowed Ichikawa's immersive techniques and tricks, but polished them and added a few of his own to make a cinematic event. You can watch *Goal!* and know afterwards what it felt like to have been there.

Sometimes a masterpiece is created out of chaos; this film falls into that category.

Señoret paid FIFA £15,000 for the rights to the tournament, a sum that was hardly inconsequential then and the equivalent of a quarter of a million pounds now. The production costs, estimated at £120,000, steadily rose. Señoret was barrel-scraping for cash, almost going flat broke, before a 'business angel' rescued him. The avant-garde experimental novelist B. S. Johnson, a Chelsea fan who wrote about the game for the *Observer*, tapped out the script. When Señoret read it, he sacked him, tactfully citing 'artistic differences'.

Johnson wanted to dot *Goal!* with scenes of London life: panoramic views of high-rise flats; close-ups of old bomb sites still strewn with rubble and weeds; the shopfronts of Carnaby Street. The Post Office Tower was preciously emblematic for Johnson, but neither he nor his unproduced script hinted at why. Oddly, he had also planned to flash the laws of the game across the bottom of the screen whenever a foul was committed.

The '66 World Cup was the last to be played without substitutes, but Señoret was able to bring on a late replacement for Johnson: Brian Glanville. By then, *Goal!*, roughly cut, was being stitched together in windowless studios in Cricklewood, rather than Hollywood.

In places such as Sunderland and Middlesbrough and Liverpool and Birmingham, Señoret sought the sensitive, ravishing and aesthetic beauty that Ichikawa had found in Tokyo. He was not interested in producing an epically long, colour version of *Match of the Day* in which the highlights, fastidiously catalogued, are shaped and made digestible. Señoret saw himself as some footballing Tolstoy capturing the vast, wide sweep of a story swarming with characters. Of *Goal!*, he said: 'No fiction writer could ever dream up such a story . . . No producer ever had so many stars.'

Goal! is impressionistic yet crammed with fine detail – little subplots – that only the camera caught and which otherwise would have slipped by unnoticed: a defender's desperate sideways glance after a mistake is made . . . a forward's anguished, frustrated howl . . . a player, hands on knees, gasping to get his breath back on the halfway line . . . the nervous twitch in a manager's eye.

The entrepreneur in Señoret meant he didn't care which country won the World Cup, providing the box office would be sufficiently huge to turn him a profit. He was also smart enough to know that the best films about sport are never about the sport itself but 'the human condition'. To mine it, he used 117 cameras, which allowed him to get multiple angles, from pitch level to behind the goals. He hired two directors. One knew next to nothing about football. The other was a movie artist who'd worked in Moscow with the frizzy-haired Eisenstein, who made *Battleship Potemkin* and *October: Ten Days That Shook the World*. *Goal!* was a triumph because both of them, painterly in approach, thought every frame should look like a picture hung in a gallery.

The 1960s was a decade in which football interested intellectuals. The philosopher A. J. Ayer, a Tottenham supporter, wrote about the game in *The New Statesman*. The Austrian-born musicologist Hans Keller succeeded him. The celebrated art critic David Sylvester, who curated Henry Moore and posed for Giacometti, worked for the *Observer*. That newspaper also employed Alan Ross, who covered matches, wrote a poem about Stanley Matthews and became editor of the *London Magazine*. Karl Miller, the future editor of the *London Review of Books*, adored Chelsea, loathed Fulham and played on Sundays in Battersea Park, striving to be 'another Denis Law'. The playwright Harold Pinter had the tiniest of crushes on Millwall and also on Derby County's post-war inside forwards – Carter, Stamps and Doherty. He could recite, without flaw, the England teams of Walter Winterbottom's early era.

Glanville was another high-brow scholar. He wrote novels as well as plays, travel articles, social commentary and literary criticism. Aware his words had merely to complement the splendour of the images in *Goal!*, Glanville reduced them to bone and sinew. His phrases are taut and pithy. His drollness is drier than desert sand. The Brazilian manager, the jowly Vicente Feola, is 'plump and brooding, like a Buddha'. Jimmy Greaves is a 'world-class forward allergic to World Cups'. France are a 'moderate team travelling hopefully'.

Glanville saw Alf Ramsey as 'tension personified', but he noted the advantage he possessed: that 'everyone' was 'afraid of England in England' – especially when the qualifying group was ostensibly a free pass into the last eight.

The actor Nigel Patrick was the average American's idea of the typical upper-class, plummy-voiced Englishman of the '60s. He was known for playing mannered, patrician toffs or urbane villains, cads, con men and scroungers in films as diverse as *Spring in Park Lane, It Takes a Thief* and *The League of Gentlemen*. Patrick narrated Glanville's lines so suavely, his diction perfect, that you'd think he was doing it while reclining across a Chesterfield sofa in the Garrick Club.

Señoret relished the sounds of the game too: the thudding whack of boot against ball, the quick, ripping noise of a shot against nylon netting, the shout for a pass, the thump of a body collapsing on to the grass after a tackle.

Señoret gave us a new way of seeing football. He surpassed what *Tokyo Olympiad* had achieved, treating the World Cup – 16 teams, 32 matches, 20 days – like a theatrical play. Drama, pathos and suspense roll through it, always gathering pace. The film was Señoret's passion project, his only credit on the Internet Movie Database. He shot 46 hours of film, winnowing it down to 148 minutes. No one since '66 has seen the 43 hours that didn't make the cut. Nor does anyone know how to find them.

Goal!, a visual feast, presents you with the soul of the competition. There is Pelé, constantly bumped over and battered from head to toe; Eusébio, the European Footballer of the Year, in his muscular, surging glory; the assured stride of Franz Beckenbauer, only 20 years old but with a tint of entitlement inherent in him; the very blond Helmut Haller, play-maker and goal-poacher; the Black Spider, Lev Yashin, gracious in his farewell World Cup; the improbable North Koreans, amazed to have sent Italy home to a pelting of rotten fruit and fresh tomatoes.

It also provides the scratch of antiquity, a flavoured portrait of yesterday – a sight of the way England used to be not so long ago, but already so different from George Orwell's and J. B. Priestley's descriptions of it. From Orwell you got long shadows, misty mornings, maids cycling to Evensong, deep meadows with elms and larkspur, and pub landlords pulling gallons of warm beer. In the early 1930s – the Devil's Decade – Priestley embarked on *English Journey*, his snapshot of the England that had struggled to rise out of the Great War and was about to fight in another. He began on Southampton docks, 'where a man might well land' on one of those hulking transatlantic ships.

Goal! shows how much has changed in a little over 30 years. It celebrates the still nascent jet age, beginning on the tarmac at Heathrow Airport, before heading north. You see a forest of chimneys on terraced houses, a low smoky sky, new towns of pale brick and ugly skyscraper flats, newspaper-sellers wearing white coats that make them look like Billingsgate fishmongers, and bowler-hatted businessmen marching across the Thames, as though Magritte has asked them to pose for a group portrait. Alive again, too, is the old Wembley, the flags atop the Twin Towers caught in the swell of a breeze.

The modern World Cup is a ticker-tape parade of banknotes. The opening ceremony is always a monster of a thing, akin to a big musical production from Hollywood's swanky heyday. Everything is done to excess, intricately choreographed, lit and co-ordinated in primary colours, the fireworks and fireboxes obligatory. In '66, the ceremony was like a small town's summer fete, lacking only the triangled bunting, hook-a-duck and a tombola. It was home-spun and home-made: a low-key parade around Wembley's greyhound track, a military brass band, a short speech from the Queen. *Goal!* gives you all that too. It also takes you inside the boozers to film those who wanted their football but also wanted their pint.

Between them the BBC and ITV showed every game live, the daily exposure to the game unprecedented. With replays, previews and expert analysis, it was impossible to escape the World Cup unless you unplugged your set or tore down your aerial. Coverage on the two channels totalled more than 50 hours. The competition was the first sporting event in the country to generate a pub culture. Even landlords who had previously forbidden TVs in the saloon bar now installed them, fearful their regulars would otherwise stay at home.

No World Cup had been so heavily merchandised before; the mascot, World Cup Willie, stared at you everywhere. As well as the predictable attire of the terraces – caps and hats, rosettes and scarfs – there were tea towels and T-shirts, cufflinks and key rings, bath mats and bedspreads, car badges and cake decorations. There was World Cup ale and World Cup cigars, World Cup figurines in pottery or plastic, World Cup braces and belts, and even a set of World Cup horse brasses to mount beside your fireplace. That is a pared-down list. The

The World Cup created a culture of watching football 'at the local'

FA advertised another 35 'official' souvenirs, but in all 120 companies produced 180 different items. The tournament even seeped into the everyday lives of men and women who, until it kicked off and gained full propulsion, didn't know the difference between Jack and Bobby Charlton and couldn't have told you whether Geoff Hurst scored goals or stopped them.

Before England's opening game against Uruguay – a goalless draw that was less attractive to look at than a slag heap – *Goal!* saunters along Olympic Way, which is as crowded as a Brueghel painting; there's too much to take in all at once.

In a modest, but lovely, vignette, it finds one of the traders selling merchandise. A squashed, brown felt hat, like an upturned basin, is pulled almost beneath his eyes; you'd think he was camera-shy. He's much older than the century; he'd have been approaching 40 when Uruguay claimed the first World Cup in Montevideo's Estadio Centenario in 1930. In one hand he holds a white board smothered in rosettes. In the other is a pocket harmonica. He is playing 'Ee-Aye-Addio, We Won the Cup'. The tempo is optimistically buoyant, as though he already knows how the tournament will end.

* * *

A fortnight earlier, the BBC had asked Alf Ramsey the obligatory question: did he *still* believe England would win the World Cup? 'Of course,' said Ramsey, irritably. 'I've been saying it every day for the last three months, haven't I?'

Eventually, Ramsey came to believe his original prediction 'wasn't a bad thing to have said' and had even proved 'valuable' because it demonstrated 'such confidence' in his team.

Ramsey was only convinced England would become World Champions after Spain were defeated in Madrid. With every unbeaten match that followed, his belief became more certain. England won seven of eight friendlies and drew the other. Notable among those results were the defeats inflicted on West Germany, beaten 1–0 at Wembley in late February, and Scotland, beaten 4–3 at Hampden Park in early April.

Arthur Rowe didn't think his friend was deluding himself about England's chances. Among the First Division's leading managers, however, only Matt Busby backed England. The others – Don Revie, Ron Greenwood, Joe Mercer and the two Bills, Nicholson and Shankly – sat on the fence, picking splinters out of their backside. Bets were hedged. They talked favourably about Ramsey's chances without committing to him. It was as though everyone, except Busby, was slightly afraid of looking like an idiot if England let them down. Revie's forecast was sufficiently Delphic to be open to several interpretations. England 'can win', he said, spoiling the moment by quickly adding: 'I'm not saying they will win.' He rattled on about 'luck', about the possibility of a loss in 'form' from one match to the next and also about how 'so much' depended on imponderables that no manager, even Ramsey, could foresee or control.

Busby didn't blather on about 'ifs'. He talked decisively about 'when' England would win, insisting that afterwards the new World Champions ought to be christened 'Ramsey United'. Busby predicted Ramsey was about to produce 'the greatest team you will see' at the World Cup. As well as the benefit of home advantage, he thought England's incredible 'stamina', their ability to 'run the legs' off any opposition, had been grossly underestimated because everyone was pointlessly harping on about wingers. Busby explained that Ramsey had been underestimated too. Cowardice deters the faint-hearted from difficult tasks, but Busby also recognised how criticism – and the doubts of those who had made it – toughened Ramsey rather than made him timid.

Busby's absolute conviction about Ramsey and England was not widely shared. Even after that friendly win over West Germany, the newspapers turned on both of them. If the *Daily Express* had blanked out the score, you'd have assumed England had been humiliated. The newspaper called it 'a gutless showing' without 'scope ... enterprise ... or imagination'.

Ramsey had used 43 different players up to and including his 4–3–3 triumph over the Spaniards. He added another five new caps, including Geoff Hurst and Martin Peters, before the World Cup began. Hurst had been picked to face the Germans. The *Express* was not much kinder about him either. Their verdict was: 'He too was lost in a plan that was never identifiable.' In the last paragraph of the match report, Ramsey's tactics were trashed as a 'sorry soccer scheme'. The *Express* was still going for the throat when, a week before the opening match, England beat Denmark 2–0 in Copenhagen. 'There can be only one word for England's football flop here tonight,' it said. That word was 'shocking'.

At some point over the next seven days, the *Express* had one of those inexplicable and miraculous, road-to-Damascus conversions. Or perhaps it was a patriotic strategy to keep the public interested. It declared England would win the World Cup, which must have baffled any reader who kept a scrapbook. The *Daily Mail* believed so too – or at least Brian James did. With his support of England and Ramsey, based on the certainty he'd be proved right, James gamely swam against the prevailing current in Fleet Street. That current swept almost every other expert clutching a press pass towards Brazil. Instead of congratulating its correspondent for his independent thinking and trusting his instincts, the *Daily Mail* became paranoid that James's enthusiasm for the home team could make the newspaper look like chumps when the post-mortem was written. If England failed, James was advised, his 'position' at the newspaper could be at risk. He tackled that ultimatum – chilling to anyone with a mortgage to pay and a family to feed – by tactfully ignoring it. James would not tone down or tailor his opinions to satisfy someone else's.

Brazil were such far-out favourites that *The Times*'s tipping of Italy looked weirdly wonky. The weekly magazine *Soccer Star* chose Brazil and didn't fancy England to even reach the semi-finals. The *Daily Telegraph* thought 'there were grounds for hoping' as far as Ramsey was concerned, but the author of the article conceded reluctantly: 'I still have to persuade myself that this [becoming serious contenders] will happen.' In the *Sunday Express*, Danny Blanchflower wrote that 'if England do not win the World Cup . . . then there can be no acceptable excuse for them'. You read the line and know instantly what Blanchflower is doing: he isn't waving a flag for Ramsey but making a rod for his back.

Brazil were considered too highbrow to be beaten – especially by a team as supposedly lowbrow as England's. But Ramsey didn't fear the World Champions. 'If we play them, we will beat them,' he said to Harold Shepherdson. His 'intelligence corps' had told him the Brazilians were riven by internal splits, trivial spats and suspicions, which had worsened during an anarchic national tour. Their squad, 40-strong, had criss-crossed Brazil like an exhibition side on a lap of honour. Cliques had formed, dividing the established players such as Santos and Garrincha, from the newcomers, such as Tostão. Brazil didn't have a settled side. Their defence of the trophy was over-reliant on Pelé, insured by his own FA for £250,000 and who, only two seasons before, had admitted that the expectations perpetually heaped on to him had become suffocatingly onerous. 'Sometimes I feel like a veteran ... tired, exhausted ... I would like to give up football,' he'd said.

Ramsey was wary of only three teams: Portugal, Argentina and West Germany.

The Portuguese were capable of scoring explosively because of Eusébio. He was their sun, around which revolved António Simões, José Torres, Mário Coluna, Jaime Graça and José Augusto, each of whom was talented in his own way. Ramsey referred to Portugal privately as the 'dark horses', so much of their magic dependent on their mood.

Argentina still had Antonio Rattin, of Boca Juniors, as well as Ermindo Onega, of River Plate, and Jorge Albrecht, of San Lorenzo. Rattin, the captain, looked as though he'd been hewed out of a long block of concrete. The leanness of his muscled frame made him seem taller than his 6ft 3in. With thin lips, a rather over-large nose and a flattish face, the cheekbones barely a bump, Rattin could appear slightly sinister, even when smiling. Onega was the play-maker, clever and technically skilful, able to cleave the opposition open in only three yards of space. Albrecht defended uncompromisingly, the kind of player who would sacrifice a limb to save a goal. But a dark thread ran through all the gifts the Argentinians had been given. The nickname Rattin got, 'El Caudillo' – the Governor – massaged his bloated sense of superiority. He was self-obsessed, certain he could both manage the team and legitimately referee any game while also playing in it. Ramsey had seen him do this so intimidatingly during that Little World Cup in South America. The Argentina team came with woes too. Their preparations for the tournament were disorganised and divisive. Their manager, Juan Carlos Lorenzo, was appointed only a month beforehand. Rattin loathed Lorenzo – and vice versa. The distrust between them, sprouting multiple roots, began at the 1962 World Cup, where Lorenzo also managed him. After Argentina lost to England in that tournament, Lorenzo accused Rattin of failing to man-mark well enough; Rattin had accused Lorenzo of imposing a flawed, illogical system on to him. During their warm-up tour of Italy, it was as though everyone had a squabble with someone else; Rattin even punched a fellow player.

Argentina could caress passes and dominate possession. The team, though, were over-fond of playing the man before the ball and disciplined only when it came to disrupting, niggling, roughing up and riling the opposition. It was a monstrous waste of talent.

The Germans, 25–1 outsiders only six weeks before the finals, troubled Ramsey's sleep much more. Franz Beckenbauer was not yet a Kaiser, but certainly a Prince. Helmut Haller and Uwe Seeler were constantly dangerous. Haller was portly, prone to pile on the pounds, and far from being the swiftest to the ball – except when he sniffed a goal. He sought acclaim and could be overly theatrical in his search for it, but there was a panache about him. He'd left his home town, Augsburg, to sign for Bologna, a deal which he described as being trapped in a 'golden cage' (he would later claim, after moving to Juventus, to be Germany's first 'millionaire' footballer). 'I got my pockets full of all the money you could dream of . . .' he said. Haller wailed nonetheless, hopelessly homesick. In Bologna, where he won a Serie A title, his palatial flat was only 300 yards from the railway station. From a window he could – and did – wistfully watch the trains as they left for Germany. Seeler, of Hamburg, was an old lag, playing in his third World Cup. He was smart, solidly built and difficult to shove or body-check off the ball; he rode a rough tackle like a surfer riding the curl of a wave. At 29, he'd successfully made a comeback after tearing his Achilles tendon 18 months before. That injury almost always meant the death of a career back then because surgery, being far less refined, could seldom repair it.

Ramsey also saw similarities, which he admired, between himself and West Germany's coach, Helmut Schön. As a forward, Schön had won the league and cup with Dresden. He considered it a 'tragedy' that Hitler had interrupted them 'at the pinnacle of their achievement'. After switching to coaching, he became assistant to Sepp Herberger only two years after West Germany's 'Miracle of Bern' defeat of Hungary in the 1954 World Cup final. A decade later, Schön succeeded Herberger, taking over a sickly side that had won just three of its previous eight matches. He was only five years older than Ramsey, but already had the slightly sagging, melancholic look of a bloodhound that's reluctant to visit the vet. On his bald pate he often wore a colourfully chequered flat cap, like a golfer's, that seemed half a size too small for him.

Much like Ramsey – through trial, error and good fortune – Schön found his best side. In his first five games he used 33 players, including 14 new caps. In the friendly at Wembley, Schön had experimented again, picking only half of the team that would start the World Cup. He'd fought against his own football association too, convincing it to revoke a ban on players in Italy, such as Haller and Roma's Karl-Heinz Schnellinger, known as 'The Volkswagen' because of his reliability. Schön had been innovatively brave by bringing in Beckenbauer for his debut in the critical game in Sweden, which Germany won to qualify for 1966. Soon he added Siggi Held and the outside left Lothar Emmerich too.

Ramsey sensed the danger of Schön's Germany before anyone else.

The World Cup groups were fortunately in Ramsey's favour. Brazil and Portugal had to slug it out together, in Group Three, beside Hungary and Bulgaria. Group Two matched West Germany with Argentina (Ramsey ignored Spain and Switzerland, regarding them as irrelevant). No one in Group Four sent him into night-sweats either. Not Italy – too vulnerable, despite the attacking acumen of Sandro

Mazzola and Gianni Rivera, the Golden Boy of Serie A. Not Chile – too prosaic. Not the Soviet Union – too reliant on Lev Yashin. And certainly not North Korea, who Ramsey thought – along with everyone else – must have booked their tickets home as soon as the draw was made, certain of the date and hour of their departure.

England sat so comfortably in Group One that some suspected collusion, the draw done with a gambler's marked deck. It wasn't so, but Ramsey couldn't have ended up with more hospitable opposition if he had hand-picked them. Uruguay, France and Mexico were as good as it could possibly get for England.

The squad was kept on the tightest of leashes at Lilleshall. Two weeks of intense graft started daily at 10am and finished at 6pm. Ramsey temporarily recruited Wilf McGuinness, of Manchester United, to work alongside Harold Shepherdson and Les Cocker. McGuinness was England's youth coach, a role given to him on Matt Busby's recommendation. His inclusion is important in retrospect because of the evidence he provided afterwards about Ramsey's confidence.

When McGuinness was about to leave Lilleshall, Ramsey told him: 'Trust me. We *will* get to the final. When we do, I want you to be there. We're going to win.'

McGuinness said: 'I think he was expecting, even then, to play West Germany. He probably even knew what the score would be . . .'

* * *

Most of the photographs of that World Cup, like most of the film of it too, are in black and white.

Two tell you the story of the competition's group stages.

The most intimate is of Pelé, the camera capturing him in wretched defeat. His chest is bare because he's just exchanged his shirt. The crucifix he always wears dangles from his neck. He is walking off Goodison Park, where a dishevelled Brazil have lost 3–1 to Portugal. Their tournament is over. A calf-length, dark raincoat is draped across his shoulders like a vampire's cloak. The sleeves are twice as long as his arms. He is hunched. His gaze is lowered. He looks like a man sheltering from a downpour in a doorway. For Pelé, the World Cup became 'a war'. Afterwards, he said that for a while 'my heart wasn't in playing football'. The brutality of Brazil's exit, their first match like kick-boxing, stays with you long after you see it. Their opposition, Bulgaria, lost on goals – 2–0 – but won on fouls 20–19. Most of those fouls were committed on Pelé. His ankles, shins, calves, knees and thighs were whacked and hacked. He took a blow to the back of the head, stumbling forward as though he'd been coshed. Pelé hobbled about, like an invalid on crutches, slowly taking little jumps one half-yard at a time. He couldn't play against Hungary, who beat Brazil 3–1. Against Portugal, the few bits of him that still worked didn't do so effectively enough to make a difference.

The other photo is no work of art. It's one of those standard snaps that were a cherished staple of newspaper back pages in the days when so few games were televised. Getting the 'goal shot', from behind the net or beside the post, was the objective then. In this one, taken at Ayresome Park, you see the goalkeeper's flapping dive for the ball, which is already past him, and two defenders, as well as the scorer. Their eyes are following the low drive as it slips into the bottom corner.

Italy 0, North Korea 1.

Before the tournament began, you could have polled 30 million people in England without finding anyone capable either of identifying even one of the Korean players or spelling his name correctly. The public knew just this about them: they had qualified only after beating Australia, and because other Asian and African nations had withdrawn en masse, insulted by FIFA's decision to offer them a solitary place in the finals. They were fussier about their training pitches than Goldilocks had been about her porridge. One was too hard and bumpy. On another the grass was too long. A third had too little grass. They had been quartered for two years in military barracks, their vow of celibacy unbroken. The Koreans were a Tom Thumb team. Their

The goal that shook the World Cup. Pak Doo Ik of North Korea sinks the former champions, Italy

average height was 5ft 5in. Their 'keeper, the Flying Panther Lee Chang Myung, was only 5ft 7in. When the Soviet Union steamrolled them 3–0 in their opening game, the Koreans got the admiration and pity always attached to plucky losers. Their 1–1 draw with Chile, though gallant, was never considered preparatory work for the most substantial shock the World Cup had witnessed since England surrendered in Belo Horizonte 16 years before.

The Italians were handicapped for more than an hour; an injury forced them to play with only 10 men. The neutrals didn't care. In an instant, the scorer Pak Doo Ik, as well as Hang Bon Zin, Pak Deung Zin and Chang Myung, became names you could accurately match to faces. If the result had been registered as an earthquake, the Richter scale would still have needed recalibration. 'This is the essence of football,' said Ramsey. 'Does it not remind us that there are no certainties in this World Cup?'

Ramsey, describing it as an 'unimaginable' outcome, had never-theless been right about Brazil. He'd been right about Portugal too. And West Germany quickly lived up to his expectations. Each game revealed a different facet of their strength. Against Switzerland, a stroll for them, the Germans won 5–0, captivating those in the uncovered Hillsborough 'Kop', which was so steeply banked it seemed to touch the sky. Against Argentina, at Villa Park, where the South Americans were cautiously defensive, the Germans were maturely even-tempered – despite crude, venomous provocation – but came away with welts, cuts and a 0–0 draw. Against Spain, again at Villa Park, the difficulty of beating Schön became even more apparent to Ramsey. A goal down, the Germans fought back to equalise, took control of possession and claimed the winner six minutes from the end, a close-range effort from Uwe Seeler.

In a tournament now without the holders, Germany had become more fancied than England.

* * *

One of Alf Ramsey's favourite films was John Ford's *The Man Who Shot Liberty Valance*. John Wayne – of course – is a rancher in a dusty town that is being terrorised by the eponymous gunslinger, played by Lee Marvin. James Stewart, a newcomer, finds his reputation is forged from a falsehood not of his own making. Everyone believes he shot dead the trouble-making Liberty Valance because Wayne allows him take the credit for it. He becomes a US senator as a consequence. In the final reel, the reporter sent to interview Stewart's character realises the story about him is a lie, but he can't bring himself to expose it. He won't shatter the myth because he can't. The myth is so well estab-lished that it is not just more powerful than the truth, but also the only narrative his readership wants and would be willing to accept. He defends the decision to spike his own exclusive with one of the most seminal lines ever written for a Hollywood movie:

When the legend becomes fact, print the legend.

The legend of Bobby Charlton is a bit like that.

He was a natural, so good he barely needed coaching. He was always disciplined and caused not one jot of trouble for Ramsey.

That, though, isn't entirely true. He wasn't always the infallibly reliable player that history has made him out to be. The making of Charlton required a strenuous level of application from Ramsey.

Since Charlton was so uncooperative while putting together his own *Book of Soccer*, Kenneth Wheeler lugged a tape recorder around with him while interviewing Charlton's family and friends, his team-mates, coaches and also Matt Busby. Wheeler ghosted Ramsey, too, working with him on two articles about tactics. He knew both the player and the manager as well as anyone who reported on England regularly. Wheeler came to the conclusion that Ramsey – not Busby – had harnessed Charlton's 'stupendous but erratic talent' and given him 'real responsibility . . . transforming him overnight from a patchy pin-up to a master footballer'. He changed his character too. Wheeler wrote of how Ramsey, after taking over, 'knew' Charlton as 'something of a joker in the pack, too brilliant to leave out or to fit in'. He described him as an 'enthusiastic individualist' who 'wanted the ball all the time even at the expense of a teammate in a more favourable position'. He could make 'exciting runs' but 'just as easily' lose the ball while attempting to perform 'some extraordinarily complicated feat'. He tended to 'stray out of position' or get 'in the way' and unsettle the 'rhythm' of his own team. Wheeler was certain of this: 'He was without doubt one of the biggest problem-players any manager ever had to cope with.' It's such an uncommon verdict of Charlton, his early career wreathed in romantic mystique, that the assessment seems skewed. Ramsey, though, agreed with it.

He rarely criticised an individual in front of anyone else, but he was not a soft touch. On the eve of one international Ramsey played in a five-a-side game – despite being 45 years old and despite a frost that was glittering across the grass, the cold air as sharp as glass. George Cohen was unaware of how tightly Ramsey was marking him. He turned abruptly, not only poleaxing Ramsey but also launching him upwards, like someone hit by a car. He came down in a tangle, landing head-first on the hard pitch, and said to Cohen. 'If I had another fucking full back, you wouldn't be playing tomorrow.'

When Gordon Banks misjudged his positioning at a free kick, costing England a goal, Ramsey went into a rage. 'One of these days,' he told him, 'I shall lift up a dagger and fuckin' well kill you.'

With Charlton, he gave him lessons in the practicalities of a footballer's life. He was one of seven players – the others included Bobby Moore, Banks and Jimmy Greaves – who defied a 10.30pm curfew to go out drinking before England left for the Little World Cup. Recollections of the night vary. Charlton said: 'We were relaxed, which is how we were told we ought to be.' Banks said: 'It was past one in the morning' when he and the others 'slipped away' to their rooms, 'thinking we'd got away with it'. Greaves said: 'It was just a social drink, really,' which ended 'near midnight'. Next morning, each player's passport was placed on his pillow. 'It was a shocking sight,' said Charlton, making it sound as though he'd found the severed head of a horse there. Ramsey tore into his rebels: 'If I had enough players in the squad, none of you would be in the side. In fact, I don't think you'd be here at all.'

Charlton was so shaken that afterwards Ramsey, thinking a lesson had been learnt, gave him the benefit of the doubt – even after he continued to exasperate. There were 'many discussions', said Ramsey, about how Charlton could 'provide better opportunities and better results for the team'. Charlton would 'listen' to the advice and 'agree' with it, but either his concentration would wander or he'd become distracted. 'Everything we had spoken about would last five or ten minutes on the field,' added Ramsey 'then it would go completely out of his head.' The 'day the penny dropped' for Charlton, he explained, came only three weeks before the World Cup began.

Facing Yugoslavia at Wembley, Charlton was standing in the cen-tre of the field, when England lost the ball and found themselves back-pedalling. The Yugoslavian attack was targeting England's left flank. 'By instinct,' said Ramsey, Charlton would 'normally have moved towards' the ball. Ramsey tracked his path, watching him take 'just one pace' towards the play before stopping, lifting his gaze towards the other touchline and readjusting his position. 'Instead of following the ball, Bobby came back and picked up the man working on the blind side of our defence. This was the moment when I thought he became a great player . . . the great player I wanted him to be.'

* * *

Rather like Bobby Charlton's transformation, the moment England's World Cup properly began can be anchored to a specific date too: July 16, 1966.

It can also be fixed to a precise time: 8.07pm.

You could have strolled up to the turnstiles and bought a ticket for England's opening match against Uruguay – priced at seven shil-lings and sixpence – less than ten minutes before kick-off. The crowd was only 87,148. Five days later, the tournament now ablaze after its slow-burn start, 92,570 were waiting for something to happen when England took on Mexico.

With half-time eight minutes away, the game was inert and goalless. England were like blocks of wood.

And then . . .

Roger Hunt shoves a pass to Charlton near the halfway line. After the tedious stalemate with Uruguay, Charlton had walked off the field feeling the 'sudden fear of anti-climax'. That fear was about to lift. Anyone who has seen Charlton's goal, live or recorded, will always be capable of recalling it – the poised run, the power of the shot. If Charlton had a 'tell', it was this: when he was just about to push the ball beyond someone, he would give a little skip. First Division defenders learnt this, waiting and preparing for it. The Mexicans were either unaware of his habit or had lost a page from their briefing notes.

After Hunt delivers the ball to Charlton, he peels off and drags the Mexican markers with him. Charlton, fatally left to his own devices, has a clear path towards the box. He trusts the pitch, knowing the ball will bowl smoothly across it. He rapidly travels 25 yards, his buccaneering run unchallenged before the bazooka shot. No one is gutsy enough to go and tackle him. It's as though the Mexican defence has frozen; only Charlton is moving. Jimmy Murphy, his coach at Manchester United, always told him: 'Don't place a shot. If you don't know where it's going, how can the goalkeeper?' When he is 30 yards out, Charlton looks up, thinks again of Murphy's advice and strikes the pale ball without breaking his stride. It rises beautifully off his boot, zooming through the night air with grace and destruction. Had the net not been there to catch it, a fan on the West Stand's shilling terraces would have been decapitated.

Until then, England hadn't remotely looked like conceding a goal, but no one had been entirely convinced Alf Ramsey's team would score one either.

10

THE HAWK AND THE BUTTERFLY

Jimmy Greaves published more words than Shakespeare. Standing side by side on a bookshelf, his collected 'works' about his life and times would measure about a yard and a half. The British Library's catalogue lists 22 titles, starting in 1962 with *A Funny Thing Happened on the Way to Spurs* and ending in 2010 with *Greavsie's Greatest*. In between is his doorstep autobiography, *Greavsie*.

The World Cup appears in most of these books like a haunting. Greaves was always asked about it in the same way his friend, George Best, was always asked about several Miss Worlds, his drinking and the fortune he earned and squandered.

Greaves was the First Division's top scorer from 1962–3 until 1964–5. In the first of those seasons, he finished with 37 goals. In the second, it was 35. In the third, his tally was 29. He had played in 26 of Alf Ramsey's 38 internationals before the World Cup, but his ever-pragmatic manager felt he was always 'accommodating' him. Greaves became to Ramsey what the drummer Pete Best became to the Beatles. He was the loose joint, an individualist who was often out of rhythm with the rest of the band no matter how startlingly he played. Ramsey was sympathetic towards him, but gradually became fed up too.

The testimony of others, analysing what Greaves gave to England, offers several reasons why Ramsey was never entirely won over. George Cohen thought Greaves neither grasped 'the principle of discipline' nor 'the virtues of it'. If Greaves 'wasn't scoring', said Bobby Charlton, his 'contribution to the kind of performances Ramsey was now demanding' counted as 'not much more than ornamental'. Geoffrey Green, much harsher, saw him as 'aggravatingly forgetful and seemingly calculating'.

Greaves's great misfortune was contracting hepatitis in the autumn of 1965. His recovery was slow and incomplete. A patient for nearly three months, he missed 13 league matches for Tottenham and scored only 15 goals, a pauper's return by his own princely standards. He noticeably lost energy and a little weight. A severe haircut just before the World Cup, the barber over-zealous with the scissors, gave his face a pinched look too.

The tournament came a year too soon for him. Greaves believed that Ramsey would win it. He also believed he would be integral to that success. The illness, though, wrecked his 'old self', he said. Chances he would usually have taken slid away from him. Nor was he quick enough to nip free of Joseph Bonnel in the last group game with France, which, like the match against Mexico, England won 2–0. Like a gardener using a rake, Bonnel dragged his studs down Greaves's left shin. They went through his sock and tore the skin so badly that the whiteness of the bone beneath became visible. The wound, dirty and bloody, needed fourteen stitches, a whole roll of crepe bandage wound around them.

The newspapers that mourned his loss also forecast his return. But even if Bonnel hadn't gone over the ball – and even if Greaves had been fit – Ramsey would not have chosen him for the quarter-final against Argentina. 'Greaves had not shown his true form to substantiate his position,' he said.

A conversation among Ramsey and his 'inner cabinet' at Hendon Hall settled the matter.

Jimmy Armfield was almost 31 years old. Unless Cohen went lame, he knew his World Cup would be about carrying the water. Even if this turned out to be his only duty, Ramsey still wanted him there. Armfield had knowledge and nous. Humility, the lack of any jealous edge or axe-grinding, meant that whatever advice Ramsey sought from him was never tainted by self-interest, sly one-upmanship or malice. His faith in Armfield was wholly reciprocated. He was treated like a non-affiliated member of his coaching staff, always to be trusted. When Armfield was not doing the *Daily Telegraph* crossword puzzle, Ramsey found him being useful, solicitously consoling or supporting the other players. He saw the manager in him that Armfield would soon become.

Between the last group game and the quarter-finals, Armfield said he was cloistered with Ramsey, Harold Shepherdson and Bobby Moore for some post-dinner reminiscing 'about the old days, past World Cups and how football had changed over the years'. As this casual conversation meandered on, Armfield remarked: 'There's never been a successful England team without an old-fashioned centre forward. Someone who's a target man. A player who gives you options because you can play a long ball up to him and he can hold it for you.'

Everyone chipped in. Opinions and memories about Tommy Lawton were shared, as well as his partner at Everton, Dixie Dean, and the battering ram that Nat Lofthouse had once been. Armfield mentioned First Division centre forwards, among them the Welshman Wyn 'The Leap' Davies at Newcastle, who in effect 'gave you an air force as well as ground troops'. Armfield suspected, but never knew for certain, that what was said influenced Ramsey's thinking. Curiously, he never asked him about it. If he had, Ramsey would have told Armfield that he'd come to the same conclusion. He was already two thoughts ahead of him.

In the group matches, Ramsey had picked three different wingers: John Connelly, Terry Paine and Ian Callaghan. Only one of them brought him a goal: a floated Callaghan cross had induced a goalkeeper's fumble, the ball dropping to Roger Hunt inside France's six-yard box.

Geoff Hurst was no Lawton, no Dean and no Lofthouse; that trio had scored 70 international goals between them. At West Ham, Hurst had won the 1964 FA Cup and the 1965 European Cup Winners' Cup, but possessed only four under-23 caps and had made just two full appearances. He didn't think he was 'remotely close' to taking Greaves's place.

Only ten months before the tournament, he was wheeling his daughter along Romford High Street in her pushchair. He saw Greaves through a tobacconist's window. Hurst went inside and became 'so engrossed' in a conversation with Greaves – anxious to learn from someone he revered – that he left the shop and forgot his daughter was still inside it.

At 12st 10lb, Hurst was one of the heaviest players in the England squad; he admitted to having 'a fat arse'. He preferred to train in a tracksuit to sweat off a pound or three. He was, though, immensely brave, fearless even, which got him a ten-star rating from Ramsey. 'I don't like shrinking violets,' he told Hurst, who wasn't one. Ron Greenwood thought Hurst's strength, despite the weight he toted about, was the stamina in his legs. 'His endless running and his direction-changing were phenomenal,' he said. Hurst also had what Greaves did not – a ravenous appetite for work. Greenwood called him 'a coach's dream' because he 'listened and practised' and 'keep on practising'. He taught himself to take a ball, played from behind, on the half-turn. He slaved away at his heading. He was diligent in teaching himself about angles, learning how to create and use space. Particularly in his nascent days, Hurst was educated in Cassettari's, the café that stood a corner kick from Upton Park. A Formica-topped table would become a pitch, the ketchup bottles were turned into defenders, and the salt and pepper pots would try to out-manoeuvre them. Hurst said his wife always knew when he'd been there because his clothes 'smelt slightly of grease'.

The photographers missed a shot during England's opening match, the picture worth a small gold mine after it was over. On the sidelines Hurst and Martin Peters were sitting together, each wearing his grey flannel Burton's suit and unsure about whether Ramsey would ever pick them. Hurst and Peters were back-to-back neighbours – so close that you could get from one property to the next by climbing over the coal bunkers in their gardens.

In January, never believing that a place in the World Cup squad could be theirs, the friends had talked of taking a family holiday together in Cornwall. 'We'd watch the finals on TV,' said Hurst.

* * *

The goal that beat Argentina in the World Cup quarter-finals at Wembley was made on Chadwell Heath.

West Ham's training ground was a wide spread of modest grass, from which you saw the sloping red roofs of semi-detached suburban houses and square back gardens that were protected by creosoted pitch-pine fences. Ron Greenwood would ask the club's maintenance staff to pour concrete into huge paint tins the size of dustbins. While the concrete was still wet, but about to set, he'd plant tall white posts into each tin. The tins were arranged, like defenders, between the touchline and the penalty area. Martin Peters had to run at them, pushing the ball outside the tins but not beyond them. With the inside of his boot, he'd attempt to curl his cross around the tins and into the near post. His foot would go straight through where the ball had been rather than following the direction of flight. 'It was like putting side on a snooker ball,' explained Peters. Geoff Hurst would make a decoy dash, abruptly changing direction to lose the defender marking him. 'We did that routine thousands of times,' he said. 'He knew where I'd be. I knew where the ball was going . . . we acted out of habit.'

In the 78th minute, while thoughts were turning to extra time, this is how Peters and Hurst broke the Argentinians. As soon as Hurst bursts into the box, you know where the ball is about to go, glanced with a flick of his head into the far bottom corner.

But you only think about that goal after you've thought about everything else: Argentina's pointless, self-defeating aggression; Antonio Rattin's sending-off; the intimidation West German referee Rudolf Kreitlein experienced.

Geoff Hurst marks his World Cup debut with the winning goal against Argentina.
The photographer's artistic crop is deliberate

When he was about to retire, Kreitlein could only estimate how many matches he had refereed – 'about 1,200', he said – but he knew exactly how many players he had sent off: '14'. Rattin was number 11 on that list. Kreitlein was resigned to the fact his whole career would be remembered only for that. 'This is my tragedy,' he'd say.

What ought to have been a lovely dance of styles, European versus South American, became football *noir* on an afternoon of intensely bright sun and intensely dark shadows. Wembley was deliciously hot, the temperature peaking at 30°C.

Watching the BBC's film of the game won't show you how crude Argentina were. You do see Rattin tripping Alan Ball and thrusting out a leg at Bobby Charlton. You do see Ermindo Onega shove and jostle and niggle Nobby Stiles, as close to him as Fred Astaire used to get to Ginger Rogers. And you do see mistimed tackles, some awful play-acting, dissent and the farce of protests and contemptuous, beseeching appeals. Statistics do occasionally lie or skew the truth.

England committed 33 of the 52 fouls and infringements that Kreitlein punished, which fingers them as the aggressors until you see that most of these were not sinister – just a bit of pushing or holding down.

You won't see what Argentina did off the ball, attempting to provoke England into retaliation: the kidney punches, the ankle taps, the hair-pulling, the treading on someone's foot, the ear-twisting, the pokes in the eye, the elbows in the ribs, the kicks on the shin before a corner is taken, the slaps on the head and the perpetual, pathetic spitting. No one in that World Cup could spit as far or as accurately as the Argentinians; for them, spitting was a sport within a sport. No England player escaped. According to Stiles, you got spittle on your face, down the back of your neck and across the front of your shirt.

In their group game against West Germany, the Argentinian defence had rugby-tackled Helmut Haller, sent Wolfgang Overath spinning into the perimeter wall behind one of the goals and chopped down both Franz Beckenbauer and Uwe Seeler; the tackle on Seeler was so outrageously high that it could have sliced off his right leg above the knee. Argentina finished that game with ten men; Jorge Albrecht committed one spoiling foul too many.

Their tactics were stealthier at Wembley. As a corner came over, Jack Charlton was hauled to the floor as he jumped for the ball. Four defenders, like a gang assaulting their victim in a back alley, ran past Charlton, each one giving him a kick in a different place. Alan Ball, 30 yards away from play, was barged over by a defender who then stood on the back of his calf. Not far from the England bench, Stiles was gobbed on. Alf Ramsey, fearing Stiles would react with his fists, instinctively looked away, waiting for the crowd to tell him the worst. Stiles merely wiped his cheek, using the left arm of his shirt like a handkerchief.

The BBC had imported a slow-motion-replay machine from the United States. The new technology confused some of the viewers it was bought to impress, and the corporation's switchboard received baffled calls that asked: 'Is this match really live?' The replays dwelt on the good – the goals, the near misses, the spectacular saves – but mostly ignored the ugly. The Argentinians, despite their subterfuge, would later be caught out because the cameraman responsible for feeding the director with close-ups was filming the worst of it. In a shameful act of self-censorship, however, the producer was 'warned' by the high-ups in Broadcasting House to 'cut' these 'incidents', sanitising the game and protecting the perpetrators.

The World Cup never found out how well Argentina could have played. It was as though they did not completely trust their own abilities. Kreitlein thought the South Americans, led by Rattin's malevolent example, 'deliberately' planned to be destructive. Tyrants are prone to tantrums, which explains why Rattin challenged everything with a wagging finger. Rarely pausing for breath, he jabbered away, questioning whatever decision the picked-upon Kreitlein made. Rattin would pat the back of his shorts, where a pocket might have been sewn, as though suggesting Kreitlein had been bribed. He'd spit on the grass close enough to where Kreitlein stood without splashing him. He'd use his height to intimidate, like a policeman standing over a small boy. The 5ft 4in referee had to either crick his neck to speak to Rattin or talk to his chest. Even in the tunnel, before kick-off, Hurst said that Rattin gave England 'a look of sneering hate'. Kreitlein received that look too.

Only two months earlier, Kreitlein had refereed the European Cup final between Real Madrid and Partizan. That honour was forgotten after Wembley. He was ridiculed as a 'comic figure' because of his baldness, his height, his demeanour. He was criticised for being 'pompous' and 'fussy', 'pedantic' and 'punctilious', and as a 'preposterous taker of names'. In fact, he booked only three Argentinians.

It is difficult to know what Kreitlein could have done differently. Rattin's state of mind was mutinous. *Goal!* captures the melt-down after his sending-off only ten minutes before half-time. Already cautioned for a needless foul on Bobby Charlton, Rattin rages again at the referee after another Argentinian booking and is dismissed for dissent. Rattin points to his captain's armband as though, like diplomatic immunity, it gives him every right to behave abominably and say whatever he likes. He tags Kreitlein, following him like a stalker. Every gesture – his hands pressed together as though in prayer, his palms raised and open, the slow head-shaking – is that of the secular martyr. Kreitlein has to run backwards to avoid Rattin and the mob gathered behind him. Rattin still refuses to go; and his team refuse to play on without him. Rattin claimed he had been promised an interpreter, and Kreitlein would later criticise FIFA for not providing one. If an interpreter had been present, this was the message he would have passed on: 'Argentina would get one minute, or two minutes perhaps, to continue playing . . . otherwise the match is abandoned,' said Kreitlein.

Eight and a half minutes drag on before Rattin leaves the field. It takes another two – *Goal!* shows us 93 seconds of this – for him to walk from the halfway line to the head of the tunnel. Occasionally, he breaks his ponderous step to look back at the match. He's puzzled and a little forlorn. After playing as though in some demented trance for more than half an hour, he now seems to have awoken from it, disconsolately aware of both the trouble he has caused and the consequences of it. When Rattin passes the corner flag, he pulls on the fabric the way a countryside rambler might distractedly pull a petal off a flower, his mind elsewhere.

Hostilities did not halt with the whistle. By trade, Kreitlein was a tailor; he had hand-sewn his own uniform. One Argentinian ripped the front of the referee's shirt. Another kicked him in the calf. A third grabbed Kreitlein by the throat when the two of them were inside the tunnel and the referee no longer had a police escort. Ramsey was spat on. A chair was hurled at the door of England's dressing room, breaking a window. The Argentinians pounded on that door, attempting to goad England into a fist fight. Some of them even pissed against the dressing room's outside wall.

Rattin, the rotten loser, portrayed himself as a persecuted victim. 'England won because they were the host team, because the matches were played at Wembley, because everything was prepared to damage the opposition, because it was not fairly played and because everything was arranged beforehand,' he said. The statement, delusional and self-justifying, is only worth recommending to anyone who has difficulty laughing.

Madness ran through Rattin that day.

* * *

The other quarter-finals adhered to the form book.

At Hillsborough, West Germany cracked open Uruguay, winning 4–0. The Uruguayans, already behind, self-harmed more severely even than Argentina did: two of their players were sent off in the opening ten minutes of the second half. At Roker Park, the Soviet Union, efficient and muscular, subdued the too-fragile flamboyance of Hungary, beating them 2–1 after a late Lev Yashin save, a leap to his left that was 'remarkable for its grace . . . his arms and body in a smooth stretched arc'. At Goodison Park, where the drama was surreally but ecstatically epic, Portugal killed off North Korea 5–3. Scoring with their opening attack, the Koreans were 3–0 ahead in 27 minutes, but behind after an hour. Losing didn't shame them because Eusébio, energetic but composed, instigated the Portuguese comeback. Since the daunting task so obviously did not terrify him, his teammates eventually stopped being terrified of the opposition too.

* * *

At present-day World Cups, the players are hidden behind high walls or fences, sometimes topped with barbed wire, or tucked into remote compounds protected by security guards, often with guns and batons and pepper spray. There is electronic surveillance, too, the see-all, beady eye of CCTV.

Neither technology nor bouncers with thick biceps surrounded the teams of 1966.

In the Peak District, West Germany practised tranquilly beneath the hills. You could stand on the touchline to watch them. Franz

Beckenbauer went horse-riding. Helmut Haller accepted an invitation to eat Sunday lunch with a local family. Uwe Seeler sat on a ball to sign autographs. In rural Cheshire, where Brazil were based, you could get almost as close to Pelé as the defenders who marked him. Often bored, he would go in goal, talking in polite, broken English to whomever gathered around the posts. The Brazilians cycled around the village of Lymm on borrowed bicycles.

The Chileans went regularly to a ten-pin bowling alley in Sunderland. The North Koreans wrote and sang their own patriotic songs, issuing the same press bulletin from their hotel in Middlesbrough every morning: 'We are all fit and very happy.' Though the term 'selfie' had yet to be invented, Lev Yashin smiled and wrapped a long arm around fans posing beside him for a photograph at Durham University, where the Soviets trained.

At Hendon Hall, you could walk into the hotel and hang around the lobby, collecting the England players' autographs. Even Alf Ramsey signed – though with reluctance, sometimes.

The crowds came to watch Pelé kick a ball, but discovered he liked saving shots instead

Ramsey usually had the kind of equilibrium that was difficult to break even with an ice pick. He demonstrated this in ways that were both significant and inconsequential.

Less than a week before the World Cup began, after England had beaten Poland 1–0 in Katowice, Ramsey emerged from the shower dripping and still naked, a towel in his hand. He came face to face with a cleaning woman, who, entirely unperturbed, continued to sweep the dressing room with a long-handled broom, as though a middle-aged man caught in his birthday suit was an everyday hazard to be taken in her stride. Anyone else would have sworn or cursed or blustered. Ramsey, without a blush of emotion, turned to Harold Shepherdson and said: 'How absurd.'

Ramsey was also remarkably unperturbed when, less than two hours before the game against Uruguay, Shepherdson revealed he had forgotten to count England's little red 'passports'. These were identity cards that had to be shown beforehand to the referee. Under FIFA's rules, a player without one wouldn't be allowed to play. Shepherdson, usually meticulous, found seven passports were missing. The police were sent to Hendon Hall to fish them out of various hiding places: jacket pockets, the drawer of a dresser, a suitcase, the shelf in a wardrobe and even someone's spare pair of shoes.

When England reported to Lilleshall – which became known as Stalag Lilleshall to those inside it – Ramsey read out a list of dos and don'ts almost as strict as in a high-security prison. 'Anyone who feels he cannot commit to the rules here can leave now,' he said. He then pointed to the door. 'That is your way out, gentlemen.' One of those house rules was 'no drinking' unless Ramsey permitted it. When Nobby Stiles and Alan Ball were caught breaking that order, Ramsey ripped them to pieces but let them go free; he knew he couldn't do without either of them. He was just as lenient when Stiles and Jack Charlton became locked in a row on the training pitch that had begun trivially, the odd shot of abuse fired, before escalating to the brink of war. Stiles had what he regarded as a 'rough working relationship' with

At the Bank of England's training ground, Alf Ramsey hid the anxiety he
experienced during the competition

Charlton. In mud-slinging contests, the two of them matched one
another clod for clod. Stiles said a 'typical' exchange between them
would be: 'Come on, you little bastard' and 'Fuck off, you big twat.'

No one, not even Stiles and Charlton, was quite sure what lit the
touchpaper of this particular bout, but it revolved around two matches
at the end of the season that didn't concern England: Manchester
United's European Cup semi-final with Partizan and Leeds's Fairs
Cup semi-final against Real Zaragoza. Both Uniteds lost, prompting
Charlton and Stiles to be less than complimentary about each other's performance. 'We were like five-year-old schoolboys,' admitted
Stiles. 'It was a good job we didn't come to blows because I would
have dropped him – if I'd had a stepladder to reach him.'

Assuming the argument was about to tail off, Ramsey allowed
them to trade insults until fisticuffs became a probability. 'I think
that's enough. Let's get this sorted out,' he said, marching them off to

a quiet corner. Geoff Hurst recognised Ramsey's peace-making as 'a great piece of man management'. He explained: 'If he'd cut them off, the resentment would have bubbled. He let them get it out of their system.' Hurst saw it as integral to Ramsey's success. 'If this squabble had not arisen and been allowed to blow itself out, England would not have won the World Cup six weeks later.'

The face Ramsey showed to the world during the build-up to the tournament looked calm and dignified, but he was not temperamentally suited for the celebrity that came with it. It was a daily, hourly grind for him. He saw his wife for only four days in two months. When the closing stages of the World Cup were about to begin, he confessed: 'I did not think the strain would be so great. Even trivial things became a chore, the constant demands for autographs and the hundreds of letters telling me who to play and how to play.' In the days between England's first and second matches, his mail arrived in bulging post-office sacks. He returned from one training session to find three of them stacked in his room; no one knew where else to put them.

Arthur Rowe always thought that Ramsey's 'bland and peaceful exterior' hid 'an absolute cauldron of emotion'. It surfaced twice after the match with Argentina. Firstly, in the photograph in which Ramsey steps between George Cohen and Alberto González and prevents them from swapping shirts. Cohen's hand is still in the sleeve of the shirt. The arm, though, is impossibly stretched, like a piece of India rubber. Secondly, when Ramsey, interviewed by the BBC, infamously branded the Argentinians as 'animals'. A hater of falsity and deceit, he couldn't hold back the swell of his anger. Post-match criticism of any team was out of character for Ramsey, so this was a hint of the stress the tournament was causing him. His choice of the word 'animals' was also so inflammatory that the promise he made alongside it made little impact.

'Our best football will come against the right type of opposition – a team who comes to play football,' he said.

Portugal were about to do just that.

* * *

It took a while for Cupid's arrow to sink in, but the country came to love Nobby Stiles during the World Cup.

Before the tournament he'd received letters that branded him as 'the filthiest player in the Football League'. Out of one envelope slipped a penny. The accompanying note read: 'This is all you are worth.' In the build-up to the semi-final of the 1966 FA Cup at Bolton, another critic wrote: 'Dear Ugly, don't look round when you come down the tunnel at Burnden Park on Saturday because I'm going to bury a hatchet in your head.'

The public's perception of Stiles the player persisted until it learnt more about him as a person, a character with a common touch.

In whatever he did, Stiles was dedicated. Early each morning during the World Cup, he left Hendon Hall and walked briskly 'through nearly empty streets'. He 'loved' the smell of the summer grass and also the sound of birdsong along the route he took to Golders Green. George Cohen claimed that after going into that part of north London, which 'probably had more synagogues than Israel', Stiles returned to admit: 'I found a church, but I'm not sure it was one of mine.' The story stuck because it was funny, which also made it too good to deny. Stiles never minded and played along with it.

Another Catholic church stood closer to England's hotel, but Stiles mostly took Mass at St Edward the Confessor, half an hour away. St Edward, perpendicular Gothic in style, is known as an architectural gem. Its 27ft square, 80ft tall lantern tower rises above the landscape. Inside, there are statues of English saints, placed in niches, and a memorial stained-glass window over the high altar.

Stiles was 'playing out the last acts of boyhood', he explained. It was 'the conclusion of the rite of passage' which began at St Patrick's Church in Collyhurst and led him to pray there for the Busby Babes after Munich. Each night during that July, Stiles said he 'battled with the problem of whether or not' to attend Mass the next day. He felt a 'conflict' between his 'desire to be as well rested as possible' and his 'fear' that changing 'anything' about 'the rhythm of my daily life' would lead to 'all kinds of disaster'. He chided himself for being 'a bit hypocritical at times', because 'if I want something I go to church and ask for it'.

Stiles would wear a knitted shirt and a pair of slacks rather than his tracksuit. 'No one bothered me,' he said. 'People said hello, but they gave you some room of your own, a little space.'

From the back pew at St Edward's, where he always sat, Stiles prayed silently for his family (his wife gave birth to a son during the World Cup). He prayed that he would get through a match with some credit and without getting hurt. He prayed that England would win.

Alf Ramsey was accused of having 'a fixation' with Stiles, his bulldog, and also of being over-loyal towards him. He did it because Stiles was loyal in return, which was a quality no manager or coach could teach.

When Stiles's father made his last appearance for his beloved St Patrick's, he forgot his boots and had to play in a borrowed pair. Nails stuck up inside the soles, but he wore them anyway. The son remembered his father's feet being a 'bleeding mess' afterwards. Stiles played like his father had done in that match, oblivious to pain.

Some considered Stiles too destructive a competitor and accused him of being too susceptible to 'blowing up' under provocation. The prosecution wasn't short of evidence. In the game with Uruguay, he was needled by Pedro Rocha and swung an inept punch at him. In the match with France, he upended Jacques Simon from behind as though committing a street mugging. Watch the clip on YouTube and – while those 80 seconds are blurry – you'll shiver a little at the sight of it. You'll also wonder how the FIFA official, sitting in the stand, recognised the horror of it while the referee didn't. On impact Simon's eyes must have rolled into the back of his head. What the philosopher Thomas Hobbes said about life in the 17th century – 'nasty, brutish and short' – described Stiles in that moment. 'I felt I had to nail him, but not hurt him,' he said. 'I wanted a tackle, a fifty–fifty, that could shake him.' He mistimed the challenge on the wet, skiddy surface, never appreciating the sharpness of Simon's turn. It was a 'terrible, terrible' assault, he confessed. 'I couldn't go and say sorry to him. That would have been hypocritical.' Stiles was so ashamed that he couldn't make another challenge after it. 'I didn't even get involved in the game.'

The next 72 hours were 'like a form of crucifixion' for him, he added. It began on TV. Danny Blanchflower said he was embarrassed by Stiles. From then on, Stiles called him 'the Reverend Danny Blanchflower', thinking his pious reaction stemmed from an afternoon at White Hart Lane when he'd simultaneously taken out Blanchflower, the ball and 'about 3ft of turf' from the pitch.

The Football Association is supposed to have insisted that Ramsey drop Stiles for besmirching England's reputation. Ramsey is supposed to have refused. So staunch was his support for Stiles, he is also supposed to have threatened to resign. Ramsey called the accounts 'exaggerated'. 'There was no pressure on me,' he said, to 'eliminate' Stiles. 'I had complete control of the team and this was never challenged.' The conversation that took place lasted less than a minute. He reminded the FA of the power he'd been given and told them: 'You will not be choosing my team, now or ever.'

Ramsey appeared on the BBC to support Stiles, describing him as a 'great player'. After hearing him say it, Stiles, who had no advance knowledge of the compliment, 'felt the tears coming to my eyes'.

He would have done 'anything' for Ramsey, he said.

* * *

The following exchange has come to define the semi-final against Portugal almost as much as the goals from Bobby Charlton, which gave England their 2–1 win:

Alf Ramsey: I want you to take out Eusébio.
Nobby Stiles: Just for this game or for life?

At least three, slightly conflicting variations of that conversation exist in print – the phrasing is slightly different – but this one endures because, like that story of Stiles confusing a synagogue for a Catholic church, it's the one everyone prefers and so doesn't want to doubt. You're attracted to the black humour and the rapier wit, the flash of repartee. Ramsey and Stiles become a convincing vaudeville act.

Stiles's own version was a little more long-winded and lacks the punchline, which he couldn't recall. 'I don't remember saying that. It is possible – but only as a joke.'

Stiles v. Eusébio is like watching a hawk discreetly following the flight of a butterfly.

An enterprising editor took a 12-minute slice from the match – a Portuguese commentary is dubbed over the English one – so he could break down the contribution Eusébio made and compare it with Bobby Charlton's. The film tells you as much, if not more, about Stiles as it does about both of them. The question of how tight *is* tight bedevils defenders. Too close, and you'll be beaten on the turn or by a quick lay-off or sudden acceleration in pace. Too far away, and the attacker will punish you for every half-yard of space you give him. Stiles did not stick limpet-like to his target. He calculated, as though to the exact quarter of an inch, the distance he needed to be from Eusébio to stifle him. He stood off, giving ground that was soon reclaimed through anticipation. His presence is overbearing. Whenever Eusébio collects the ball, Stiles is waiting to confront him. He polices him along the touchline. He whips the ball away from him. He blocks a run or intercepts a pass. He forces him to go a little deeper than usual to collect possession. 'I was never without support,' Stiles said generously, outlining how England triangulated their defence, squeezing Eusébio into small pockets of space.

Seven of the 14 goals Portugal had scored before the semi-finals belonged to Eusébio. His eighth came from a penalty in the 82nd minute. Portugal were 2–0 down when Jack Charlton threw his fist at a header the way a tired boxer flaps at a punchball.

The night before, West Germany had beaten the Soviet Union 2–1 at Goodison Park, a game spoilt by collisions, fouls and tackling of 'audible ferocity'. What clung to that match was an 'abattoir odour'. Wembley was perfumed. The game flowed. On grass as smooth as glass, England pushed passes about and played expansively, a job done with zest and self-belief. Bobby Charlton flourished. 'That night I felt I could run *all* night,' he said.

He scored in the first half, making his side-footed shot from the edge of the box – through a tangle of players – look as nonchalant as a goal-line tap in. 'If I'd whacked it, I would have missed it,' said Charlton. In the second, he ran on to a short, rolled pass from Geoff Hurst and drilled the ball in.

And yet . . .

In the dying moments, Stiles feared England 'had started to get a bit lost' and became 'too complacent'. The defence, dozing off, let in António Simões. He was ten yards out. The equaliser looked so inevitable that Ramsey was resigned to extra time. 'I felt sure the ball was going to finish in the back of our net . . . It didn't seem possible that anyone could get to him,' he said.

Somehow Stiles stuck the toe of his boot in front of Simões and robbed him of the opening. He called the tackle 'desperate and a little dangerous' because 'a foreign referee was likely to give a penalty' unless he took the ball without taking anything of the man. 'He would have scored, you know,' said Stiles. 'He was a good player and good players don't miss chances like that.'

Ramsey regarded it as one of the best pieces of defending he had ever seen. 'I cannot think of another player in the world who would have saved the situation. It made me realise what a tremendous asset he was to me.'

* * *

On the eve of the World Cup final, Alf Ramsey is asked yet again: will England win? For the first time since 1963, Ramsey doesn't know how to answer. He folds his arms and freezes. His eyelashes flutter. Finally, after a second or two, he says, 'Yes,' but it comes out with an agonising slowness.

You'd think each letter of the word had burnt his lips.

11

GET OFF YOUR ARSES

One of the most evocative photographs of the World Cup final is rarely seen and seldom mentioned. It was taken inside the tunnel less than 15 minutes before kick-off.

We can summon at will and without effort so many of the scenes from Wembley, shuffling them like cards before our eyes. We know them as well as the pictures in our own family album. But this intimate photo, a still image grabbed from film that Pathé News shot, is treasurable because it flirts with your imagination.

You get only the back view of the players, but your mind automatically conjures up their faces, each in their Dorian Gray-like prime.

The teams are walking up the slight concrete slope that links the dressing rooms to the wide cinder apron of the pitch. Anyone who was fortunate enough to stand at the bottom of the tunnel in the old Wembley will remember how gloomy it could be there and also how cold it felt, even on a balmy day. It was rather like being stuck in a hole. The darkness made the huge rectangle of light at the far end seem intensely inviting, pulling you towards it. The tunnel was slightly claustrophobic too, just sufficiently wide for the teams to go out shoulder to shoulder without bumping into one another. The crop of this photograph, deliberately tight, cleverly gives you a sense of that. You feel as though you're among the players, a participant rather than a spectator.

You see the white number 16 on Martin Peters's shirt and the black number 10 on Siegfried Held's. Ahead of Peters is Bobby Charlton. Ahead of Held is Franz Beckenbauer. None of the players nearest to the camera can see the whole of the pitch yet, only a sliver of the vivid grass that lies ahead. They are still a dozen steps from experiencing the beautiful noise of the crowd too, a blast of warm, sticky air and all the glazed brightness of the day.

Each player stares fixedly ahead. No one meets another's eye, as if each is afraid a sideways glance might betray something about their own state of mind.

In the far distance is the long curve of the stands and the squat, skeletal floodlights stuck on top of them. In the foreground is the crossbar of the nearest goal and the pale spidery web of the net. Flanked on either side of the mouth of the tunnel are fans with silk flags, creased and flapping in the summer breeze. The sky, which takes up more than half of the picture, is the colour of milk. The weather is being contrary; brief showers, some of them quite hard, interrupt the sunshine.

Whenever we remember the final we are instinctively carried to its end rather than the beginning. But this photograph captures the moment *before*, the prelude to everything, which makes it so valuable. You could have memorised every damn detail about the final but still take from this beguiling photo the sense of immense possibility; the idea that *anything* could be about to happen – or not; that somehow a game played decades ago is about to begin again, and just for a second or two you aren't quite certain who will win it.

You find it impossible not to speculate about what everyone is thinking. You know they want the formalities, the pageantry and the anthems to be over quickly. You know each player is telling himself not to make a hash of things; no soft, terrible mistake like Moacir Barbosa's for Brazil in 1950. You know they're all daring to believe that fate might anoint them as the hero, a match-winner like Helmut Rahn in Switzerland in 1954, or Pelé in Sweden in 1958, or his unlikely goal-scoring understudy, Amarildo, in Chile four years later. You also know they're trying to bury their butterfly nerves, disguising every flutter.

If the photograph came with thought-bubbles, this is what we'd see:

That George Cohen is experiencing a 'feeling of finality' and one recurring thought: 'By Christ, I hope I play well.'

That, despite half a dozen cups of tea, Jack Charlton's throat is parched; he feels as though he's swallowed a sheet of sandpaper.

That his brother Bobby is thinking about how closely he will chaperone Beckenbauer. That Beckenbauer is thinking about how closely he will chaperone Charlton.

That, after repeatedly throwing a ball against the tunnel wall and catching it again in his pale grey gloves, Gordon Banks is cursing the rain. He prefers to play in bare hands, sticky chewing gum coating his fingers and palms – a tip learnt from Lev Yashin. He is conscious of 'a band playing . . . somewhere in the distance', the drums and brass peculiarly muffled.

That Bobby Moore, staring at the shallow archipelago of puddles on the concourse, is relieved it is wet because passes will 'zip a little' now, the pitch as fast as waxed linoleum. He thinks the German flags outnumber England's. He hears only the blare of German klaxons and not the clack-clack of English rattles.

That Nobby Stiles is constantly turning over the same, confused, jumbled thoughts; they came to him in church that morning. He is thinking about 'all the days that had gone before' which 'brought me' to this one.

That Alan Ball is re-reading in his mind the four-word telegram from his father that was waiting for him in the dressing room: 'Be magic little man.' Ball has one fear: 'That my good fortune will not last.' Though not 'a religious person in any sense of the word', he is praying to God as fervently as Stiles did hours before.

The absence of someone in a photograph can be as important as their presence. Only Geoff Hurst's left collarbone is visible. His head and the rest of his lean body is obscured. But because you know this day, his greatest, will shape every other in his life afterwards, you're compelled to search for him. The night before, Hurst had turned sleeplessly in his bed, playing and replaying the match across the ceiling. Now, about to go into the great bowl of the stadium, he feels the hairs on the nape of his neck stiffen. 'It was like walking into the blast of a fire.'

* * *

Even those who don't call themselves football fans are able to identify the World Cup final. The game is the equivalent of a landmark building everyone can name or one of those landscape paintings, famous even if you've never seen it hung in a gallery because endless reproductions decorate biscuit tins or chocolate boxes.

Like the biographies of great men, the facts of their lives so overfamiliar to us, you'd think almost all there is to know about the game *is* already known. The 4–2 scoreline, of course; the goals and the time of each of them; the goal-scorers; England's cadmium red shirts; the pitch, as smoothly trim and verdantly green as the lawns of Hampton Court Palace; the dingy grey of the stadium; the tableau of outstretched legs, grimacing faces and half-closed eyes as the West Germans equalise, the seconds slipping away; the ball thudding against the underside of the bar and coming down again, the making of an unresolved controversy; the exhaustion; the pain; the tears; the glory; the glint of the gold trophy; the lap of honour.

In any game, though, there are always 'what ifs', largely forgotten afterwards.

In this one, the 'what ifs' are abundant. They loop over, below and wind around one another like the strings of a cat's cradle. Without them – and without extra time – history would treat the final less reverentially. It would be an ordinary, even slightly scruffy affair, lacking much of a climax.

Those 'what ifs' begin as early as the 12th minute.

What if Ray Wilson, jittery under what he described as a 'Fourth Division ball', floated in exploratorily by Sigi Held, hadn't dropped his 'marshmallow' header towards Helmut Haller, as though presenting him with an unwrapped gift?

As England were about to set off from Hendon Hall, Denis Follows – still unable to recognise one full back from the other – said to Wilson: 'Good luck, George.' Wilson accepted Follows's handshake without correcting him.

The man who was George believed his friend Ray could normally

Ray Wilson (right) celebrates winning the 1966 FA Cup final, hugging teammate Alex Scott

have played 'in a collar and tie' and a pair of dress shoes without noticeably impairing the level of his performance. Only ten weeks before,
Wilson had won the FA Cup in one of the ancient competition's most
inspiring finals. Everton, two goals down to Sheffield Wednesday in 57
minutes, were 3–2 ahead after 74. He knew Wembley better than his
own front yard. On any other day, Wilson in his isolation would have
nonchalantly nodded the ball away or let it drift harmlessly behind
him. His mistake triggered another. Jack Charlton was caught in a
'split second of mental hesitation'; he was unsure about whether to
block Haller's under-hit shot or let Banks safely gather it. Charlton
dithered and stepped in front of Banks, unsighting him. The ball
bobbled past the goalkeeper before he could properly stretch for it.
Charlton 'dare not look' at Gordon Banks. Wilson can't look at either
of them. England's two oldest players – combined age 63 – have made
novice miscalculations. As Wilson admits: 'I'd committed the cardinal
sin of not attacking the ball . . . If I'd been younger, the mistake would
probably have destroyed me.'

   What if Helmut Schön hadn't made a tactical mistake?

   Schön sacrifices too much German creativity by forcing Franz
Beckenbauer to bind himself to Bobby Charlton. The decision stems
from his shaking fear of the hurt Charlton can inflict. Being stolidly
pragmatic costs Schön the romantic heart of his team. Able to go only
where Charlton goes, Beckenbauer becomes like a younger brother
hanging around his older sibling. 'Bobby? Fancy a trip to the corner
flag?' he once flippantly asked, desperate for a respite from the monot-
ony of marking him.

   *What if Schön had chosen neither Hans Tilkowski nor Horst-Dieter
Höttges?*

   Tilkowski is constantly running his right hand over his left shoulder,
injured in the semi-final. The pills he takes beforehand only slightly
dull his pain. Schön sticks with Tilkowski only because the goalkeeper's deputies – including a 22-year-old Sepp Maier – are considered too
inexperienced to replace him. Even fully fit, Tilkowski is vulnerable to

high crosses, corners and free kicks. With his bruised shoulder, he is a liability. In the ninth minute, Geoff Hurst, aware of Tilkowski's discomfort, body-checks him legitimately in mid-air. Tilkowski becomes groggy, his eyes vacant and his mouth full of blood, like a boxer who has succumbed to a sucker punch.

Höttges, his tendon strapped but sore to the touch, frets about whether he is fit enough to play at all. The blame for England's equaliser, six minutes after Haller's goal, belongs to both him and Tilkowski. When Bobby Moore takes two slightly stuttering strides before languidly clipping his free kick towards Hurst, there is no explanation – except gross incompetence – for the room the England striker gets. Höttges is four yards adrift of the position he ought to be in; he has gone to sleep while standing upright. Tilkowski is glued to his line, as though afraid of another battering.

Höttges is also at fault for England's second goal in the 78th minute. At the very point at which Alan Ball's out-swinging corner reaches the top of its flight, the Germans have nine defenders in the box and another in the D. There's a half-clearance, the corner skimming off Wolfgang Weber's head . . . an attempt to charge down the rebound that Hurst seizes . . . and then Höttges, who has enough time and sufficient protection to kill the ball dead, topples backwards while making a flailing, sliced clearance with his left foot. It spins towards Martin Peters . . .

What if Roger Hunt had been on form?

In the 87th minute, Ball sends the simplest of short inside passes to Hunt, who has half the field to run into. The Germans, opened as easily as a tin can, are over-stretched; only Willie Schulz guards Tilkowski. Bobby Charlton, galloping almost parallel with Hunt, begs for the ball. If Hunt finds him, the game is over. He delays, clinging to possession three seconds too long before miscuing the pass. Hunt's inadequacy in that brief but crucial half-minute typifies what has gone before for him. Ball is always searching for Hunt's 'backside', the size of which, he said, meant it 'wasn't difficult to find'. Against the Germans, though, he seldom sees it. Hunt roams the pitch like a lost dog. He doesn't impose himself on the match at all; he's out of step with the tempo of it. He'd been tasked with pushing up on the sweeper, admitting at half-time to Ramsey: 'I'm not getting a kick.' The occasion and the atmosphere seem 'so unreal' to him. He can't 'take it all in', he admits. In the closing minutes of the first half, Hunt found himself with a close-range, angled chance. He pushed it so tamely at Tilkowski that Peters, unable to suppress the thought, lamented the absence of Jimmy Greaves. 'What would Jimmy have done with a chance like that?' he asked himself.

What if Jack Charlton had not challenged Sigi Held?

When Peters scored his goal, Charlton was on his right shoulder, expecting the ballooning deflection off Höttges to come to him. Afraid he would send any shot 'over the bar', Charlton's first reaction was the unpoetic 'Oh, shit.' A similar response arrives, unbidden, whenever you see Charlton's challenge on Held in the last minute. It is needless, reckless, blatantly stupid. Charlton doesn't have to topple into Held; he merely has to stand off him. Held is facing his own goal. Even if he'd taken the ball down, his options were almost non-existent. When Charlton makes contact with Held, his body is almost horizontal. His boots are three feet off the ground. His left elbow is planted into Held's back. With loudmouth irritation, Charlton has complained about nearly every decision given against him in the final – even this one – but he is caught bang to rights, a victim of his own impatience. Moore couldn't contain his anger. 'Don't ever fucking do that again,' he shouted. 'It was the only time,' said Charlton 'that Bobby ever swore at me.'

What if England had put only four, rather than five, players in the defensive wall?

However powerful and accurate Loather Emmerich's left foot might have been, he wouldn't have beaten Banks from 30 yards unless his shot travelled and then dipped at fantastic speed. No one got a ball past him from that kind of distance. Banks, however, is over-cautious. He decides he needs five players to guard his goal. Nobby Stiles arranges the wall. He pulls and pushes it, like someone trying to drag a pantomime horse on to a stage. The rest is farce: Emmerich's drive ricocheting off Cohen to a grateful Held . . . Held's feeble drive becoming a cross after grazing the back of Karl-Heinz Schnellinger . . . the ball drifting past the goalmouth . . . Uwe Seeler, amid a traffic jam of players, straining to reach it first . . . Weber unmarked at the far post because England have thrown too many players into the wall and now have too few inside the box. The goal, so late it almost counts as posthumous, would have psychologically reduced to rubble 95 per cent of teams.

Arthur Rowe defined what made a truly 'great' manager: 'It isn't only what he knows about football, but what he knows about men,' he said.

What if Alf Ramsey hadn't possessed that quality?

Here is the most significant 'what if' of all.

* * *

Arthur Hopcraft was sitting among the crowd at Wembley, rather than in the press box. He longed for the atmosphere he usually found on the Kop or at Villa Park. Hopcraft heard men 'with Home Counties accents' and 'obsolete prejudices' who spoke their opinions in 'decently educated voices of ignorance'. Some of them were unable to identify England's players. He suspected these 'fans' had bought their tickets to 'see the successors of the Battle of Britain pilots whack the Hun again'. Waiting for extra time to begin, Hopcraft registered the sense of deflation around Wembley. The fear England would lose was palpable among those who could not bear the prospect of defeat against *the Germans*.

It was impossible to escape the feeling – however implicit – that the World Cup was a coda to the Second World War. In that morning's *Daily Mail*, the columnist Vincent Mulchrone was aware of it too. He began his piece with the sentence: 'If Germany beat us this afternoon at our national sport, we can always console ourselves that we have recently beaten them twice at theirs.' Like Hopcraft's neighbours in the stadium, you'd have thought Mulchrone was about to revel in his clever observation before defending it.

He was not.

Only 18 months before, Mulchrone had produced a line of verse to describe the scenes at Sir Winston Churchill's funeral: 'Two rivers run silently through London tonight, and one is made of people.' He summoned as much style to denounce jingoism too. The World Cup, he said, had 'encroached more deeply into the inward-looking British temperament than any international event since the one we know now as the Second World War. Indeed, it has been war. And a very valuable little war too, if only because it showed us how nationalism can raise its idiot cry over a cowhide.' Mulchrone denounced the 'partisanship' he'd felt and witnessed around him: 'Housewives who went all Greer Garson' . . . 'children who were being brought up as woolly-minded internationalists' . . . and anyone 'half-stoned out of their Rule Britannia minds' at England's results.

In the 1960s, it was possible to walk into W. H. Smith's and find 'war' comics fighting old battles, their covers plastered with phrases such as 'Take that, Kraut' or 'Knife for a Nazi' and illustrations of either a swastika or the lightning bolts of the Waffen SS. The war shadowed nearly every life, even some of those who were involved at Wembley. Martin Peters's father-in-law lost his parents, three sisters and his brother-in-law to a direct hit from a bomb. Nobby Stiles was born in a cellar during a Luftwaffe raid; his mother was too scared to flee the shelter, letting her friends become midwives. Jack Charlton remembered hiding under the stairs in Ashington, covering his ears against the sound of the explosions. Bobby Moore was only four days old when Barking Power Station, where his father worked, was targeted.

No one, though, was more sensitive about the war than Helmut Schön. The appearance and behaviour of his team in England became 'essential' to him 'at all times', said Hans Tilkowski. By his own admission, the idea of *Heldentod* (the hero's death) had not appealed to Schön during the war. He worked in the marketing department of a pharmaceutical company. In his last game for Dresden, he was jeered by the crowd, who claimed he was *kriegsverwendungsfahig* (fit for service). In October 1944, Schön was conscripted as a grenadier into Dresden's *Volkssturm* (the People's Army), but discharged after three weeks to distribute medical supplies. He nevertheless got to show the sort of cold courage that those of us who have never been close to combat wonder if we possess too.

Dresden was called 'the German Florence' because of its art and baroque architecture: the decorative pavilions of Augustus the Strong's Zwinger Palace; the Semper Gallery within it – the palatial home for old masters such as Rembrandt and Raphael; and the sumptuous dome of the Frauenkirche. Schön's 87-year-old father, an art dealer, insisted the Allies would never bomb Dresden. They were 'too civilised' and the city was 'too beautiful' to be destroyed.

On February 13, 1945, the RAF and the United States Army Air Forces arrived.

Schön was an air-raid warden, stationed at a factory nine miles away, when the three-night apocalypse began. He heard the aircraft approaching but thought Leipzig or Berlin might be their destination. He then saw what were incongruously called the 'Christmas Trees', the flares that identified bombing targets. These looked 'so peaceful and dream-like but terrifying' to him. More than 4,000 tons of explosive created a firestorm that roared across streets of brick and sandstone and wood. Seven months later, the photographer Richard Peter borrowed a camera, scrambled on to the roof of the Wiederaufbau Neues Rathaus and crouched beside a robed statue. His photo, *Allegory of Goodness*, is horrific. The city far below is burnt, blown-out, skeletal. The land is as craterous as the moon. Schön drove through the inferno, finding his wife in a shelter. Five days later, he found his father too, sitting amid still-smoking rubble. Schön looked at the blackened bodies of women still holding their children – he compared them to 'Egyptian mummies' – and saw 'dead men everywhere'.

One German commentator in 1966 criticised the English press for being 'tin soldiers', adding words such as 'troops' and 'storming' into their reports or using phrases like 'advancing on' or 'military-style', as though creating an image of a panzer division. Alf Ramsey, who admired Schön, never referred to the war in his team talks before the final or during it. He made no reference to it afterwards either. Ramsey always rated 'dignity' as 'a very important quality'. He thought it was 'sadly lacking in a lot of people'. But Schön, he knew, possessed it.

The television coverage of today's football is as obsessed about managers as it is about players – if not more so. There is no hiding place for them. The cut-away reaction shot towards the technical area is done as automatically as the director's pressing of the rewind button as soon as a goal is scored or whenever a decision requires a review. How a manager responds – and what his character tells us about him – personalises the game and is integral to the melodrama. It wasn't so in 1966. During the World Cup final, you hardly glimpse Ramsey or Schön until extra time begins. You don't see what Schön called the 'respectful glances' he and Ramsey exchanged. Nor do you see the two of them, after Wolfgang Weber's goal, turn to one another 'with their arms outstretched', each giving a 'shrug' of their shoulders. To Schön, the sign language silently conveyed the message 'What can you do? That's football.'

When Weber scored, Schön's first thought was a most curious one. 'I wondered what the Queen thought,' he said.

* * *

Like a tangle of ivy, so many myths and misconceptions grew around Alf Ramsey and the 1966 World Cup that it became impossible to get at the truth beneath them. Some – even the most fanciful – are still repeated today.

'You've won it once. Now go and win it again.'

We should always be suspicious of smart remarks unless they come from recognised speech-makers. Ramsey was no Winston Churchill. What he's reputed to have said before extra time began was nonetheless rousingly Churchillian, which is why it became famous, passing into established fact. What Ramsey actually said was: 'You've let it slip once. Don't let it slip again.' The repetition of 'slip' doesn't chime as well as 'won' and 'win', the authentic sentences losing a little of the polish and punch of the fictional one. But it wasn't those lines that ought to be chiselled on a bronze plaque, but two others.

George Cohen thought that playing at Wembley was like 'running on several layers of lush carpet'. The dense weave of the Cumberland grass made it 'about two yards slower' than any other pitch, but paradoxically the ball travelled 'two yards faster' compared to anywhere else. A player felt the pull of the turf on his legs, especially in his calves. When Ramsey walked on to the pitch before extra time, he found some of his team sitting on it. He looked across at the Germans, many of whom were lying on their backs like sunbathers in a park. Ramsey's instruction to his team was:

'Get off your arses. They'll think you're knackered . . . Look at them. They are knackered.'

Ramsey did his sums. In the last quarter of an hour of the second half, England should have won the game 3–1 or 4–1. The Germans ought to have been 'paralysed' because 'so often we had more attackers than they had defenders', he said. At half-time, the match poised at 1–1, Ramsey said no more in the dressing room than: 'You've played well, but you can play better. If you do, you'll win.' He now thought England, despite being in command, had been guilty of making 'vital mistakes' and failing to 'take advantage of our footballing ability'. Outwardly, he was calmly professional, relaxed without being arrogantly confident. Inwardly, he was seething. 'I was absolutely furious because I knew how many chances of scoring we had missed. But I knew I must not show my anger. I also knew that I must not indicate, either by word or expression, the least bit of sympathy for the team because they had to go on playing. I knew they could do it. They knew they could do it. But even a casual "hard luck" might have put doubt in their minds.'

Ramsey held England together with language, delivered with the stiffest of upper lips. His composure was extraordinary. Harold Shepherdson, glancing at his watch, thought only four seconds of the match remained when Wolfgang Weber's shot struck the net. Others calculated time was up before the ball reached him. Unarguable is this fact: there were only 39.88 seconds between Weber's equaliser and the whistle, which means that Ramsey – while rising from the bench and taking 14 strides on to the pitch – had less than a minute to decide what to say and how to say it.

Here are another two 'what ifs':

What if Ramsey had used the wrong words and the wrong tone?
What if he'd looked as crestfallen and angry as he felt?

* * *

Watch the BBC's coverage of the game again in its entirety and you'll notice a few things that are often overlooked.

Some of them are trivial.

The hole in the West German flag flying from Wembley's Twin Towers and also the wind that sends it flapping like a galleon's sail.

How easily the pitch becomes scarred. It had been drenched in one downpour after another during the previous 48 hours and got soaked all over again that afternoon.

The weak sun, which occasionally breaks through and casts watery shadows, before the clouds crack and slide off, filling the stadium with strong, warm light.

The way the full backs always protect the posts at corners.

The fact the referee, Gottfried Dienst, is so fallibly human, confusing fair tackling for fouls – and vice versa.

You'll also realise something important. While Geoff Hurst is the principal character, he is not the star performer. In fact, despite his goals, he is only the third-best England player on the field.

* * *

After Alf Ramsey left him out of the second and third group games, a distraught Alan Ball telephoned his father. This was the crux of their conversation:

Son: I'm coming home.
Father: Fight for your place like a man.

In a horrible huff, thinking his World Cup was over, Ball shot off to a bookmaker's, backed a long-shot horse and won £50. He brought the cash, paid in five-pound notes, back to his room and spread it on the carpet in front of Nobby Stiles. He did a dance, circling his winnings, while singing a song out of tune. The lyrics comprised only three words:

Fuck Alf Ramsey.

Stiles watched him, saying nothing but aware that his friend's escape to the bookies, like his reaction to it afterwards, was not a defiant act but one of inarticulate despair. 'He wasn't kidding me,' said Stiles. 'I only had to look at his face to know inside he was breaking up.' Ball was 'a moping, walking nightmare', his mind a mess. He believed his World Cup was over. 'There was no way I could get back in,' he said. He was wrong; Ball was reprieved, saved from his misery, for both the quarter-finals and the semis.

Only 21 years and 79 days old when he faced the West Germans, Ball was the last to learn he'd been picked. The news was only given to him on Saturday morning. Every other player, bar one, was told the day before – the confirmation given privately to him, either after training or that evening when Ramsey trooped them off to the Hendon Odeon to watch *Those Magnificent Men in Their Flying Machines*, a 138-minute, tediously overlong comedy about the pioneering age of aviation (Ramsey considered it to be 'the greatest film I ever saw' – though perhaps this was his defence against a charge of unnecessarily inflicting suffering on his own team).* One of the many World Cup myths, springing up as a result of the delay in letting Ball know of his selection, is that Ramsey thought Jimmy Greaves would be fit. That is nonsense. Ramsey decided to pick an unchanged team on his way back to the hotel after the semi-final. While Greaves was tested during a midweek practice match on Arsenal's training pitch at Colney – an elaborate stretching exercise for all of England's reserves – Ramsey did not dwell on him. He did, however, want to confuse Helmut Schön. Ramsey convinced himself – wrongly – that Schön believed Greaves would play and had consequently devised an intricate tactical trap for him.

It was merely sound management to hold Ball in suspense. If Ball had known he would be playing the night before, Ramsey judged that he would have become too hyperactive to sleep and would have started bouncing off the walls.

He certainly bounced around Wembley.

Ball described the match as 'the most instinctive' performance he ever gave. He followed no prearranged pattern, stuck to no orders. 'I just worked and ran.' Ball barely stopped to take a breath; he was always in motion. He switched from one touchline to the other or frequently started a move and then contributed to it again 60 or even 70 yards further on. On occasions, Ball was so animated, so frantic, that he made some of the players around him seem like still-life objects. He went on seven dribbling sprees, created six chances and won five free kicks.

* Bobby Charlton was clearly very bored. Afterwards, he said the team had gone to see *The Blue Max*, a film about a First World War German fighter pilot. It was not shown in Hendon that week.

Only the incomparable Bobby Moore surpassed Ball's performance. 'Stand big,' Moore was told as he learnt to become a defender.
No one stood bigger than him at Wembley. He dominated the pitch.

A West Ham fan was once stupefied to find himself welcomed into
Moore's company. His questions elicited a series of humble replies, the
last of which directly referred to his modesty. 'When you're good at
something you don't have to tell everyone about it,' explained Moore.
His performance at Wembley proved that. It was something as near to
perfection as you will ever see. Goodness, he was good. The final gave
us the quintessential Moore, the player Ramsey called the 'greatest' he
ever knew 'in terms of reading the game'. He read that final as though
he'd already seen or played in it the afternoon before. The 'touch map'
for Moore reveals he covered two-thirds of the pitch. He stroked 64
successful passes, some with scientific exactitude. His passing accuracy
was an astonishing 93 per cent. He made 17 'ball recoveries' and six
clearances, often stealing possession back with the courtesy of Raffles
stealing jewellery. Of course, he also made two of England's goals.

Statistics are cold things. The privilege was not so much in totting
up what he did, like an accountant dealing with figures, but watching
how he did it. He takes distinguished responsibility without grand-
standing; everything is done, serenely and at his own pace, with a
certainty of purpose. The TV viewer is drawn to Moore because he
commands nearly every scene. In the opening minutes, Karl-Heinz
Schnellinger strikes an arching, 50-yard pass upfield. Moore, despite
the presence of Uwe Seeler, stretches out his right foot and draws
the ball towards him as though nothing is at stake and no one need
worry. In the closing minutes, Moore decides to duel with Wolfgang
Weber in England's box when anyone else would have kicked the
ball between the Twin Towers. He beats Weber to it, shakes him off,
shields possession and turns back towards his own goal-line, giving
a George Best-like shimmy. He dummies to go to his left while swiv-
elling to his right. Moore, avoiding Weber again, finally flicks a short
pass to Martin Peters with the outside of his boot.

In between, Moore is guileful in his positioning, his interceptions and the way he creates almost as much as he defends. He makes the most crucial tackle of the final, a piece of work not found in many match reports afterwards because the game gave reporters too much to write about. With four minutes to go before half-time, the match poised at 1–1, Lothar Emmerich breaks from 45 yards out, vaulting over a tackle from Jack Charlton and clearing a route to goal for himself that is of motorway-like width. Moore not only moves across the pitch as fast as his slow legs will take him, but he also makes a sliding tackle so well timed, so immaculate, that he dispossesses Emmerich and passes to George Cohen at the same time.

Moore was the only player whom Ramsey didn't quietly drag aside and swear to secrecy about his selection, as if afraid Schön had bugged every room and all the telephones. 'If Bobby Moore didn't know he was playing without me telling him so, he's not the Bobby Moore I know,' he explained.

In paying him that compliment, Ramsey offered Moore an apology without anyone noticing it. Only a month before, Norman Hunter had played in the first game of England's tour of Scandinavia. Ramsey weighed up the possibility of continuing with Hunter, dropping Moore and appointing Bobby Charlton as captain. Moore was on trial. In retrospect, the idea seems madly inconceivable, as though Ramsey had lost his senses, but his mood then reflected the sometimes edgy relationship between them in the past.

* * *

Alf Ramsey saw himself as parenting his side as devotedly as a single father. In England's family, however, he looked on Bobby Moore as a prodigal son. The two of them admired one another without being perfectly compatible in a decade that, like no other before, made generational differences stark. As Ramsey saw it, Moore was over-fond of the tinsel and glamour of the 1960s, which wasn't always compatible with the responsibilities demanded of an England captain. There were silences, suspicions, fallings-out and reconciliations. Moore had once protested, like a rebel shop steward, about what he considered to be Ramsey's overbearing and too strenuous training methods before and during the Little World Cup. Ramsey bided his time. As punishment for what he perceived as a botched mutiny, he delayed naming Moore as captain for the first two internationals of 1964–5. Peace talks had to take place between them; Moore buckled to Ramsey's will before being forgiven.

Moore was always grateful to him for what came next. Anyone who asked Moore 'How are you?' would get the same reply: 'All is well.' He continued to say it even in the late autumn and winter of that same season.

He awoke one morning with what his wife Tina, who was seven months pregnant, described as a 'yelp'. Her husband was doubled up beside her. Moore pretended – as he did for the rest of his life – that his 'twinge of pain' was the consequence of a 'minor groin injury'. Within 24 hours of seeing a doctor, Moore had surgery for testicular cancer. Even those journalists who knew that one of Moore's testicles had been removed didn't report that fact; they believed an opponent's high tackle had made his operation necessary and urgent. The headlines accompanying their stories – 'Surgeons Decide Moore's Future' – were factually correct, but the content beneath them didn't come close to the truth. Moore's refusal to share it was entirely understandable. In the 1960s, cancer was a taboo subject – the unmentionable. Suffering from it could be socially isolating, the disease considered to be a death sentence. Moore played for West Ham again within three months. Ramsey was solicitous, kind and positively supportive. 'When he knows he has your loyalty, you see a different side to him,' said Moore.

Though he did not mean to do it, Moore also created upheaval immediately before the World Cup. Despite the silverware West Ham had won, and also despite the kudos Ron Greenwood gleaned from it, the club got stuck in the league, never contenders for the championship. In six seasons, West Ham only twice finished above halfway. Moore feared the team under Greenwood was 'going on the blink'. He wanted an increase in salary from £80 a week to £100 and a £10,000 signing-on fee, which Tottenham were prepared to give him. Greenwood refused to allow him to leave under 'any circumstances'. In a move made accidentally on purpose, he sneaked out news of Moore's unrest and stripped him of the captaincy in early April. The leak – premeditated intimidation – showed where the power between club and player still lay. Moore's contract expired on June 30. Ramsey had to dispatch Moore and Greenwood into a room at Hendon Hall to sign a month-long deal, enabling Moore to play in the finals. That piece of paper, which Greenwood whisked away, ought to be classified as a document of national importance and placed behind glass in the British Museum.

As Ramsey said: 'If people say England would not have won the World Cup without me as manager, I can say it would have been impossible without Bobby Moore.'

* * *

The film *Goal!* doesn't follow the narrative you'd expect when documenting the final. It begins not with the players but with one of the groundsmen. You find him at 7.30am, climbing the concrete steps into the stadium, a jangling set of keys in one hand. He is wearing an old tweed jacket and a brown trilby, placed at a natty slant, as though he's Frank Sinatra about to do a gig at Carnegie Hall. With those keys, he unlocks a small green door beside a row of turnstiles.

Wembley is open for business.

For a minute or two, he takes a seat on the red bench that Alf Ramsey will occupy that afternoon and looks around the pitch. In the Royal Box, typed place cards are being laid on every velvet seat. So are tartan blankets, ready to protect the dignitaries from the possibility of a chill. Chrysanthemums – a great blast of yellows and reds – are arranged as decoration.

Goal! also goes inside the England dressing room, where cheap wire coat hangers are being slipped into each red jersey and stuck on the pegs, their white numbers facing the camera.

You even see what – with hindsight – is one of the most affecting little scenes of the day. The ground staff begin assembling the goal at the tunnel end. A roll of netting appears, along with the posts, the stanchions and the crossbar. The crossbar is balanced on the shoulders of two workers and wobbles a bit. Next, you see one of the grounds-men on the top step of a ladder, taking the weight of the crossbar. He very carefully lowers it on to the iron rod protruding from the top of the left-hand post. He snaps them together, connecting bar to post as snugly as two pieces of a jigsaw. No commentary accompanies this. The makers of *Goal!* considered adding one – and even wrote a paragraph for it – but then decided to let the audience realise the significance of it for themselves. This is the crossbar Geoff Hurst will belt the ball against in the 102nd minute. Watching the frame of the goal being put together in the early morning gives you an appreciation of how well it held together in the late afternoon.

That goal? Everyone knows it so well.

Alan Ball, his socks jammed around his ankles, crossing low for Hurst . . . Hurst moving on to it with a surprising litheness . . . The shot, the force of it unbalancing him . . . The crack of the ball against the underside of the bar . . . Roger Hunt, the prime eyewitness, on the half-turn, his right hand raised in appeal. Much of what Hunt did went uncredited – but not this. His is the first voice to claim the goal, and his body language is confident and persuasive. When Hunt went back to the halfway line, Jack Charlton was waiting for him. 'Was it a good 'un?' yelled Charlton. Like an angler exaggerating the size of his catch, Hunt spread out his hands a yard apart and winked at him.

You can't excoriate the referee for giving England the benefit of the doubt. The linesman, Tofiq Bahramov, made Gottfried Dienst's decision for him. He did so from a position that was not as clear as Hunt's and nowhere near as close; Bahramov was almost level with the edge of the six-yard box. You can't blame him either. Every photograph published then or since, plus nearly every foot of film, hasn't settled in almost 60 years the issue that he and Dienst had barely 60 seconds to think about.

There is a photograph, taken from the stands, that belongs in the category of magnificent optical illusions: the ball looks as though it is about to land at least two feet over the line. Others, taken from almost parallel with the posts, suggest it will fall short by an inch or two – unless the rules of geometry change in the last yard of its descent. The TV pictures are next to useless. The BBC had just seven cameras at Wembley: two on the gantry, one on the stadium's west side, another in front of the scoreboard and one in 'The Pit', which was a pitch-side 'hole' beyond the touchline; there were also cameras planted behind each goal. Even *Goal!*, which seemed to put lenses everywhere, didn't have a camera in a place where the evidence could be definitive. The only reel of film worth examining belongs to Movietone. Their commentary is as distinctly neutral as Switzerland. After explaining what all the fuss was about, Movietone passes no judgement but suggests: 'Another angle may help you decide for yourself.' Hey presto,

From this angle, Geoff Hurst's shot looks to have dropped well over the line. The camera is lying

it provides pictures taken flush on the goal-line. Go through them frame by frame, stop when appropriate, and play spot the ball. Those who still believe the whole of it crossed the line need to book an optician's appointment.

No, it wasn't a goal, but the debate about it will never end satisfactorily. Most of us don't want to know whether it was legitimate because not knowing preserves the mystery and the cult status of the final.*

* * *

While Nobby Stiles was waiting for extra time to begin, he trotted past Franz Beckenbauer, who was still sitting on the grass. Beckenbauer 'smiled broadly' at him, in a manner Stiles considered to be conceited and condescending. He thought Beckenbauer had convinced himself that England were broken, too exhausted and demoralised to win. But the effect of another half-hour's effort on the body was more apparent in the West Germans. Their limbs were heavy. Their breathing came in gasps. Their attempts to break down England were so paltry that Gordon Banks was never stretched. He had only to punch away one corner and receive a shot that dribbled feebly into his gloves. Germany's efforts, as the clock ticked away, were acts of quiet desperation. Indeed, Beckenbauer symbolised the Germans' draining physical strength. He could run into England's half, but – lacking surplus energy – he had to walk or canter back into his own. In contrast, Alan Ball, buzzing effervescently, had enough mileage left in his legs to play until Sunday night.

These 30 minutes, like the previous 90, belong to Geoff Hurst, but once again are really about Ball and, especially, Bobby Moore.

In the few seconds that remain, Moore, lordly in his step, takes down on his chest a tired, punted ball from Willi Schulz and brings

---

* Yes, I know. In 2016, technology supposedly 'proved' that Geoff Hurst's shot crossed the line. I don't believe it.

it out of the box after an exchange of passes. He does this so casually, his approach almost blasé, that it boggles the mind. Jack Charlton
is shouting at Moore to 'kick the fucking thing anywhere'. Any other
defender on God's earth would have done it; Moore ignored the
advice the way a stage performer ignores a heckler.

Here is the final 'what if':

*What if Moore had held on to the ball or thrashed it towards the West
German corner flag?*

The pass he plays to Hurst instead, which only he sees, contains
within it something of the whole essence of his brilliant career. Off
Hurst goes, running into a sun now so low that his shadow resembles
the distortion in a fairground mirror. He can't see him, but Hurst hears
the pounding sound of the boots that belong to Wolfgang Overath,
who is chasing him – working overtime to no avail.

After the semi-final, Hurst half convinced himself that he would
be sacrificed; that Jimmy Greaves would take his place. In 1960, still
a tender 18, Hurst had come to Wembley for the first time to watch
England, who were facing Alfredo Di Stéfano's Spain. On a rain-
soaked pitch, Greaves scored in the opening minute. Greaves was a
thoroughbred. Hurst, on the other hand, admitted he was regarded
at West Ham as not much more than 'a packhorse'. In his early career
in the First Division, the supporters taunted him on the terraces and
even by post. Anonymous letter-writers claimed he was 'wasting the
club's time and would never be a footballer', said Hurst. At Upton
Park, his fiancée Judith, soon to be his wife, brandished her umbrella
at his critics, as though she might club them with it.

As though suffering from imposter syndrome, Hurst described the
torture of thinking that Greaves was certain to be back for the final: 'If
you've ever been sentenced to death and then spent three days waiting
for the Governor to walk in and announce a reprieve, you might know
how I was feeling. How I got through those days, I will never know.'

He might also have been 13 miles away from Wembley, wearing
white rather than red. Four years earlier, Hurst had made his County

Championship debut for Essex against Lancashire, and for a while he thought cricket would assume priority over football. That afternoon, Essex were playing Surrey at the Oval.

Hurst always insists he 'mishit' the shot that brought him his hat-trick. He didn't care where the ball ended up because nothing would have been left of the match after the Germans retrieved it. You have to believe him, but what Hurst did is a contradiction of what he said. He sets his body for the shot as though posing for a photograph in the Football Association's coaching manual. Seen side-on, it is a per-fect example of how to shoot. The furious power he puts into the very last kick of the match lifts him a foot and a half off the floor. Hans Tilkowski tries to second-guess Hurst. Believing he will blast the shot across him, Tilkowski fractionally transfers his weight on to his left leg. When the shot is walloped past him to his right at head height, he can't throw himself that way to attempt a save. Tilkowski only shuffles; it's as though his feet are stuck in two buckets of cement.

Hurst gave a dramatic description of his last goal and what fol-lowed it.

'If I'd had the energy, I would have chased the ball into the net and kissed it,' he said. 'I felt my legs shaking, my whole body droop . . . Then I noticed the crowds pouring on to the pitch . . . the Germans in little clusters of white shirts and grey faces . . . it was over . . . Nothing made sense . . . There was a glazed look on every face, nothing seemed quite real or in proper focus . . . I was conscious only of everybody talking at once, yet saying nothing that made sense. I could hear my own voice, but I didn't know what I was even trying to say.'

Those paragraphs appear in Hurst's biography, published only 14 months later.*

* *The World Game*, written with Brian James. James once complained to Hurst that a bad back was stopping him from cutting his lawn. Arriving home one afternoon, James was met by his son. 'Dad,' he said, 'you'll never guess who's been to cut our lawn.' As Hurst said: 'The relationship between players and journalists was different back then.'

Here's the thing: he said none of it.

His ghost-writer had tried but failed to push Hurst into bringing back 'The Day' in Technicolor for him. After a sentence or two, groping for words, he had faltered and dried up. His ghost-writer had screwed up his eyes, reliving what he had seen and reimagining on Hurst's behalf. When Hurst saw the finished pages, he said: 'That's it or as close as anyone is ever going to get. The whole thing was a blur . . . I can't tell you any more.'

Ghosted books are like sausages: you ought never to know how they are made. But this story needs telling because it reveals the profound effect the World Cup had on those responsible for winning it. The final proved so overwhelming for him that Hurst was almost less of an authority on the history he wrought than the millions at home who witnessed him make it. He wasn't alone in that experience. Others were similarly overwhelmed. Emotion and exhaustion came to them in such a wild rush that what happened could neither be stored nor processed accurately afterwards.

Ray Wilson described the final as 'just like a dream to me'. He was unable to 'recall' what he 'most wanted to remember', he said. His mind was full of blanks where imperishable images should have been. Wilson traced part of the reason back to the 'delayed shock' he suffered. 'I felt numb for weeks afterwards.' The delirious reaction of the crowds brought home to him 'all the responsibility' he and the others had been 'subconsciously shouldering' for so long. 'It was obviously the greatest day in English football, but it simply did not have the same impact on me . . . I wish I could have shared it.'

An hour later, George Cohen, his boxed medal sitting in the well of his hand, said aloud: 'It's bloody ridiculous. I don't feel anything. I really don't.'

For Roger Hunt, the aftermath of the game amounted to no more than 'back-slapping and singing'.

Nobby Stiles, sitting in the dressing room with the trophy in his lap, was so dazed, distracted and tearful that a policeman was able to take it from him and hand back a replica. Stiles neither resisted nor asked for an explanation.*

And after watching a clip of himself in conversation with Alf Ramsey before extra time began, Bobby Moore confessed: 'I can't remember a single word we said to one another.' Sublime moments never last. You have to catch them as they fly. But Moore subsequently explained, as though it embarrassed him slightly, that some of his memories, lost and unrecoverable, were reconstructed from TV replays. Regularly, he struggled to distinguish between them; an image he'd seen on film would come to him, a substitute for the real thing.

Only Alf Ramsey mapped the match in Ordnance Survey-like detail. He could replay the game kick by kick without the need of the recorded highlights, his power of recall practically infallible. He remembered everything, minute by minute – each shot and save, each miss in front of goal and all the misplaced passes, each tackle, corner, free kick and even the throw-ins.

He could describe the lot – except how the day made him feel.

* The World Cup was swapped to avoid a second theft of the trophy (see page 267).

12

WINE AND ROSES AND
MILK AND HONEY

Alf Ramsey confessed without embarrassment: 'I feel all the sorts of things that others do, but I just don't show them. I suppose I have always been like this.' Ramsey said he was like his mother, who didn't reveal 'much emotion' but was 'very human'.

At the very moment Geoff Hurst's third goal went past Hans Tilkowski in a phosphorescent flash, a photographer on the halfway line pointed his camera at Ramsey. What he caught in a microsecond was a portrait of a man apparently made out of stone. All around Ramsey is a spontaneous display of uninhibited joy, which, like too much alcohol, can easily make a fool of you. Everyone is standing up. Everyone is shouting. Harold Shepherdson leaps into the air. Beside him, Ramsey's face is so sombre, and his body so rigid, that you'd think someone had just whispered news of a death into his ear. His gaze is hard and unblinking. He is focusing on something far off, his thoughts entirely elsewhere. His hands are clamped against his knees. His expression betrays absolutely nothing. There is no smile; no facial movement whatsoever, in fact. He is about to turn and utter the two sentences that count as the least celebratory in the history of the game.

'Sit down, you silly bastards. I can't see.'

Ramsey was the only person in Wembley who wasn't following Hurst's gallop towards goal, but admiring 'the spirit' of Wolfgang Overath. He was 'astonished' at the energy the German summoned in pursuit of a lost cause. 'My reaction at the final whistle may have appeared cold-blooded, but this is me,' explained Ramsey. 'My pleasure

At the very moment England win the World Cup, Alf Ramsey looks as though
someone has given him some bad news

was to *see* what was happening. I was looking at the players. Amazed at
their reaction, getting so much enjoyment just from watching them ... I
was just as thrilled as anyone, but for a while everything was confusing.'

Ramsey waited near the foot of the stairs to the Royal Box. In a bloom
of late sunshine, his arms folded high and tight against his chest, he
watched Bobby Moore take the World Cup gently in his hands. When
Moore returned with the trophy, he tried to give it to Ramsey, who at
first declined the offer, as though accepting would be inappropriately
boastful. Nobby Stiles attempted to pull Ramsey towards him, gripping
both his right forearm and his left shoulder. Stiles said: 'You did it, Alf.
We'd have been *nothing* without you.' Ramsey ignored the sincerity in
that statement: 'It's your day, not mine,' he told both of them.

He would not be chaired around the pitch. He refused to join the
team photo, even when other players physically tried to drag him
into it. The BBC cameras missed the only small intimacy he allowed

himself. When, finally and reluctantly, he took the World Cup from Moore, he 'did what he clearly regarded as an excessively flamboyant gesture; he kissed the trophy', wrote Arthur Hopcraft.

When Ipswich won the League Championship, Ramsey was persuaded by the club's well-lubricated directors to take off his jacket and run around an empty Portman Road. The directors 'were the only audience and they cheered every stride I took', he remembered. At Wembley, Ramsey briefly held the World Cup aloft before slipping into the tunnel. He lingered in front of the door of England's dressing room, waiting for the lap of honour to end. As each player arrived back, he shook them by the hand again, calmly and undemonstratively. The dressing room was like Piccadilly Circus after the pubs and bars had closed on a Saturday night. The racket was too much for Ramsey: 'I don't think I have ever in my life heard such a noise. Just *so much* noise,' he said. 'There were more people in there than there should have been and everyone was talking at once.' Observing him amid the chaos, Hurst found Ramsey phlegmatic in both word and gesture. You'd have thought England had won nothing more spectacular than 'third prize in a flower show', he said.

When Ramsey was asked how he felt, he gave a strangulated reply. The experience was 'all rather *nice*', he declared. What came next was punctuated by pauses. He gave away as little as he possibly could without being monosyllabic. He had won the World Cup without being over-generous with descriptive phrases; he wasn't about to tear through the dictionary now. 'I don't know . . . it's very difficult . . . this had become a desire . . . I think it leaves you a little flat . . . at the same time you have this tremendous feeling of satisfaction.' No newspaper was going to make a blazing headline out of anything else he said either. Ramsey regarded how he 'felt' as no one's business apart from his own.

Ray Wilson remarked of his manager that day: 'I swear he smiled – twice.'

Just how grounded Ramsey remained was evident when one correspondent decided to pay him a compliment in the belief he would receive one in return. Thinking Ramsey would be a sucker for flattery, he thanked him for his co-operation during the competition. He added that he and his fellow writers had 'never' doubted that England would be successful.

Ramsey sniffed the air, looked coldly at him and asked: 'Are you taking the piss?'

He was more animated about what happened after England left Wembley. There was a jeroboam of champagne, which he opened at Hendon Hall and poured for each of his players, like a waiter. There was the bus ride from Hendon to the Royal Garden Hotel, where the World Cup banquet was held. 'Never in my life will I forget that journey,' said Ramsey. Crowds, banked more than a dozen deep, waited along the route. 'Everywhere there were people lining the pavements and waving and shouting . . . I felt the excitement then, and there is nothing quite like it.' There was the supporter who stood in the middle of the road with his arms in the air. He ran towards the bus. The driver had only two options: to stop or to run him over. 'He put his head through a window and all he could say was "I love you all" over and over again. It was about fifteen minutes before we could move on. He was quite a chap,' explained Ramsey. There was also a young girl in a very bright red mini skirt. Ramsey saw her dancing on top of a car parked 'slap across the middle of the road like a barricade'. And there was a pub, outside which 'about 40 customers' raised pints in a synchronised toast; Ramsey raised his hand to them in response.

He and his wife Victoria did not arrive back at Hendon Hall until two o'clock on Sunday morning. They talked and drank for the next two hours. 'We couldn't stop talking,' he said. Ramsey found it almost impossible to sleep. 'I don't know what I thought when I lay in bed . . . I can't remember my thoughts. They were just a jumble. I kept wondering if it was really true and if we had really done it.'

The players, most of them also without sleep, got on the bus again at 10am to go to a film studio in Soho's Wardour Street. They watched the colour newsreel footage of the final, which was about to be rushed into every cinema. The auditorium was so congested that Ramsey politely insisted the usherette took his seat. 'I know what happens,' he told her. He stood in the aisle.

There was no open-top-bus parade, no glad-handing in the back garden at Downing Street with the prime minister and no taking of afternoon tea with the Queen in the White Drawing Room at Buckingham Palace.

On April 18, 1930, listeners, tuning in their wireless for the news, were informed by the BBC's announcer: 'This Good Friday . . . There is no news.' A piano recital, lasting five minutes, was played to fill the gap. In 1966, the BBC wasn't so idly casual about story-gathering. The corporation's weekday schedules, however, amounted to only two – occasionally three – news programmes per day, each ten minutes long. News came from the papers, but even Fleet Street's attention didn't linger long on July 30 once the bunting had been taken down and the drunks had staggered home and sobered up.

The Sunday 'red tops' splashed on the result with relish. The high-end broadsheets were more circumspect, uncertain whether the triviality of a football match had a right to occupy space beside foreign and domestic politics. The *Sunday Times* led not on Ramsey's England but on Rolls-Royce striking a trade deal with the USA worth £35 million. The headline in the *Observer* was the ridiculously parochial 'London Goes Wild for Cup', as though anyone north of Watford or west of Windsor either hadn't seen the game or wasn't interested in it.

On Monday, the 16-page *Guardian* gave England's success no more than a single column on the front page and four stories, totalling 33 paragraphs, on page 10. The *Times*'s page-one coverage was peculiarly perverse. Readers of the 'newspaper of record' were given an illustrated account of the homecoming 'ovation' the West Germans received in Frankfurt. Written by their correspondent in Bonn, it name-checked neither Ramsey nor any of his players.

If England won a World Cup today, the *Daily Mirror* and the *Daily Mail* would produce editions thicker than an old-fashioned telephone directory. In '66, the *Mirror*'s sole front-page story about the match concentrated on the bride and groom who had wheeled a portable TV into their church ceremony. The paper devoted only four pages to the game, each of them containing a generous slab of advertising. The *Mail*, claiming one in five of the world's population had watched England's success, didn't appreciate that its own readership might want to know more about it than the scraped-back bones. The final's page-one presence was a snippet of 67 words. Inside, a thumbnail profile of Ramsey ran to 387 words. On the back page, the match report, a news story and a column amounted to fewer than 3,000 words.

By the middle of that week, the World Cup was being treated like ancient history. The dogs had barked and the caravan had moved on.

Ramsey quietly went home to Valley Road, where he locked the front door and hid behind the curtains. 'We didn't want to see anyone,' he said. 'We put the telephone in a little room where it was difficult to hear it and determined that we wouldn't answer it for a week. We could hear a faint buzz almost all day, every day. We probably lost a lot of calls we would have liked, but it couldn't be helped. It was the only way we could get any peace.' A TV crew 'camped' at the top of his drive for two days, patiently expecting him to not only appear, but also give them an interview. The Ramseys left the house only after the TV crew ran out of patience and 'there wasn't anyone about'.

The adoration of strangers can go too far. Soon Ramsey found coach tours crawling past his house. 'A lot of people peering in,' was how he put it. 'Fortunately, during the summer, our hedge gives us a lot of cover.' The postman brought letters, cards and invitations. The Ramseys 'enjoyed reading them aloud' to one another and sharing the writing of thank-you notes. When he returned to his office at Lancaster Gate, he found even more letters, heaped up like a snow drift. There were nearly 2,500 pieces of fan mail. Several hundred were franked with overseas postmarks. The Football Association was obliged to publish an item in the *FA News*. The small piece, highlighted in a box, apologised for the fact that Ramsey would be unable to answer every correspondent. Some names and addresses were illegible; others, in their haste to write to him, hadn't included a return address. It took Ramsey six months to clear his desk of letters. As soon as he'd replied to 50, another 25 would arrive. He confided that every morning he felt 'some trepidation' about how many more would be waiting for him.

He was discovering that fame, which he had neither wanted nor sought, came with a high and disagreeable rent.

* * *

On the morning of the World Cup final, the *Financial Times*'s op-ed page published a 1,200-word article that was headlined: 'Who's Made Money Out of the World Cup?'

It began with two facts: the TV audience was likely to reach 400 million (26 countries were taking the game live, another 30 were showing the highlights); and Wembley's gate receipts would exceed £200,000, a 'record for a soccer match'. The newspaper pointed out that attendances at England's six games were guaranteed to exceed half a million.

While the *FT* could not offer precise figures, it was certain the competition had been particularly rewarding for businesses such as the Post Office, which had designed and produced 200 million World Cup stamps, which were about to sell out. It had also raked in revenue from sending between 3.5 and 4.5 million words by telex (worth £50,000) for media organisations and connecting around 8,000–10,000 overseas calls (another £50,000).

The *FT* concluded that British Rail had enjoyed 'a field day', cashing in on 77 long-distance and 100 local 'specials' to take fans to matches.

Hoteliers, 'the most difficult to gauge', were not out of pocket either – despite complaining that some of their clientele were a bit stingy. 'Many opened their doors in the hope of Brazilian coffee millionaires,' said the *FT*, but 'found they were hosting fans of more modest means'.

WINE AND ROSES AND MILK AND HONEY

There were some unlikely successes, big, small and quirky. Sales of postcards in the Birmingham branch of Rackham's department store climbed from 23 per day to more than 800 on match days. In Manchester's John Lewis branch, Brazilians bought Wilkinson Sword razor blades 'in bulk' (the *FT* added the gratuitously offensive line: 'but then the Brazilians are a swarthy race'). Fine china, such as Royal Worcester and Wedgwood, and also silver, made in Sheffield, saw a significant lift in sales. So did tourist hotspots; the number of visitors to Chatsworth was 'overwhelming', the paper said. All this was minor compared to the sale of World Cup Willie merchandise, which the *FT* estimated had brought in £2 million.

The Midas organisation, however, was the Football Association, which was suddenly awash with cash. The *FT* broke down the reasons for that: attendances across all the matches would total 1.46 million, bringing in an estimated £1.5 million; the TV revenue was £500,000; and the FA would reap about 5 per cent in royalties from World Cup Willie's popularity. Its gross income from the competition would be about £2 million; after paying expenses and settling debts, the FA would bank half of that.*

There was one glaring and bizarre omission from the *FT*'s investigation: Alf Ramsey and his players were not mentioned among the beneficiaries of the World Cup's cash machine. The original question of who'd made money from the tournament produced a clear answer: not the England team.

There was a pungent whiff of the country's recent past in the way the FA's generals regarded the poor bloody infantry. No lavish boats were launched on their behalf. Before the World Cup, the FA gave each player:

---

* The FA was forced to pay £249,167 in corporation tax out of its World Cup profits because it didn't share the money among the counties and the clubs. The FA admitted it had been 'caught napping by the tide of events' and was 'vulnerable to criticism' on that issue.

A suit
A raincoat
A kit bag
£60 per game
£2 per day spending money
Permission to keep their match shirts and shorts

Every member of the squad was 'requested to bring with them' the following: towels, athletic 'slips', gym shoes, shin guards, spikes and football boots (two pairs), which should be 'properly studded', as well as 'a suit for travelling and a dark lounge suit for evening wear'. After the World Cup, the FA awarded the players a less-than-generous bonus of £22,000, which the 22-strong squad unanimously decided to spilt evenly among themselves. Ramsey handed over the money in brown envelopes at the end of a lunch that ITV organised and screened live on the Sunday after the final. When it was over, Ramsey had to ask ITV 'for a room' so he could 'say goodbye to the players' privately and give each of them their money.

In 1966, the average wage had risen to between £20 and £27 per week. The average house price was £3,620. The sum each England player received was equivalent today to £15,000 – a miniscule percentage of the seven-figure windfall the World Cup gave the FA.

Adidas, the boot manufacturer, exposed the FA's miserliness. Every boy has a memory of his first boots. Jack Charlton's were second-hand, bought after his mother saw an advertisement in a local newspaper. When Charlton went to claim them, he found the boots were 'almost brand-new' Mansfield Hotspurs, then the crème de la crème of sports footwear. He paid eight shillings for them. Alan Ball's mother took her son to buy a pair of Pocock Internationals, which he cherished. Geoff Hurst's 'pride and joy' were his Tom Finney boots, which he 'spent hours' cleaning. Charlton, Ball and Hurst could barely believe Adidas would give them £500 in cash – half of the FA's 'thank you' for the whole tournament – to wear their distinctive three-striped boots in the final. 'I thought about those Mansfield Hotspurs,' said Charlton, 'and how precious those eight shillings were at the time.' Ball met the Adidas rep, went back to his hotel room and hurled his fee into the air, showering beneath the banknotes. 'I remembered those Pocock boots and the sacrifice it took to pay for them.'

The money from Adidas proved important because the Inland Revenue taxed the extra income from the FA at 40 per cent. Ball, who paid super tax in 1966–7, complained he was left with only £460. Gordon Banks, the only member of the side not to wear Adidas boots, fell into conversation with one of the T-shirt sellers who had turned Olympic Way into a street market. The trader's earnings were £1,500. 'I and every other member of the team would have played for nothing,' insisted Banks, stung nonetheless by the discrepancy between the scale of the achievement and the pittance of a financial reward he received for it.

The FA's parsimony, as well as its lack of understanding, empathy and tact, still shocks. It failed to do what would have been fair and decent. You can't be certain whether a lack of will or an absence of intelligence was behind it, but the FA's constant arrogance, ineptness and imbecility tilts the balance of probability only one way. Any jury is always likely to find the prosecution case to be the most convincing. At its Annual General Meeting that year, the FA even voted unanimously against a motion to raise international match fees from £60 to £100.

In the *Wizard of Oz*, the actors playing the Munchkins were paid only $50 per week. Toto, Dorothy's Cairn terrier, got $125 a week. 'The dog had a better agent,' said one of the Munchkins.

The England players knew what it was like to lose out to man's best friend. They got less for winning the World Cup than the dog Pickles had earned from finding the trophy four months earlier. In that great seven-day panic, the cup – on display at a Stanley Gibbons Sport with Stamps exhibition – was stolen from the Methodist Church Hall at Westminster. Pickles, a mixed-breed black and white collie, sniffed the thing out beside the front wheel of a parked car in Beulah Hill. His owner collected £5,000. Pickles got a year's supply of dog food.*

Both owner and dog were also invited to the World Cup banquet at the Royal Garden Hotel, a perk denied even to the wives of the players. The wives were socially distanced from their husbands, pushed into the hotel's restaurant, the Chophouse, which was on a different floor. Each wife received the kind of curious gift from the FA that you'd pass on to someone else at Christmas: a pair of scissors in a cardboard box. You wonder why they bothered ...

Nothing, though, was more egregious than the saga of the commemorative mats. This was farce in a top hat, and so unbelievably petty that only the FA could have been responsible for it. In Lancaster Gate's storeroom, Ramsey noticed a stack of blue presentation boxes containing an eight-piece set of table and drinks mats. Each mat showed an aerial photograph of one of the grounds used during the World Cup. Ramsey asked Denis Follows to send the boxes to his coaching staff and also to his squad. Follows told him each set was reserved 'exclusively' for 'FA council members and visiting officials'.

'We won the World Cup,' protested Ramsey, 'not the officials'.

Follows would not budge.

Some of the mats were never given to anyone. They remained in the storeroom, gathering dust and mildew for the next five years.

* * *

The *Football League Review* quickly labelled the post-1966 period as the 'age of the pop star footballer', but the tone the magazine took was disapproving – almost scolding, in fact – which made it sound like a Victorian gentleman tut-tutting after his first glimpse of a lady's ankle.

---

* Pickles died in 1967. He was strangled by his choke chain and lead. The lead got caught in the branch of a tree while he was chasing a cat.

The *Sunday Times* wrote of football's 're-birth', identifying television as the midwife. It said the game was now 'common gossip' because the BBC's World Cup coverage had 'converted' previously 'unsympathetic viewers' to its 'virtues'. The opening fortnight of the competition proved so popular that the BBC occupied five of the top 10 places in the audience ratings, a figure unprecedented since the arrival of ITV.

Bobby Moore described the axis-shift in attitudes differently. The World Cup was the English game's 'big bang' moment, hurtling in change so transformative that it instantly became 'less of a sport and more of a business'.

'The promotion and advertising men moved in on that day with deals we had never dreamed of,' he said.

This hadn't seemed likely on the Sunday after the final. Moore held a small party for his friends at home and then sat with a glass of lager in front of the TV while his wife Tina did the clearing-up. 'Everything just felt a little flat,' she admitted. Jack Charlton drove home with his parents, stopping off at a greasy spoon for egg and chips and a bread roll. Nobby Stiles and Alan Ball ate the same meal at a motorway services café. Martin Peters made plans to go furniture shopping later in the week. Geoff Hurst washed his car in soapy water and cut the lawn, a dutiful husband doing the household chores. The winners of the World Cup went back to the banality of their quotidian lives, unaware of how different things were about to become for them.

As the anointed 'Golden Boy', Moore didn't have to try to cash in; the wine and roses and the milk and honey just came to him.

Even those who are worshipped will always worship others. Moore saw a little of himself in the actor Steve McQueen. After watching *The Thomas Crown Affair*, he had two shirts made identical in colour and style to those McQueen wore in the film. The critic Barry Norman thought McQueen, the King of Cool, could 'light up' a scene while standing still and without speaking. This was the image Moore sought for himself. His photogenic qualities had already made him a handsome face for hire. Moore also sensibly established himself as a limited company to make the most of it. He had, if only momentarily, been a Brylcreem Boy, paid £450 to appear on a poster – even though his blond curls were unsuited to the slicked-back look. He had a signed column in *Tit-Bits*. The pages of that weekly magazine, which once published P. G. Wodehouse, had cast off whimsical humour in favour of the glamour of movies, celebrity, showbiz, photographs of long-legged women dressed as skimpily as 1960s taste would allow, and stories of spice and scandal, such as 'Her Visions Solve Murders' and 'Jilted Lovers' Sensational Revenge'. Moore had a corner of *Tit-Bits* all to himself.

In the aftermath of the World Cup, he seldom had to buy his own drinks in a public place or pay for a taxi or parking ticket. Though given a Ford Escort, the World Cup Willie logo emblazoned across it, he preferred to drive a Jaguar. As a dandy, he modelled suits for the Queen's designer Hardy Amies, wearing a Lorenzo hat and cape. He was named in the top 10 of the country's best dressed men, a list which included Michael Caine and the society photographer Cecil Beaton. He plugged hair tonic, sports watches, jewellery and Kellogg's cereal, and supported the anti-smoking cause. He owned a sports shop. He snipped ribbons to open supermarkets and car dealerships. He plunged into businesses such as shirt-making and the suede and leather trade. Moore did not bring the bread home alone. His wife Tina extolled the meaty flavour of Bisto gravy, and the couple promoted the conviviality of a pint in the pub and a game of darts in a TV commercial called 'Look in at the Local'. The Moores could eventually afford an £11,000 Georgian-style home in Chigwell, which had a staircase with such a majestic sweep that Tina said it was 'like something out of *Gone with the Wind*'.

Hurst lacked Moore's Hollywood appearance, appeal and earning power. He nevertheless found that life post-1966 was prosperous 'pandemonium'. He'd been used to shopping at a supermarket in Romford, where West Ham fans would occasionally recognise him and politely request an autograph. When he went there with his wife after the final, Hurst was 'mobbed', cornered in the 'biscuit aisle' while attempting to 'shake a hundred hands at once'. Like Moore, he opened shops, collecting in return a 'small' cheque, a tea set or a box of shirts. He called the numbers in a bingo hall. He handed out prizes. Hurst had previously been the recipient of letters which, after fulsomely praising him, brazenly asked for Moore's signature rather than his own. Now he was the focus of attention. He calculated that the number of invitations he received to go somewhere or do something would have 'occupied every evening of the week for about two years'.

The financial advantages of winning the World Cup quickly became apparent. Hurst signed a six-year contract at West Ham worth £140 a week; six months earlier, his salary at Upton Park had been £45 a week. Adidas paid him £300 every time he pulled on their boots in an international. In the decade when a player wearing anything other than black boots was mocked as a poseur, Hurst was paid to champion a pair of green ones too. The *Evening Standard* gave him a weekly column. He swapped his semi-detached chalet bungalow for a £12,750 house, sensible enough to know property was the safest investment. His present to himself was an Austin 1100, priced at £1,000.

Hurst was otherwise cautious. Asking himself whether he wanted to 'embrace' the ritzy glitter of the 1960s or 'concentrate' on his playing career, he decided his football emphatically had to come first. The thought of turning his fame into money 'didn't appeal to me', he insisted.

Peters shared his friend's sentiments, but also awoke to find himself treated as public property. He soon discovered how uncomfortable that burden could be. Peters said he 'tried to hold on to my old life as much as possible'. It proved 'difficult', he added. 'Nothing prepared me for the level of adulation.' Even being pestered for autographs proved 'embarrassing' because 'it wasn't what I wanted . . . I didn't feel like a star or a celebrity.' Peters preferred to be 'left alone' and to live 'in peace and quiet'. He realised 'this wasn't going to happen', forcing him to 'gradually' accept his responsibilities without ever relishing them.

'I didn't try to capitalise on, or exploit, my new status.' The daily post still brought him the same kinds of invitations that Moore and Hurst discovered on the door mat. Peters avoided most of them, not wanting to be gawped at during 'guest appearances'. Any extra money he got exacerbated the guilty conscience he carried with him too. Out of gullibility, rather than greed, Peters had sold his complimentary tickets for the World Cup final to the London tout 'Fat' Stan Flashman, the man who bragged he could get 'anyone into anything' for the right price – from a Wembley international to Wimbledon's Centre Court, and from the Last Night of the Proms to a royal garden party.* Peters's stupidity meant his parents were two of the 32.3 million people who saw the final on a black-and-white TV at home. 'I don't remember what he gave me for the tickets,' said Peters. 'Whatever it was, it was no compensation for the shame I've felt . . .'

West Ham gave him a salary rise that was only a notch or two below Hurst's. His pay climbed from £45 a week to £100 – enough to have bought his parents a whole row of seats at Wembley.

Ball became a £110,000 player only 16 days after the final. Don Revie had inappropriately tapped him up during the competition. Frantic to take Ball to Leeds, Revie advised him to 'make yourself a rebel' at Blackpool, deliberately worsening a contract dispute so the club would be 'glad' to sell him. As though he'd read – and taken seriously – too many John le Carré and Graham Greene novels, Revie arranged clandestine meetings with Ball at a wild spot on the Lancashire moors. He handed over £100 on each occasion, compensating him for loss of earnings while the deal Blackpool had offered remained unsigned. Revie claimed he 'wept' when Ball signed for Everton, who outbid Leeds's timid directors, the board unable to see what Revie saw – the golden vision of an 'unbeatable' midfield of Ball, Billy Bremner and Johnny Giles.

* It was claimed he even got tickets for a customer to attend Princess Anne's wedding in Westminster Abbey in 1973.

Bobby Charlton said: 'We lived in the glory of the World Cup.' It was instantly beneficial for him. By 1968, he was collecting £15,000 a year from Manchester United alone, which was £1,000 higher than the prime minister's salary. His brother Jack bought their parents a house in Ashington worth nearly £3,000. The new home, which their mother Cissie named Jules Rimet, contained all the spic-and-span mod cons denied to them before.

Not everyone, though, was courted as fervently as the triumvirate of Moore, Hurst and Peters, or possessed the spending power of Ball and the Charltons.

Nobby Stiles relied on his World Cup bonus to buy himself out of an underfloor heating company; according to Stiles, the business had never turned 'much of a profit'. He blocked the release of a novelty record that described him as 'rough and toothless' because the lyrics upset his wife. He did become a heart-throb to 'every grandmother' he met. 'They all want to give me a kiss,' he said. 'I'm not much to look at, but I'm younger than their husbands.'

The reward for being an England international: George Cohen puts his name to a dressing-room indispensable

George Cohen advertised the unpretentious Elliman's Athletic Rub, the 'perfume' in every sporting amateur's dressing room. He plugged it as 'a must for me'. Roger Hunt lived as he had lived before, but added an extension to his house. He was 'not one for the bright lights', he said. 'I like to get home . . .' There were still fans who got hold of his telephone number and rang him for a 'chat or to ask for tickets'. Two supporters roused him from his bed at 2.30am, desperate to talk in his front garden. Hunt wanted everything to be low-key and unfussy. 'I don't suppose my life out-side football sounds very exciting. That does not bother me. Every man's life is his own affair and too many find themselves doing too many things they don't want to do,' he explained. Hunt didn't even leave Wembley with his own World Cup shirt; he'd traded it for Wolfgang Weber's.

Ray Wilson came home to banners strung along his street, a sight which he likened to 'the end of the war'. His two sons, aged eight and six, who hadn't been interested in the game before the World Cup, now became 'fanatics', like 10 million other schoolboys. Whenever Wilson heard the knock-knock on his front door, he knew 'autograph hunters' were 'around my house'. His wife was 'suddenly Mrs Celebrity', hearing others call out to her on the street. Wilson, like Hunt, got on with his life and waited for the delirium to pass. 'I didn't make any money,' he said. 'I got a £10 cheque for signing a football.'

He summed up his reaction to it in a single sentence so wonderfully laconic that it surpasses all others.

The World Cup?

'It almost changed my life,' said Wilson.

* * *

Just three weeks after England beat West Germany, the new league season began. *Match of the Day* chose the fixture that made most sense for television: the east–west London derby that took Chelsea to West Ham. Chelsea won 2–1, but the result was immaterial beside the fact that the 35-minute-long highlights endorsed what Bobby Moore called 'the '66 effect'. Recognising the game's newly acquired status, the BBC switched the programme from the small offshore island of BBC2 to the mainland of BBC1. Conscious that a fair slice of his audience were still learning their footballing ABCs, Kenneth Wolstenholme reassured them in an avuncular fashion: 'I will explain some of the technical points of the game as we go along . . .'

West Ham allowed Moore, Geoff Hurst and Martin Peters to run out alone, emerging from the heavy shadow of Upton Park's West Stand and into the sort of sunshine that sizzles the skin, the temperature 29°C. The headline news was that 36,000 supporters were there to acknowledge them. The previous season, West Ham's average attendance had been 24,000.

The English game was being played in the light of a fresh era. A boom had begun. During the 1965–6 season, a little over 27.2 million watched matches in the Football League. In 1966–7, the number increased to 28.9 million – the highest figure since the 32.5 million of 1959–60. By 1967–8, it had shot up still further – 30.1 million. Between the end of the 1965–6 season and the start of 1968–9's, Liverpool's attendances climbed from 40,000 to nearly 50,000; Everton's from 38,000 to 49,000; Tottenham's from almost 38,000 to 42,000; Manchester City's from 27,000 to 37,000; Arsenal's from 29,000 to 37,000. Nottingham Forest's City Ground packed in an extra 12,000 supporters.

Photographs began to appear not only of crammed terraces, but also unusual vantage points near grounds that fans – either immune from vertigo or ignoring the risk – eagerly occupied: scaffolding that was temporarily cladding a building; a motorway overpass with a steep fall below; a precipitous grassy bank; the top of a thin wall. One of the most eye-catching photos saw two men, who had been erecting a TV aerial, sitting on the roof of a house overlooking Blackburn Rovers' Ewood Park.

The World Cup made more money for the Football Association too. Before it, England's average attendance at Wembley was 61,666. Afterwards, the figure soared to 86,111. England's first nine games as champions earned the FA £537,650.

A market bazaar of products emerged to satisfy the addict, especially those demonstrating the zeal of those new supporters. New brands of boots and footballs were launched. Replica kit became more widely available. The usual uniform inside a ground of scarf, bobble hat, rattle and badge could now be augmented at home by the kind of paraphernalia that World Cup Willie had inspired – everything from branded bath salts to tea cosies, wallpaper and tablecloths. The literature of the game expanded too. Football took over from pop music on the newsstand. In 1966, *Charles Buchan's Football Monthly* was the best-seller

The best seat *outside* Blackburn Rovers' Ewood Park

among three mainstream soccer magazines. Between the '66 World Cup and the 1970 finals in Mexico, the market swelled sufficiently to support five newcomers – including *Goal* and *Shoot* – and the circulation of *Football Monthly* almost tripled, from 110,000 to 325,000 copies. The *Football League Review*, which recorded a modest 50,000 readers before the World Cup, was soon totting up almost half a million. Even the Football Association's *Laws of the Game*, previously selling 20,000 copies per year, began shifting 40,000.

The agent Ken Stanley capitalised on a craving for the printed word almost before any of his competitors got out of the blocks. He was a slim, slight-looking man who seemed, like Alf Ramsey, to be a little older than his years because of his receding hairline. Born in 1922, he grew up as one of nine children in a terraced house in south-west

Manchester. If the war hadn't got in the way, Stanley would have been a stellar figure in table tennis. He was a boy star, competing in his first world championship at 17 years old. He toured in exhibition matches staged at Butlin's holiday camps and shared a basketball court with the Harlem Globetrotters and a sawdust ring with circus performers.

Aware that you got nowhere without self-promotion, Stanley taught himself to become a business impresario. He had previously been a manager at Mitre, which then dominated the market for panelled footballs. It was a golden key that opened many doors, bringing Stanley back into contact with men such as Ramsey and Matt Busby, both of whom he had last seen in khaki during the war. He struck out alone, opening a suite of offices overlooking Huddersfield's St George's Square.

Stanley unashamedly said his trade 'was all about contacts'. He made and retained them not only because he was a workaholic – 16-hour days were common – but also because he was trustworthy. Even Ramsey, wary of everyone, liked Stanley, whose moral compass, like his own, pointed towards true north. He would rather lose money than do anything unscrupulous or unethical. He deplored the spivs and cheats, calling them 'semi-con-men' who exploitatively lined their own pockets by taking advantage of a player's financial ignorance.

Ramsey was fond of Stanley for another reason too. Like Ramsey himself, he was a dapper chap. He shined his shoes, made sure the creases in his suit trousers were sharp and wore a plain shirt and a plain tie.

Stanley recognised that 'the modern player' possessed the 'glamour and appeal' of the Hollywood movie stars of the 1940s and '50s. 'If you want to sell something, footballers have just about the biggest pulling power in the country,' he said. He made sure any commercial venture never interfered with the football, another reason First Division managers readily accepted him into their office.

In 1966, Stanley was the agent of three of England's World Cup team: Gordon Banks, Jack Charlton and Alan Ball. Also on his books were

Billy Bremner, Denis Law, Billy McNeill of Celtic and John Greig of Rangers. His big-name client was George Best, who made more money than the whole of Ramsey's World Cup team put together. Stanley got Best to endorse an entire department store of products. As well as football merchandise, there were slippers, chewing gum, lollipops, lamps, crisps, sunglasses, sausages, eggs, oranges and pies. Best's own fashion line clothed 'the man who sought style in the '60s'. By 1968, he was earning £100,000 a year. By the end of 1969, it was £250,000.

Stanley forged a deal in publishing. He launched *Soccer Annuals*, branded with the names of his clients. Best's sold a whopping 120,000; Ball's 75,000; Bremner's 40,000. In the two years that followed the World Cup, everyone in England's team – apart from George Cohen and Gordon Banks – published an autobiography. Among the titles were *Ball of Fire*, *Hunt for Goals*, *Soccer My Battlefield* (Nobby Stiles), *My Life in Soccer* (Ray Wilson), *For Leeds and England* (Jack Charlton) and – the dreariest of all – *Forward for England* (Bobby Charlton). Even Harold Shepherdson was recruited. *The Magic Sponge* was one of the few books worth the ink and paper used to produce it.

There was one notable omission from the list.

Not even Stanley could persuade Ramsey to become an author.

* * *

His team referred to him as 'Sir' a full five months before the New Year's honours list confirmed it.

Alf Ramsey was one of 31 knights. This was not a list sprinkled with stardust, but mostly an anonymously rum collection of unglamorous men in suits whom few of the public knew existed. Among those joining Ramsey were the chief inspector of taxes, the chairman of the South of Scotland Electricity Broad, the principal of King's College London and the chairman of the White Fish Authority.

A previous sporting knight, the Yorkshire cricketer Len Hutton, complained that becoming 'a Sir' always put 'ten shillings on the bill', the tip he felt obliged to leave in restaurants as a consequence of his newfound status. Ramsey dithered before accepting his knighthood – though not because of the extra cost of dining out. 'One did not know what was involved. This concerned me to some great extent,' he said. It was as though Ramsey thought becoming a knight would embrace demands more onerous than putting on a tailcoat, a top hat and turning up punctually at Buckingham Palace. He arrived there looking a little like Stanley Holloway about to sing 'Get Me to the Church on Time' in *My Fair Lady*.

Even after learning his anxieties were baseless, Ramsey was determined not to do anything that might vulgarise the honour, which meant never exploiting it.

During the night of the World Cup banquet, he took a telephone call from the sports editor of the *News of the World*. Wanting an exclusive story, the newspaper was prepared to hand him £10,000 for a conversation it promised would last no longer than ten minutes.

'No,' he said.

That 'no' came out so emphatically that his caller knew Ramsey's refusal was not a negotiating tactic designed to jack up the price. He could not be bought.

The Football Association guaranteed him a bonus of £6,000 for winning the World Cup. It took them until Christmas to pay up, but Ramsey was never lured into making a quick buck elsewhere. No publisher could persuade him to produce his life story – despite waving a cheque for as much as £20,000 in front of him. Ramsey gave each of them the same answer. He felt a book would be 'inappropriate at this time'. He would 'do nothing' and 'say nothing' that could possibly either compromise or imperil 'my relationship with my players'. Ramsey was also sensitively aware that any publisher would expect chapters about his upbringing, his family background, his marriage, his likes and dislikes, and 'revelations' about those he admired and those he didn't. Without them, it would be a Swiss cheese of a book, the holes all too visible.

Ken Stanley suggested that Ramsey produce an annual, in which he contributed only one or two pieces himself and 'edited' others to give the book a wider appeal. Ramsey dismissed even that idea. The man responsible for creating the zeitgeist in the English game refused to capitalise on it.

He could have made a near six-figure sum after the World Cup; he just couldn't bring himself to do it.

PART FOUR

13

DID YOU BRING YOUR OWN KETTLE?

The first thing you see is a head shot that fills the screen like a full moon. The camera, positioned at his feet, is thrust directly into his face. For five seconds, you're up close and very personal with Alf Ramsey. You can't escape the heavy eyebrows, sorely in need of a trim, and the spots and small blemishes on his waxy skin.

It is March, 1969; Ramsey has made a decision he will regret.

He is sitting on the bench at Wembley. England are destroying France 5–0 in a friendly, overcoming mist and rain and the mud of a deteriorating pitch.

The game neatly bookends a 45-minute biographical film with a title so soporific – *Sir Alf Ramsey: England Soccer Team Manager* – that it contains no hint of how generously he co-operated with it.

Ramsey nonplussed everyone by letting London Weekend Television into his life. The producers won Ramsey over with a few blandishments and a specific argument. Even the Queen, breaking protocol, was succumbing to the same TV scrutiny. The 'intimate' peek at her, called *Royal Family*, would be screened later that year, supposedly casting some sympathetic light on the magic of the monarchy and making everyone who was part of it seem both a little less remote and a little more like the rest of us.*

Ramsey was similarly persuaded that no harm would be done if a camera stalked him too, demystifying what he did for the benefit of the

---

* The film has not been broadcast in its entirety on TV since the 1970s. The Queen's view of it was said to be unfavourable.

ordinary fan. The phrase 'fly-on-the-wall documentary' wasn't yet in common usage, but the profile of Ramsey is one of the early prototypes.

Here he is getting off the train from Ipswich, stepping on to the underground escalator, finding a seat on the Tube and strolling into Lancaster Gate. Here he is on the training pitch in his tracksuit . . . in a team meeting . . . on the team coach . . . inside the dressing room . . . walking along Wembley's tunnel.

Here he is again at home, where the director pans across family photographs in polished silver frames, medals displayed in their presentation boxes and dolls attired in national costumes. Even Ramsey's dachshund makes a guest appearance.

Like the man himself, his house is a model of order. Framed on the wall is the back page of the *Sunday Express* that proclaims 'England – World Champions'. There is a limited-edition print of the 1962 FA Cup final, a painting which the Football Association commissioned to mark its centenary. Most conspicuously of all, there is an original oil portrait of Ramsey. The artist, Vasco Lazzolo, had studied at The Slade and painted figures as diverse as the Duke of Edinburgh and the 'showgirl'-cum-model Christine Keeler, who became infamous during the sex-and-spying Profumo scandal. In the painting, which Lazzolo copied from a photograph, Bobby Moore is passing the World Cup into Ramsey's hands. It is not a piece of fine art. The brushstrokes are loose. The colours are either too pale or too gaudy. Only Moore looks like himself; Ramsey's face is far too gaunt.

TV reviewers found the documentary hypnotic. Ramsey had previously been considered to be the least known of the country's best-known men. So every triviality – even that prawn cocktail and grilled Dover sole were his favourite dishes – was considered revelatory. The *Daily Mirror* rated the documentary as 'delicious', thinking it 'softened' the 'enigmatic cold fish' Ramsey had previously seemed to be. The *Sun*, describing him as 'a man even his best friends don't know', called the material on him 'heaven-sent' and came to the conclusion that Ramsey would have 'finished top in any field he chose'.

The programme was written and narrated by the *Daily Mail*'s Ian Wooldridge. As a teenager, growing up in Hampshire, he'd considered Ramsey as one of his 'heroes at Southampton'. In his commentary, while watching Ramsey cross the platform at Liverpool Street, Wooldridge describes him as looking 'like a bank manager who had forgotten his briefcase, a major in mufti or the man from the Pru'.

From the comfort of his armchair, dressed in a shirt, tie and cardigan, Ramsey, who looks and sounds a little Pooterish, discusses Ipswich, the World Cup and managing England. Wooldridge asks who he admires outside football. The cogs of Ramsey's brain turn, but not fast enough to produce a name. 'Don't ask me that . . . you see how limited I am and how narrow my life is . . . Let's talk about football.'

Wooldridge also sought out those who knew Ramsey: FA councillors, the game's administrators, John Cobbold, his 84-year-old ex-landlady, former teammates and current players, among them Ted Ditchburn, who is seen with a lit fag between his fingers. Another interviewee, who is unidentified, reiterates the well-worn classic about his course of social improvement. He tells Wooldridge that Ramsey at The Dell was 'a broad cockney lad' who decided 'as the years went on' to 'do something about that'.

Wooldridge believed the changes Ramsey wrought on himself were entirely to his credit. But, after the documentary aired, he was plunged 'deeply' into Ramsey's 'black books', he said. Wooldridge couldn't quite believe that Ramsey, unbearably sensitive about how he sounded, thought he'd been ridiculed and now looked so 'thunderously' at a programme that otherwise 'eulogised his achievements'.

The significant segment in the documentary was not about the past, but how uncomfortable the present had become for Ramsey. After France were beaten, Wooldridge noted that Ramsey gave a 'fleeting smile' before 'the mask drops again'. With a comedian's timing, he added: 'After all, it's only 5–0 to England.' The press conference afterwards confirms another of Wooldridge's observations: that Ramsey could be 'charming', but only 'when he wants to be'. Cordiality turns to hostility when Ramsey says 'the public' have been 'brainwashed' by the negative coverage that he believes is being disseminated by 'all and sundry' in the media. When questioned about a remark he made two years earlier, Ramsey reacts as though he's been poked in the eye with the sharpest of sticks. 'I don't quite understand you,' he tells the reporter. 'Having said a thing, you harp on it time and time again. This is ridiculous.' He concludes with another little flare of anger. 'I hate to think what you would have said about me and the England team if we hadn't got the goals tonight.'

Anyone else, after such a handsome win, would have gone for the gentle touch. Ramsey refused to be conciliatory because his critics, despite 1966, had stopped giving him the benefit of the doubt.

In early June, 1968, England lost 1–0 in a friendly with West Germany on a bone-hard pitch in Hanover, and lost again – more significantly – to Yugoslavia in the semi-finals of the European Championships in Florence. Knowing England couldn't be out-played, Yugoslavia decided to out-kick them.* The game, a savage affair, rarely rose out of the gutter, which is where England had to grub around to play it, blow for crude blow and stud for stud. There were so many fouls that you stopped counting them. Yugoslavia's winner came in the 86th minute.

The makers of *Sir Alf Ramsey: England Soccer Team Manager* were especially canny in choosing the fixture against France as the game to glue their documentary together. England had won only one of six matches in eight months, failing to score in three of them.

---

* Alan Mullery infamously became the answer to a quiz question that outlived his career: 'Who was the first England player to be sent off in an international?' In the semi-final against Yugoslavia, after being hacked down yet again Mullery had one last chance to reciprocate – and so he took it, swinging his right boot into his assailant's groin. In the dressing room afterwards, he expected Ramsey's condemnation for his lack of discipline but instead was congratulated for giving back to 'those bastards' a taste of their own cruelty. Ramsey paid the £50 fine that the FA – blind or ignorant to the injustice – handed to Mullery, denying him an appeal.

And the World Cup in Mexico was approaching at disconcerting speed.

* * *

Alf Ramsey made his decision to defend the trophy in the month after he won it. He had said that 'one day' it 'may be fun' to 'start all over again' and 'help a little club up to the top', à la Ipswich. But at that point, there was nowhere else for Ramsey to go except back to his office at Lancaster Gate.

A World Cup winner did not swap England for a 'little club' in the bottom half of the First Division – and no vacancy existed at the luxury end of the table. Ramsey was not attracted to the prospect of making a fortune overseas either. 'I will not go abroad,' he said. 'I am an Englishman.' His attitude towards money often made him sound like one of the landed gentry who, banking with Coutts, thinks discussing the question is rather undignified. 'I can still only eat three meals a day,' was how he responded to rumours that he could quadruple his Football Association salary in Italy or Spain.

Two other factors influenced his decision to carry on. He felt it was his 'duty' to try to retain what was now his. He also asked himself, who could do the job as well as him? He could think of no suitable candidate.

In a statement that the FA later chose to forget in a convenient bout of amnesia, its secretary, Denis Follows, said of Ramsey: 'He has a job with us for life . . . no one will ever really be able to repay him for the riches he brought to English – no, British – soccer.'

The game wasn't as wholeheartedly grateful to Ramsey as Follows imagined.

After the World Cup, Ramsey promised 'the best was yet to come' for England. The results and insipid performances didn't stack up beside such bullishness. As soon as England lost 3–2 to Scotland, only nine months later, it was gloomily suggested his future might already be behind him. Denis Law teased England: 'Hey, as we've beaten the World Champions, does that make us World Champions instead?' he asked. The *Daily Telegraph* said the gap between mid-summer 1966 and spring 1967 was 'time enough, indeed, for a great football team to wither away and die . . . We knew . . . that this was bound to happen one day. It was the timing that surprised us.'

For a corpse, England had a startling amount of life still in them. They won their next four matches without a conceding a goal. This remained insufficient for those who hadn't uncorked the champagne to celebrate the World Cup. The naysayers, condemning Ramsey as a villain, included *The New Statesman*'s Hans Keller, who at least encapsulated his distaste for both him and England's 4–3–3 formation in a sentence of such marvellous, deft concision that it deserves repetition. In a column published 48 hours before the final, Keller wrote: 'Next week I shall describe how England won the World Cup and what we can do about it.' He was far from isolated in believing Ramsey, eschewing wingers, had committed a criminal assault on the English game.

On the very night of the Royal Gardens Hotel banquet, a Middlesbrough director was heard to complain: 'The way England played was absolutely dreadful.' A First Division chairman roasted Ramsey for a 'system' that 'can only bring negative football to our grounds . . . We must escape from 4–3–3.' George Best branded the final as 'a turgid, disappointing anti-climax' and dismissed England as 'a bunch of hard-grafting runners with . . . very few world-class players'. Malcolm Allison considered England to be 'a good side' with 'some ordinary' figures in it. Jimmy Hill predicted forwards would take 'five years' to learn how to break the defensive grip 4–3–3 now held them in.

After Laurence Olivier watched his wife, Vivien Leigh, win the best actress Oscar for *Gone with the Wind*, he admitted: 'It was all I could do to restrain myself from hitting her with it. I was insane with jealousy.' Some of Ramsey's detractors, similarly motivated, would gladly have picked up the World Cup and struck him with it too. According to them, England's success should have been invalidated on the basis of a lack of artistic merit. Regularly damned for not being Brazil, Portugal or Italy – or even the Hungarians of 1953 – Ramsey's sides came to be regarded the way pessimists regard the English weather. The prevailing attitude was: 'It could be worse.'

Ramsey was outraged about having to defend himself for not winning the World Cup in a style satisfactory to purists with classically high standards – especially as those same purists hadn't thought winning it was even possible beforehand. It may not have been an aesthetic triumph, but Ramsey sought to prove it was a worthy one. 'Stifling opposing individuals is what the game is all about. It's always been so. We just did it better than anyone else,' he said. To accusations that he was defence-minded, Ramsey's retort was: 'That's rubbish. I want to win every game.'

The Football League's Luddite tendencies, which were obviously Alan Hardaker's, also resurfaced. The League behaved as though it would have preferred the game to be obscure, played for a niche audience, rather than popular. Reading the *Football League Review* was like listening to an ornery malcontent. The League complained because the total wage bill of the 92 clubs fell only a 'few pounds' short of £5 million. It complained about agents, whose demands had contributed to those fatter pay packets. 'These gentlemen are becoming more than just a source of irritation . . . Mr Ten Per Cent has no place in football.' It complained about transfer fees, which were soaring even faster than salaries: in June, 1968, Allan Clarke went from Fulham to Leicester City for £150,000; a year later, he moved to Leeds for £165,000. It complained about Kenneth Wolstenholme's use of 'wing back, centre back and sweeper up' during commentaries on *Match of the Day*. Why, the League asked, was Wolstenholme doing this? 'Who in the English game is using such phraseology?' The BBC were 'attempting to force these terms on to the viewer' and 'to modernise the game'. It complained – as ever – about the clamour for more live TV matches. Hardaker was certain any increase would wipe fans from the terraces. He was piqued because those who opposed him at the

FA used logic to nutmeg him. Advocating that TV had 'done more for football than people were prepared to admit', the FA actually thought the BBC and ITV ought to cough up enough cash to screen matches live – even 'on a Saturday'.

The pull between club and country, the perpetual bickering about rearranging fixtures, was another subject on which Hardaker tub-thumped – this time with a Janus face. He was vocal in his support of Ramsey's needs while doing as little as possible to accommodate them.

A *Football League Review* polemic, published in the first issue of the 1966–7 season, was unequivocal in its condemnation of the World Cup too. 'The tumult is over, the shouting too. The combatants have departed. The flags have gone. We are back to normal, thank goodness.' The writer moaned on: 'It has suited Alf Ramsey's purpose, in playing the foreigners at their own game, to resort to the abomination of 4–3–3 . . . But let there be any widespread adoption of these tactical notions in England and swift retribution will follow . . . We are still old-fashioned enough to prefer the stuff we were raised on, namely the ball coming in from the wings.'

Even Geoffrey Green looked back and saw that the 'gradual decline' of the game began when managers in all four divisions tried to copy Ramsey. Too many of his imitators were mediocre and adopted 4–3–3 without possessing the personnel to make it successful. Never were so many square pegs hammered into the wrong-shaped holes. The game became 'tighter, meaner, less attractive', said Green. Five years before the World Cup, clubs had scored an average of 69 goals per season. Five years after it, the number had dropped to 57.

This wasn't remotely Ramsey's fault, but he got punished nonetheless for being so good that everyone else wanted to emulate him.

* * *

Every story requires a full stop, but the one applied to England's World Cup winners arrived with almost indecent haste. The team played only three more matches together. The last of these was a 5–1 win against Wales at Wembley. It came only 108 days after the final.

George Cohen made just another seven international appearances. His career ended at Anfield, where he attempted to control a ball that flew at him at height and spun like a child's top. He wrenched his knee and tore his cartilage. 'I hit the deck screaming,' he said. Cohen, unbelievably, was treated with a sponge and a bucket of water, and he hobbled about for a further five minutes. His consultant compared the inside of his knee to a 'sago pudding'. Cohen couldn't even kick a ball in his own testimonial match.

Ray Wilson's farewell was abrupt too: there were only another dozen caps for him. In the summer of 1968, he had a cartilage removed, making only six more league appearances for Everton.

Nobby Stiles played just three times for Ramsey between 1967 and 1969. One knee injury after another sapped his 'old confidence' in his own 'indestructibility', he said. Stiles tried to be philosophical after discovering 'football, like life, gives and takes away', but he admitted: 'You think of your wife and your kids and wonder how you are going to look after them when you lose the only job you can do – the only one you ever wanted to do.'

Roger Hunt quit international football in January, 1969 – the same month he scored his 234th goal for Liverpool and established a new club record. He'd claimed only three goals in his previous 17 matches. Hunt, though only 30, sensed his superpowers waning as he aged.

Ramsey sprinkled new caps about: Colin Bell, Francis Lee and Mike Summerbee of Manchester City; David Sadler and Alex Stepney of Manchester United; John Hollins of Chelsea; Cyril Knowles of Tottenham; Tommy Wright of Everton. He also went back to figures already familiar to him: Keith Newton of Blackburn Rovers; Brian Labone of Everton; Norman Hunter, still Jack Charlton's central defensive partner at Leeds; Alan Mullery, who had moved from Fulham to Tottenham; and Chelsea's Peter Bonetti, the deputy to Gordon Banks.

Ramsey was still held over the fire for not accommodating Jimmy Greaves. In that iconic photograph of Ramsey, immobile on the bench at the final whistle at Wembley, the only other person not celebrating is Greaves. Even in the next frame, in which Ramsey is smiling, Greaves looks as though he doesn't belong. He came on to the field afterwards without giving the impression that he wanted to be there, and without knowing either what he was supposed to do or where he ought to put himself. It was a mark of his popularity that Greaves's decision to collect his bags a few hours later and surreptitiously do a moonlight flit, leaving an empty chair at the World Cup banquet, did not alienate him from the rest of the squad, who made allowances for his melancholy. Greaves said he 'didn't want to spoil' Ramsey's celebrations by 'letting him see the hurt in my eyes'. Ramsey considered it disrespectful, but said nothing.

He still continued to select Greaves for his squad without picking him in his side. Whether he played or not, he continued to be the problem child. The football writers of the 1960s regularly gushed over Greaves, but never enough to name him as their Footballer of the Year. He was cast as a victim of his own genius, possessing too much fizz for a personality as flat as Ramsey's.

Greaves and Ramsey were always untangling crossed wires in their relationship – most of them, it has to be stressed, left in a messy state by Greaves, who seemed to assume the manager could read his mind. In one of his autobiographies, Greaves said he finally told Ramsey: 'I would rather not be called up unless I was going to play.' Citing one more epic miscommunication between them, he then claimed to be 'astonished' when Ramsey announced: 'Greaves . . . has told me that he does not want to play for England.' In another of his books, his account differs. Greaves admits: 'Effectively, I said I was retiring from international football.'*

---

* In neither book does Greaves disclose how Ramsey persuaded him not to quit the game prematurely. At the start of 1968, Greaves went through a

Even Greaves's divorce from England didn't separate him from Ramsey, who was constantly reminded about the man who wasn't there by newspapers who wanted him back.

* * *

By the end of the 1960s, when the average computer was still the size of a wardrobe, a fad emerged for using technology to predict the outcome of football matches and other sports events.

A month before the 1970 World Cup began, the *Observer* fed a computer – called Elliott 803 – with every 'relevant fact' about the tournament: past results, current form, probable teams and tactics, and also the effects of altitude and heat. Paper was inserted, buttons were pressed and, amid some flashing blue lights and electronic gurgling and whirling, Elliott 803 digested the lot and spat out the result of the final:

England 3, Brazil 2 (after extra time).

In fairness to Elliott 803, Alf Ramsey envisaged a similar result.

Drawn together in the same group – beside Czechoslovakia and Romania – Ramsey saw England and Brazil meeting again in the Azteca Stadium, the world's best defence clashing with the world's best attack.

Ramsey thought of his squad, containing eight survivors from the World Cup-winning team, as being superior in strength, ability and experience to the 22 he had mobilised four years before.

The Charltons had a combined age of 67 now. At 35 years, one month and three days old, Jack became the oldest player to get a

---

tough lean spell – two league goals in 12 matches. Tottenham dropped him. 'If you want to transfer me,' he told them, 'I won't argue.' He turned to Ramsey for comfort, confessing he was 'in two minds' about 'giving up' altogether. Ramsey 'talked to me like a father', said Greaves. He quoted the nub of the advice he got: 'Don't do it . . . It's a bloody daft idea.'

game in that tournament. The previous April, Bobby had won his 100th cap.

Bobby Moore was 29. Geoff Hurst, now 28, had scored 16 league goals – twice as many as anyone else at West Ham – in a side that finished 17th in the table. Martin Peters, at 26, had left Upton Park and gone to White Hart Lane. The £200,000 deal, struck only two months before, had made him the country's most expensive player.

Alan Ball arrived in Mexico with a League Championship winners' medal; Everton had taken the title by a mammoth nine points.

Ramsey was confident enough to think that England's most gruelling struggle would be against the 'heat', which cooked the skin; the 'altitude', capable of shrivelling unhealthy lungs; and the glare at noon, making it almost impossible to stare for long at a polished surface outdoors without damaging the naked eye.

He didn't discount the claims of Italy, who had a rickety build-up but were motivated by the dread of going home from a second successive World Cup in sackcloth. He did not discount West Germany either. Gerd Muller brought 38 goals with him from the Bundesliga. Franz Beckenbauer was immaculate in his early maturity. Ramsey nevertheless still locked his gaze on Brazil – even when the Brazilians themselves were unconvinced about how great their team would be. With the Mexican sun on their backs, rather than the Merseyside rain of 1966, Ramsey saw the sharp threat in them. Six wins and 23 goals had got them to the finals.

Since early 1969, Brazil had been managed by João Saldanha: politically left-wing, a card-carrying communist in a country stuck with a right-wing dictatorship. Pelé described him as 'a unique character', which was rather an understatement. His unconventionality was legend. As boss of Botafogo, Saldanha had erratically fired a pistol into the air to spook an opposition player suspected of match-fixing. As boss of Brazil, the pistol appeared again to intimidate a club manager who had insulted him with the words 'You are a coward'. Saldanha was a habitual smoker and drinker, diagnosed

with pulmonary emphysema, but as an ex-journalist the one tempta-
tion from which he could never turn away was newspapers. He read
every paragraph, regarding the criticism he found there – the kind
he had regularly meted out to others – as heresy best settled with
his fists. His enemies began piling up, including Pelé, from whom
he became silently estranged, and also Brazil's military-controlled
regime. The government was led by a general who wanted to choose
the team the way he chose his cabinet. Saldanha couldn't survive.
No one knew whether he was being sincere about it, but his pre-
announced plan to drop Pelé meant he was dropped instead. Only 77
days before the World Cup began, Saldanha was replaced in a fumbling coup by Mário Zagallo, who had won the 1958 and 1962 World
Cups as a player. Without being too radical, Zagallo made vital nips
and tucks and undertook some organisational reshaping. He admitted Brazil went to Mexico in a 'kind of fearful' fugue, nervous about
what would happen there.

What did happen was sublime.

What we talk about when we talk about the beautiful game is Brazil
in 1970. You only have to recite the names to bring everything back:
Carlos Alberto . . . Jairzinho, the Hurricane . . . Rivellino . . . Tostão . . .
Gerson . . . Clodoaldo . . . *and* Pelé.

In their opening match, Pelé came within eight inches of lobbing
the Czechoslovakian goalkeeper with a shot struck from ten feet
inside his own half. Against Uruguay, his outrageous dummy mis-
directed their 'keeper to the extent that he almost found himself in
Munich four years ahead of the next World Cup. Any defensive wall
allowed Rivellino to show how audaciously he could bend a free kick
around it. On parks, along roads and down backstreets mesmerised
boys everywhere tried to master his technique.

Their formation, nominally 4–3–3, was ever changing – football's
equivalent of improvised jazz. How lethal it was, and how irresistibly
gorgeous too. No one encapsulated it in words like Gerson, a player
who smoked so much that he liked to have a lit cigarette waiting for

him at half-time, and again at full-time. 'Those who saw it, saw it,' he said of that Brazilian side. 'Those who didn't will never see it again.'

* * *

For England, the 1970 World Cup revolved around four pivotal events.

The save Gordon Banks made in Guadalajara.

The saves he was not there to make in León.

The consequence of Alf Ramsey's misguided substitution of Bobby Charlton there.

The 18-carat gold bracelet that Bobby Moore didn't steal from a 12ft by 12ft jeweller's store in the lobby of a Bogotá hotel.*

Moore's saga, a tediously long story with a short and obvious explanation, involved the police, the British Embassy, the British and Colombian governments, a magistrate, three nights of house arrest under armed guard and the re-enactment of the 'crime' of lifting a £650 bracelet that no one ever found. Moore was the mark in a rudimentary piece of 'street grifting' designed to extort money, a sting that at least one of his accusers had pulled before. The same accuser couldn't decide whether the bracelet was studded with diamonds, emeralds or both. A second swore Moore had put the bracelet in his left blazer pocket – but his blazer did not have one – and a third claimed to have witnessed the theft through the shop's front window. Moore lost five pounds in weight while waiting to be freed, but won the astonished admiration of everyone after arriving in Mexico – 72 hours behind the rest of his team – with the sangfroid of someone who had suffered

* In *Bobby Moore: The Definitive Biography*, Jeff Powell, doyen of the *Daily Mail* and a close friend of Moore's, says Moore speculated that 'Perhaps one of the younger lads with the squad did something foolish, a prank with unfortunate circumstances.' Moore's wife Tina said: 'The story wasn't what Bobby told me . . . [and] I truly was the only one he trusted . . . I am positive that he would have disclosed that to me, as he did the rest of his innermost thoughts and feelings at the time.'

nothing more traumatic than the inconvenience of a mislaid bag. He was embarrassed only by his appearance: unshaven and wearing the creased clothes he'd been unable to change for four days.

The misfortunes that befell Banks, Bobby Charlton and Moore – the spine of the side – were symbolic of a shambolic World Cup for England. Whatever could go wrong, did so. Alf Ramsey never got a grip on it.

This was the first World Cup in which England fully embraced the sort of sponsorship from which the team could directly benefit. Ken Stanley convinced Ramsey to let him establish a players' pool.

In 1966, the Football Association hadn't possessed the commercial intelligence to realise that a glossy team photograph of the World Cup winners with the trophy just might be something magazines wanted to publish and the public wanted to own. Two months passed before a picture was cobbled together at Roehampton instead of Wembley. Rather than placing the team in front of the Twin Towers, the backdrop was autumnal shrubbery and trees, many denuded of their leaves.

Among the first deals struck in 1970 was an exclusive arrangement with the *Daily Express*, which wrapped a photo of the whole squad around the front and back pages of the newspaper. The edition sold out. Motorists drove around to waste petrol (then the equivalent of 33p per gallon), simply so they could fill up again and satisfy the craze for collecting 30 World Cup coins that Stanley had persuaded Esso to mint. The squad's World Cup song, 'Back Home', dislodged Norman Greenbaum's 'Spirit in the Sky' as the chart number one and held off competition from Elvis Presley to stay there for three weeks.

Every player was given a cream-coloured Ford Cortina 1600E, the three lions badge adorning the front doors. Ramsey wouldn't accept one. He also refused to appear on *Top of the Pops* to mumble the lyrics of 'Back Home'. Still thinking of sponsorship as a little unsavoury, and wanting his hands to be as clean as possible, he even turned down his cut of the money from everything so that his team got a little more of it. He lent his name to only one thing: a factual *World Cup Guide*, sponsored by Park Drive cigarettes.

Before setting off for Mexico, Ramsey considered England to be in a deliciously prime position. 'Nothing has been left to chance,' he said. The FA, however, had no one capable of saving the manager from himself. Nearly every press conference he gave started a small fire difficult to extinguish.

There are no foreign lands; only the traveller is foreign. No one became more aware of that than Ramsey. He knew which Aertex shirts to wear in Mexico, which Zeiss sunglasses would block out most ultraviolet light, which vaccinations were needed, which pills to swallow to combat infection and which energy drinks best tackled dehydration. He also knew everything there was to know about altitude and temperature. Ramsey was neurotically risk-averse too. Ice in drinks was banned. Room service was banned. Walking between 12pm and 3pm was banned. Sunbathing was strictly rationed. A player was allowed to spend ten minutes on his back and another ten minutes on his front, each timed as precisely as the boiling of an egg (the blast of a playground whistle was the signal to flip yourself over). These precautions, though necessary, made Ramsey look to the Mexicans like an old-school Englishman suspicious about 'abroad'. He gave the impression of being a reluctant tourist on one of the earliest package holidays, who doesn't speak the language, isn't brave enough to try a local dish, doesn't want to learn about the customs and the culture, prefers not to drink the water and sits uncomfortably on the beach in socks and sandals, a white knotted handkerchief protecting his head.

Bobby Charlton described Ramsey as being 'at war' with his environment in Mexico. 'He didn't warm to the Mexicans and they, in their pride and sense that he rather despised them, responded in similarly hostile fashion,' he explained.

Ramsey was constantly agitated, as though on the edge of picking a fight. He felt he was 'on trial', he said. Relations with the Mexican media and the public steadily deteriorated, and he made no sustained efforts to improve them. Unlike the average politician, Ramsey could not fake sincerity and lacked the stagecraft to learn it. His face seemed set in a permanent scowl of disapproval.

A year before the World Cup, England had embarked on a South American tour that began in Mexico, stopped off in Uruguay and ended in Brazil. This fact-finding mission was supposed to be a charm offensive too.

It turned out to be more offensive than charming.

In Mexico City, after a goalless draw, Ramsey chucked Mexican reporters out of the England dressing room like a pub landlord evicting drunks at closing time. He berated his hosts essentially for what he perceived was their lack of respect towards the World Champions. 'There was a band playing outside our hotel at five o'clock this morning. We were promised a motorcycle escort to the ground. It never arrived. When our players went out to inspect the pitch, they were abused and jeered by the crowd. I would have thought the Mexican public would have been delighted to welcome England.'

His diatribe was arrogant and patronising. The bad smell it left still lingered in 1970.

Nothing Mexico did or offered to Ramsey pleased him. The team bus wasn't good enough; England brought and drove their own. The food wasn't good enough either; the FA agreed a partnership with Findus, owned by the Swiss company Nestlé, that saw containers of frozen meat – and even fruit – shipped over from Europe. Ramsey and the FA had given the Mexican media a sword; they plunged it into England with relish. When customs officers incinerated Findus's beef burgers, bacon and sausages – all regarded as unfit – mock concern was expressed about England suffering malnourishment. A newspaper advised its readers to 'wash' any 'rotten fruit' it planned to throw at them. A TV station, apologising for the absence of a red-carpet welcome for England, assumed Ramsey had arrogantly packed his own – and brought a band with him to play the national anthem. At one press conference, Ramsey was asked if he'd brought a kettle to brew 'English' tea. 'Don't be stupid,' he said, sounding like one of his favourite characters, Captain Mainwaring, in his favourite TV comedy, *Dad's Army*. At another, tossed a softball question about Mexican hospitality, he answered with a provocative silence. Everything was a hassle for Ramsey. The noise outside England's hotel. The heat of the day. The reporters and TV crews, always wanting another word.

Ramsey did not care what anyone thought about him because he believed it did not matter. He made England the most unpopular team in the competition.

* * *

Not only the ball travelled faster through the thin air of Guadalajara, which is 5,212 feet above sea level. So did the apple cores, coins and orange peel hurled at Gordon Banks's goal before England faced Brazil. It was strewn across his six-yard box and piled up inside the back of his net, forcing him to go litter-picking.

The Mexican crowd, determined not to be impressed, jeered England on to the pitch and off it again. The roaring hostility towards them abated just once because the locals were catching their breath, too stupefied to speak.

There is a hierarchy even in the performance of miracles; some are less common than others, notably the one Banks performed.

Less than eight months after winning the World Cup, he had been neither thanked for his service nor allowed to argue his case when, without warning, Leicester City forced him out of Filbert Street. There was no apology or any ceremony about it. His manager, Matt Gillies, told Banks: 'The directors and I have been talking . . . We think your best days are behind you . . . You should move on.' Leicester had Peter Shilton, a prodigy already well aware of his own potential greatness. Shilton, still not 18, was conscious that half his career could be over before Banks retired. Leicester let Banks go purely so Shilton could take over from him.

After the shock wore off, what Banks felt was 'that dreadful feeling of betrayal' and incomprehension. 'I'd won the World Cup. I was still England's number one.' He was also driving nothing more plush than a Standard Eight and paying Leicester £3 – from his £35-a-week salary – to rent his semi-detached home.

Banks was linked with Manchester United, who flirted with him, and also West Ham, but he expected Bill Shankly to outbid both of them. Leicester priced Banks at £55,000. Shankly sheepishly claimed that Anfield's directors regarded the sum as 'too high' for a goal-keeper, an excuse that was barely credible. As if Shankly ever listened to his board . . .

Banks went to Stoke City, who paid a £2,000 signing-on bonus after Gillies also reneged on a verbal promise to compensate him for his loyalty. The episode shockingly exposes how undervalued and under-appreciated goalkeepers continued to be. It cost Tottenham only £25,000 to steal Pat Jennings from Watford in 1965. In 1966, Manchester United made Alex Stepney the country's most expensive 'keeper after buying him from Chelsea. The fee – identical to Banks's – was £60,000 below the price United had paid to purchase Denis Law from Torino three years earlier.

Goalkeepers were like cheap furniture – necessary but disposable. Alf Ramsey may not have found Ted Ditchburn the most affable company at Tottenham, but Arthur Rowe reminded him that recruiting the best goalkeeper you could find was integral to successful management. 'It's hard enough to score a goal. Don't give them away for free,' he'd said. Ramsey was one of the few contemporary managers who viewed goalkeepers as specialists, needing to be treated differently. 'Alf's convinced me that my mind hasn't got to wander,' said Banks, acknowledging how much sharper his concentration became under Ramsey. So did his positioning. So did his agility. So did his command of the box and his confidence in himself.

* * *

Gordon Banks was not even in his prime when he produced the save of all saves in Mexico.

Every time you watch Pelé rise to meet Jairzinho's measured cross and make powerful contact with it, you expect the ball to whizz past Banks. The laws of physics and geometry conflate in your mind to make any other outcome impossible. How close Pelé is . . . the speed of the header . . . the sight of it spearing towards the bottom corner . . . the distance Banks has to travel across his line. No, he can't get there; he'll be left groping at hot air, the ball already behind him before he can throw himself at it.

Pelé knows all this. He supplies his own commentary to the moment: 'Goal,' he screams.

The figure is disputed, but Pelé insists he scored 1,283 career goals.* 'And I am always asked,' he said, 'about the one I did not score.' He did not score it because Banks was there to redefine what a goalkeeper is capable of doing.

An old joke persists in football. On the rare occasion when something momentously era-defining occurs in a game, you should record the date, not the time, for posterity's sake.

June 7, 1970.

In a nanosecond, Banks did the maths. He calculated how fast the ball was moving – and how fast he had to move in response to it. He knew how high the header would bounce because he also knew how hard the sun had baked the pitch. He knew what he could not do, which was to catch the ball. He had to push it up and around the post with the fingers of his brand-new dimpled gloves.

Off he dived – and made history.

Sandwiched between England's opening group game against Romania, who were beaten 1–0, and their third, a copycat result over Czechoslovakia, the contest between the current World Champions

---

* Pelé published this figure in a tweet in 2015. The *Guinness Book of Records* puts his total at 1,279 goals.

and the former World Champions is even now all about Banks v. Pelé. You think of the save before you remember Bobby Moore tackling Jairzinho off the 'wrong' foot. Or the game's only goal, also Jairzinho's, which not even Banks could reach. Or the sitter, which ought to have given England a draw, that Jeff Astle snatched at and fluffed.

'He got up like a salmon out of clear water,' Banks said of Pelé. It reads like a line invented by a hack ghost-writer, but Banks made that analogy himself. The other language he used about the save was always plainer, modestly wanting to make the incredible seem mundane. 'All your experience and technique take over,' he explained, putting it down exclusively to instinct.

* * *

Alf Ramsey made uncharacteristic errors in preparation, selection and tactics.

There was also his confusing slip of the tongue before the game with Brazil. Ramsey announced, very formally, that the side to face them would be the one that had 'finished' the match against Romania. He forgot that Peter Osgood had replaced Francis Lee in the second half. Osgood thought he was playing; Lee believed he'd been unfairly dropped. During the team talk, Ramsey began discussing what Lee needed to do to push through Brazil's defence. 'But I'm not playing,' protested Lee. Embarrassed, Ramsey had to correct his error, apologising both to him and Osgood.

The plot was well and truly lost when England were about to leave Guadalajara for León – and even more so after the squad arrived there for the quarter-final against West Germany. One rotten decision from Ramsey rolled itself into the next. What happened can be condensed into 12 words: first the man took a drink – then the drink took the man.

But which drink and how?

Gordon Banks could never say with complete certainty what made him so sick that he couldn't get out of bed in León, where whatever was in him began coming out of both ends. More than likely, it was the Coke with ice he drank before dinner – rather than the bottle of beer he drank during it. What followed was a shambles of Ramsey's own making. He believed what Mexico's World Cup officials – disliking England and wanting to be awkward – had told him: it was 'impossible' to fly from Guadalajara to León because the runway at the airport was 'not long enough'. England would have to motor 200 miles along dust-flaked roads for four and a half hours. He neither challenged nor checked that lie. West Germany's plane had landed in León without a hitch before the competition began. When it was too late to do anything about it, Ramsey then became frantic about the standard of the hotel England had booked. He sent Harold Shepherdson and the team doctor to León to inspect the rooms and the kitchens.

This was another mistake.

Banks had gone to bed with stomach cramps. He awoke, looking as pale as parchment, in extreme pain. There was no one to treat him because England's doctor was in a taxi heading to León. Banks received no medical attention until he reached León himself at 1pm that day, only 23 hours before the match. His face was the colour of stagnant water. His temperature was also 38°C, but he arrived shivering and 'in a clammy sweat'.

Believing Banks would shake off the bug, like a mild cold, was Ramsey's third miscalculation. Peter Bonetti had not played a competitive game in the six and a half weeks since Chelsea beat Leeds in the FA Cup final replay at Old Trafford. His last England cap – only his sixth – had come the previous December. In training, Bonetti had found the ball's late wobble and extra speed difficult to read. Frequently, it embarrassed him. He wasn't equipped to play. Not psychologically. Not physically.

On the morning of the match, three hours before kick-off, Banks went through a fitness test. He said it took place on a 'strip of lawn dotted with acacia trees' that bordered one side of the hotel. You'd have thought England were a Sunday pub team on a beery outing to the south coast. Banks was asked to jog 12 yards from one tree to another. He stretched his arms. He jumped up and down. He collected a ball that was gently rolled underarm to him. Banks never forgot the conversation that followed:

Ramsey: How do you feel?
Banks: Fine.
Ramsey: Splendid. You're playing.

Banks went back to his room, fell backwards on to the bed and got up again to vomit. In the team meeting, held in Ramsey's bedroom because the hotel couldn't offer an alternative, Banks was in agony – perspiring, holding his stomach, afraid of being sick. After becoming dizzy, he fainted.

Slightly different versions exist of what Ramsey muttered after England lost 3–2 to West Germany without him. The gist was: 'Of all the players we had to lose, why him?' Ramsey considered Banks to be England's 'greatest strength' – even more important to him than Bobby Moore and Bobby Charlton.

If that was the case, you can only answer Ramsey's 'Why him?' with a question of your own: why didn't England take better care of him?

* * *

Alf Ramsey described England's defeat to West Germany as 'one of the mysteries of football'.

But there was no mystery about it whatsoever. England, 2–0 ahead until the 69th minute, wilted in the noonday heat.

Ramsey made the wrong substitutions at the wrong time, particularly his decision to unchain Bobby Charlton from Franz Beckenbauer, saving him for a semi-final that England had yet to reach. Charlton, who said he still felt 'fantastically well' and 'full of running', was annoyed not about being dragged off, which he'd expected, but because he thought England were complacently 'pissing around too early', believing the game was won. Bobby Moore thought Charlton's withdrawal heralded 'the making' of Beckenbauer. 'Psychologically, he used to fear playing against Bobby,' who could 'run forever', he said. Without Charlton there to emasculate him, dominating his every thought, Beckenbauer was 'suddenly free', added Moore. 'It was like taking lead weights off his feet.'

Helmut Schön made better choices than Ramsey. He brought on a fresh right-winger, Jürgen Grabowski, to torture the fatigued Terry Cooper, who was made to look shuffling and ungainly. And Peter Bonetti was abysmally at fault for all three German goals.

The first, from Beckenbauer, crept softly under him. The second, the fluky back-header from Uwe Seeler, went over him. Gerd Müller's extra-time winner, struck from close range, seemed to go clean through him. Bonetti came off his line so reluctantly to face Müller that you'd have thought premature rheumatism had already hardened his joints. The photograph everyone knows, taken from behind

West Germany's winner, which Peter Bonetti doesn't see because his eyes are closed

the net, could have been choreographed by Diaghilev: Müller is air-borne, twisting his slim frame at an angle so he can get over the ball; Bonetti still has one foot on the turf and his ungloved hands can't stop a ball that's already past him. The photograph few have seen is a landscape, snapped a spilt second before the other one. This shows why Bonetti was so easily beaten: his eyes are tightly shut, as if bracing himself for a blow. As Gordon Banks once said: 'You can't stop a shot if you can't see it.'

In their World Cup dirge 'Back Home', England had promised to 'give all we've got to give', but it was never going to be enough once the Germans took command. England chased them through every compass point without retrieving the ball. By then, like a gambler with a diminishing number of chips, Ramsey had wasted all his bets.

* * *

In the hotel, still in ferocious pain, Gordon Banks lay propped up on pillows to watch the game on a 'delayed transmission'. When the first half began on TV, the match in the stadium was already deep into the second. Oblivious to the abrupt reversal in fortunes, Banks was thinking about the semi-final when Bobby Moore, Alan Ball and Alan Mullery pushed open the door to his room, looking grimmer than pall-bearers at a state funeral. Assuming this was the feeblest of practical jokes, Banks asked: 'So how many did we win by?'

Alf Ramsey never blamed individuals – apart from himself. He didn't criticise Peter Bonetti,* not that day or afterwards. In the dressing room, almost silent apart from the sobbing, he shook hands with everyone. When Ramsey reached Bonetti, he said, very chivalrously: 'Thank you for everything you have done for us.'

The careers of three World Cup winners ended on the aeroplane home. Ramsey, who sat alone for most of that flight, went over to

* Bonetti did not win another cap.

Bobby Charlton: 'I just want to say thank you for all you have done for England.' The meaning of that sentence was immediately apparent to the recipient. 'He did not tell me that my England career was over, but then there was really no need . . . there was no way I would play in the next World Cup.' Jack Charlton didn't wait for Ramsey to come to him. He fortified himself with 'a few drinks' before planting himself in a vacant seat beside him. He made a small, rehearsed speech about how his time to retire internationally had finally come. Ramsey, barely looking at him, said only: 'Yes, I totally agree.'

Nobby Stiles had gone to Mexico as emergency cover for Mullery. Only 28, Stiles knew his battered knees were already 'shot through'. He called it his 'career crisis'; even his place at Manchester United was in jeopardy.

But Stiles, an observer attuned to the moment, recognised that failure in Mexico marked the beginning of the end for someone else too.

'Alf's spell had been broken,' he said.

14

THIS IS THE END OF THE
WORLD AS WE KNOW IT

The attributes that won Alf Ramsey the World Cup – obstinacy and his implacable belief that he was always right – meant he would never win another.

The careers of most top football managers, like those of most top politicians, end in failure because of a flaw fatal to continued success: their ego begins to slowly poison their judgement. It happened to Ramsey in Mexico, but the signs were even more conspicuous as soon as he arrived home. After watching the gorgeous fiesta of the World Cup final on TV from his own sofa – Brazil beating Italy 4–1 – Ramsey responded to it with a quote so asinine that either his eyesight or his sanity should have come under scrutiny

Even the faintest praise for the new champions, however grudging or ungracious, would have been preferable to what Ramsey offered. 'I don't think we can learn anything from the Brazilians. As far as our football is concerned, we have nothing really to concern ourselves with,' he said. The view was so blatantly at odds with the evidence that it sounded like the agitated ravings of a man who had spent too long under the Mexican sun without wearing a hat.

If you were being especially kind, you could claim that he was only reminding everyone not to undervalue the merits of the English game. But no excuse can entirely explain away the dumb idiocy of the statement because during the next two years – and then again in the 18 months following them – almost everything Ramsey did confirmed how much he believed it.

With the kind of magical thinking that would not have disgraced the plot of a South American novel, Ramsey also constructed an alternative outcome to the World Cup, which was built around a healthy Gordon Banks. With Banks in goal, rather than Peter Bonetti, England hurdled over West Germany and nimbly side-stepped Italy in the semi-finals. In the Azteca, his tactical acumen subdued Brazil, as though administering an anaesthetic to them, before a counter-attack or two retained the trophy. This is the way Ramsey truly saw things.

He also reached the conclusion that Banks's illness was not acciden-tal but deliberate, a well-executed plot to nobble the favourites. The perpetrator was the CIA. According to Ramsey, the motive, vaguer than mist, had 'something' to do with improving Latin American rela-tions; England were just the patsies. If you're willing to believe such guff, as Ramsey did, you must be willing to believe anything – even that the moon is made of green cheese. In 1966, *Life* magazine published a piece about the World Cup that congratulated 'Britain' on winning it. By 1970, the United States' knowledge of 'soccer', though improved, remained relatively unsophisticated. Only guesswork would have led the average American to pick out Ramsey in an identity parade. Nor was the CIA's in-tray so empty that spiking Banks's drink would have become a priority on those very few days when nothing much was going on in Vietnam, behind the Berlin Wall or inside the Kremlin and the Lubyanka.

Ramsey went with the Sherlock Holmes argument – 'When you have eliminated the impossible, whatever remains, however improb-able, must be the truth' – because it suited his purpose. Settling on sabotage as the reason for England's downfall was the only way Ramsey could rationalise his loss. A conspiracy theory, however cranky, enabled him to pretend – at least to himself – that he'd been cheated rather than defeated.

Mexico was the beginning of what was unnecessarily dragged out into a long end for Ramsey. In the grip of error, he increasingly looked

Sir Harold Thompson, looking surprisingly benign, slightly jovial and innocent

to be blind to – or detached from – too many of the realities facing him. When turning points arose, he merely chose not to turn.

He hopelessly misread the opposition, not only on the pitch, but also off it.

* * *

By the end of 1971, Professor Sir Harold Thompson could no longer contain himself. He wrote a 3,000-word report, half 'state of the nation' summary, half personal manifesto, that was called 'The Function and Policy of the Football Association'.

Thompson continued to be a quite brilliant chemist – adviser to governments at home and abroad – and a quite odious man. He was now the FA's deputy chairman – a prince to the king – but his overbearing, bombastic personality dominated meetings and browbeat colleagues whom he considered to be lesser beings with inferior minds.

The FA's chairman was Andrew Stephen, a bespectacled Scot who looked like the amiable manager of a market-town bank. He was a doctor with a diffident but pleasant bedside manner. Stephen, also chairman of Sheffield Wednesday, had succeeded Joe Mears, head of the family dynasty that ran Chelsea. Mears had died of a heart attack only a fortnight before the start of the 1966 World Cup.

Among the FA's other chief figures were Len Shipman of Leicester City and Dick Wragg of Sheffield United. Shipman, the president of the Football League, was accused of belonging to the 19th century after advocating the return of 'the birch' to deal with the 'wild animals' of hooliganism. Wragg, a builders' merchant, joined the FA Council in the year Ramsey was appointed as England's boss and became head of the International Committee in 1969. There was much less to him than met the eye. Pitting this trio against Thompson was like deploying a squadron of archers to stop a tank. He out-thought and out-argued them. If he couldn't do either, he thumped the conference table with the flat of his hand, sending cups and teaspoons bouncing out of their saucers.

He deplored not only England's defeat in Mexico, but also the mess it left behind. Thompson, who wasn't there, did his investigative homework afterwards by talking to the British and Mexican embassies. In a three-page, typed letter to the FA secretary, Denis Follows, he wrote: 'There can be no doubt that we have damaged our own reputation and the name of the UK ... The faults were to some extent on our own side and could have been avoided.' Without identifying them, Thompson blamed doddery FA councillors who 'apart from their physical incapacity' also lacked 'the necessary experience, training or ability' to 'cope' with the 'worldly relationships of modern football'. He thought 'some members' had been 'allowed to go on far too long', and added that their 'retirement ... is in my view overdue and fundamental'. Thompson also believed that 'ordinary members' of the FA Council should be allowed to 'express their opinions' without being 'told to shut up' by 'those who have nominally "led" our team and refused to admit their own incompetence'.

There was one person Thompson did name in his report.

'Even Sir Alf Ramsey, as a paid servant of the FA, has a responsibility to the FA Council and silent arrogance is as inappropriate here as it was in Latin America,' he said.

Thompson had spent his whole working life writing theses and documents, along with letters to the gentry, politicians in ministerial posts, diplomats, civil servants, other academics and also academic institutions. He knew how to pick his words for maximum effect, how to weigh each sentence and select a phrase, the full purpose and meaning of which was partly disguised. The remark about Ramsey's 'silent arrogance' might suggest – to those who didn't know Thompson well enough – mild irritation. Those who did know him were aware the message signalled his sharp distaste for Ramsey and what he saw as his inadequacies as both a man and a manager. And the phrase 'paid servant' qualified what Thompson believed was Ramsey's below-stairs status in Lancaster Gate.

Thompson hadn't even considered Ramsey to be England's best candidate when the FA appointed him. His preferred choice was Wolves' Stan Cullis. While not exactly pen pals, he and Cullis occasionally exchanged correspondence about the future of the game.

Now, it seemed to Thompson that the FA would never be rid of Ramsey – unless he orchestrated his departure.

From its opening paragraph, 'The Function and Policy of the Football Association' continued that theme. Thompson was primarily concerned about how the FA was perceived by the press and public alike, how 'his' organisation had been unfairly maligned for operational failings and how its relationship with the curmudgeonly Alan Hardaker and the Football League required recalibration. Thompson still couldn't resist parading a few of his prejudices and taking the cheapest of shots at Ramsey.

In his own handwriting, Thompson highlighted the sensitivity of his report's content and the importance of making sure there were no indiscreet leaks that would turn his comments into a Fleet

Street headline. Above the title, Thompson scrawled 'PRIVATE & CONFIDENTIAL' in large capitals, dragging his pen across the paper at least twice to fatten each letter.

'The wave of euphoria which followed England's World Cup victory nearly six years ago has long since passed,' began Thompson, reminding the FA's hierarchy of Ramsey's decline. 'Of course . . . the enormous popularity of the game is still beyond argument. Yet its image has become blurred, almost tarnished. Is this due to the behaviour and discipline of players, crowds or supporters; to visions of prima donnas in our leading teams; to higher wages and still higher transfer fees being paid by clubs which claim to be on the verge of insolvency; to the idiosyncrasies of an England team manager . . .?'

The line about Ramsey and his 'idiosyncrasies' again showed how much he disliked him.

That feeling was reciprocated. Neither man could stand the sight of the other.

* * *

Alf Ramsey welded himself to the England job out of choice, a decision based around the pride he took from it. 'Money wasn't my motivation,' he said.

If it had been, Ramsey could have been boss of Manchester United.

Less than six months after the 1970 World Cup, Sir Matt Busby demoted his prodigy, the 31-year-old Wilf McGuinness, from manager to reserve-team coach and reluctantly took over as caretaker, a post he didn't want for reasons of inclination and health. When asked who would succeed him, Busby replied: 'The bigger the name, the better, and who is bigger than Sir Alf Ramsey?' That declaration was so startling that Busby was forced to clarify it immediately afterwards. He wasn't suggesting United were bidding for Ramsey; he simply represented 'the calibre of candidate' the club wanted to appoint. Busby, though, had already approached Ramsey clandestinely shortly before

McGuinness was put out of his agony (United, European Champions in 1968, were 18th in the table and Third Division Aston Villa had knocked them out of the League Cup).

Busby and Ramsey had known one another for nearly 30 years. Busby was the first club manager to step inside the England dressing room after the World Cup final. The idea of hiring Ramsey made perfect sense to Busby, who thought the knights would get along without aggravation. Knowing, too, how highly Ramsey thought of McGuinness, he suggested the two of them might become a team. McGuinness would benefit from working alongside him and could repair his career.

Busby was not the first suitor to promise Ramsey a cash windfall and total control. When Jimmy Hill decided to step aside as boss of Coventry City in 1967, after steering them to the Second Division title, he tried unsuccessfully to persuade Ramsey to replace him. Ramsey said he had no intention of leaving Lancaster Gate. Busby got the same answer. Ramsey was preparing for the European Championship group games against Malta, Greece and Switzerland. He also wanted to go to a third World Cup.

Busby asked Ramsey to think about his offer. His England contract expired in June. If United hadn't found another candidate by then, would Ramsey reconsider?

Again, he declined.

* * *

In the early 1970s, English football took a hard look at itself and didn't like what it saw.

In a beauty contest, the decade was always going to be an ugly sister to the 1960s, giving it an inferiority complex from birth. Grappling to gain an identity of its own, the '70s became distinctive in ways that were hugely less attractive and more aggressively rebellious. The decade wasn't entirely drab. After all, you could laugh at the fashions

– blaringly loud tank tops, the flap of bell-bottom trousers, wide lapels, panda collars on shirts and silk kipper ties in psychedelic patterns that, if looked at long enough, seemed to swirl like a lava lamp. It wasn't entirely an economically desperate time either; for some the standard of living outstripped both the '50s and '60s. The chief difference lay in attitudes and perceptions. The emblematic, feelgood thrill of the '60s was that today was good but tomorrow would be better still. The '70s, pessimistic even in its infancy, put a hobnailed boot into that theory and kept on kicking. Social and industrial unrest filled acres of newsprint. Post Office workers walked out for 47 days in their first-ever strike. Rolls-Royce went bankrupt. Inflation nudged towards a 30-year high of almost 9 per cent. Unemployment topped one million for the first time since the Great Depression. This was only the prelude to the miners' dispute, the lights going out and the introduction of the three-day week, which benefited only those who manufactured candles or batteries for the 'wireless', and pupils who got to bunk off school earlier than usual.

Football, not immune to the downturn, faced an existential reckoning too. Millions had gone missing from the terraces since the late '60s. At the start of 1972, the Football League studied statistical projections that terrified them: the number of spectators attending over the course of a season could fall below 25.5 million – or, perhaps, dip lower still. The League and the Football Association were always butting heads over TV, arguing about how many games should be shown and also how much the BBC and ITV should pay for them. On those two questions alone, Alan Hardaker egregiously declared 'war' between the League and the FA.

There was also the blight of hooliganism, both inside grounds and on the way to and from them. In pubs and bars, on streets and at railway stations, a football scarf too often became feared by those who were not fans. John Arlott gave up covering the game, which he thought had become 'a bit seedy'. He experienced an epiphany after the *Guardian* asked him to go to Luton's Kenilworth Road on Boxing

Day: 'I thought what a nasty obit to have: "He was clubbed to death outside the Luton ground."'

England under Alf Ramsey offered no balm for the wounds. Even after Ramsey began winning again, there were still calls for him to step aside.

Between mid-autumn 1970 and the early spring of 1972, England went unbeaten in 10 matches, a respectable enough run, studded with the occasional modest thrashings of East Germany (3–1), Greece (3–0), Malta (5–0) and Scotland (3–1). Ramsey relied on his five remaining World Cup winners – Banks, Moore, Ball, Hurst and Peters – as the structural pillars of a new side in which both the tried and untried appeared and then disappeared again. It was all very similar to the preparations Ramsey had made before 1966; he shuffled the deck as rapidly as a street card sharp in a game of Find the Lady.

In came strikers such as John Radford at Arsenal and Joe Royle of Everton. There were new central defenders, among them Derby's Roy McFarland and Larry Lloyd of Liverpool. The midfielders included Ralph Coates, about to move from Burnley to Tottenham, and Arsenal's Peter Storey, who was also capable of switching to right back. Chris Lawler of Liverpool was called up. So was Leeds's Paul Madeley, so outstandingly versatile that he could slot in anywhere. Even Colin Harvey of Everton and West Bromwich Albion's Tony Brown were tossed a fleeting chance, each making only a solitary appearance. After Mexico, Peter Shilton won the first of his 125 caps.

Ramsey nonetheless took stick for racking up results and goals against no one likely to bother England in the forthcoming World Cup. The victories, though adequate, were thought to be superficial, like a coat of varnish on old furniture, because functionality rather than flair was still Ramsey's default position. He took few risks, never playing the players the public would have paid to see. The ordinary fan concluded with regret that, if Ramsey had ever watched Rodney Marsh at Loftus Road or Charlie George at Highbury, he had immediately closed his eyes. He didn't seem overly fond of Frank Worthington or

Tony Currie either. Here was a quartet of non-conformists predisposed to taking the piss on the field every Saturday afternoon and going on the piss most Saturday nights. Like his friend George Best, Marsh would beat a defender twice for no reason other than he could do it. With his lank hair and long face, which made him look like a groomed Afghan hound, George performed ridiculously audacious tricks with a ball. So did Currie, confusing defenders with a shuffle that spun them around as though they were trapped in a revolving door. Worthington disliked shin pads, rolled his socks to his ankles and wore sideburns in honour of Elvis Presley, his hero. He went for cheeky goals; volleys and chips became his speciality. He was good enough to have scored them in his cowboy boots, part of an off-field outfit that made him look like an actor auditioning for a Sergio Leone western. His philosophy on his anything-goes lifestyle was summed up in the title of the autobiography he eventually published: *One Hump or Two?* On the cover, Worthington is pictured demurely holding a tea cup.

Ramsey said: 'When people ask me why I don't play so-and-so or so-and-so, the answer is because the player concerned never quite satisfied me.' This was his way of saying that Marsh and company didn't perform consistently enough for him. The likes of Worthington might warrant top marks in the *Sunday People*'s player ratings only once every three or four weeks, which is why Ramsey so mistrusted mavericks. He thought of them as vaudeville acts who would entertain for 10 minutes and go AWOL for 80. Jimmy Greaves, drawing on personal experience, could testify about that line of thinking. Ramsey's critics on the terraces and in the press box, who were still disgruntled, resurrected Greaves's case as evidence that nothing in the manager's attitude had changed – and nor would it change in the future. They saw no remedy for Ramsey's dourness or lack of adventure.

There were other, worrying signs that Ramsey was not the smooth, quiet operator he had once been. The dossiers he kept were evidently out of date. During Arsenal's Double-winning season, he telephoned

Bertie Mee to ask whether his goalkeeper, Bob Wilson, was eligible for England's Under-23 team. Wilson's next birthday would be his thirtieth, and he was about to win his first cap for Scotland, qualifying because of his parents.

* * *

Hindsight always brings the clarity of 20–20 vision, so anyone who finds England's European Championship quarter-final against West Germany on YouTube will recognise immediately what the game represents: the closing of an era. The match, which the Germans won 3–1, was heavy with symbolism.

There was Bobby Moore, 31 and slightly tubbier than before, giving the ball away for the opening goal after 26 minutes and conceding a penalty with a mistimed challenge in the 84th. There was Gordon Banks, failing to get a glove on a deflected shot that his younger self would probably have palmed away. There was Geoff Hurst, substituted shortly before the hour; he never played for England again. His wife Judith, sitting in the stand, cried that evening. 'I knew somehow that was the end,' she explained.

England equalised in the 78th minute, but the result didn't overly flatter the Germans, whose overall performance gave anyone who saw it an awareness of how much their football had changed creatively and also how many thousands of light years separated it from our own. It was world class v. third class.

After Mexico, Helmut Schön decided the Germans needed to be bravely innovative. He switched Franz Beckenbauer to sweeper. 'We needed a different approach,' he explained. Schön called the Wembley win 'one of the national team's greatest matches'. If he 'ever wanted' to watch a game 'from the past', he slid the video of it into his machine.

The Germans were technically superior and craftier, possessing a swagger and a finesse the opposition embarrassingly lacked. One individual, the so-called Rebel on the Ball, possessed more charisma than England could muster collectively; he ran the show. If Günter Netzer had been born in Manchester, rather than Mönchengladbach, he might never have worn an international shirt under Ramsey. He played the way he lived, which was with a casual, hedonistic ebullience and a disregard for convention. He went where he wanted to go. A back-to-back title winner with Borussia Mönchengladbach, Netzer was dropped for the 1973 German cup final, ostensibly because of a lack of fitness. Defying his manager, he put himself on as an extra-time substitute, banging in the winner a minute later. He opened a nightclub named Lover's Lane. He drove a Ferrari. He seldom drank but liked long parties (you can only imagine what would have happened if Netzer, Frank Worthington and Rodney Marsh had gone on a boys' weekend together).

Netzer, only 5ft 10in tall, wore size-12 boots, and his straight hair flopped on to his shoulders. He could move with a languid, elegant nonchalance before suddenly revving off like one of his Ferraris. On that Saturday night at Wembley, he collected a pass from Beckenbauer ten yards outside his own box and – after outstripping Francis Lee for speed and vaulting over a tackle from Alan Ball – finished up ten yards outside England's in less than seven seconds, leaving defenders to gag on his dust. Without looking up, he would launch attacks with incisive short passes or a long ball, placed rather than punted, that curled off the outside of his boot.

Ramsey didn't bother to name-check Netzer in his pre-match talk. He believed his old adversary Schön was coming for a disciplined bore-draw ahead of the second leg in Berlin. The English press alarmed Schön, who found its preoccupation with the war still persisted. After he promised to 'lay as firm foundations as possible', Schön read pieces that predicted England would need to 'storm the Siegfried Line' to break Germany down. He winced again when the tactical battle between him and Ramsey was described as 'Monty against Rommel'. Schön played a very loose 1–3–3–3 formation. If Netzer dropped back, Beckenbauer went forward.

Without anyone shadowing him, Netzer was free to roam, controlling the flow and tempo of the game. His first touches were so beautiful that some of England's looked amateurishly clumsy in comparison, like watching someone trying to play a piano with their toes. You willed Netzer to get the ball simply so he could bewitch you all over again. England, stiff and passive, bludgeoned high balls upfield to escape from their own box, exposing again their paucity of thought.

The English game entered a state of emergency not seen since the Hungarians had frightened it witless. Parallels were drawn in newspapers with the humiliation of 1953. The phrases used were so depressingly similar that you fancied someone had gone through old bound copies of newspapers, cutting and pasting whole passages from them. The Football Association's response was also so similar that it seemed no one had learnt anything from recent history. A shiver went through Lancaster Gate, but it failed to find a spine to run up.

It wasn't a writer but a pocket cartoonist in the *Daily Mail* who caught Ramsey's dark mood and his reluctance to look anywhere else but backwards. Ramsey is depicted on the phone, while holding a piece of paper that contains the names of his retired '66 winners. He is working his way through them and has reached Nobby Stiles. The caption reads: 'Nobby, are you available for May 13 . . .' That was the date of the return match in Berlin – an irrelevance because the tie was already lost and England didn't have anything left to give; it was all about preserving a little dignity.

Just as he'd attempted to claim parity with Brazil after Mexico, Ramsey would make another equally delusional claim. After England came away with a goalless draw in Berlin, he announced: 'I am proud of my team. On the day I would not have changed any one of them for a member of the German side.' Not even Netzer . . .*

---

* England adopted an age-old tactic to stop Günter Netzer in Germany: they kicked him. 'Most of the England team autographed my right leg,' he said.

* * *

No Fleet Street newspaper bashed Alf Ramsey harder or more frequently than the *Sun*.

Words such as 'humiliation' and 'embarrassment' were used everywhere in reference to England's performance against West Germany, but one of that paper's headlines boiled into seven words what others were taking 2,000 to say:

The Man Ten Years Behind the Times

Having grasped Ramsey warmly by the throat, the *Sun* refused to let go. Over the next 18 months, there were more headlines that came viciously to the point:

Ramsey, You're Killing our Soccer
We're Not the Greatest
Ramsey's Boring the Pants Off Us
Pack It in Ramsey – Everyone Laughs at You Now

If Ramsey wasn't replaced, said the *Sun*, 'they will soon be tearing down our soccer stadia, making bingo halls, bowling alleys and office blocks out of them'. Watching Ramsey's team was about as entertaining as 'a chess match', it added. There was no shortage of stories about who should follow Ramsey. The favourites, predictably, were Don Revie and Brian Clough. A third candidate was Malcolm Allison. No one wanted Ramsey's job more than Clough. Nor did he hide his vaulting ambition. 'I would love it. I'd jump at being England manager,' he said.

The advice Clough gave to other bosses was the succinct 'Say nowt, win something and then talk your head off.' Clough had won something – a League Championship – but talking his head off was a daily occurrence long before that happened. He had an opinion about everything, including social affairs and politics, the royal family, the state of British TV and the Apollo moonshots.

Ramsey could barely say Clough's name without choking; he referred to him as 'the Derby County manager'. And Clough had a particular loathing for him too, both personal and professional. Anyone needing to compose a story knocking Ramsey only had to find Clough, who thought of Ramsey as a 'strange' man and also a 'cold' one. He regarded his approach to football as 'negative' and 'sterile'. 'I found it difficult to watch England play and even more difficult to listen to Ramsey talk. Blimey, he was dull . . . Like his team, he sent you to sleep.' Clough said he never knew what Ramsey was thinking because he could never tell 'what he was feeling'. It was like 'talking to an iceberg'.

Shaken by the vilification he received after losing to West Germany, Ramsey's relationship with the newspapers – such as it was – sank to even lower depths. He tried to give back as much criticism as he got, confiding after one tempestuous press conference: 'I have just given those bastards some terrible bloody stick.'

Ramsey's biggest fight was still going on inside Lancaster Gate.

* * *

Like a lot of very bright people, Sir Harold Thompson had a constant need to remind everyone of his intelligence. A show-off arrogance was not his only defect, but the others stemmed directly from it.

Arthur Rowe had worked with Pegasus in the mid-to-late 1950s. He found Thompson meddlesome, annoying and ignorant about football, a rank amateur who reckoned his technical knowledge was equal to any professional's. He was also almost impossible to shake off. Thompson couldn't let go of the club, afraid that someone else might succeed without him. He gave his opinions without waiting to be asked. He barged into conversations about Pegasus in the same way he barged into their dressing room, making suggestions about tactics and the opposition in between smoking one cigar and lighting up another. He sent notes containing written advice. Often too polite for his own good, Rowe feigned interest until Thompson found someone else to demean.

A smack of cruelty or a sneer was present in a lot of the mischief Thompson perpetrated. With patience, he picked his moment to goad and bait those he perceived as vulnerable, as though it was a blood sport. He would probe away at them with questions or criticisms.

Alf Ramsey usually made his excuses and left whenever he saw Thompson approaching or sniffed the pungent whiff of his cigars, which arrived in a room shortly before he did. Often Ramsey would close his office door and make a lengthy telephone call. When a conversation with Thompson could not possibly be ducked, he used as few words as possible.

How Thompson addressed him – and others – was only one bone of contention for Ramsey. Thompson retained the public-school habit of referring to nearly everyone, especially any person he considered to be beneath him, by their surname only, never prefixing it with the politeness of 'Mr'. Ramsey always called him Thompson because Thompson always called him Ramsey. Thompson made no concessions with the players either. It was 'Moore', not Bobby, and 'Banks', not Gordon. When Thompson clicked his fingers, which he did occasionally to seize someone's attention, you'd have thought he was summoning a waiter to fetch him a whisky.

Thompson came to resent Ramsey. This hardened into a distaste that became impossible to conceal. For him, it was a question of class and upbringing. He didn't like Ramsey's manner, his voice or his lack of subservience to those who paid his wages. He didn't like the fact he'd been awarded his knighthood for winning the World Cup – or the protection that triumph afforded him in the Football Association. He didn't like Ramsey's approach to football either. In particular, he didn't like – at all – the fact that someone who'd left school before starting to shave had more authority than he did within the FA.

Ramsey tried to work around Thompson, but found him to be a 'bloody pest'. There were a succession of small battles, which

Thompson instigated to be awkward. He started to telephone FA councillors on spurious pretexts that didn't disguise the point of the call, which was to quote whatever criticism he'd found of Ramsey in the newspapers. On an England trip to Prague, he puffed on his cigars at breakfast, vexing players who were trying to eat while inhaling cumulus clouds of smoke. He smoked again during a team meeting, which he attended uninvited. As a German speaker, he had ambitions to handle England's public relations during the 1974 World Cup. 'Over my dead body,' said Ramsey. Thompson wanted to know, usually in writing, about England's training methods . . . how Ramsey prepared for matches . . . how he decided which players to watch and which team to pick . . . the roles of Harold Shepherdson and Les Cocker . . . a breakdown of Ramsey's working week . . . his long-range strategies, building up to future World Cups. As though he was of blue blood, Thompson suggested to Ramsey that it would be 'respectful' if the players 'stood up' whenever he entered a room.

On each occasion, Ramsey rebuffed him, knowing that every request would only be followed by another soon enough. Thompson's tactics were blatant – and there was no way to stop them without getting into the sort of shoot-out that Ramsey had seen in so many westerns.

He did commit one mistake. In a London hotel, Thompson asked Ramsey to carry his bag. For some reason, he did it. The small incident emboldened Thompson in his conflict with him.

* * *

Except for the occasional retrograde slip or two, the language of modern football has learnt how to use 'tragedy' in its proper context rather than attaching it fatuously to descriptions of own goals, missed penalties and last-minute defeats. The game now saves that word for occasions the *Shorter Oxford English Dictionary* defines as 'A terrible or fatal event in life, a calamity, a disaster'.

On Sunday, October 22, 1972, a tragedy occurred on the B5038 between Whitmore and Trentham in Staffordshire.

Gordon Banks had spent the morning at Stoke's Victoria Ground, where he received treatment for a minor shoulder injury sustained the afternoon before at Liverpool. Impatient to get home, he put his foot on the accelerator of his Ford Consul, trying to overtake a line of traffic at a spot where experience ought to have taught him to wait. The road, wet after drizzle, 'was flanked by trees and dipped before taking a sharp turn to the right', he said. His car, which was on the wrong side of the road, smashed head-on into a van that contained a husband and wife and their three-year-old son. Banks remembered two sounds: an 'almighty bang' and then 'glass shattering'.

Photographs of the car show it so mangled, the metal wrenched apart and twisted, that Banks's survival – and also that of the family in the van – is miraculous. But shards of glass from the windscreen tore at the flesh on his face. Two of those shards punctured his right eye. Banks underwent a three-hour operation. He needed 202 stitches, from chin to scalp, and 108 micro-stitches in and around his eye socket. He was blind for 50 hours. When he first tried to open his eyes, 'nothing happened', he said. 'It was as if someone had glued down my eyelids.'

In hospital, Banks, attempting to pick up a cup of tea from his bedside table, was unable to gauge correctly either distance or angle. He grasped at 'thin air', he admitted. Twelve weeks later, when stretching his arms at full length, he could see the spread of his fingers with his right eye, but a blur of indistinct shapes lay beyond them. He wore dark glasses to protect the eye from sunlight. Plastic surgery – 'smoothing out a few bumps', he said – couldn't cover the groove of a diagonal scar across his forehead. A dozen people – one of them from Brazil – offered to donate an eye for a transplant. 'That was unthinkable,' he said.

In the ambulance that took them from the scene of the crash, Banks had made both an apology and a confession to the wife of the van driver:

'I'm sorry. It's all my fault.' In court, he was found guilty of dangerous driving and fined £40, as well as being made to pay £29.80 in costs.

Banks was the current Footballer of the Year – just the second goal-keeper to receive the silver statuette since Bert Trautmann 16 years before. The honour acknowledged the fact that, without him, Stoke would never have won the League Cup at Wembley, the club's first major trophy.

Now half blind and 35 years old, Banks chose to retire because he could no longer 'meet the standards I set for myself'. The problem for Alf Ramsey, about to start the 1974 World Cup qualifying campaign, was that no one else could meet them either.

* * *

It hurt Alf Ramsey to have to confess how much he misjudged the Football Association. He came to regret not only his lack of financial foresight after 1966, but also the trust he placed in the FA to behave decently towards him. He conceded that he should have 'made a stand' for more money from a 'position of strength' years before, rather than in the autumn of 1973. 'Perhaps foolishly, I regarded it as an honour and payment enough to manage England,' he said.

At Derby County, where he collected generous bonuses, Brian Clough earned nearly £20,000 a year; he also drove a company Mercedes. Having failed to land Ramsey, Manchester United had moved for Frank O'Farrell, paying him a sum not far short of £17,000. Don Revie got much the same at Leeds. Ramsey's pay was £7,200, which included a cost-of-living bonus of £1,100. His annual increase at Lancaster Gate was £100.

It was Ramsey's perfectly understandable belief that his 'salary should be commensurate with the position', which it demonstrably wasn't. 'The England managership ought to be the best-paid job in football,' he said. 'Not among the worst, with a reward less than some managers receive in the Third and Fourth Divisions.'

The FA disagreed. It reacted to his request for a rise with the same horror as Mr Limbkins, the head of the parish board, after being told that Oliver Twist was demanding another bowl of gruel in the workhouse.

Its flat refusal was not based solely on footballing reasons.

The forced retirement of Denis Follows as secretary meant the arrival of Ted Croker, slickly smart in a pin-striped suit. Croker was a former RAF pilot who had survived a wartime crash in the Pennines; he'd crawled 200 yards down a cliff with two broken ankles to seek help for his fellow flyers. He was also a former player – eight appearances in defence for Charlton – and a qualified FA coach. It was his business experience, more than his football background, that attracted the FA, which ached for more commercial insight (its revenue from business 'enterprises' was a measly £24,000 per year then). Croker had developed a successful snow-blowing machine before switching to the concrete business. To no one's surprise, apart from his own, he found within the walls of Lancaster Gate a dysfunctional ragtag organisation. The FA even 'neglected to tell' Follows it would be appointing a new secretary until the advertisement for his job appeared in the newspapers. Its telephone number was also ex-directory, which, according to Croker, made buying tickets for internationals 'about as hard as trying to get into MI5'. The FA had a workforce of 56 people, but there had been 42 changes of staff in the previous 12 months. Ramsey was not their only underpaid employee. 'All the staff were underpaid,' revealed Croker.

He came with big ideas and a sparkling vision of a bold, brave new world. This was jolting for some FA councillors – and for Ramsey. Croker saw the benefits of shirt sponsorship. Ramsey saw it as a desecration. Sticking a company's name and logo beside the England badge was sacrilegious. A pure white shirt – 'the shirt of *my* players', he said – was non-negotiable for him. Ramsey was old enough to remember men walking up and down the streets with a huge sandwich board strapped across their shoulders, advertising everything from smelling salts to beer. 'We can't be like them,' was his view.

The FA had consistently played on Ramsey's weakness, which was his loyalty. Their attitude now ought to have been like a blinking red light, a warning that his employer no longer thought so highly of him and also perceived his opposition to shirt sponsorship as damaging to them.

Ramsey still put the FA's rebuff to one side, determined to be firmer after he reached the World Cup finals in West Germany.

Disjointed and out of sorts, England had so far failed to dominate a three-team qualifying group beside Wales and Poland, the current Olympic champions. Wales had inconvenienced them at Wembley, drawing 1–1, before Poland inflicted the serious damage in Warsaw, winning 2–0. Bobby Moore had toe-ended a Polish free kick, skewing a clearance that Peter Shilton saw too late to save. In the second half, occupying enough space to dig out a swimming pool, Moore had asked for a pass but languorously mis-controlled it. He couldn't drag the ball back before Włodzimierz Lubański robbed him to score.

After beating Wales too, the Poles were only a point away from eliminating England. No one, though, expected them to get that point at Wembley.

If not a formality, Ramsey was so confident about the outcome that he was ready to confront the FA with an ultimatum afterwards: if his salary didn't improve, he would consider quitting before the finals.

* * *

High intelligence wasn't required to form a low opinion of Alan Hardaker. In the name of the Football League, he kept saying things so obviously half-witted that you had to be a half-wit yourself to take any of them seriously. In the build-up to the World Cup in Mexico, Hardaker made a point of announcing with apparent pride that he would be staying at home because he saw nothing to be gained from going. 'World Cups – we can live without them,' he said. Hardaker was 'annoyed' by what he perceived as the unnecessary hype around the competition. 'What possible difference can it make to our football?' he asked, selectively overlooking the difference 1966 had made.

Before England faced Poland at Wembley, Hardaker climbed back on to his soap box to repeat his charge that the World Cup was an overblown circus, barely worth bothering about. 'Let's keep our sense of perspective. Everyone is going hysterical. It's a football match, not a war.' Not qualifying, he insisted, would be 'a terrible thing for about six weeks and then everybody will forget about it'. Hardaker was speaking partly in self-defence. The League had declined to cancel the previous Saturday's round of matches, which would have given Alf Ramsey at least seven days to prepare his team.

As things turned out, the contest with Poland became a sequence of such astonishing unlikelihoods – impossible to legislate for – that England could have spent a month on the training pitch without that extra work making a difference. That Ramsey never got to repeat his appeal for more money to the Football Association confirmed what he'd quietly feared. Ramsey could be a little superstitious. At Tottenham, he'd occasionally played with a rabbit-charm tucked into a sock. Ever since the defeat to West Germany in León, he'd talked disproportionately about 'luck' too – specifically bad luck, as though he and his team were cursed. It's the only explanation for the 1–1 draw Poland got; nothing else makes any sense.

You could sit through that game every day for the rest of your life and not know how England failed to rack up a cricket score. On the same pitch, just three weeks earlier, Austria had been crushed to powder by their hosts, losing 7–0. Ramsey expected something similar against the Poles.

Martin Peters found he was rarely the critics' choice for international honours, his name absent from newspaper pieces about who ought to be chosen. His wife once remarked to him: 'The only person who ever picks you for England is Alf Ramsey.' For this game, Ramsey made Peters captain. He was the only survivor from 1966. Alan Ball, sent off in Poland, was suspended. Bobby Moore was dropped as punishment for his performance in Warsaw. The conversation was painful but unavoidable for Ramsey, like telling a favourite son that it was time he packed up and left home.

Ramsey had gradually remoulded his side. He had tried Rodney Marsh, but dropped him again. He'd made Emlyn Hughes his left back. He'd brought in Tony Currie, letting him share some of the creative duties with Colin Bell. He'd persevered with Allan Clarke and Martin Chivers up front and pushed Mick Channon of Southampton alongside them. He gave Moore's shirt to Norman Hunter.

This England was not the kind of side that made you gasp in excited anticipation. Neither were the Poles.

Without the injured Włodzimierz Lubański, who had embarrassed Moore, the team was reliant on the seductive flair of the captain, Kazimierz Deyna and admirably reliable contributors such as Robert Gadocha and Jan Domarski. The goalkeeper, Jan Tomaszewski, was eccentrically unorthodox – though not the 'circus clown in gloves' that Brian Clough had called him to grab another headline. Some of Tomaszewski's saves could be slapstick or slapdash. He was prone to punching the ball away while facing his own goal and relying on any part of his body, including his head and his shoulders, to stop whatever came at him. He was also an athletic shot-stopper and would have dived on broken glass for the sake of his country.

England had 35 attempts on goal to Poland's two. They rattled post and bar. Efforts were kicked or scrambled off the line; somehow Tomaszewski parried or blocked a dozen others. When he was beaten, the referee rescued him, spotting at least one trifling infringement that even his linesman, who was closer, did not detect.

The goal Poland claimed, after 57 minutes, belonged to the Theatre of the Absurd, a pile-up of mistakes crashing and banging into one another. At any other time and in any other place, Hunter would either have whipped the ball away from Gadocha or lifted him with a kick right into Ramsey's lap on the front row of the England bench.

Hughes would have reacted more smartly and much faster, moving rather than lunging to shut down Domarski and preventing the shot. Shilton's drop to the turf would have been quicker too; he'd have taken the ball comfortably against his stomach, not let it skid beneath him

When Ramsey watched and rewatched the film of the game, he always went back to the goal. 'I tried to explain to myself how it could have happened. I couldn't. Not really.' Nor could he explain how, after so much pressure and possession, Clarke's penalty was the only goal England claimed.

Nearly everything about this game was extraordinarily bizarre. Nothing, though, topped Ramsey's reason for his delay in replacing Chivers with Kevin Hector of Derby. The decision came so late that England's hopes lay practically dead. Hector so nearly changed history. With Tomaszewski out of position, adrift in no-man's-land, his header bounced off the bended knees of the defender guarding the post.

Ramsey insisted it wasn't his indecisiveness that pinned Hector to the bench and left Chivers on the pitch for so long; he claimed his wristwatch had stopped. Like most grounds, Wembley didn't have a clock. 'I thought there were 12 minutes to go . . . there were only two,' he said.

If expert evidence didn't categorically contradict Ramsey, you'd be minded to believe him. Moore offered a different version. He'd urged Ramsey to 'stick a left-sided' attacker on. Ramsey said he'd pushed Hunter forward and then added: 'I don't think we can do any more.' He also asked: 'How long to go?' A voice – Moore couldn't remember whose – told him: 'Five minutes.' Moore's account of the rest of the conversation ran like this:

Ramsey: Too late now.
Moore: It's never too late. Get Kevin Hector on . . . Come on . . . Just get him out there.

The *Sun*, continuing its campaign against Ramsey, said beforehand it would be better if Poland performed a 'mercy killing' on him and

England. The following morning, the newspaper didn't celebrate. Its front-page headline – 'The End of the World!' – drove the story, but the photograph beside it was heart-breaking. Ramsey, wearing his beige mackintosh, is walking along the perimeter track, every step excruciating for him. The bulb of the photographer's flash gives his face a dead whiteness. He is staring into the night sky, his expression blank because his thoughts have not yet become feelings.

UNDER ATTACK . . . Sir Alf dodges beer cans from disappointed fans last night as he leaves the ground.   Picture by PETER JAY

15

ONE NIGHT AT THE CAFÉ ROYAL

Without knowing it, Brian Clough did Alf Ramsey a colossal favour.

If Clough hadn't resigned from Derby County only 48 hours before the World Cup qualifier against Poland, Sir Harold Thompson would have launched his campaign against Ramsey and ousted him before Oxford Street had switched on its Christmas lights that year.

Clough, along with his assistant, Peter Taylor, quit because his directors demanded he curtail his newspaper work and numerous TV appearances. Derby's chairman, Sam Longson, had originally glowed in the publicity Clough created, often by elevating rudeness into an art form. Envy set in for Longson when, very belatedly, he realised his manager was beginning to out-star his club. Resentment came next; Clough started chastising his own board too frequently for Longson's liking.

Convinced the team he'd constructed were on the cusp of a long trophy-winning spree, the League Championship merely a prequel to it, Clough regretted his decision to leave in the same week he made it.

He had been the overpowering presence on ITV's panel of talking heads during the defeat to Poland. With a typically provocative flourish, he'd produced a theatrical prop before kick-off. 'I've got a nail here in my hand and I want it to go in the Polish coffin – or, perhaps, it could go in Sir Alf's,' he said. Clough had condemned Ramsey's team selection in Warsaw. 'He picked a side with seven defenders, a side which screamed out to anyone who could read the programme: "We have come here not to lose. A draw will do."' Clough still reckoned Wembley would become a waltz for England, but helpfully warned

The gang's all here. England, looking disorganised, at the Café Royal

what failure would mean for Ramsey: 'I'm afraid it will be the end of the road . . . I don't see how he could continue . . .' Afterwards, Clough lambasted Ramsey for choosing 'the wrong team' again and added that he would 'never forgive' him for what had happened.

Clough was banking on fan power to force Derby's board out and bring him back in. The Football Association feared the same kind of fan power could be stirred if Ramsey were sacked, conceivably putting them in an impossible position: obliged to hire Clough, now unexpectedly available as a 'popular', ready-made replacement. This scenario was the cause of grisly nightmares at Lancaster Gate. The FA councillors were capable of reciting, verbatim, the gossip in Football League boardrooms about how completely Clough took control and how contemptuously he treated most directors. He was already on a charge of bringing the game into disrepute after writing a newspaper article that attacked in equal measure Leeds, Don Revie and the FA itself.

When Ramsey was asked about his future, he answered coyly, telling reporters: 'I don't know . . . we'll see, won't we . . .?' He was bracing himself for the sack. None of the FA's councillors had appeared in England's dressing room at Wembley to present Harold Shepherdson with a silver salver in recognition of his distinguished service. Their excuse – the huge crowd had made it impossible for them to walk there – entirely lacked credibility. 'They made it over here in 1966,' said Ramsey. He concluded: 'The writing was on the wall . . . I was a dead duck.' He found that 'suddenly the handshakes stopped', and he 'sensed a coldness among the FA Councillors' too.

He didn't want to be succeeded by the people's choice. He thought Clough talked like a patriot without acting like one. Before the European Championship qualifier against West Germany in 1972, Clough had withdrawn Roy McFarland from England's squad, claiming he was unfit. Ramsey had planned to partner him alongside Bobby Moore. Only 48 hours later, McFarland played in Derby's final league match of the season, a win over Liverpool that was ultimately critical in landing Clough the championship. Ramsey received six identical reports of that game; McFarland showed 'no sign or semblance of injury', he said.

Much to the FA's relief, Clough compounded his original error with another. After rushing to leave Derby, he also rushed to join Third Division Brighton. You normally only went to the seaside resort for 'a holiday or a dirty weekend', admitted Clough. He was going there for more than £25,000 a year.

* * *

The traumatised Football Association had assumed that World Cup qualification – plus the cash windfall that went with it – was a foregone conclusion. The FA had no contingency plan about what to do with Alf Ramsey or how to fill the financial hole – about £500,000 deep – now confronting them.

What is more, Ramsey still had support inside Lancaster Gate.

Dick Wragg and Len Shipman fought his corner, reporting the response of other councillors quietly to him. Since Sir Harold Thompson's opposition was hardly classified information – Thompson labelled Ramsey as a 'loser' who 'must go' – Wragg and Shipman concentrated instead on more malleable colleagues who might be persuaded to forget the 1974 World Cup and plan for 1978. It helped Ramsey's cause that the FA, squirming at the thought of committing regicide, were incapable of answering with forthright conviction three fundamental questions:

Who possessed Ramsey's calibre and matched his international pedigree?

Who did the FA actually want – and would their choice even accept the job?

How much was the FA prepared to pay a successor?

The field was quite shallow. There was always a reason not to tick the card of a particular candidate. Bertie Mee, at Arsenal, and Bill Nicholson, still at Tottenham, were both older than Ramsey. Ron Greenwood was only a year younger – and he hadn't won a trophy for West Ham since 1965. At Ipswich, the 40-year-old Bobby Robson, without any silverware, was considered too callow. Burnley's Jimmy Adamson, the FA's original choice a decade before, was no longer a plausible option either. Don Revie, the obvious pick, had triumphed both domestically and abroad, but there were FA councillors who mistrusted his 'shady' character and disliked his 'dirty' team.

In mid-November, on the morning after England had lost 1–0 to Italy in a friendly at Wembley, the FA's senior International Committee gave Ramsey the dreaded Devil's Kiss – a vote of confidence. Wragg described it as 'unanimous'. Of course, it wasn't.

It would take another 167 days before Thompson got rid of Ramsey, the sacking carried out in super-slow motion.

* * *

Failure in a team game is seldom one man's fault, but Sir Harold Thompson was determined to pin it on Alf Ramsey.

Thompson was not at Wembley when England drew with Poland. He was being interviewed for a BBC programme about the persecution of scientists in the Soviet Union.

He certainly knew how to persecute Ramsey.

His attitude towards him was identical to Brian Clough's. 'Don't tell me again that he won the World Cup in 1966. That is not good enough,' said Clough. Thompson, made to look a little stupid, had underrated Len Shipman and Dick Wragg, who both blindsided him with their private lobbying for Ramsey. He'd supposed the International Committee would simply confirm his removal. Wragg's announcement of the FA's backing for England's beleaguered manager enraged him.

At the FA's next meeting, held a fortnight later, Thompson challenged the minutes of the previous one, which he said 'did not represent the feelings of all the council members'. The vote of confidence given to Ramsey 'should not preclude a wider discussion by the council or some other select group at a later date', he added. The 'later date' Thompson suggested was actually there and then. The 'select group' he mooted was a subcommittee he intended to dominate.

On St Valentine's Day, the FA created a panel to 'consider our future in relation to the promotion of international football'. Along with Thompson, it comprised Andrew Stephen, Wragg and Shipman, West Bromwich Albion's Bert Millichip and Brian Mears, the son of Joe, who had become Chelsea's chairman in 1969. Mears drove a car that proclaimed his allegiance to his club: his personalised number plate began with the letters 'CFC'.

Called the Future of Football Committee, it was less of a brains trust and more of a lynch mob, charged with selecting which rope to use and calculating the drop. Thompson let it be known that the 'future' he envisaged didn't have Ramsey in it. He found it 'impossible' to communicate with him, he said. Ramsey's philosophy was 'old hat'. He was 'yesterday's man'.

Of course, the FA had 'retired' Denis Follows at 65, but the councillors themselves hypocritically refused to bow out with dignified grace at the same age. More hypocritically still, Stephen – siding with Thompson – pointed out that Ramsey would be 58 when the next World Cup finals were staged, which made him too old to continue as manager. Stephen was already 67. The average age of the committee was 61 – a figure that would have been even higher without its youngest member: Mears was only 43.

Wragg, watching the tide turn and rise against Ramsey, tried to save him from drowning. He suggested sacrificing Harold Shepherdson and Les Cocker, constructing a new coaching team around Ramsey and then allowing him to choose his own successor. Wragg was feisty, knowing he needed to be. Shipman was in no shape for a brawl. At 72, Shipman had suffered a heart attack the previous December, spending two weeks confined to bed. Still fragile, he wasn't fit enough to beat off Thompson, who blew and raged and bullied. 'What can you do when your hand is forced?' asked Shipman, disconsolately.

As early as March 1, Ted Croker was drafting an advertisement for Ramsey's job.

* * *

The Football Association vote that formally condemned Alf Ramsey was a bad replay of 1966: it finished 4–2 against him. The meeting was held on April Fool's Day.

The first ballot ended in a 3–3 stalemate. Dick Wragg, Len Shipman and Brian Mears backed Ramsey. Sir Harold Thompson, Andrew Stephen and the ambitious Bert Millichip did not.

Much to Thompson's chagrin, Wragg and Shipman tried to revive their alternative plan to break the stalemate: Ramsey should be allowed to hand-pick an assistant who would succeed him after either the 1978

World Cup or the 1980 European Championships. 'Thompson,' said Mears, 'was adamant that Ramsey had to go.'

'We must get rid of him now,' Thompson repeated, parrot fashion. He also shot down suggestions that a new role should be created for Ramsey, leaving him on the FA's payroll. Thompson's argument against that suggestion was right – Ramsey's replacement would feel like a newly married husband forced to live with his mother-in-law – but it was made for entirely the wrong reasons.

Knowing he would never break Shipman and Wragg – the allies were too close to be divided – Thompson concentrated on Mears, the weakest link. Mears finally buckled under Thompson's verbal pressure, caving in and switching his vote. 'Should never have happened,' said Mears of Ramsey's ousting. 'The emotion that I felt when I left that meeting was of shame.' His conscience pricked an hour too late, his lame capitulation always staying with him; he'd allowed Thompson to settle a grudge.

Afterwards Thompson even betrayed his ignorance about possible replacements for Ramsey. He asked Shipman: 'Who's your manager at Leicester? Is he a suitable candidate?'*

* * *

It took the Football Association another 19 days to tell Alf Ramsey of his sacking. He claimed 'not to be surprised'.

The FA, without giving a reason, originally summoned him to Lancaster Gate on a Friday, his day off. He stalled them for 24 hours.

As a doctor, Andrew Stephen had given patients bad news, but he fluffed every line when delivering it to Ramsey. He was the most incompetent of executioners. Stage fright gave him a shaky hand, a dry throat and a weak bladder. As he always did, Ramsey arrived early for the

---

* Jimmy Bloomfield was Leicester's manager. He was subsequently interviewed for the job.

meeting, which was planned for 10.30am. Stephen was nowhere to be seen and, like a game of hide and seek, Ramsey went hunting for him. He finally found Stephen in the secretary's office, which he'd searched only minutes before. Stephen walked Ramsey into the chairman's room. He began the conversation by half stammering out an apology; he needed to go to the toilet (where Ramsey assumed he had previously been). He returned wringing his hands, as though still drying them, and then began silently pacing the floor. There was another delay. 'I'm thirsty,' said Stephen. 'Would you care for a drink?' Ramsey did not. Stephen fumbled with the cap on a bottle of tonic water, barely able to look at him. At last, he gave up, placed the bottle on his desk and stared at a space about two feet above Ramsey's head. The speech Stephen gave was short and perfunctory, the words gabbled out very quickly while he still possessed the courage to say them. The FA had 'reached a decision . . . a change was required . . . a new manager . . . a new start'.

Stephen wanted Ramsey to manage the squad, which he'd already picked, during both the forthcoming Home Internationals and the summer tour of Eastern Europe. 'No, thank you,' said Ramsey, displaying the utmost restraint. He later explained: 'If I'd done it, it would have been intolerable . . . I'd have been on a hiding to nothing.'

Two things become obvious to Ramsey: the FA had no idea who would succeed him and had no intention of offering him an alternative position. The exchange with Stephen, lasting less than five minutes, ended when Ramsey rose to leave. 'I couldn't understand how anyone could be as naïve as to replace a manager without a thought or consideration for the players,' he reflected.

That Saturday afternoon, the headline game in London was Arsenal against Derby County at Highbury. Ramsey chose to watch the unglamorous Second Division fixture at Selhurst Park between Crystal Palace and Hull City. He acted as though nothing untoward had happened to him – or was about to.

No announcement about Ramsey's dismissal would be made until May 1, enabling him to tell his family and his friends before being harassed by the newspapers and TV.* Ramsey cancelled all his appointments – except for one: four days later, he presented the Texaco Cup to Newcastle, who beat Burnley in the final at St James's Park. 'I found it agonising to talk about the future of England – a future in which I knew I wouldn't be playing a part,' he said. Ramsey had to fend off speculation that either he was about to quit or the FA was about to sack him. 'No one has said a word to me,' he lied.

In that same week Stephen 'confidentially' sounded out Sir Matt Busby about becoming England's caretaker manager. Busby, though aware Ramsey had his own sources among the FA councillors, didn't want him to find out about the approach from anyone else. With the utmost circumspection, he rang Ramsey, telling him he'd refused the FA's offer.

Ramsey minimally tweaked the statement the FA had written to announce his farewell (Ted Croker refused to read this aloud to him; he played a tape recording of it instead). He asked for one word to be changed. Even though it made no difference – 'they amount to the same', he said – he wanted to be 'replaced' as England manager rather than 'dismissed' from his position.

It is a curiously bland document – written and edited by a committee – of only 262 words. One of those words is 'unanimous', used again only five months after the FA had chosen it to declare total support for him. The first five paragraphs essentially amount to a claim of self-defence and self-justification and also reveal the news that Joe Mercer, then general manager at Coventry City, had agreed to do what Busby had not: he'd become England's caretaker boss. The last lines, which Ramsey never saw until their publication, seem tacked on, like a scribbled PS at the end of a letter. The FA expresses

---

* In a *Sunday Mirror* piece published in March headlined 'Where's Sir Alf?', Brian Clough asked: 'Is he doing six months penance in a monastery or riding a donkey in Tibet?' Clough urged Ramsey to publish a 'blueprint' for the 1978 World Cup, unaware that Thompson's plot to unseat the England manager was already unstoppable.

its token thanks for his 'unbending loyalty . . . dedication and high level of integrity'.

Ramsey had sworn that his only responsibility to England was to 'get results'. He had stopped getting them. Knocked out of the World Cup, he'd won only two of his previous eight games. His removal was necessary, but it was ineptly done and edged with malice. And, forgetting Ramsey still had more admirers than detractors, the FA was tone deaf, totally blind and especially dumb to believe a World Cup winner could be kicked into the cold as easily as a manager who hadn't won a tin button.

The ordinary fan saw how manipulative the FA had been during the previous six months and also how disingenuous its gratitude for Ramsey looked on the page. When more details emerged, the FA's attitude began to seem unnecessarily callous and deliberately spiteful. It was as though the whole thing was meant to be demeaning and that certain councillors considered his sacking as righteous revenge for his autocratic rule. The public learnt of his request for a salary rise and were reminded about why he needed it. Sir Harold Thompson's vindictiveness was made plain too. That Thompson had taken charge of the process diminished Stephen, turning him into his glove puppet.

Stephen was selective with the truth when, after four weeks had passed, he laid out the reasons why Ramsey had to go. 'We had to look at the quality of our game and we realised we had been falling behind the rest of the world, particularly since 1970,' he said. 'We all decided we needed a team manager who would be flexible enough in his attitude . . .' Stephen insisted he had remained pro-Ramsey until the draw against Poland, a spurious claim designed to defend Thompson, whom he also pretended was not 'solely responsible' for the sacking. This was no more believable than Stephen's next point: 'There is no way we would insult a man who has done such a good job for us by looking for a successor behind his back.'

These were weasel words indeed.

Thompson was specifically asked whether he had led the assault against Ramsey. He turned very shy. 'People will have to think what they imagine about that,' he said. They certainly did; they also came to the conclusion that he and the other men in charge of the FA were an unpleasant, vengeful and ungrateful bunch of heartless incompetents.

Ted Croker should have been bright enough to know what was coming. Removing Ramsey was like pulling down a public monument. Since it had been done so shabbily, Ramsey elicited sympathy and even pity. Croker said he found that those who had previously 'pilloried' Ramsey in the media 'now made him a martyr'. In the *Sunday Express*, even Danny Blanchflower called the FA 'mean to a man'. The *Daily Mirror* said of Ramsey: 'Those who dance on his coffin are fools.' Croker's predecessor, Denis Follows, piled in too: 'I do not believe [the sacking] was handled in a diplomatic way. Had I still been at the FA, I would have made sure it was done differently.' Jock Stein embarrassed the FA with the severity of his condemnation. 'This must send a chill down the spine of every manager,' he said. 'It is the interference of the professionals in football by amateur legislators.'

Shortly afterwards, Croker was the chief speaker at the Football Writers' Association dinner. His antenna registered the hostility towards him as soon as he entered the room. The guests regarded Croker as a villain and Ramsey as a victim. Croker, who had intended to talk light-heartedly, rewrote his speech in a sweat and on the hoof. It flopped. 'I knew at once my speech was a disaster . . . when I sat down there was muted applause, not for what I had said but because I had stopped,' he confessed.

The Official FA Year Book, published three months later, not only gave no explanation for Ramsey's dismissal, but made no direct reference to it either.

* * *

The Café Royal, opened when Queen Victoria was still in her tender 20s, had offered swish hospitality to everyone from Oscar Wilde to Auguste Rodin, George Bernard Shaw to Virginia Woolf and Winston Churchill to David Bowie. Wilde, dizzy there after one glass too many of absinthe, imagined himself walking across a field of tulips. The bohemian Bowie chose the Café Royal to mark the retirement of his alter ego, Ziggy Stardust.

On the eighth anniversary of England's World Cup win, it hosted a party for Alf Ramsey.

The place had been smarter. The gilt was flaking, some of the plaster moulds on the ceilings needed touching up, the carpets were a little frayed or bare in spots and some of the mirrors were tainted in their frames. But the soft, tallow light of the chandeliers and the wall lamps hid most of these defects.

A 'Special Testimonial Dinner' was being staged to raise £10,000 for Ramsey after the FA had – yet again – failed him, a lack of respect evident in his pay-off: £8,000 and an annual pension of £1,200, the first instalment due in far-off 1985. Ramsey described it as 'a tissue handshake' rather than a 'golden' one. As he did with most of his savings, he put the money into his local building society.

The souvenir brochure for the evening, as well as documenting Ramsey's results, contained an alphabetical list of the 101 players capped during his reign, starting with Jimmy Armfield and ending with Gerry Young. A total of 62 of them came to the Café Royal, including 18 of his World Cup squad. Among the 500 guests, who paid £100 per head to be there, was the vice president of the High Wycombe Referees' Society, who also happened to be the prime minister, Harold Wilson.

When Joe Mercer had arrived at Lancaster Gate, the receptionist didn't recognise him. 'Do you have an appointment?' he was asked. 'Yes,' replied Mercer, 'for seven matches.' With his short tenure already over, the FA had appointed Don Revie as Ramsey's successor, putting aside their misgivings about him. Revie came to the Café Royal clutching a contract worth £12,000 more than Ramsey's had been.

Ramsey also gave invitations to the FA's handyman-cum-caretaker, who had worked in Lancaster Gate for 35 years, and England's coach driver. 'Sir Alf has always taken the same size in hats,' was the driver's tribute to Ramsey's gesture.

His sacking had provoked a reaction not unlike '66's: a thousand letters to answer; TV and newspaper reporters staking out Valley Road; friends sneaking along a 'secret' route through his back garden to visit him.

In the week and a half between his summons to Lancaster Gate and the official news of his dismissal, he had tidied and cleared his office. His important possessions fitted into a cardboard box and a briefcase. Ramsey then escaped to the south coast to 'think and plan', he said. He 'died a thousand deaths' there, expecting every day to pick up a newspaper and discover the story had 'broken unofficially'.

The loss of his job was like a bereavement, the detachment from it terrible for him. The first stage of grief – denial – was conspicuously present, which meant the other four – anger, bargaining, depression and acceptance – were biding their time but would arrive shortly. In that brief limbo period, when only he and the FA knew what was coming, Ramsey experienced a huge sense of unreality, as though a mistake had been made and everything would quickly go back to the way it had been before. He couldn't process either what was happening to him or what his response to it should be.

On some days, he didn't want to leave the house. Though he did everything not to show his distress, the mask as firm as he could make it, Ramsey was not unlike the Beatles' Eleanor Rigby: he kept his public face in a jar, putting it on before leaving home.

Suitors did try to court him.* Ajax, the former European champions, offered £30,000, a sum he had previously turned down to manage

---

* The first of these was a boys' team from Staffordshire, mostly under-11s, who brazenly asked him to coach them. 'There is no pay and no expense allowance,' he was warned.

the Greek national side. He was soon linked with Aston Villa, Athletic Bilbao and Portsmouth too.

He took £21,000 from the *Sunday People* for three interviews, the first of which ran under the headline:

At Last! Sir Alf Tells All

He didn't, but he told enough to make the newspaper's investment in him worthwhile in sales. Ramsey retained his integrity, making precise points and recollecting facts in a measured, even-tempered voice. He rejected publishers who were prepared to hand him twice as much as the *People* had done for more details. They wanted 'all the dirty washing', said Ramsey, who was not prepared to peg it out for them.

He appeared on ITV's expert panel during the World Cup, occasionally beside Brian Clough. 'He was still a funny bugger,' said Clough, 'but I saw a different side to him.' He felt sorry for Ramsey, who looked a 'lonely man'.

* * *

The diners at the Café Royal were served Arbroath smokies, cold tomato soup and saddle of lamb. Geoffrey Green serenaded Alf Ramsey on his mouth organ, giving him a rendition of 'Moon River'. The entertainment was provided by the comedian 'Cheerful' Charlie Chester, whose heyday spanned the late 1940s to the early 1960s. As one correspondent reported, Chester 'apparently imagined he was addressing a stag do in Bradford' rather than a bow-tied audience in central London. The BBC had once warned Chester to tone down his act, which was too close to the knuckle for their liking. If performed today, his routine at the Café Royal would have got him culturally cancelled before the third joke.

Harold Wilson presented Ramsey with an £800 replica of the Jules Rimet trophy. A screen showed highlights of England winning the World Cup, each clip taken from *Goal!*

The team that had beaten West Germany, plus Harold Shepherdson and Les Cocker, posed with Ramsey while he cradled his trophy. A photograph, appallingly lit, was taken in a room that had a ceiling mural of cherubs and a carpet so heavily patterned that the sight of it could induce a bilious attack. The photo reminds you of a boys' boarding school in which the pupils can't sit still and the masters, resembling wax figures, pretend not to notice. In the front row, Bobby Charlton and Bobby Moore, neither of them looking at the camera, are having a conversation. Alan Ball is staring into the far bottom corner of the room. In the middle row, Nobby Stiles, wearing his owl-like glasses, is trying to attract George Cohen's attention. In the back row, Geoff Hurst is covering his face with his hands. Jack Charlton hunches his shoulders, as though attempting to make himself look a foot shorter.

How different they all look. How long ago '66 already seems. How much had changed in each life since then.

Six months earlier, Moore had made his last appearance for West Ham, tearing knee ligaments in an FA Cup tie. After pledging to give him a lucrative free transfer, the club asked for a fee of £25,000. 'West Ham wanted their pound of flesh,' said Moore, livid about a betrayal that he believed was both parsimonious and disrespectful. He signed for Fulham, taking the downward step into the Second Division.

The Charltons had already been there, scrapping it out as managers. Bobby had been relegated at Preston, who finished second from bottom. He was beaten twice by his brother – 3–0 and 4–2. Jack won the championship for Middlesbrough and the Manager of the Year Award for himself, bettering big beasts such as his mentor Don Revie and Bill Shankly. He was the only one of Ramsey's World Cup side to realise in advance that the FA had fired his old boss. In April, he'd telephoned him for advice, ending the call with a promise to meet Ramsey at Hampden Park for the Home International. When Ramsey replied, 'Maybe,' Charlton instinctively knew what had occurred.

Both Charltons were integral to Stiles's late career. The first transfer deal Jack struck sold Stiles to Bobby, who made him player-coach. At

Beer, cigarettes and a tactical talk. Jack (left) and Bobby in an unusually serious mood

Middlesbrough, Stiles had described himself as a 'fading football star'. He tried to 'nurse and protect' a 'knackered knee' and confessed: 'I was no longer in the glory business.' At Preston, where he took a £50 drop in wages, he 'survived . . . but only just' with a 'broken body'.

Still struggling to come to terms with the loss of his eye, Gordon Banks had become a youth coach at Stoke. His separate, specialist brief was to take care of up-and-coming goalkeepers. He soon identified a problem: Stoke had no full time apprentice 'keeper. 'I was dumbfounded,' he said.

Only three of the World Cup winners remained in the First Division: Hurst at Stoke, Ball at Arsenal and Martin Peters at Tottenham (Peters had made what would be his last international appearance two months before).

George Cohen found football 'too hazardous and, at times, duplicitous'. He understood it 'wasn't going to provide a great living' for him.

He not only left Fulham behind, but also the game itself. He went into the property business, swotting up on planning law, how to assess land ripe for development and how to beat off the competition to buy it.

Anyone could track down Roger Hunt or Ray Wilson. The telephone number of the Hunt haulage company – Hunt Bros, a family firm founded by his father – was printed in the *Yellow Pages*. Hunt had already gained his Heavy Goods Vehicle Licence, and he discovered the solitude of the cab suited him. 'It took me a long time to get over leaving Liverpool,' he admitted. When he did, he preferred not to 'hang around' grounds like 'some old players' do. Despite buying season tickets at both Liverpool and Bolton, he rarely went to games. The man who once thought he 'couldn't live without football' did not miss it because watching held so little appeal for him.

Wilson appeared in the *Yellow Pages* too – at Leeches House Funeral Home in Huddersfield. When his sacking from the FA was still raw, chafing him daily, Ramsey had attempted to bring perspective to it. 'Despite everything that has been said, football is not a matter of life and death,' he said. No one knew that more than Wilson. His world, far from the din of crowds in huge stadiums, had become about the silence of chapels and churches, crematoriums and coffins. About consoling the bereaved. About how the living must take care of the dead. Wilson had worked for his father-in-law's firm of undertakers during those close seasons early in his career when it was necessary to supplement his income. He knew how to embalm, dress and prepare a body. He fitted out the coffins and lined them in silk. He became used to the phone ringing late at night or early in the morning, the sadness and the sobbing summoning him to yet another stranger's home.

Wilson had been caretaker boss of Bradford City. He thought about, but declined, the offer to move permanently into management. The reason he gave was: 'I did not have that fanatical feeling about the game that's needed to put up with all the stick.' On being an undertaker, which 'could be very unpleasant', Wilson said: 'The job takes a lot of getting used to . . . You know very early on whether you can cope with it. Fortunately, I could.' He still found it 'stressful' to meet the grief-stricken – 'it's like pre-match nerves' – but he didn't 'worry about trivial matters any more'. He took 'real job satisfaction' from the work, sounding as though football had seldom given him that.

For the photograph, Ramsey got his team into the room and organised them with the briskness of arranging a training session. In his testimonial brochure, he had written: 'I owe my greatest show of gratitude to the footballers of England.' He singled no one out. How he felt about 'his boys' of '66 was nevertheless on display at the Café Royal. He shook their hands on arrival and on departure.

What everyone remembered about the dinner was the opening line of the speech Ramsey gave:

'This is an evening I shall never remember.'

Ramsey paused, before correcting himself. 'Sorry, forget,' he said.

Some thought it was just a slip of the tongue. Some thought he meant it.

16

YOU ARE WHAT YOU ARE

Telford United's ground, Bucks Head, was the kind of place where things tended to end for footballers rather than begin.

Telford had won the FA Trophy in 1971, but five years later the Southern League side was so hard up that players' wages – about £25 per week plus a £5 win bonus – were chopped in half out of financial necessity. The team contained men who had day jobs: furniture removal, sales, advertising, a mechanic, a chartered accountant.

The only draw in Telford was Geoff Hurst, who had become player-manager. Hurst had left Stoke for West Bromwich Albion, and had also appeared for Cape Town City, Cork Celtic and Seattle Sounders in the still-fledgling North American Soccer League. He was approaching 35 years old. Telford was his way of 'starting somewhere where I could see a way of going up'. Sometimes he got frustrated with himself. 'I wind myself up for a shot I know I would have buried 10 years ago and miskick it. Or I scoot past someone and he comes tanking back to catch me.'

Hurst used a bag of autographed footballs – mementos of his hat-tricks and the great appearances of his own career – as practice balls at Telford. His World Cup medal dangled as a charm on his wife's bracelet.

Telford on a cold Monday night in mid-October wasn't the most salubrious spot for a reunion of the World Cup winners. Hurst had arranged the match on behalf of his new club's centenary. Neither the town nor his own players could quite believe it. 'Being on the same pitch as Bobby Charlton is all they can talk about,' he said.

It was 1976.

The tenth anniversary of the World Cup had slipped by without much acknowledgement, the decade just gone barely a wrinkle in time. Sir Harold Thompson was now the Football Association's chairman. He – and it – held no celebratory dinners. The BBC replayed the final, but only to mark the corporation's landmark – 40 years of TV broadcasting. Two months later, ITV screened a gloomy documentary, *The Rise and Fall of English Soccer*. The 'fall', it implied, had begun at the same time as the 'rise' in 1966.

In the two years since the Café Royal dinner, Alan Ball had lost his place in the England team, breaking the last link with '66. Don Revie slowly became the punishment the FA inflicted on itself for sacking Alf Ramsey in such a disgraceful manner. Ball called Revie's infamous dossiers 'masterpieces in planning' that 'never worked out', rating them 'the most boring bedtime reading of all time'.

Ball was about to swap Arsenal for Southampton. Martin Peters had already swapped Tottenham for Norwich, the club becoming an 'absolute joy' to play for, he said. Bobby Moore remained at Fulham, nervously unsure about what awaited him next. Gordon Banks was following Hurst into the North American Soccer League, enticed there by Fort Lauderdale Strikers. The doctor conducting his medical was astonished to find a metal plate in one of his knees and another in an elbow. He was more astonished still after asking Banks to cover his left eye and read the top line of the sight chart with his right – no one had told him about Banks's partial blindness. Nobby Stiles had been retained as a coach at Preston after Bobby Charlton departed by 'mutual consent'. He'd begun taking his coaching badges at Lilleshall. The coach in charge of his sessions screened the film of Wolfgang Weber's last-minute goal and criticised England for putting 'too many men in the wall'. Stiles was 'on the point' of responding aggressively before wisely deciding to remain mute. 'The previous year, one of the lads had argued,' said Stiles. This student had subsequently 'failed' the course for being too outspoken.

No one's life had changed more than George Cohen's. On one of his daily five-mile runs he became extraordinarily tired, struggling home while suffering from a 'tight' stomach and diarrhoea. He self-diagnosed a 'touch of colitis'. The doctor diagnosed bowel cancer. Cohen, who'd regarded himself as 'indestructible', was only 36. 'This can't be happening to me,' he said. Cohen was now in recovery, living from one week to the next.

The 8,000-strong gate, the tickets sold on nostalgia, and the length of the queue for autographs afterwards demonstrated that the public were still enthralled by '66, grateful for the emotions it stirred. The FA, which should have been equally grateful, was just indifferent. It neither knew what to do with the players nor much cared about what happened to them. The World Cup winners had understandably felt entitled to wear authentic England shirts at Telford. Instead, they had to put on a predominantly plain white shirt, lacking the three lions badge. The FA refused to recognise the match.

In the end, it didn't matter. 'We played again as though '66 was yesterday. It was just . . . well, beautiful,' said Hurst. Afterwards, drinking 'a few sherbets', toasts were made to an absent friend: Alf Ramsey wasn't there.

At the start of the year, Ramsey had made the oddest of moves. He'd become a director at Birmingham City, despite sharing no history or affinity with either the club or the West Midlands. His role was so nebulous that no one – not even him – could define it. 'I go to meetings. I watch matches. I make suggestions. I try not to get in the way.' Ramsey gave Birmingham a modicum of gravitas. He was a 'trophy hire' for a team that rarely won a trophy of its own. Since 1875, it had seldom needed to lift the lid off a tin of silver polish.

Perpetually asked about a managerial comeback, Ramsey would say at one moment 'my feet are itching' and at another be less committed: 'If I am offered a job I think I would enjoy, I would take it.' As he'd been offered half a dozen of them, accepting none, that prospect seemed unlikely.

The most improbable twist had occurred when Brian Clough spent his 44 days at Leeds, where he'd replaced Revie. From the beginning, Clough faced a dressing-room revolt – the consequence of his inflammatory criticism – while striving to quickly reshape the side. Without Peter Taylor, who had stayed at Brighton, Clough tried to take Ramsey to Elland Road. 'He would have been like the Rock of Gibraltar at that ground. No one would have been able to move him,' he said. Clough rang Ramsey at home. His wife answered the phone and took a message. Clough was sacked before he could try again – and Ramsey, unsurprisingly, never returned his call.

Ramsey attended few matches in person then, preferring to watch on TV at home. 'I never ask clubs for tickets,' he said. 'If I can buy a seat, I do so. Otherwise, I pay and stand on the terraces.' If Ramsey went to a ground, he did so 'quietly', 'unannounced' and incognito. He put on a bowler hat – he'd originally bought it in 1961 for the Queen's visit to Ipswich – because his hair had begun to thin. Wearing a bowler, rather than a cloth cap, would have been as noticeable on the terraces as turning up at a society wedding in a Harris tweed suit and pair of brown brogues. Ramsey nevertheless insisted the bowler acted as 'a sort of disguise'. He was 'almost never recognised'. Among the sway of the fans, he saw the game differently. 'Listening to the comments around me, I have learnt a lot. The public are not necessarily looking for the same thing we, as professionals, want.' Ramsey heard comments which 'irritated him', but did not engage in arguments. 'I enjoy football this way. Free of responsibility.'

At Telford, Hurst insisted, the conversations – some of which went on until dawn – were not all 'do you remember stuff' about Ramsey and '66. He and the others had already 'sort of buried the past, great though it was', he said. What rankled him was the necessity to be cautious or self-abnegating when publicly discussing the modern game. 'We have to keep our mouths shut,' he added, aware of the risk of sounding like 'old men trying to turn the clock back'. Hurst explained why. 'Because of Alf. We are all regarded as his team, his time . . .

Anything we say about England football now comes out as though we are just defending him. In a way, when they fired him, they fired us, too. Made us part of the past . . .'

Hurst spoke the simplest of truths. It became more apparent as the years passed.

* * *

The world moved on from 1966, but Alf Ramsey and his team didn't – or couldn't – always move with it.

Fate did not often scatter her blessings on them either.

Ramsey said his concern was always for 'my players', who 'were more important to me than anyone'. He soon realised he was not the lone victim of the occasion that made him a national hero. Others struggled too.

Consider this fact: in May, 1986, twenty years on from Wembley, Franz Beckenbauer was about to manage West Germany in the World Cup in Mexico. Bobby Moore had just resigned in exasperation as boss of Fourth Division Southend United.

Why the English game insulted Moore so transparently and for so long is as mystifying now as it was then. Moore believed promises had been made – and broken – over a vacancy at Watford. He did become boss of lowly Oxford City in the Isthmian League, where he worked from a 'portable building'. His inducement to stick it out was a salary of £14,000 and a company Daimler. The surface dazzle of those trappings didn't obscure the lack of substance beneath. His assistant, Harry Redknapp used to sit in the dug-out and wonder: 'What am I doing here?' He'd then look across at Moore and think, much more pointedly: 'What are *you* doing here?'

Moore, having finally left Oxford, only got into the Football League again after a six-year absence; Southend offered him what he thought might be his 'last chance'. It was like an Oscar-winner running a village amateur dramatics society. Southend were spectacularly on their uppers. There was no training ground. Their finances were chaotic, the club bouncing between the possibility of a visit from the bailiffs and outright bankruptcy (there wasn't much for the bailiffs to take; the TV in Moore's office was black and white). The chairman wanted to pick the team. Moore got heckled from the Southend directors' box about a performance his dissenter rated as 'a load of crap'. He even arrived late, and obviously drunk, before a match.

Before going to Southend, Moore would still get calls from First and Second Division directors asking about his availability. 'Then I would hear nothing except whispers that they'd been warned off me,' he said. The warning-off had nothing to do with his footballing talent. He'd passed his FA coaching badge at just 21 years old, but each tilt at management was a flight of fantasy not dissimilar to his attempts to become an entrepreneur. Often these business projects merely became ostentatious ways of shredding money in public. One ostensibly sure-fire investment in a country club lost him £100,000.

Moore was too trusting to make business or management profitable. As a player, he had inner strength in reserve. As a boss, he needed to overcome his natural inclination to be pleasant and respectful even when others, pulling a fast one, were taking advantage of him. He eventually became 'sports editor' of the Sunday Sport, a newspaper that was all tits and bums and preposterously wild stories, such as 'Adolf Hitler Was a Woman', 'Aliens Turn Soldiers to Stone' and 'World War II Bomber Found on Moon'.

George Cohen underwent a second operation for bowel cancer 18 months after his first. He wore a colostomy bag. Cohen was commendably candid about this. Once read, his graphic description of a 'colostomy bath' is not easily forgotten: 'I lay back in the water and thought: "Jesus Christ, I'm the only professional footballer I know who can have a bath and watch himself take a crap at the same time." I burst out laughing . . .' Later, the bullet of another cancer hit Cohen. It was cancer of the pelvis. His response to each terrible setback was always 'to get on with the business of making a living'. In doing so, he was fortified by the formidable strength of his wife, who reminded him: 'George, you have your life. Things could be rather worse.'

Ray Wilson, still an undertaker, rang Cohen. Aware of his friend's situation, he indulged in some black humour. He pretended the primary reason for the call was business. 'I was ringing to offer you a deal,' he laughed.

Wilson lived in a whitewashed, isolated home, accessible along an unmade road. 'To me, this is paradise,' he said of the hills and fields that surrounded him. He walked his dogs across the moors. Coal and logs burnt in the grate of his living room. He drank a pint in a pub with horse brasses, where the regulars knew him and the strangers didn't. The beard Wilson grew, soon speckled with grey, and the tweed hat and country clothes he wore usually guaranteed him the anonymity he sought. He liked that sense of invisibility. He liked, too, the benefits of living his life without anyone watching him do it. Once, travelling on the Underground with Bobby Charlton, he saw other passengers nudge one another and whisper Charlton's name. 'He didn't bring me into it, thank Christ,' said Wilson, who watched Charlton fulfil his obligation to be polite. 'The truth is, I was bloody pleased to get on my train and sit on my own.' He couldn't 'cope' with the 'fuss', he added. Wilson once sat through a news item about 1966. His was the only name not mentioned. He neither minded nor cared.

Roger Hunt carried on with his haulage business, a map of the United Kingdom pinned above his desk in a plainly furnished, paper-strewn office. He stored most of his souvenirs in his loft and packed his England and Liverpool shirts into a suitcase that belonged to the same era in which he had worn them. On the wall, beside the stairs, hung photographs of Bill Shankly's Liverpool of the 1960s. The Kop awarded Hunt a 'people's knighthood', anointing him 'Sir Roger'. The title was used so naturally in conversation at Anfield that you'd have believed the Queen really had tapped Hunt on each shoulder with the tip of a ceremonial sword. Hunt developed a routine to satisfy those fans who sought what he couldn't give them – irrefutable evidence to validate once and for all England's third goal. 'I saw the replay just last night,' he'd say. 'And I'm more sure than ever that the ball was over the line. Maybe it had something to do with the fact I wasn't wearing my glasses.'

It was only human for Martin Peters to ask himself the question others perpetually asked him: how much did he regret *not* being known as the player whose goal won England the World Cup? The handful of seconds that separated Peters from the record books – he'd have been the eighth player to claim the winner in a final – dictated the shape of his life: money, prizes, recognition, kudos. While he was still playing, Peters discovered that everyone remembered Geoff Hurst's hat-trick, but could not necessarily identify who got the other goal. Some people were even surprised to discover he'd been in the team. Peters had been nicknamed 'the Ghost' on the basis of his ability to suddenly materialise in the box without anyone apparently noticing him. But the title he chose for his autobiography – *The Ghost of '66* – partly reflects the public's lack of awareness of him and also his career. 'It would be wrong to say I dwell on it,' he claimed, 'but it [scoring the winner] would have made a hell of a difference . . . my life would have been quite different . . . People get labels, don't they? And they stick.'

No one but the woefully ignorant ever blamed Peters for the relegation Sheffield United suffered, dropping into the Fourth Division, after he took charge of a side that lacked a beating heart at the end of the 1980–1 season. In charge for 16 games, Peters admitted he lacked the 'knowledge' to make a difference, a comment that proves how bashfully unassuming he could be. He never got another chance in management. He coached at seaside holiday camps – in resorts such as Skegness and Clacton – and played in the Magnet and Planet Eastern Counties League, the crowds so small that you could have shaken hands with everybody there in less than fifteen minutes.

The job Peters eventually took – selling insurance warranties – sent him to Suffolk. He'd visit Alf Ramsey, drinking tea in his kitchen. One morning – for 'no obvious reason', said Peters – Ramsey apologised for the substitutions he'd made in Mexico in 1970. 'I've thought about it for a long time,' he said. 'Everyone thinks I was wrong, don't they?'

Unassuageable sadness, the kind which makes you incoherent through incomprehension, engulfed Alan Ball shortly before he retired as a player, and then again not long after his managerial career ended.

In 1982, his father Alan Ball Sr – 'the main man' – died in an accident an hour after arriving in Cyprus to accept a coaching role. He was 57. He was travelling on the road between Larnaca and Limassol when his driver, attempting to overtake, lost control of the car. It spun down an embankment and into a dry river bed. Ball said his mother was 'never the same' afterwards; she became afflicted with a 'mental illness'. Ball underwent 'three episodes' of mourning: the death, the return of the body and the funeral. His father was cremated wearing his 'best suit', a ten-pound note folded in the top pocket of his jacket. He'd asked for the note, explained Ball, 'just in case' there was 'anything going on up there'.

Ball managed 13 clubs, among them Southampton and Manchester City, for a total of 666 matches. Accepting his managerial career was finally over in 1999, he conceded that he felt 'a huge sense of relief'. He could now devote himself to his passions – golf, horse racing, walking the dogs on a Hampshire beach and, above all, time spent with his wife and family. In 1966, he had been the only member of the World Cup-winning team to be engaged rather than married. He and his wife-to-be, Lesley, were teenage sweethearts. Northern lad met northern lass, each knowing the other was 'the one'. 'The only girl I had ever loved,' he said of her.

In 2001, Lesley was diagnosed with ovarian cancer. She 'fought her illness with resolution and without complaint', said Ball. She died in 2004, aged 57. Alone with her in the last moments, he 'saw her as I did on the day I married her 37 years earlier . . . no man could have had a better wife . . .' She left farewell letters to her three children. These were written on identical floral cards. The PS on each of them was identical too: 'Look after your Dad,' it said. During her illness and chemotherapy, Lesley had reassured Ball that life would go on without her. But for him, lonely and adrift, it never really did.

During the summer of 1977, while he was painting Telford's main stand, Geoff Hurst was called to the phone: a 'Mr Greenwood' was waiting to speak to him. Ron Greenwood had been made England's caretaker manager after Don Revie quit to become boss of the United Arab Emirates. The pressures, which Alf Ramsey had absorbed, sent Revie fleeing from Lancaster Gate, his appointment proving to be one of the least successful since Caligula made his horse a Roman senator. In his resignation letter to Sir Harold Thompson, Revie wrote: 'For many reasons I have found the job intolerable.' As though the discovery had surprised him, Revie also claimed that not everyone in the Football Association was 'pulling in the same direction'. He went on to complain about the 'constant criticism'. His four-year contract in the UAE, worth £340,000, was plump compensation for his previous suffering.

Greenwood, at 55, wanted Hurst to bridge 'the big age gap' between him and the England squad. He was invited back into the aristocracy of the FA. That coaching position also led to another. The Telford stand was being repainted again – another brush in Hurst's hand – when, in 1979, Danny Blanchflower, manager at just-relegated Chelsea, rang to take him to Stamford Bridge. Hurst left the Southern League for the Second Division. Chelsea didn't expect him to splash tins of Dulux on to the back of The Shed, but the amount of cosmetic sprucing up and practical repairs required on the pitch spoke to the long-term neglect of both club and team. Blanchflower, often wearing a 1950s-style trilby, had immediately become aware that modern management was trickier than writing a thousand words for the *Sunday Express*. He couldn't revive Chelsea. When Blanchflower got the sack, after winning only five of 32 matches, Hurst replaced him.

As for so many of the '66 side, he found taking one step forward eventually led to taking two giant ones either backwards or sideways.

He lasted 20 months as Chelsea's manager. He lost his £28,000-a-year wage, replacing it with £25 per week from the dole office.

Hurst already knew that fame came with sharp or awkward edges. Not long after the World Cup final, he'd been introduced as 'George' Hurst when he presented a car to a competition winner. When he went to purchase a pen in a department store, he found a queue of shoppers waiting for him to sign autographs with it. He asked the sales assistant whether he could pay for the pen with a cheque. 'If you have some form of identification, sir,' she replied.

After '66, his relationship with his parents 'profoundly changed' too, said Hurst. He described it, painfully, as a 'source of great sadness'. He was 'increasingly treated' more 'as a celebrity than a son'. His parents' visits to his home dwindled and then stopped. What Hurst called 'the rift' did not heal. 'We had not changed,' he said of his wife and himself, 'but their perception of us had.'

Hurst sold insurance. He'd practise his patter at home, knocking on the kitchen door while his wife pretended to be a prospective customer. A real customer refused to deal 'with former footballers'. Another wanted to know what the initials MBE stood for on his business card. 'Mechanical Breakdown Expert,' he told him. Making a cold call on the phone, the recipient, believing it was a wind-up, barked: 'If you're Geoff Hurst, then I'm fucking Marilyn Monroe' (a sentence with an unintended double meaning).

Even with only one eye, Gordon Banks was the best goalkeeper in the North American Soccer League in 1977, chosen for the All Star team after conceding just 29 goals in 26 games. The NASL was the last hurrah for Banks. The optimism he brought back, along with the spirit of the sunshine in Florida, gradually dissipated in England, where it was hard enough to find work and harder still to retain it.

Banks succeeded Hurst as manager of Telford. After sacking him, the club was unable to pay him off. It gave him a job selling tickets in a booth in a local supermarket instead. 'Talk about from hero to zero,' said Banks, who called it 'the most humiliating time of my life'. He then coached at Port Vale, thinking he'd get the manager's job there. Again, what he got were his cards.

The World Cup gave him a 'marvellous sense of pride' that was 'soon forgotten', said Banks. He added, mournfully: 'I began to wonder what we got out of it, and it wasn't much.'

He fell back on after-dinner speaking. Banks would tell his audience that, after tipping Pelé's header around the post, Moore had been less than impressed. 'Banksy, try to hold them. No silly corners,' he told him. The gullible believed that.

On a spring afternoon in 1989, Nobby Stiles contemplated suicide. He was driving in the outside lane of the M6, 'somewhere between' the Hawthorns and his front door in Sale. Stiles considered himself to be caught in a slow, futile rotation of ever-decreasing circles; hope was always extinguished by disappointments that pushed him into clinical depression. He'd been sacked by Preston in 1981. He'd gone to West Bromwich Albion and taken on a miscellany of roles, briefly even becoming manager.

But he was broke.

West Brom gave him neither a car nor the money to put fuel into the one he owned. Not long before, needing to buy petrol, Stiles had slotted his bank card into a hole-in-the-wall machine. Back came the illuminated message: 'Insufficient funds'. Often, driving along the same stretch of motorway seven days a week, he began to ask himself: 'What the fuck am I doing? What use am I to anyone?' It culminated in those suicidal thoughts that day – and in the impulse to respond to them. He decided to slam his foot down on the accelerator, shut his eyes and end his life. The speedometer showed he was travelling at 70mph. Stiles closed his eyes – for no more than a second or two, he thought – and opened them to find the road ahead coned off. He moved into the inside lane, almost swerving into a lorry. His car, scraping against it, was 'battered all along the left side'. He owed a debt to the skill of the lorry driver, who prevented a fatal accident with quick reactions and a smart manoeuvre.

Stiles drove home very slowly, parked his car and told his wife what had just happened. What came next is like the melodrama of a soap-opera script. Stiles drank half a bottle of brandy that night. He awoke the next morning with a horrible hangover – and to a phone call from Alex Ferguson. If he wanted it, there was a coaching job for him 'with the kids' at Old Trafford.

The *People*'s front page of January 29, 1978, carried headlines hot enough to burn a hole through a newsagent's counter:

The Tragic Secret of Soccer's Golden Boy
Drink Is Killing Me, Says Jimmy Greaves

While owning up to his alcoholism, Greaves detailed his 'minimum' daily intake – or as much of it as he could remember. It amounted to a bottle of vodka, which he started to consume as soon as the alarm clock went off, and 12 pints of beer (he subsequently adjusted that total upwards to 20 pints). If Greaves ran out of supplies, he would rootle through his dustbins in the hope that a few last drops could be drained from the empties. 'I was drunk from 1972 to 1977,' he said.

Reading Greaves's story reminds you of the protagonist of Charles R. Jackson's novel *The Lost Weekend*. It's about a man who, 'somewhere around thirty', makes the 'upsetting discovery that life wasn't going to pan out' the way he'd expected. He self-medicates on drink until becoming addicted. Greaves was 31 when he played his last game in the First Division. Drink led him into bankruptcy, divorce and a one-bedroom flat in east London. He faced two options: to continue drinking and die; or to stop, sober up and adhere to abstinence. In choosing sobriety, Greaves had the overwhelming support of anyone who had ever seen him score a goal. That club was so big that a thousand Wembley Stadiums wouldn't have accommodated the membership.

Fondness for Greaves meant he received compassion rather than condemnation. It wasn't common in the 1970s to make public confessions of the kind that exposed your soul. Greaves earned sympathy

364

even from those who didn't understand why someone given so much would be so foolish as to drink it all away. The witticism that implies the gutter is the best spot from which to study the stars could have been coined for him. For Greaves got out of the gutter and made himself into a star all over again. He became a TV pundit capable of containing constructive criticism within a wicked gag.

Greaves was regularly drawn back to '66. He would talk about serenading Alf Ramsey with his rendition of Cilla Black's 'Alfie', which he sang from a seat near the back of the England bus. He would also explain how a stray remark betrayed Ramsey's lack of erudition. During a debate about the merits of club chairmen, Greaves had damned them collectively with the phrase 'There's little choice in rotten apples.'

Ramsey scolded him: 'Jimmy, we are English . . . we speak the language of Shakespeare.'

'That is Shakespeare, Alf,' he said.

Greaves didn't realise that glib frivolity and gloating were unlikely to endear him to Ramsey. He also didn't realise his own slight misquoting of *The Taming of the Shrew*.*

Like so much else surrounding the World Cup, you couldn't make up the fact that the player so contentiously left out of the final went on to have a more successful post-football life than most of the 11 who got a shirt that day. But you're still left with the impression, however much he hid it, that Greaves would have willingly traded every moment of his TV fame for a place in that team. He gave his most revealing interview to Ian Wooldridge, who was moonlighting for the BBC. Wooldridge nudged him towards an emotional edge. He prepared the ground, and Greaves poured a little of his heart over it. It wasn't so much what Greaves said but what you saw in his eyes when he said it. In '66, he was the 'loneliest man in the stadium', he admitted. 'All I wanted to do was . . . go away and be alone.'

---

* Hortensio's quote in *The Taming of the Shrew* is actually: 'There's small choice in rotten apples.'

No one came close to matching the success of the Charltons. Their stock was nearly always on the up. Jack buttressed the achievement of '66 with more trophies and awards. He became the Footballer of the Year. He won the league title, the FA Cup and the League Cup, the royal flush of the English game. Every tongue brought in a different tale about what he said, thought or did. Some were genuine; some were myths. No one especially cared, including Jack himself, because nothing diminished the affection in which he was held. Much of the rapscallion boy he'd once been remained in Jack, who was still huntin', shootin' and fishin', and for whom Geordieland was home. 'I could never move south,' he said. His popularity in the country of his birth was surpassed only in the country he adopted and which adopted him in return. The big miracles he performed with the Republic of Ireland, taking them to the World Cup quarter-finals in 1990 and into the last 16 in 1994, converted neutrals into supporters, their passports turning green overnight. England fans speculated about what Jack might have done for the Football Association, a question that almost made your head ache. We never got to find out because Sir Harold Thompson didn't bother to reply to the application Jack posted to him following Revie's disappearing act. Almost a decade later, after he'd taken the Ireland job, the FA tried to demean him again. Bert Millichip made the snidest of remarks to his counterparts at the Irish Football Association: 'You've made a mistake appointing that man.'

Even if Moore had lived into old age, and even if Hurst had scored four goals instead of three in '66, Bobby Charlton would still be the emblematic figure of English football at the point at which it ruled the globe. His European Cup winners' medal, collected ten years and three months after the Munich disaster, confirmed that. But as magnificent as his talent for playing had been, Bobby possessed no magic as a manager, and little aptitude for it either. Aware of this, he turned himself into a salesman instead. Bobby, though far less interesting a character than Jack, took on the role for which his personal history made him perfectly suited. He became the professional football diplomat, an ambassador for club and country, an advocate for the game.

In different ways and for different reasons, the Charltons of Ashington became national treasures. The fact they barely spoke to one another for 30 years added sad drama to the life the brothers had once shared, as though welded at the hip, before refusing to share it at all. Here were siblings united in the end only through mutual dislike and mistrust, the cause of the feud raw and obvious only to them.*

* * *

Alf Ramsey was never the same man after his sacking. His antagonism towards the Football Association did not abate but piled up ever higher, deepening like a coastal shelf. Even when nearly everyone who had got rid of him was gone from the FA too – either retired or dead – he still wanted nothing to do with it. What happened in the early spring of 1974 was a constant presence throughout the rest of his life and also governed the way he lived it.

Ramsey avoided discussing 1966, often citing the excuse to filmmakers and authors that he was 'working on a book' and would be in breach of his publisher's contract if he spoke to them. The book did not appear because it did not exist.

It would be a kindness to Ramsey to pass over the rough times he endured while attempting to re-establish himself and prove the FA wrong: an inglorious half-season as boss of Birmingham City in 1977–8 and a fractious 13 months as technical director of Panathinaikos in Greece, which began in 1979. The courtesy of forgetting all that can't be done, however, because the wilderness years acquainted Ramsey with the sort of ordinary, everyday defeats and bleak anticlimaxes that were unbecoming for a World Cup winner.

---

* The most likely explanation is a falling-out over their different attitudes towards – and treatment of – their mother.

Winless and pointless after four games of the 1977–8 season, Birmingham sacked their manager, Willie Bell, a former left back at Leeds and a Scottish international. He left an empty chair that Ramsey, still a club director, was conveniently there to occupy. He tried to dodge it, attempting to recruit Jack Charlton instead. Recognising that the job wouldn't be just about repairing superficial cracks at St Andrew's, Charlton let him down gently.

Ramsey claimed to be 'as sharp as ever', but also said: 'There is not much future in me at 57.' He sounded like the Ancient Mariner, home from the sea. Bob Paisley had just won his first European Cup, aged 58; he was about to win his second, aged 59. His role as manager, Ramsey insisted, would be temporary and not permanent, a promise that perished after the seduction of some early success.

He had been away from the First Division for nearly 15 years, his era at Portman Road now seen through a sepia tint. He was unprepared for the shifting dynamics in club dressing rooms. Players wanted more and were less tolerant of any attempt to deny it to them. No prospective new buy was content with a hundred quid or so to 'sign on', the notes stuck in his back pocket to avoid tax. The 'standard' amount had climbed towards £20,000–25,000. Agents were becoming ubiquitous too; some were far less accommodating than Ken Stanley had been. Dealing with them anguished Ramsey, who didn't know how to bargain.

Birmingham's lone 'star' was Trevor Francis, who'd been only 12 years old in 1966. There were players in the youth team who had little or no memory of the World Cup. On the practice pitch, Ramsey wore a suit and a collar and tie. He resembled a senior civil servant about to collect his retirement clock. 'I'm too old for a tracksuit,' he explained.

This was the season Brian Clough matched what Ramsey had achieved at Ipswich. After bringing Nottingham Forest out of the Second Division, he immediately won the First. Ipswich, under Bobby Robson, took the FA Cup. Clough was 43, Robson 44. Alongside them Ramsey looked antique.

He resigned his directorship and formalised his position with the team, taking the title of consultant manager. But the bounce he gave Birmingham – four wins in his first five league matches – couldn't be sustained. He lasted only six months and 26 games.

Ramsey had wanted to flog Francis and use the £500,000 Arsenal were prepared to pay for him to rebuild Birmingham.* He was constantly peeved by the speculation about Francis's future that appeared on the back pages of the tabloids. He was equally peeved whenever Francis commented on events. Every newspaper writer who had heard what Ramsey memorably said about the saga was reciting the quote for a month afterwards – and imitating his voice too: 'Trevor Francis has had his say. His wife has had her say. Now I am waiting to hear from his fucking dog.'

Birmingham's board originally agreed to sell Francis, but developed the coldest of feet and backtracked, too afraid of the fans' adverse reaction. It gave Ramsey his ready-made excuse to resign.

His career was over.

Ramsey fell out of favour and out of fashion. How else can you explain why his only other managerial 'job' came in the comic strip *Roy of the Rovers*? Roy Race, whom age changed but never withered, had been shot by an unknown gunman. In stepped Ramsey, whose likeness on the page – his face was rather fat – was even less convincing than Vasco Lazzolo's painting of him 16 years before.†

* * *

A man's character will determine his destiny. Alf Ramsey's destiny might have been much changed if he'd been a little less curmudgeonly and a little more conciliatory in the corridors of Lancaster Gate.

---

* Less than a year later, Francis was sold to Nottingham Forest for £1 million.
† Ramsey got Melchester Rovers to play without wingers. He won his opening match 14–0.

The obvious point, which bears restating, is that compromise of that sort wasn't in him. Asked whether he should have done things differently with England, Ramsey replied in the only way he could: 'I have reflected a lot on this and wondered how much of it was my fault. I think it came down to principles. I did what I believed to be right . . . You are what you are.' The telling phrase is the last one. 'You are what you are' should remind anyone reading it that *who* Ramsey *was* made England world champions.

'At heart,' said George Cohen, 'he was a simple, rather shy man who didn't expect too much from life beyond the achieving of a little respect and the acceptance that he had always done what he could.' The description fits. Ramsey didn't go into hiding or completely disappear. He chose a kind of honourable exile at home in Valley Road, becoming accustomed there to a slower rhythm of living. No one, it seems, can remember him attending any of Ipswich's player reunions. He seldom saw a match at Portman Road – despite the two seats the club reserved for him there. He never appeared as the subject of *This Is Your Life*, clutching the big red book, or as a guest on *Desert Island Discs*. He declined to trade confidences on a chat-show sofa. He deserved a grand, Holbein-like oil painting, but never sat for one. The National Portrait Gallery owns only uninspiring photographs of him.

The FA eventually added a few more pounds to Ramsey's pension to buck up his income, but he still had to scratch around for money where he could. The *Daily Mirror* paid him £150* for a column that often exemplified the fury and frustration of the patient man.

As though picking at grievances, he was often scathing about England in his columns, and also about the third full-time manager to succeed him, Bobby Robson. The two men lived so close to each other that Bobby Charlton in his prime could almost have launched a pile-driving shot from Ramsey's back garden into Robson's. Try as he

---

* In the same period, the *Nottingham Evening Post* was paying Brian Clough £500 per column. I wrote it for him.

might, which he frequently did, Robson couldn't set up a line of com-
munication with his near neighbour. He wrote to Ramsey and, not
trusting the Royal Mail, asked his secretary to hand-deliver the letter.
Ramsey did not reply. Offering him a lift home from Stamford Bridge,
Robson's charity was met with a curt put-down: 'I came by train. I'll
go home by train,' said Ramsey.

No one could criticise the views Ramsey gave to the *Daily Mirror*
because winning the World Cup was an impregnable shield, protecting him against return fire. You could, however, legitimately question
the morality of expressing those opinions so explicitly. His rudeness
could be devastating. If the things he said about Robson had been said
about him during the 1960s, Ramsey would have gone into apoplectic
shock at the blatant disrespect.

One story often gets re-aired as evidence of his hostility towards the
Scots and Scotland. 'Welcome to Scotland,' was the greeting Ramsey
got after arriving in Glasgow. 'You must be fucking joking,' was the
reply he gave. Jock Stein emerged as the unimpeachable character witness for Ramsey, denying the charge that he was anti-Scots. 'I never
found him that way in any talk we had,' he said. Alex Ferguson said so
too. Before Ferguson took Scotland to the 1986 World Cup in Mexico,
he travelled to Valley Road to talk to Ramsey about how to prepare
for it. 'He could not have been more helpful,' announced Ferguson.
Ramsey offered no similar support – and gave no advice – to Robson.

'I have no idea what Alf had against me,' said Robson. 'The mystery will have to stay unsolved.' His only theory was actually the
right one: 'Maybe he wanted nothing to do with the people who had
just fired him.'

Whenever Ramsey went to Wembley, he would try to swap his
ticket – even with a stranger – to make certain his seat was as far
away as possible from any FA councillor's. You could hardly blame
him for that. It was Ramsey's misfortune that Sir Harold Thompson
remained as FA chairman until 1981. It was his further misfortune that
Bert Millichip, who had also voted against him in 1974, took over from

Thompson and clung on to power for 15 years and 170 international matches. Still nervous about Ramsey's independent streak, the FA under Millichip allowed his experience to go to waste in the 1980s. It calculated that hiring Ramsey as a consultant or a superior sort of scout might turn out to be infinitely more trouble for them than it was worth. By coaching from the pages of the *Daily Mirror* instead, Ramsey demonstrated to the newspaper's readership the expertise England were missing, but often his pieces also conveniently gave the FA an excuse not to go searching for olive branches.

'I only ever wanted to be a winner. And I was,' said Ramsey, looking back on the 1960s. 'I had the chance to make so many people happy. And I did . . . I achieved something I set my heart on. I like to think I changed the game in England too. Gave us some glory, an identity to be proud of.'

This, an elegant summarisation of his legacy, only hints at the depth of Ramsey's love for managing England. You get the feeling he would have willingly died broke to keep on doing it. He considered his sacking to be 'the saddest day of my life'.

Something far sadder, though, lurks beneath it.

'Over the 11 years, I never really enjoyed working for the FA,' he said.

The fact Ramsey believed he had won the World Cup in spite of his employers is the most astonishing admission of all. With great personal achievement came great personal sorrow.

How different it should have been.

Epilogue

ONCE WERE WARRIORS

The posters, stuck in shop windows along the High Street, are beginning to curl at the corners. The show advertised – one of those ubiquitous Elvis impersonators in full regalia – has already been and gone from Dudley Town Hall; in fact, Elvis left the building more than a week and a half ago.

Tonight, though, the old place is relying again on attracting those of us who want to be borne back into the past.

We're about to swing into 1966.

The patterned walling of the Town Hall, built almost a century ago, has a touch of the Venetian about it. Inside, the very recently refurbished theatre has a high, curved ceiling, decorated with roundels, a balcony and clear glass windows flanked by barley-twist columns. It resembles the kind of auditorium where, rather than hip-shaking Elvis, you might see an old-style variety performance: a stage hypnotist, a performing dog, a lewd comedian offering leaden innuendo and a magician about to saw his sequinned assistant in half.

Dudley and its Town Hall are, paradoxically, both an odd and an appropriate setting for 'An Evening with Sir Geoff Hurst'. Odd because the spot seems a little low-key for such a legend – even one so lightly modest about his title and his status. Even on this clear blue day, the mildest so far this autumn, Dudley is a bit sombre. This corner of the Black Country is feeling the post-pandemic pinch: empty or boarded-up shops; few customers wandering around the streets; a surplus of nail bars, vape shops, tattoo parlours and mobile-phone stores, but a noticeable absence of much else.

Appropriate for two reasons. The town is only six miles from the Hawthorns, where Hurst briefly played for West Bromwich Albion. It is also the birthplace of Duncan Edwards, who is commemorated in the Market Place. Edwards's statue, in front of the fruit-and-vegetable stalls, is a triumph. Somehow, the sculptor imbued movement into solid bronze. In a short-sleeved England shirt, Edwards draws back his right boot in preparation to kick the brown ball at his feet. I thought, if I stood there long enough, it would actually happen; his shot would fly down the road in the same way it flew into West Germany's net from the edge of the box in Berlin's Olympic Stadium in 1956.

For Hurst, this is the start of a 23-date provincial tour that will take him as far north as Darlington and as far south as Portsmouth. He insists these gigs will be his last. In another two months, he will be 81 years old.

His appearance here couldn't be more timely.

It's just over three weeks since the death of the Queen. During the 10 days of official mourning that followed, Buckingham Palace chose a few photographs that symbolised her platinum reign. Wembley '66 made the cut, edging out only about a billion other images. Resplendent in her sun-bright dress and matching hat, the Queen was shown presenting the World Cup, the image offering proof to those born long afterwards that football flourished well before the Premier League and the Champions League were a glint in anyone's eye.

Yesterday, an anniversary slipped by almost unnoticed, another reminder about how little endures. The date marked 20 years since the demolition of the old Wembley began, the Twin Towers reduced to unsightly heaps of rubble.

It's also exactly 50 days until the kick-off of yet another World Cup that England won't win.

While Hurst was still so young that old age must have seemed as far off to him as another galaxy, he promised not to go 'harping on' about '66 and his hat-trick. There is no need for him to apologise for breaking that vow. When he said so, during the mid-1970s, England's

triumph seemed a little dated, the attitude towards it already lique-
fying into indifference. A decade later, the players began journeying
around the country, hosting events like this one in groups of three or
four. Sometimes the bouncer on the door had to throw the patrons in.
One evening in Newcastle, the 'hot bed of soccer', only 13 seats were
filled. We still nurtured then a false expectation of regaining the trophy. Our repeated failures hadn't yet made us appreciate the value of
the original achievement.

Perhaps we still haven't; not fully, anyway.

As Hurst points out, 'the longer' our disappointment lasts, the
'stronger' our memories of '66 ought to become. But the capacity of
the Town Hall is 980. I take a rapid headcount and estimate it isn't
even a quarter full. Those who have come occupy only the stalls, leaving the upper circle empty and cavernous-looking.

* * *

Hurst is standing on a stage so bare – a plain table and a couple of
wooden chairs are the only pieces of furniture – that you'd think we
were about to watch a Samuel Beckett play. He doesn't look his age.
He is still trim, straight-backed and smartly dressed in a grey suit and
matching open-necked, pale grey shirt. He's already shaken hands with
most of us, signing books, programmes, replica footballs and shirts. In
1966, there was no sustainable market for sporting memorabilia. The
concept barely existed and only a few private collectors considered
even medals as treasure.

I once asked Jack Charlton about his World Cup medal. It was safe
from any burglar, he said. There was no possibility of anyone finding
it except by accident. Charlton couldn't remember into which drawer
at home he had casually shoved it 'a while ago'. He didn't know either
whether the medal was still in its box. The box, he added, was made
from cardboard, a fact that surprised him when he received it; he'd
been expecting a smooth leather case with a soft silk lining. Charlton

added one last thing, as though he needed to explain why the medal apparently seemed so insignificant to him. While insisting he would never sell it – a pledge he kept – he also said it was less important than his memories of the match, a remark that was to become in hindsight so bitterly poignant.

Hurst sold his medal, along with other bits and pieces, for £150,000. He sold his World Cup final shirt for £91,250. One weekday morning, with Manchester living up to its reputation for miserable weather, I went to the National Football Museum to look at it.

Outside, along the Walk of Fame, rain lay between the raised grooves of the brass plaques embedded into the concrete in front of the main entrance. I dodged from one World Cup winner to the next, ticking off the engraved names and faces. Inside, the few fans there that day were being photographed beside the Premier League's bulbous trophy, with its hideously ugly gold crown – a superfluous piece of bling.

The museum was much changed since I'd last been there, the exhibits switched about and remounted. I wandered about aimlessly before finding the relics of '66, which were arranged behind huge plates of protective glass. Here was Roger Hunt's winners' medal, so small it would hardly fill the palm of an infant's hand. Here, too, was the replica – the original was lost in Brazil – of the Jules Rimet trophy, no taller than a milk bottle. I found it neither attractive nor alluring. I wouldn't stick it, like an ornament, on the corner of my mantelpiece.

Hurst's shirt was displayed on a tailor's dummy. It was still so richly red you'd have thought it had just arrived fresh from the factory.

I was drawn to one thing in particular: the match ball, which rested on a metal ring suspended at eye level. The ball, a Slazenger Challenger, was a little misshapen, like a balloon desperate for some air. The bright brown-orange leather of each panel was wrinkled, the fissures like the tiny spread of crow's feet. Other scars of battle were minor chips, flaking and scuff-marks. I was told the name of the last person allowed to handle it without the need to wear a pair of white gloves: of course, it was Hurst.

The ball had taken a circuitous route to the museum. Filched on the pitch by Helmut Haller, who thought no one was looking, a BBC camera caught him walking towards the tunnel with it. Haller gave the ball to his son as a fifth birthday present. For nearly 30 years it lay in a cellar. The ball was brought back to England only after the *Sun* and the *Daily Mirror* got into a tabloid tug-of-war over it – a squabble involving helicopters, a car chase, two hideaway hotels and a sum of £80,000.*

I was wonderstruck by the sight of it. This, I thought, really was the same ball Hurst had headed, Gordon Banks had held and Bobby Moore had caressed with passes of such self-assurance. I spent so long examining it, very slowly and from various angles, that I noticed the steward discreetly beginning to nudge a little closer to me. It was as though, suspicious of my motives, he was afraid I could be planning some sudden smash-and-grab raid.

In the beginning, I couldn't have told you why the ball was more important to me than any shirt, any sod of Wembley turf, even any medal. But as I left the museum, I realised that, more than anything else, it was a genuinely precious object. Just think: if that ball could talk, we'd know whether or not Hurst's shot crossed the line.

* * *

The audience in the Town Hall is predominantly male and predominantly of a mature vintage. These are pensioners who were teenagers in the summer of 1966. Even before he starts to speak, Hurst has listened courteously to a lot of stories that begin: 'I remember ...' When he does speak, I anticipate what will happen, but at the same time am slightly surprised by it. As he relives everything, it's as if *Goal!* is rolling on a big screen behind him. Hurst's words come with pictures.

I'm soon aware – as I'm sure everyone else is too – that fragments of the game still come as clearly to him as they did then, each one

---

* The *Daily Mirror* won.

personal to him: the spinning ball, appearing just below the lip of the stand after Bobby Moore flights it towards him for the first goal; the arc of the sky as he turns and falls on his backside after striking his second; the whiteness of the posts up ahead in the game's last breaths.

Hurst is following a memorised script, his patter rehearsed and performed on countless occasions before, but his delivery veers off at lovely tangents. It's like the kind of conversation we all have with ourselves sometimes: a big memory pushes you towards random, smaller ones, these recollections not always sequential but themed and without punctuation.

We get what we've come for. Like that Elvis tribute act, treading these boards before him, Hurst knows he's expected to belt out all the hits.

He saw a clip of film 'only a month or two ago' of England's opening match against Uruguay. 'There was booing when we walked off,' he says, emphasising that England's triumph was no foregone conclusion. Nor, he stresses, was his own part in it. His admiration for Jimmy Greaves, 'the supreme goal-scorer', still sounds like love in its first flush. Even after all this time, it's as though Hurst is unable to quite believe that he played against West Germany and Greaves didn't. He shares an anecdote about Greaves which he thinks illustrates both his impudence and his comic timing. Asked about the most important instruction he'd ever received at half-time, Greaves said it came from Alf Ramsey, who'd loomed over him in the dressing room and snapped: 'Jimmy, put out that fag.' Even those of us with limited imaginations are able to summon up that scene.

He discusses Argentina and 'the late' Antonio Rattín. 'He's not dead,' says Hurst, 'but that's how we always described him among ourselves because he'd take you out fifteen minutes after the ball had gone.' He goes on to explain 'what people tend to forget' about his late, headed winner against the Argentinians: 'Martin Peters was chiefly a right-footed player who produced the perfect left-footed cross.' His wife once passed Christmas dinner over the fence to Peters, who had

Hurst and Peters: friends and neighbours

been sick shortly before the festive season. Which is why 'every time' he looks at the 'famous photograph' of himself and his dear friend – Peters is grabbing Hurst around the waist and hoisting him in celebration – he thinks: 'That's my neighbour.'

He tells us about Ramsey, striding on to the field before extra time, and that barked order to 'get off your arses'.

The prelude to his description of England's third goal is a conversation shared with Roger Hunt that was notable for its brevity. 'You don't seem to score with many headers,' observed Hurst. Hunt's reply was the light-hearted: 'I don't score many headers, Hurstie, because I'm too busy doing all your fucking defensive work.'

Hunt was always wheeled out as the plausible witness, denying accusations of conspiracy to defraud over a goal that Helmut Schön always called 'false'. Franz Beckenbauer insisted Bobby Charlton had apologised for it, patting him on the back before muttering: 'Sorry.' A decade later, as West Germany's captain, Beckenbauer came to Wembley again. The night before the match, the Germans arrived to practise on the pitch and discovered the ground staff had neither marked the lines nor assembled either goal. 'See,' said Beckenbauer. 'They've removed the evidence.'

After the '66 final, the linesman Tofiq Bahramov was asked why he gave the goal. It's claimed he smiled before answering in a single word: 'Stalingrad.'

It was a joke, innocently fabricated, that got stretched too far and repeated too often. I thought of the interview I'd watched less than a month before, while hunkered in the basement of the British Film Institute in London. It had been shot 20 years after Bahramov's decision tipped the balance of the final. His moustache was shaggier. His hair was whiter, and unruly too. He could have been Einstein's love child. He sank his body into a low armchair while the goal was replayed for him on a 21-inch TV. 'It's clear the ball crosses the line . . . I saw it very clearly,' he declares, turning his face towards the camera.

What else could Bahramov have said? And what else can Hurst say, except reiterate the line he's always taken? Hunt was 'certain', said Hurst, 'the ball had crossed the line . . . That's always been good enough for me. Honestly, I couldn't see it. I had the worst view in the stadium.'

He begins to talk about Kenneth Wolstenholme.

Quoted almost as often as anything Oscar Wilde ever said, Wolstenholme's 14 words – 'Some people are on the pitch. They think it's all over . . . It is now' – still impress Hurst like a line of gorgeous poetry. 'I defy anyone,' he says, 'to watch that last passage of play and come up with a better description of it.' Wolstenholme's commentary leads him towards the deliberately facetious answer he gave to 'the stupidest question' ever put to him.

'Did you know there were people on the pitch?'

'Yes. I stopped, stuck my foot on the ball, looked around for a bit and saw them before I put the shot into the net.'

Hurst adds that, above the din, he heard – and still hears – the squeaky voice of Alan Ball. Unmarked and in space, Ball was screaming at him and pleading: 'Hurstie, Hurstie, pass me the fucking ball.'

'I just pretended not to hear him,' he says, casually. 'Otherwise, I wouldn't have got the hat-trick.'

* * *

At times, Hurst seems to yearn for the impossible. To have everything as it had once been. To relive the experience of July 30 afresh, gathering it in through touch and sight to better remember an afternoon that came and went too quickly, each hour rushing by 'like a minute'.

In a football sense, some of that 1966 team would never find such happiness again. Alf Ramsey presciently told Alan Ball: 'You'll play a lot of games in your life. You won't play one better than that.' Ramsey's prediction came true. 'That was not only the day of my life, but the day that made my life what it became,' admitted Ball. 'Sometimes I long to be 20 again, when everything seemed so easy.' Ball would have given 'almost anything' to go back in time because 'I didn't really understand what was going on . . . I was quite naïve.'

He wasn't alone.

Roger Hunt thought the World Cup was 'too big' for him. 'It took years to sink in.' Martin Peters confessed that 'no other day' in his career came remotely close to providing him with 'the same sense of achievement'. For Gordon Banks, during the chilly realities of his old age, '66 symbolised the 'simplicity of how football used to be'. He added a lament for his lost youth: 'When I was young, older people were always wondering about where the years had gone. I used to wonder what they were talking about. Now that I am their age, I am the same.'

Banks also explained what he called the 'secret' of England's success. It was 'how much we liked one another'. This is apparent in the affectionate accounts Hurst gives us. As well as 'Banksy', he refers to 'Bally' and 'Mooro' and 'Big Jack'. Ramsey is 'Alf'.

His stories play up everybody else's abilities, while generally playing down his own. It's as though Hurst wants us to believe that scoring three goals in a World Cup final was just down to luck – a game of chance on a par with picking the right lottery numbers.

It's not a melancholy night in Dudley because Hurst, so entertaining, extracts and accentuates the humour from '66. He avoids the pathos. Hurst is, regretfully, the only survivor healthy enough to do a public event. When, not so long ago, Hurst gave an online interview, he nonetheless scrolled through the comments afterwards and discovered that one of them read: 'Geoff Hurst? I thought he was dead.' Last autumn, he was fitted with a pacemaker after his pulse climbed to 200 beats per minute.

I begin to dwell again on how and why my unexpected interest in the World Cup was rekindled during that first Covid-19 lockdown. And, as the evening wears on, I begin to think less about Hurst's presence and more about the absence of others who once were warriors too.

Bobby Moore died in 1993, shockingly young at 51. An operation for bowel cancer revealed a secondary tumour in his liver. He never asked how long he had to live. When the unthinkable occurred, the metal gates outside Upton Park were festooned with claret and blue scarfs and flags, rosettes and shirts, and the sort of floral farewell that wouldn't be seen again until the death of Diana, Princess of Wales.

Alan Ball suffered a heart attack in 2007 while beating down a bonfire built to burn garden rubbish. He was 61.

Six of the team died between May, 2018, and September, 2021.

Banks, who was 81, had twice been diagnosed with kidney cancer. Another tumour, found in his stomach, was said to be 'the size of a meatball'. Roger Hunt and Ray Wilson were both 83. Martin Peters was 76. And in 2020, only 102 days separated the deaths of Nobby Stiles, at 78, and Jack Charlton, whose passing – at 85 – was commemorated in newspaper supplements.

Like Wilson, Peters and Stiles, Jack had Alzheimer's – that slow, slow, slow dying of the light before the quiet vanishing. His memories were taken piecemeal, a depressingly common occurrence among players of his generation who headed a much heavier ball.

In the beginning, Jack was at least aware that his dementia meant that talking to him was often like addressing a 'brick wall'; he 'could not remember'. Each case of Alzheimer's was slightly different. Wilson, who had always sung around the house, began singing more often. He collected flowers for his wife, especially daffodils and bluebells in the spring, and constantly drew pictures in ballpoint pen. One of these was captioned: 'I am a happy man.' Peters died in his sleep. Stiles was too ill to attend the opening of Nobby Stiles Drive in Collyhurst.

At first, absorbing the fulsome obituaries for Stiles, I couldn't work out why I was so moved by them, and also by the photograph almost every newspaper published of him: he was leaning against a post, glancing down and pulling a face for the benefit of the camera. I think it was because, after interviewing him all those years ago, I discovered Stiles did not remotely conform to the stereotype into which I'd stupidly boxed him. I had assumed the player I'd seen on the pitch – spiky and argumentative – would be the same man off it. He turned out to be unimposing, kindly and softly spoken. There was a disarming shyness about him too. He treated me, a nobody, as though I was a somebody. I've never forgotten that.

Along with another seven of the World Cup winners, Stiles sold his medal. He cried when announcing its sale. After football was finished with him, he relied on after-dinner speaking to squeeze out a living. As well as dementia, he suffered a stroke, a heart attack and

Nobby Stiles deliberately poses for the photographer

prostate cancer. Harry Redknapp once saw Moore being 'slung out' of Upton Park because he didn't have a ticket. A steward was dispatched to the wooden bench seat that Moore occupied in E block. 'The secretary', the steward informed him, wanted to know if he had 'a ticket'. Moore did not. 'Then I'm afraid I've been told to ask you to leave,' he said. The snubs Stiles received from Manchester United and England were not committed so publicly. When he asked United for seats – he wanted to take his granddaughter to a match on her birthday – the club asked him to pay for them. When United wanted to book Stiles to speak at a dinner, it expected him to work for them for free. On the 50th anniversary of the World Cup win, the Football Association offered to send a form to his home so he could be assessed for means-tested financial benefits. His wife declined.

I imagined Stiles setting off for church on the morning of the final, a 24-year-old with the better part of his career and a whole lifetime ahead of him. I also saw him walking through the wooden doors and sitting in a pew. I wondered how many of the other worshippers, if any, had recognised him in prayer. When comparing the unparalleled triumph of '66 against how things worked out afterwards for Stiles, I thought of the words attributed to St Theresa of Avila:

More tears are shed over answered prayers than unanswered ones.

St Theresa had a point – even though she made it in the 14th century.

Those who make history become history, but in Stiles I saw more distressingly than ever how the game so often failed the team of '66.

England's next World Cup winners can expect knighthoods or CBEs. Postboxes will probably be painted in fancy, Olympic-like gold. It took the country 24 years to reward the 'Forgotten Five', who had gone unmentioned in previous honours' lists. Cohen, Wilson, Ball, Hunt and Stiles were given the MBE, which seems rather mean and also rather arbitrary. Peters got an MBE in 1978. Bobby Charlton was awarded a knighthood in 1994. Hurst, already an MBE, became Sir Geoff in 1998. Moore, Jack Charlton and Gordon Banks were made OBEs in the 1960s or '70s. It also took 43 years for FIFA to acknowledge that squad members – as well as the manager and coaches – should receive winners' medals.

Banks, in particular, bridled at how little England got for winning in '66 and how much the Germans received for losing: reputedly, £10,000 each and a Volkswagen. If England ever won another World Cup, his view of what would happen afterwards was the despondent: 'They'll stop dusting us down and bringing us out every four years.'

The 'they' were the FA, which had a good memory for the fanfare of anniversaries and a bad one for remembering much else in between – especially the responsibility to be altruistic.

Talent and experience went untapped because bugger-all was done with it – or for it. No apology, which would be too late now anyway, can either make good that deficiency or suppress the scandal of it. The FA was fortunate that those members of the team who enjoyed the success, but got no financial security from it, didn't go in for picket-line protests or sob stories. Stiles was typical of that. When Alf Ramsey picked his 'greatest' England team, Stiles was one of only two World Cup winners that he didn't select.* He didn't grumble about that. If anything, he always seemed too magnanimous and too reasonable. He came from the same era as Duncan Edwards, which is why his response was highly characteristic of those footballers who, expecting less than they deserved, didn't look back in anger. 'I don't begrudge what the lads get today,' he said. 'We shouldn't necessarily have earned more in our day. It was a different time.'

* * *

A different time . . .

Hurst is reflecting on that fact too. 'So long ago,' he says. There is a pause while he looks blankly into the stalls. Either the thread of one thought is momentarily lost or he has lapsed into another, which he prefers to keep private. 'So long ago,' he says again, adding that he never expected to be discussing something that 'happened nearly 60 years ago'.

He talks about the grounds, the goals, the ball, the boots, the tackling, the pitches and the pay. Hurst never earned more than £10,000 a year as a player, he says.

He goes on to explain: 'It was a bruising game then. You had the tackle from behind. And most of the centre halves I faced were very big lads. Some of them had a bolt through their neck . . .'

He remembers, after a Saturday match, how he would drink with Bobby Moore and Martin Peters in the Black Lion, a pub in Plaistow, not far from Upton Park. 'We'd have a pint with the fans. You wouldn't believe that, would you?'

Actually, I would.

---

* Stiles's place went to Alan Mullery. Francis Lee was preferred to Roger Hunt.

There are great champions in any age, but we've always related to these World Cup winners because, on one level at least – any lack of pretension – they seem so much like the rest of us. They never saw themselves the way we saw them – eleven ordinary immortals managed by a twelfth.

I wait for someone in the Town Hall to ask Hurst about Alf Ramsey. No one does. I do the asking myself.

It was said of Ramsey that his best friends were his players. 'He thought like them' and 'put them first', explained Moore. I want to know what separated him from his contemporaries to such an extent that those players knelt so devotedly before him. Hurst's reply is instant. 'It was his discipline that made him special,' he says. 'He saw what was required to win the tournament. He knew what he wanted from everybody and he told you what that was. He made things very straightforward. If you gave him your respect, you got his respect back.'

Hurst gave Ramsey credit for simply being himself. He added that his influence on him continued well after his playing career ended. 'When I went into business I tried to follow the same practices and principles he laid down. He was strict about making sure the team was more important than any individual. I did that too.' Hurst's admission makes you realise the fortune that could have awaited Ramsey as a managerial guru for swanky corporate clientele – if such a thing had existed back then and he'd been inclined to exploit it.

What did await him was Alzheimer's. His story, from first act to last, contains all the elements of a Shakespearean tragedy. The rise. The fall. The neglect. The death.

Much the same can sadly be said about those who helped make him the manager he became.

John Cobbold at least lived long enough to watch Ipswich win the FA Cup. Before the final – against Arsenal in 1978 – his mother Lady Blanche was asked whether she would like to meet the prime minister. She replied, in all sincerity: 'I'd rather have a gin and tonic.' Four years later, Cobbold died of cancer of the spine, aged 56. During his last months, he recorded his life story on a series of cassette tapes. In his book, published posthumously, Cobbold said he'd been advised by a friend to 'command the attention of readers as quickly as possible, probably on the opening page'. He wrote what he considered to be a humdinger of a line:

'"Fuck," said the Duchess, waving her wooden leg.'

Arthur Rowe received a testimonial from Crystal Palace rather than Tottenham, who weren't so generous. His friend Ramsey was there to make the presentation to him. Rowe became a scout who paid at the gate rather than take his free seat in the stand. At home, he displayed no photographs and only one trophy: a football mounted on a plinth awarded to him by the magazine *Sport*. Rowe died, at 87, in 1993. He, too, had dementia. On a winter's night a policeman found him on a London bridge. He appeared to be trying to walk to White Hart Lane. 'My old club is in trouble,' he told the officer. 'I've got to see them and sort them out.'

Ramsey's Alzheimer's became detectable to his old England side on the last occasion he and they came together – at a Buckingham Palace garden party. It was held in the summer of 1992 to celebrate 40 years of sporting success during the Queen's reign. 'One by one we noticed there was something wrong,' said George Cohen. 'We were seeing . . . the passing of our chief.' Standing beside the palace's lake, Ramsey's wife Victoria protected him with stage-like prompts. She announced the arrival of each player and his partner by name: 'Oh, look, Alf, here's . . .'

In the last year of his life, he was handed a photograph of the 1966 World Cup-winning team. It was an attempt to coax a memory out of him. He took the photo and looked at it perplexedly for a minute or two. He then pointed at a face in the front row.

'That's Alf Ramsey,' he said.

* * *

No one in the Town Hall needs to be told that Alf Ramsey was an exceptionally great manager. Hurst, though, feels the need to remind us that no one wins a World Cup by accident. I stare along the row and then behind it, noticing how many heads are nodding in silent agreement.

Hurst is asked another question. I hear it only dimly, and his answer not at all. I am still thinking about Ramsey.

I had visited his grave at Old Ipswich Cemetery. The cemetery was opened in the mid-19th century. Appropriately enough, the site belonged to the Cobbold family, who sold it to the town council.

Ramsey's ashes lie in Plot OC 194, a detail useless in my search for him because there were no signposts. It was early afternoon. There was a scent of cut grass and peaty earth. A breeze, mild at first, pulled at half a dozen clouds and then, gathering pace, shook its way through the trees. Despite the low hum of passing traffic, it was still and quiet; I could hear the sound of my own footsteps. I stood at the top of the cemetery and stared across the great sloping sweep of the place, the variegated greens quite beautiful in both sun and shadow and the wide paths white and dusty. From a distance, the squat copper spire of one Gothic-style chapel, made of buttressed flint, and the dull brown roof of another seemed minuscule to me, like buildings in a model village; an immense, dark spruce beside them was surely a mere sapling when Queen Victoria put on her widow's weeds.

Even with a rudimentary map, I got lost. I took one wrong turn, and then at least two others. I was left contemplating the scale of the cemetery – it covers 25 hectares – and the multiple routes around it, which in that moment were puzzlingly labyrinthine. I passed almost no one; only the odd figure, glimpsed far off, came and went again, their head often lowered.

In the end, I found him only because there was no other spot left to search. I walked to the bottom of the hill. I had stopped now and again to admire the grandest of the monuments: the obelisks taller than a man; the fenced-off tombs on top of which lay an effigy, hands together in prayer; an angel with an enormous spread of wings; the huge crosses, lichen-stained and weather-beaten; the ornate, Roman-like urns that stood on thick stone blocks; the wide, high slabs of granite or marble that, long ago, a mason had chiselled for a month or more to create the most filigree decorations.

Ramsey's gravestone resembled none of those. It reflected his absence of vanity, his distaste for splashy showing-off and the need to not draw attention to himself. I was certain it demonstrated, too, his restraint and the sense of proportion he maintained, a Kipling-esque determination to treat triumph and disaster 'just the same'. Perhaps, it sustained him.

Even though I'd seen a photograph of the gravestone, the humble modesty of it was still a shock. The stone was a very pale grey and also very small, not even half the size of the two grander graves that stood either side of it. In a plain gilt, capitalised font the inscription recorded not achievement but endearment:

MY DEARLY LOVED HUSBAND SIR ALFRED
RAMSEY 1920–1999. ALTHOUGH YOU HAVE
GONE BEFORE ME, THE MEMORIES & LOVE WE
SHARED WILL ALWAYS BE WITH ME
UNTIL WE ARE TOGETHER AGAIN WHERE
PARTING IS NO MORE

A wooden bench, heavily creosoted, stood in front of the grave. The long branches of another big spruce, its bark and leaves especially dark, overhung it, offering shelter. The wind had blown over a metal pot of plastic red roses, which someone had placed on the shallow plinth of the grave. I righted it again and tidied the flowers a little, brushing away some surface dirt. I regretted not bringing a fresh spray.

Ramsey died aged 79. The small, formal announcement in the personal column of *The Times* said he 'passed peacefully away'. He had prostate cancer. He'd also suffered a stroke. He was initially an NHS patient, treated at Ipswich General Hospital. Like Arthur Rowe, Alzheimer's meant he lost his bearings and was often unaware of his surroundings. He was once found wandering the hospital corridors. Eventually, he was moved into private care. It cost £500 a week, a sum his wife Victoria paid out of the couple's savings. Knowing her husband would have opposed it, she could not bring herself to accept the Football Association's belated offer to foot that bill. The FA, continuing to ignore Ramsey, hadn't even invited him to the 1996 European Championships, which it hosted. 'It appears we never treat our heroes very well,' said Victoria.

Ramsey once listed the three things he loved: his 'wife, football and my country'. All he ever wanted to do was 'work for' England, he explained. Instead, he was left to seek out a role and a purpose for himself alone, never finding either. Someone of such extraordinary, self-made strength got crushed between the monumentality of winning a World Cup and the FA's demonstrable failure to respect the rarity of the feat. 'He lived for football and he just felt lost. There was nothing left for him, really,' said Victoria. 'I really do think it broke him. He would have done anything to help England, but they discarded him.'

Looking at his grave, a line from Ramsey's daughter Tanya wheeled through my mind. She had written to me, saying: 'I think he was overwhelmed with the fame awarded him.' That fame did not reap a fortune. His four-page will bequeathed about £200,000, which included the value of the family home. Some of his memorabilia was subsequently sold off. It included a few great prizes – the cap he won against Hungary, his League Championship medal – and items of ephemera: an unused ticket for the 1966 final, his souvenir programme and a blue tie bearing England's badge.

Ramsey had never wanted a grandiose farewell. His funeral, held at Ipswich Crematorium, was restricted to family and close friends, emphasising Tanya's description of her father as 'a strongly private man'. There was no anthem. No flag on the casket. No bugler. A journalist, sent to view the floral tributes, counted only eleven of them. Victoria's wreath for her husband was of two interlinked hearts.

A week later, his Saturday-afternoon memorial service was held in Ipswich's St Mary-le-Tower Church; Ramsey hadn't wanted what his family could have claimed – the grandeur of the Henry VII Chapel in Westminster Abbey. 'My Way' was played on a three-manual pipe organ. The elegiac lyrics of the song could have been written for him; for in doing 'what he had to do', he fulfilled the promise he made to win the World Cup. The service, alas, reinforced not only Ramsey's estrangement from the game, but also the game's abandonment of him. Beneath its spire – a town landmark – the fans, some wearing England or Ipswich shirts, outnumbered the dignitaries. Of the 92 invitations sent to Premier League and Football League clubs, only five were accepted. The FA sent two 'minor' officials, who included – the supreme irony of ironies – Bert Millichip, who had been knighted eight years before.* In the churchyard afterwards, Jack Charlton despaired about the fact that not even Ramsey's death had given football a fresh appreciation of him. 'We forget things so quickly now,' he said. 'People don't seem to have time to remember what's important . . . that's if they care to.'

I think he was right.

Victoria believed the manner of her husband's sacking and the impact it had on him 'contributed to the ill health he suffered'.

I think she was right too.

It ought to provoke in everyone the kind of anger that starts in your stomach and climbs up into your throat.

* * *

* Even some of the FA's tributes to Ramsey were botched. Before an under-21s game between England and Sweden at Huddersfield, the electric scoreboard in the ground asked the crowd to pay tribute to 'Sir Mat Busby', spelling Busby's Christian name with only one 't'. A minute's silence before an international against Sweden at Wembley was 'cut short by the jeering of a large section of the crowd'.

Hurst is still talking, answering a question that is predictable but necessary. Yes, he 'knows, for sure', he says, that 'one day someone' else will claim a hat-trick in a World Cup final. He is prepared for that eventuality and won't mind. He will sincerely congratulate whoever does it. He remains 'surprised' no one did it before him and also that his feat has gone unchallenged for so long.

With this, he says his goodbyes, with a wave of his left hand, and thanks us all for coming. We give in return what he sincerely warrants: a standing ovation.

I have one last thing to do before I leave.

In the charity auction, held during the interval, I had acted purely on impulse, bidding for – and winning – both a framed replica England shirt, signed by nine of the World Cup team, and another shirt, signed by Pelé, such a hero of mine that I was guilty of idolatrous love for him.

Why did I buy those shirts? I'm not exactly sure. I suppose the mad-keen autograph-hunter I'd once been, hanging around in car parks or beside the dressing rooms, suddenly surfaced in me again. Once a collector, always a collector. Or, perhaps, the collection I'd seen in the National Football Museum made me want something, however small, of my own; something, indeed, that in dismal old age will give me a tangible connection to my boyhood. Whatever the reason, I ignored the financial profligacy. Instead, I instantly saw only the wall at home where these two treasures would hang.

Each signature from 1966 – only Alan Ball's and Bobby Moore's are missing – is scribbled with the thick nib of a black Sharpie pen. Pelé's signature glitters thinly in gold on green; he signed along the number 10 on the back of his Brazilian shirt.

I carried my prizes awkwardly through Dudley, which was so dimly lit that the street lamps barely cast a shadow. It was nudging 10.30pm. I surely looked to puzzled passers-by like an incompetent burglar, making his escape from the art gallery on foot because his getaway car had stalled.

* * *

I had regarded going to see Geoff Hurst as the closing of a circle, everything about 1966 resolved and neatly put away.

Of course, it wasn't.

How quickly the future leaves the past behind – even the recent past. Sometimes one event piles into another, leaving us with a hazy sense of disbelief that so much can happen, all at once, and abruptly change the landscape.

At the end of 2022, we saw a World Cup played in a country that ought never to have hosted it. We saw a tournament so engrossing that, at times, it made you wish you didn't have to wait four years for the next one. We saw a final, epic in stature, that belonged to that small bull in dancing slippers: Lionel Messi, playing in the match of his life. And we saw Kylian Mbappé become the 'someone' Hurst had spoken of on that bare-boarded stage in Dudley twelve weeks before. Mbappé's hat-trick was imperfect when compared with Hurst's (two of his goals were, after all, penalties in a losing cause). No matter. Hurst was now *the first*, but no longer *the only*.

All too soon afterwards, as our spokesman for 1966, Hurst was once again forced to fulfil the obligation longevity has bestowed upon him, which is to offer condolences for the dead. First, George Cohen, aged 83 – a gentle man and a gentleman. Then Pelé, aged 82, indisputably The Greatest (for me).

Hurst, as ever, composed simple, noble statements to convey his feelings of loss and love and grief and gratitude; his blessed luck to have shared the same pitch with both of them. On each occasion, I stood for a while in front of the two shirts I'd bought, tracing with my eyes the loops and swirls of Cohen's signature and Pelé's.

I thought about Hurst, his burden of duty and the dignity with which he always carries it. Cohen's death left him and Bobby Charlton as the only survivors of '66, and Charlton is frail and has dementia.

A week or so later, on a dark, frosty morning in January – the beginning of a year that marked the 60th anniversary of Alf Ramsey's first international as England manager – I sat through the whole of *Goal!* again.

I find it difficult to believe that something I know so well will eventually be discovered, like an archaeological relic, by future generations who, without necessarily knowing all that happened, will watch the game without any particular feeling and understand only later why the match meant so much for so long to so many who were born before them.

Here, once more, was Wembley spread out in the sun: the cut-up grass; the waving flags; the people on the pitch; the delirious, joy-of-all-joys moment of the final whistle; the lap of honour; the trophy sparkling in the late-afternoon light.

I took it all in. Banks diving at full length to smother the danger of a pass. Bobby Charlton smacking a shot against the post; his brother, Jack, mithering about a decision made against him, his expression one of disgust. Cohen spooning the ball over the bar. Wilson pinching it away near the touchline. Hunt grappling for possession not far from a corner flag. Hurst, dangling in mid-air, still barging his shoulder strongly into Tilkowski. Stiles attempting to pull off the flashy extravagance of a bicycle kick, which he miscues.

Some things that, unbelievably, I'd missed before registered with me for the first time. Moore rising to win a header in midfield. That Ball could conceivably have gone sprawling in the box and claimed a penalty (the savvy modern player would certainly have dived). Peters being booked for 'unsporting play'. And, lastly, how the soundtrack of *Goal!* turns 'Ee-Aye-Addio, We Won the Cup' into melodious jazz that begins with a jaunty blare before slowing, becoming in the last frames of the film almost mournful and heart-breaking. In the closing scene – an impeccable piece of symmetry – the groundsman who had unlocked Wembley early that morning locks it up again late that evening, shoving his keys into a jacket pocket. He descends the concrete steps, kicking aside the afternoon's accumulated rubbish

– song-sheets, team-sheets, rolled-up programmes, torn banners, discarded tin cans. Hours later, that image, purposefully unromantic, and the sound of the music accompanying it were still swimming around inside my head.

I think, rather pessimistically, that 1966 will fully regain its lustre and significance for us only on the day when there ceases to be anyone left who played in it. We'll look at them all differently then, realising – with profound regret and a little guilt – that we didn't always pay that team our proper respects. Finally, though, we'll begin to make amends, telling history afresh.

I'm certain of this too: we, who are mere mortals, live only for as long as the last person to know us remains alive. The players of '66 – and Ramsey – will be here forever, their achievement inextinguishable. And each of them will get what only the truly privileged are ever afforded: to be seen, remembered and celebrated not as old men, with wrinkled brows, but exactly as they once were – straight-backed and lithe and fearsomely fit.

Winners, shining in their youth.

AUTHOR NOTES AND ACKNOWLEDGEMENTS

That W. G. Sebald quotation, decorating the opening paragraph of Chapter 1, constantly fascinates me.

How far back do you have to go to find a beginning?

Now, I think, I know.

Of course, this book would never have been written without Channel 4's rerun of the 1966 World Cup final. But during the course of my research, I came to appreciate how much of it is rooted in my fledgling years in journalism, the start of which, even now, seems like a succession of small miracles.

I won't bore or torture you with all the preliminary biographical details, but in 1977 I was working part-time for a news agency that occupied the top floor of a building on West Bridgford's Radcliffe Road. The front window of the office conveniently overlooked Trent Bridge cricket ground, the pavilion rising in the middle distance. The main gates at Nottingham Forest were around the corner, less than a minute's walk away. Notts County's Meadow Lane was a mere stroll across the river, followed by a sharp right turn.

In those days, my early mentor, the great Matthew Engel, owned the sports arm of the business. My other early mentors, Mike Elliott and Tony Turner, owned the news side of it. When Matthew moved on to grander things – soon becoming the *Guardian*'s cricket correspondent and, eventually, editor of *Wisden* – I took over his desk, which faced a blank wall in a back room. My new boss was Roland Orton, who already ran the Leicester News Service. I was 18 going on 19. He was 64.

How best to describe Roly and his quixotic character . . .

He wore thin, gold-framed spectacles and his silver hair was always well combed. He had a remarkable talent for being able to talk while a burning cigarette dangled from the left corner of his mouth; the ash, slowly accumulating, would finally topple and spill across the wide lapels of his jacket. Sometimes, he'd be oblivious to that. When ringing me, he would start a conversation by asking: 'Now then, dear boy, what's happening?' His response to anything that either astonished or irritated him usually began with the phrase 'Quite frankly', which he tended to repeat twice.

In the trade, he'd long assumed near-legendary status. Roly was a bon viveur and a raconteur who was prepared to tell stories against himself. During one match, Roly admitted, he mistook a police-dog training exercise on the pitch – the crowd's half-time entertainment – for a major incident. He filed the story with the Press Association, which was just about to send it out on the wire when his retraction arrived in a rush of panic. He may not have been entirely sober at this point.

Roly seemed to know everyone: directors, players, Football Association officials, most of the BBC, including Peter Dimmock and David Coleman, and all of Fleet Street's senior sports staff, tabloid and broadsheet alike.

I possessed only one attribute: I could touch-type at a fairly brisk rate. Roly nonetheless showed patience and benevolence towards my naïve, greener-than-Wembley-grass apprentice self.

It's fair to say that he and I had our misunderstandings and our spats. He wrote out my weekly pay cheque, but sometimes forgot to either post or sign it (I still have one of those unsigned cheques). It's also fair to say that we got along much better after I stopped working for him. Indeed, during the last six years of his life we spoke nearly every day (even on a Sunday), and we lunched together at least once a month. He became an affectionate, grandfatherly figure to me – especially when my life or career hit some turbulence.

Here's the thing.

Roly's home patch was Leicester City. Very little occurred at that club without him knowing about it. He was particularly close to Len Shipman, who tipped him off in advance about Alf Ramsey's sacking from the England job in 1974 (the headline of Roly's obituary describes him as the 'Ramsey-Scoop Journalist'). He repeated to me all the things Shipman had told him about the myriad machinations at the FA. Once, during a lunch we shared in Leicester, he was discussing Ramsey when Shipman arrived unannounced. For the next hour and a quarter, he sat beside us, throwing in additional anecdotes.

Roly was pally with Geoffrey Green too. Though Green retired from *The Times* in the mid-1970s, he continued to be an occasional presence in press boxes and on the page. I see him as I write this: he is pole-thin and wearing a blue canvas jacket, just a little shorter than a Victorian frock coat, and a matching cap, his fashion sense somewhat Eastern European. Roly and Green had a habit of greeting one another with a single word, always a place name that evoked a past drinking session of epic proportions. Roly took me to a lunch with Green. The food came in bottles. More England and Ramsey stories flowed with the alcohol that afternoon.

Roly was not only aware I kept a diary-cum-journal (an account of when, how and why can be found in my book *The Great Romantic*), but also encouraged me to continue with it. 'Always take a note. You never know when it might be useful,' he said.

As I began going through all the things that I had scribbled down and saved back then, I came to realise this: in essence, *Answered Prayers* 'began' decades ago. It is 40-odd years in the making.

I won't rake over again the meetings I had with the 1966 team, which I highlight in the Prologue. I will stress – in case it isn't obvious – that particularly in the late 1970s and mid-1980s, the World Cup barely counted as history. It appeared to have been played only the day before yesterday. Memories were fresh and untainted by constant repetition. No one spoke about it for the sake of posterity either.

Often, casually buttonholing those writers or broadcasters who had either covered the tournament and/or knew Ramsey, they spoke of '66 with a matter-of-fact-candidness. Among them were Ken Jones, Peter Batt, Mike Langley, Frank McGee, David Lacey, Max Marquis, Hugh Johns, Brian Moore (I saw him quite often) and Bryon Butler, who had worked on the Nottingham *Evening News* and reported on Forest's 1959 FA Cup win.

I also talked to managers and former players who had a connection of one sort or another with England or Ramsey. A few were found in press boxes; others at sportsmen's dinners, football writers' lunches, testimonial banquets. Many I knew already: these included Brian Clough (of course), Tommy Lawton, Alan Hill, Jackie Sewell, Joe Mercer, Malcolm Allison, Len Shackleton, Ted Ditchburn, Ted Phillips, Nat Lofthouse, Tommy Docherty, Don Howe, Jimmy Armfield, Jimmy Adamson, Jeff Astle, Peter Shilton, Larry Lloyd, Stan Bowles, Ian Moore, George Eastham, Johnny Giles, Billy Bremner, Joe Baker, Trevor Francis, Trevor Brooking, John Connolly, Frank Worthington, Emlyn Hughes, Ken Shellito, Peter Shilton, Mike Summerbee, Colin Todd, Dave Mackay, Derek Dougan, Denis Law and Tommy Gemmell (both of whom played in the Scotland team that beat England in 1967). I interviewed Don Revie in his office at Lancaster Gate. I even had a brief correspondence with Les Cocker about coaching and training.

Some contributors stand out and shine. On one memorable midweek night in 1986, I spent two hours beside Danny Blanchflower at Selhurst Park. He painted vivid pictures of his whole career for me; I barely had to ask a question. His reminiscences began with the sentence: 'I used to play this game once.' He was infinitely more fascinating than the League Cup tie we were supposed to be watching.

More than a decade ago, researching a biography of George Best, I interviewed Wilf McGuinness, the kindest of men. That conversation, once the subject of George was exhausted, turned to Ramsey and '66.

While writing that same book, I met David Stanley, son of Ken. He mentioned that his father had known Ramsey during the war.

Ken's agency, for which David also worked, handled the promotional pushing and shoving for both the 1970 World Cup and the one England did not reach in 1974. I promised David, who quickly became a friend, that 'soon' I would ask him about his father's relationship with Ramsey. Ten years later, I finally did. He was, as ever, fantastically helpful.

In 2011, I went to Brian Glanville for advice. I wanted to know who, among 'modern' strikers, most resembled Tommy Lawton in style (Brian nominated Geoff Hurst). For the next 90 minutes, just chatting away, he guided me through the history of the English game from the 1940s until the mid-1970s. He spoke about Moore and Charlton and Banks et al. In 2012, during another fabulously long conversation, he talked specifically about Walter Winterbottom, the FA's 'selectors', the '66 World Cup and the making of the film *Goal!* In subsequent years, he was always incredibly generous with his knowledge and his insight.

My sports-writing hero, Hugh McIlvanney, was similarly fantastic. We had 'lunch' at one of his favourite restaurants (two glasses of champagne were drunk before the starter arrived) and carried on talking at his London club. Put it this way: Hugh had a rather spiky relationship with Ramsey.

A special mention in dispatches goes to Graham Rowe, who shared his memories of his father Arthur. Also, I'm especially grateful to: Kevin and Simon Wooldridge, sons of Ian; Sir Michael Parkinson (as always) and his son Mike, who kindly sent me recordings from their archive; Ben Jeffrey for some precious assistance; Stephen Tollervey of the BFI (who also makes a superb cup of tea); Derek Cattani, who ran the FA's film and photographic department; Peter Lodge, the chairman of the Wharfedale German Society, who translated significant parts of Helmut Schön's autobiography for me; John and Jennifer Williams, for both being here and offering wine, support and also newspapers when I was unable to go and fetch my own; the staff of the British Library at St Pancras and the British Library at Boston Spa; the BBC Written Archive in Reading; the Royal Society (thank you, Rupert Baker) in London; the Royal Archives in Windsor (thank you, Sarah Mitchell).

At Riverrun, Ian Bahrami's considerable editing skills and Jasmine Palmer's all-round efforts were highly valued. As for my editor, Jon Riley, I can honestly say this: I was immensely grateful for his company as well as his supreme expertise and his own passion for the game (Jon is a Spurs supporter of long standing).

I am enormously indebted, as ever, to my agent Grainne Fox for her advice, her ideas, her encouragement, her negotiating skills and her good humour.

Finally, and most significantly, neither this book nor I would exist without my wife Mandy. It can't be easy living with someone who writes for a living. Somehow, Mandy tolerates the daily disruptions and upheavals I create: papers piled everywhere (more than 4,000 sheets for *Answered Prayers*); books in towers, arranged like a city skyline; my weird working hours; my failure to get a printer to work; my ability to lose something – especially a newspaper cutting – that was sitting beside me only five minutes before; my frequent inability to find objects directly in front of my nose – most often, my glasses. She is also much more adept at using a library microfilm reader than I will ever be. She is, indeed, more adept at everything.

In fact, Mandy deserves a World Cup winners' medal of her own. Alas, all I can offer are three words: I love you.

PICTURE ACKNOWLEDGEMENTS

Page **9** Getty Images/Popperfoto, **11** Getty Images/Chris Ware Keystone, **13** Getty Images/Stu Forster Hulton Archive, **23** Getty Images/Fox Photos, **31** Getty Images/Don Morely Allsport, **61** Shutterstock/ANL, **83** Getty Images/W & H Talbot Archive/Popperfoto, **89** Shutterstock/Fortune/*Daily Mail*, **126** Getty Images/Keystone, **129** Getty Images/Chris Morphet Redferns, **137** Getty Images/Mirrorpix, **140** Getty Images/Robert Stiggins/*Daily Express*/

Hulton Archive, **146** Getty Images/Kent Gavin/Keystone/Hulton Archive, **172** Getty Images/Bob Thomas Sports Photography, **182** Shutterstock/ANL, **196** Shutterstock/ITV, **205** Getty Images/Central Press, **216** Getty Images/Central Press, **221** Getty Images/Mirrorpix, **223** Shutterstock/Dezo Hoffmann, **235** Shutterstock/Colorsport, **252** Getty Images/Mirrorpix, **259** Gerry Cranham, **276** Peter Robinson, **306** Gerry Cranham, **311** Getty Images/United News/Popperfoto, **333** the *Sun*/News Licensing, **335** Getty Images/Joe Bangay, **349** Getty Images/Bob Thomas Sports Photography, **379** Getty Images/*Evening Standard*/Hulton Archive, **384** Getty Images/Bob Thomas Sports Photography, **396** Getty Images/Hulton Archive.

All other images provided by the author.

SOURCES

BOOKS

Allison, M., *Colours of My Life*, Everest, 1975

Annan, N., *Our Age*, Weidenfeld, 1990

Arlott, J. (ed.), *Soccer: The Great Ones*, Pelham, 1968

Armfield, J., *All Stars Football Book*, World Distributors, 1966

——*All Stars Football Book*, World Distributors, 1967

——*Right Back to the Beginning*, Headline, 2004

Bagchi, R. and Rogerson, P., *The Unforgiven: The Story of Don Revie's Leeds United*, Aurum, 2002

Ball, A., *Ball of Fire*, Pelham, 1967

——*International Soccer Annual*, Pelham, 1969

——*International Soccer Annual No. 2*, Pelham, 1970

——*International Soccer Annual, No. 3*, Pelham, 1971

——*International Soccer Annual, No. 4*, Pelham, 1972

——*Playing Extra Time*, Sidgwick and Jackson, 2004

Banks, G., *Banks of England*, Arthur Baker, 1980

——*Banksy*, Penguin, 2002

Barrett, N., *I Was There: 20 Great Sporting Memories from the Writers of the Daily Telegraph*, Telegraph Publishers, 1985

Barwick, B., *Are You Watching the Match Tonight?*, Andre Deutsch, 2013

Batt, P., *Batty: The Life and Wild Times of the Guvnor of Fleet Street*, Headline, 2000

Bellos, A., *Futebol, The Brazilian Way of Life*, Bloomsbury, 2002

Best, G., *Soccer Annual No. 5*, Pelham, 1972

Blanchflower, D., *The Double and Before*, Nicholas Kaye, 1961

——*Soccer Book*, Muller, 1959

Bond, B., *1966 and All That*, Greenways Publishing, 2016

Bowler, D., *Danny Blanchflower: A Biography of a Visionary*, Gollancz, 1997

——*Three Lions on the Shirt: Playing for England*, Gollancz, 1999

——*Winning Isn't Everything: A Biography of Alf Ramsey*, Gollancz, 1998

Bremner, B., *Book of Football No. 2*, Souvenir Press, 1973

Brooks, M., *Ipswich Town: Champions 1961–62*, History Press, 2011

Brown, C., *1966 and All That*, Hodder, 2005

Buchan, C., *Soccer Gift Book, 1967–68*, Longacre Press, 1967

——*Soccer Gift Book 1968–69*, Longacre Press, 1968

Butler, B. (ed.), *The Football League, 1888–1988*, Queen Anne Press, 1988

——*The Official History of the Football Association*, Queen Anne Press, 1991

——*Sports Report: 40 Years of the Best*, Queen Anne Press, 1988

Byrne, J., *The Strategy of Soccer*, SBC, 1965

Campkin, J., *The World Cup 1958*, Fletcher and Son, 1958

Cannadine, D., *Class in Britain*, Yale, 1998

Chapman, P., *Out of Time: 1966 and the End of Old-Fashioned Britain*, Bloomsbury, 2016

Charlton, B., *Book of Soccer*, Cassell, 1960

——*Forward for England*, Pelham, 1967

——*My England Years*, Headline, 2008

——*My Life in Football*, Headline, 2009

Charlton, C., *Cissie*, Bridge Studios, 1988

Charlton, J., *The Autobiography*, Partridge Press, 1996

——*For Leeds and England*, Stanley Paul, 1970

Cohen, G., *My Autobiography*, Greenwater, 2003

Connelly, C., *Last Train to Hilversum: A Journey in Search of the Magic of Radio*, Bloomsbury 2019

Connor, J., *The Lost Babes: Manchester United and the Forgotten Victims of Munich*, Harper Collins, 2000

Crawford, R. and Wood, M., *Curse of the Jungle Boy*, PR Publishing, 2007

Croker, T., *The First Voice You Will Hear*, Collins, 1987

Davies, C., *Forgive Us Our Press Passes: An Anthology of Modern Football Writing*, Know the Score, 2008

Davies, H., *Books, Balls and Haircuts: An Illustrated History of Football from Then to Now*, Century, 2003

——*The Bumper Book of Football*, Quercus, 2007

——*The Glory Game*, Weidenfeld and Nicolson, 1972

Dawson, J., *Back Home: England and the 1970 World Cup*, Orion, 2001

Dickenson, M., *Bobby Moore: The Man in Full*, Yellow Jersey, 2014

Dimmock, P. (ed.), *Sports in View*, Faber, 1964

——*Sportsview Soccer*, 1963

Donovan, P., *The Radio Companion*, Harper Collins, 1991

Downie, A., *The Greatest Show on Earth: The Inside Story of the Legendary 1970 World Cup*, Arena, 2021

Downing, D., *The Best of Enemies: England v. Germany*, Bloomsbury, 2000

Drewett, J., *1966: The 50th Anniversary*, VSP, 2016

Durante, F., *Shocking Brazil: Six Games That Shook the World Cup*, Arena, 2014

Easterly, M., *66 on 66*, Pitch, 2016

Edelston, M. and Delaney, T., *Masters of Soccer*, Naldrett Press, 1960

Engel, M., *Tickle the Public: One Hundred Years of the Popular Press*, Gollanz, 1996

FA Book for Boys, 15, Heinemann, 1962

——18, Heinemann, 1965

——20, Heinemann, 1967

——22, Heinemann, 1969

——23, Heinemann, 1970

FA Yearbook 1962–63, Heinemann, 1962

——*1966–67*, Heinemann, 1966

Fabian, A. H. and Greene, G., *Association Football, Vol. 3*, Caxton Publishing, 1960

Feeney, P., *1966: From Good Vibrations to World Cup Victory*, History Press, 2016

Ferguson, A., *Managing My Life*, Hodder, 1999

Ferrier, B., *Soccer Partnership: Billy Wright and Walter Winterbottom*, 1961

Findler, H., The New Yorker *Book of the 40s: Story of the Decade*, Random House, 2015

——The New Yorker *Book of the 60s: Story of the Decade*, William Heinemann, 2014

Finn, R. L., *England, World Champions 1966*, Robert Hale, 1966

——*My Greatest Game*, Saturn Press, 1951

——*The Official History of Tottenham Hotspur 1882–1972*, Robert Hale, 1972

Finney, T., *My Autobiography*, Headline 2003

Foot, J., *Calcio*, Harper, 2007

Francis, T., *One in a Million*, Pitch, 2019

Frewin, L., *The Saturday Men*, Macdonald, 1967

Gallacher, K., *Jock Stein*, Stanley Paul, 1988

Gardiner, S., *Ipswich Town: A History*, Amberley, 2013

Garnett, T., *Ipswich Town Football Club*, Tempus, 2000

——*100 Greats: Ipswich Town Football Club*, Tempus, 2002

Gibson, J., *Soccer's Golden Nursery*, Pelham 1970

Giller, N., *July 30 1966, Football's Longest Day*, NGB, 2016

——*My 70 Years of Spurs: A Long Walk Down White Hart Lane*, Pitch, 2021

Glanville, B., *Champions of Europe*, Guinness Publishing, 1991

——*England's Managers: The Toughest Job in Football*, Headline, 2007

——*Football Memories*, Virgin, 1999

——*The Footballer's Companion*, Eyre and Spottiswoode, 1962

——*Footballers Don't Cry: Selected Writings*, Virgin, 1999

——*Soccer: A History of the Game*, Crown, 1968

——*Soccer: A Panorama*, Eyre and Spottiswoode, 1969

——*Soccer Nemesis*, Secker and Warburg, 1955

——Sunday Times *Book of the World Cup*, Times, 1974

——(with Weinstein, J.), *World Cup*, SBC, 1958

Goldblatt, D., *Futebol Nation, A Footballing History of Brazil*, Penguin, 2014

——*The Game of Our Lives, The Meaning and Making of English Football*, Penguin, 2014

Golesworthy, M., *The Encyclopaedia of Association Football*, Robert Hale, 1969

Graves, R. and Hodge, A., *The Long Weekend: A Social History of Great Britain, 1918–1939*, Folio Society Edition, 2009

Greaves, J., *Greavsie: The Autobiography*, Time Warner, 2003

——*Let's Be Honest*, Pelham, 1972

——(with Giller, N.) *Don't Shoot the Manager: The Revealing Story of England's Soccer Bosses*, Boxtree, 1994

Green, G., *The History of the Football Association*, Naldrett Press, 1953

——*Pardon Me for Living*, Allen and Unwin, 1985

——*Soccer in the Fifties*, Ian Allan, 1974

——*Soccer the World Game: A Popular History*, SBC, 1953

Greenwood, R., *Yours Sincerely*, Headline, 1984

Guthrie, J., *Soccer Rebel*, Pentagon, 1976

Hall, D., *Manchester's Finest: How the Munich Air Disaster Broke the Heart of a Great City*, Bantam Press, 2008

Hardaker, A., *Hardaker of the League*, Pelham, 1977

Harding, J., *For the Good of the Game: The Official History of the PFA*, Robson, 1991

Harris, N., *The Charlton Brothers*, Stanley Paul, 1971

Hattenstone, S., *The Best of Times: What Became of the Heroes of 1966?*, Guardian Books, 2006

Hattersley, R., *Borrowed Time: The Story of Britain Between the Wars*, Little Brown, 2007

Hayter, R. (ed.), *Soccer Stars of Today*, Pelham, 1970

Henderson, J., *When Footballers Were Skint*, Biteback, 2018

Henderson, M., *50 People Who Fouled Up Football*, Constable, 2009

Henderson, M. and Voller, P., *The Essential History of Ipswich Town*, Headline, 2011

——*Match of My Life: Ipswich Town*, Know the Score, 2008

Hennessey, P., *Having It So Good: Britain in the Fifties*, Allen Lane, 2006

——*Never Again: Britain 1945–1951*, Jonathan Cape, 1992

——*Winds of Change: Britain in the Early Sixties*, Penguin, 2019

Hess-Lichtenberger, U., *Tor: The Story of German Football*, WSC, 2002

Hill, B., *My Gentleman Jim*, Book Guild, 2015

Hill, J., *My Story*, Hodder, 1998

——*Soccer '69*, St Stephen's Press, 1968

——*Striking for Soccer*, Peter Davies, 1961

Hodgkinson, A., *Between the Sticks*, Harper Collins, 2013

Holmes, B., *Caesars, Saviours and Suckers: The Good, Bad and Ugly of Football's Foreign Owners*, YPS, 2016

——*The Match of My Life*, Kingswood Press, 1991

Honigstein, R., *Das Reboot: How German Football Reinvented Itself and Conquered the World*, Yellow Jersey, 2016

Hopcraft, A., *The Football Man: People and Passions in Soccer*, Collins, 1968

Hopkins, E., *The Rise and Decline of the English Working Class, 1918–1990*, Weidenfeld, 1991

Hughes, E., *Crazy Horse*, Arthur Baker, 1980

Hugman, B. J., *Rothman's Football League Players Records: The Complete A–Z*, Rothman's, 1981

Hunt, R., *Hunt for Goals*, Pelham, 1969

Hunter, N., *Biting Talk*, Hodder, 2004

Hurst, G., *Geoff Hurst's Greats*, Icon Books, 2016

——*1966 and All That*, Headline, 2001 and 2006 (updated)

——*1966 World Champions*, Headline, 2016

——*The World Game*, Stanley Paul, 1967

Hutchinson, R., *They Think It's All Over . . .*, Mainstream, 1995

Inglis, S., *The Best of Charles Buchan's Football Monthly*, English Heritage and FM, 2006

——*The Football Grounds of Great Britain*, Collins,1987

——*League Football, 1888–1988, The Official Centenary History of the Football League*, Collins, 1988

——*Soccer in the Dock: A History of British Football Scandals, 1900 to 1965*, Collins, 1985

James, B., *England v. Scotland*, Pelham, 1969

——*Journey to Wembley: The Story of the 1976–77 FA Cup Competition and Liverpool's bid for the Treble*, Cavendish, 1977

Jenkins, G., *The Beautiful Team: In Search of Pele and the 1970 Brazilians*, Simon and Schuster, 1998

Johnston, J., *The Lord Chamberlain's Blue Pencil*, Hodder, 1990

Kelly, S. F., *The Kingswood Book of Football*, Kingswood, 1992

Kelner, M., *Sit Down and Cheer: A History of Sport on TV*, Wisden, 2012

Kynaston, D., *Austerity Britain, 1945–51*, Bloomsbury, 2007

——*Family Britain, 1951–57*, Bloomsbury, 2009

——*Modernity Britain, 1957–59*, Bloomsbury, 2013

——*Modernity Britain (Book Two), 1959–62*, 2014

——*On the Cusp: Days of '62*, Bloomsbury, 2021

Laschke, I., *Rothman's Book of Football League Records, 1888–89 to 1978–79*, Queen Anne Press, 1979

Lawton, J., *On Football*, Dewi Lewis Media, 2007

Lawton, T., *When the Cheering Stopped*, Golden Eagle, 1973

Ledbroke, A. and Turner, E., *Soccer from the Press Box*, Nicholas Kaye, 1950

Leighton, J., *Duncan Edwards: The Greatest*, Simon and Schuster, 2012

McColl, G., *England and the Alf Ramsey Years*, Chameleon Books, 1998

MacDonald, R. and Batty, E., *Scientific Soccer in the Seventies*, Pelham, 1971

McGuinness, W., *Manchester United, Man and Boy*, Know the Score, 2008

McIlvanney, H. (ed.), *McIlvanney on Football*, Mainstream, 1994 and 2007

——*World Cup '66*, Eyre and Spottiswoode, 1966

McKinstry, L., *Jack and Bobby: A Story of Brothers in Conflict*, Collins, 2002

——*Sir Alf*, HarperSport, 2006

Marquis, M., *Sir Alf Ramsey: Anatomy of a Football Manager*, Arthur Baker, 1970

Matthews, S., *The Way It Was*, Headline, 2000

Mayes, H., *Empire News Footballer's Who's Who*, Kemsley, 1954

——*The FA World Cup Report 1966*, Heinemann, 1967

Mayo, J., *The 1966 World Cup Minute by Minute*, Short Books, 2016

Meisl, W., *Soccer Revolution*, Phoenix Sports Books, 1955

Miller, D., *England's Last Glory, The Boys of '66*, Pavilion, 2006

——*Stanley Matthews: The Authorised Biography*, Pavilion, 1989

Montgomery, J., *The Fifties*, Blackfriars Press, 1965

Moore, B. (ed.), *The Book of Soccer, No. 9*, Stanley Paul, 1966

——(ed.), *The Book of Soccer, No. 10*, Stanley Paul, 1967

——(ed.), *The Book of Soccer, No. 13*, Stanley Paul, 1970

——*Brian Moore, The Final Score*, Hodder, 1999

——*England, England*, Stanley Paul, 1970

——*My Soccer Story*, Stanley Paul, 1967

Moore, K., *What You Think You Know About Football Is Wrong*, Bloomsbury, 2021

Moorhouse, G., *The Other England: Britain in the Sixties*, Penguin, 1964

——*The Press*, Cape, 1964

Morse, G., *Sir Walter Winterbottom, The Father of Modern English Football*, John Blake, 2013

Motson, J., *Forty Years in the Commentary Box*, Virgin, 2009

——*Match of the Day: The Complete Record Since 1964*, BBC, 1992

——*World Cup Motty: My World Cup Stories*, SJH, 2019

Moynihan, J., *The Soccer Syndrome*, McGibbon and Kee, 1966

Nead, L., *The Tiger in the Smoke: Art and Culture in Post-War Britain*, PM Centre, 2017

Nicholson, B., *Glory, Glory: My Life with Spurs*, Macmillan, 1984

Nicholson, W., *The Professionals*, Andre Deutsch, 1964

Nicolson, J., *Frostquake: The Frozen Winter of 1962*, Chatto, 2021

Pawson, T., *The Football Managers*, Eyre Methuen, 1973

——*The Goalscorers*, Cassell, 1978

——*Runs and Catches*, Faber, 1980

Perryman, M. (ed.), *1966 and Not All That*, Repeater Books, 2016

Peters, M., *Goals from Nowhere*, Stanley Paul, 1969

——*The Ghost of '66*, Orion, 2006

Phillips, N., *Doctor to the World Champions*, Trafford, 2007

Powell, J., *Bobby Moore: The Definitive Biography*, Robson Press, 2004

Preece, I. and Cheesman, D. (eds), *The Heyday of the Football Annual*, Constable, 2015

Ramsey, A., *Talking Football*, Stanley Paul, 1952

Reng, R., *Matchdays: The Hidden Story of the Bundesliga*, Simon and Schuster, 2013

Roberts, R. and Olson, J. S., *John Wayne, American*, Free Press, 1995

Robinson, P. and Cheesman, D. (eds), *1966 Uncovered: The Unseen Story of the World Cup in England*, Mitchell Beazley, 2006

Robson, B., *Against the Odds*, Hutchinson, 1990

——*Farewell but not Goodbye*, Hodder, 2005

Ross, G., *The Gillette Book of Cricket and Football*, Muller, 1963

——*World Cup, England 1966*, Purnell, 1966

Rous, S., *Football Worlds: A Lifetime in Sport*, Faber, 1978

Rowlinson, J., *Boys of 66*, Virgin, 2016

Sandbrook, D., *The Great British Dream Factory: The Strange History of Our National Imagination*, Penguin, 2013

——*Never Had It So Good: A History of Britain from Suez to the Beatles*, Little Brown, 2005

——*White Heat: A History of Britain in the Swinging Sixties*, Little Brown, 2006

Scovell, B., *Football Gentry: The Cobbold Brothers*, Tempus, 2005

——*The England Managers, The Impossible Job*, Tempus, 2006

——Bill Nicholson, Football's Perfectionist, John Blake, 2011

——The Conquests of 1966 of Alf and Gary, Fonthill, 2016

Seldon, P. J., A Football Compendium: A Comprehensive Guide to the Literature of Football, British Library, 1996

Sewell, A., Wills Whiffs 1970 World Cup Preview, Queen Anne Press, 1970

Sheil, N., Voices of 1966: Memories of England's World Cup, Tempus, 2000

Shepherdson, H., The Magic Sponge, Pelham, 1968

Singny, D., A Pictorial History of Soccer, Hamlyn, 1968

Shackleton, L., Clown Prince of Soccer, Nicholas Kaye, 1955

——Return of the Clown Prince, GJKN Publishing, 2000

Sharpe, I., The Football League Jubilee Book, Stanley Paul, 1963

——Soccer Top Ten, Soccer Book Club, 1963

Shaw, P., The Book of Football Quotations, Ebury Press, 2014

Sheldon, P. J., A Football Compendium, British Library, 1995

Sherwood, K., Pegasus: The Famous Oxford and Cambridge Soccer Side of the Fifties, Oxford Illustrated Press, 1975

Smart, A., Best, Pele and a Half-Time Bovril: A Nostalgic Look at the 1970s – Football's Last Great Decade, John Blake, 2014

Smith, D. (ed.), The Boys' Book of Soccer, Evans Brothers, 1969

——The Boys' Book of Soccer 1966, Evans Brothers, 1965

Smith, M., Match of the Day, BBC, 2005

Smith, R., Mister: The Men Who Taught the World How to Beat England at Their Own Game, Simon and Schuster, 2016

Smith, S. (ed.), The Brazil Book of Football, Souvenir Press, 1963

——International Football Book No. 9, Souvenir Press, 1967

——International Football Book No. 10, Souvenir Press, 1968

——International Football Book No. 12, Souvenir Press, 1970

Soar, P., And the Spurs Go Marching On, Hamlyn, 1982

Soar, P. and Tyler, M., Book of Football's All-Time Greats, Marshall Cavendish, 1971–4

Stiles, N., Soccer My Battlefield, Stanley Paul, 1969

——After the Ball, Hodder, 2003

Summerbee, M., The Autobiography, Optimum, 2010

Sutcliffe, R., Revie: Revered and Reviled, Great Northern, 2010

Sutherland Muckle, D. and Shepherdson, H., Football Fitness and Injuries, Pelham, 1975

Talbot, B. and Weaver, P., 1966: The Good, the Bad and the Football, Phoenix Mill, 2006

Taylor, R. and Ward, A., Kicking and Screaming: An Oral History of Football in Britain, Robson, 1995

Tennant, J., *Football, The Golden Age*, Cassell, 2001

Thomson, D., *4–2*, Bloomsbury, 1996

Thornton, E., *Leeds United and Don Revie*, Robert Hale, 1970

Tossell, D., *Alan Ball: The Man in White Boots*, Hodder, 2017

Tyler, M., *Boys of '66*, Hamlyn, 1981

Villoro, J., *God Is Round*, Restless Books, 2016

Walker, S., *The Captain's Class*, Random House, 2017

Ward, A. and Williams, J., *Football Nation: Sixty Years of the Beautiful Game*, Bloomsbury, 2009

Webb, W. L. (ed.), *The Bedside Guardian, 21*, Guardian, 1974

Welch, J., *The Biography of Tottenham Hotspur*, VSP, 2015

West, G., *The Championship in My Keeping*, Souvenir Press, 1970

Wheeler, K., *Champions of Soccer*, SBC, 1971

——*Soccer the British Way*, SBC, 1965

——*Soccer the British Way*, Cassell, 1967

——*Soccer the International Way*, Kaye and Ward, 1967

Whitehead, R. (ed), *The Times 50 Greatest Football Matches*, History Press, 2019

Whitaker's Almanack, 1964 and 1967

Widdows, R., *The Sixty Memorable Matches*, Marshall Cavendish, 1973

Wilson, A., *Our Times: The Age of Elizabeth II*, Hutchinson, 2008

Wilson, J., *The Anatomy of England: A History in Ten Matches*, Orion, 2010

——*Inverting the Pyramid: The History of Football Tactics*, 2008 and 2013

——*The Names Heard Long Ago: How the Golden Age of Hungarian Football Shaped the Modern Game*, Blink Publishing, 2019

Wilson, R., *My Life in Soccer*, Pelham, 1969

Wolstenholme, K., *Young England: The Story of the Development of Soccer Talent*, Stanley Paul, 1959

——*Book of World Soccer*, Daily Mirror, 1962

——*Book of World Soccer*, World Distributors, 1965

——*Book of World Soccer*, World Distributors, 1967

——*The Pros*, Leslie Frewin, 1968

——*They Think It's All Over . . .: Memories of the Greatest Day in English Football*, Robson Books, 1996

Wright, B., *Book of Soccer, Number 7*, Stanley Paul, 1964

——*Football Album*, LTA Robinson, 1954

——*One Hundred Caps and All That*, Robert Hale, 1962

——*The World's My Football Pitch*, Stanley Paul, 1953

Young, P. M., *Football Year*, Phoenix, 1956

——*Football Facts and Fancies*, Dobson, 1957

——*A History of British Football*, Stanley Paul, 1968

No author and/or publisher identified:
The Big Book of Football Champions, 1953
Brooke Bond PG Tips Book of Football, 1970–71, Wolfe, 1970

NEWSPAPERS

Aberdeen Evening Express: Oct 6, Oct 25, 1962

Belfast Telegraph: April 21, 1955; Oct 1, Oct 25, 1962; May 1, 1974

Birmingham Post: Oct 2, 1962; Jan 31, 1976; March 6, March 9, 1978

Daily Express: May 2, 1957; March 15, Feb 20, March 15, March 30, April 24, Aug 2, Aug 9, Oct 1, Oct 26, 1962; Feb 28, Oct 1, 1963; May 26, May 28, June 1, June 6, June 8, 1964; Dec 9–10, 1965; Feb 8, April 14, July 10–16, July 18–23, July 25–30, Aug 1–3, Oct 4, 1966; Sept 20, 1967; May 1–3, May 6, 1974; April 15, 1986; Oct 22, 1991; May 1, May 17, July 31, 1999; July 30, 2016

Daily Herald: June 30, July 2, 1950; March 21–23, Nov 26, 1953; Aug 4, March 6, 1956; May 2, 1957; Sept 4, Oct 23, Dec 19, 1961; March 1, March 15, June 12, Aug 2, Aug 22, Oct 1–2, Oct 5, Oct 18, Oct 26, 1962; April 29, Aug 9, Aug 22, Sept 11, Sept 21, Nov 21, Nov 26, Dec 1, Dec 4, 1963; April 10, May 26, May 28, June 1, June 6, June 8, 1964

Daily Mail: Aug 22, 1955; Dec 17, 1956; March 10, August 30, 1961; April 25, July 25, Oct 26, Dec 6, 1962; Feb 2, March 19, March 21, March 29, June 1, June 6, August 19, Dec 22, 1963; May 26, May 28, June 1, June 6, June 8, Sept 25, Oct 3, Oct 23–24, Nov 4, Nov 7, Nov 9, Dec 1, 1964; Feb 10, April 7, April 12, Aug 20, Dec 9–10, 1965; Jan 4, Jan 8, Feb 10, Feb 14, Feb 16, Feb 26, March 10, March 18, April 2, June 8, June 24, July 10–16, July 18–23, July 25–30, Aug 1–3, Aug 22, Sept 2, Sept 23, Sept 30, Oct 4, Oct 22, Nov 29, Dec 7, Dec 9, Dec 30–31, 1966; Jan 5, May 6, July 21, Nov 9, 1967; Feb 26, March 25, May 22, June 10, June 15, Aug 9, Oct 21, 1968; Oct 18, Dec 16, Dec 17, 1969; June 5, 1970; March 30, April 1, Dec 21, 1972; Jan 17, Jan 20, April 28, May 3, Oct 18, 1973; April 3, May 1–3, May 6, May 31, June 29, July 29, 1974; March 25, June 16, Dec 23, 1975; March 20, 1976; Oct 31, Nov 12, 1981; April 28, 1983; July 29, 1985; June 1, 1987; Oct 8, 1990; Feb 24, June 8, 1998; May 1, June 8, Nov 12, 1999; Oct 5, 2000; April 6, 2010; Sept 16, 2011; Nov 13, 2012; Oct 11, 2013; July 10, 2021

Daily Mirror: Nov 16, 1950; Feb 1, 1951; Oct 5, Dec 21, 1953; Feb 11, 1954; Nov 15, Nov 17, Nov 23, Dec 14–16, Dec 18, 1960; Oct 23, 1961; March 30, May 8, June 6, Aug 30, Oct 13, Oct 26, Dec 4, 1962; Feb 6, Feb 14–15, Feb 19, Feb 28, June 3, 1963; May 26, May 28, June 1, June 6, June 8, Oct 23, 1964; Feb 9, May 10, Dec 9, 1965; Feb 15, May 4, July 10–23, July 25–30, Aug 1–3, 1966; Jan 2, 1968; April 28, Nov 11, Dec 9, 1969; Nov 9, 1972; Oct 19, 1973; May 1–4, May

6, 1974; Oct 3, 1977; March 13, 1978; Feb 22, March 20, 1980; April 14, 1984; March 24, 1990; Jan 27, Feb 4, 1995; Jan 12, 1996; May 1, 1999

Daily News: May 2, 1957

Daily Sketch: Nov 6, 1963; April 12, May 6, May 13, May 15, June 25, Sept 10–12, Sept 14, Oct 2, Oct 4–5, Oct 12–13, Oct 20–22, Nov 1, Nov 3, Nov 15, Nov 23, Nov 26, Dec 6, Dec 8–9, 1965

Daily Telegraph: Oct 10, 1949; Nov 20, 1950; Sept 2, Nov 10, 1952; Sept 28, Nov 26, 1953; Jan 22, Jan 27, Feb 2, May 25, Aug 10, 1954; March 22, 1961; Feb 20, March 15, March 30, April 24, Aug 2, Aug 9, Oct 1, Oct 26, Nov 19, Dec 4, 1962; March 2, Aug 10, 1963; May 26, May 28, June 1, June 6, June 8, Sept 21, Sept 28, Oct 3, Oct 5, Oct 17, Oct 26, 1964; Feb 9, Feb 12, Dec 8, Dec 9, 1965; Feb 24, April 7, July 10–16, July 18–23, July 25–30, Aug 1–4, Sept 7, Oct 14, Oct 18, Oct 20, 1966; Jan 6, April 2, 1968; Jan 17, April 17, June 3, June 7, June 10, 1969; Sept 20, 1988; May 1, 1999; March 30, 2007; Nov 9, 2010

Eastern Daily Press: Oct 26, 1962; Aug 22, 1963

East Anglian Daily Times: Oct 26, 1962; May 1, May 5, May 15, May 17, 1999; Jan 9, 2018

Financial Times: Dec 2, 1965; Feb 11, March 3, March 31, April 18, June 14, Aug 19, Dec 29, 1966

Guardian: Nov 10, 1937; Nov 25–26, 1953; Sept 29, 1955; Nov 5, 1961; March 15, April 30, Aug 2, Aug 5, 1962; Feb 24, Feb 28, 1963; April 23, May 26, May 28, June 1, June 6, June 8, 1964; May 12, 1965; July 10–16, July 18–23, July 25–30, Aug 1–3, Nov 28, 1966; March 22, Sept 30, 1968; March 14, 1969; May 4, 1970; Dec 10, 1971; Aug 24, Oct 19, Oct 21, Nov 27, 1973; April 3, April 5, May 23, May 25, 1974; Aug 4, Aug 20, Dec 31, 1976; June 4, Nov 8, 1977; Aug 20, Oct 30–31, 1978; Oct 30, Nov 18, 1981; May 23, 1985; June 11, July 29, Sept 20, 1986; April 11, 1991; Feb 21, Feb 23, Feb 25, Sept 16, 1993; Sept 15, 1995; Feb 24, 1996; June 13, June 26, 1998; May 1, 1999; March 22, Aug 21, Sept 1, Sept 3, 2001; Feb 17–19, Feb 23, 2002; May 29, Aug 23, Sept 25, 2003; Dec 30, 2005; Feb 15, 2006; July 10, 2009; Oct 13, 2012; Dec 5, 2013

Huddersfield Daily Examiner: June 15, 1990; April 27, 1994

Illustrated: Sept 2, 1950

Illustrated London News: August 27, 1967; June 1, 1968

Independent: Oct 23, 2011

Irish Times: Dec 9, 1965

Leicester Evening Mail: Oct 2, 1962

London Evening News: May 1–3, May 6, 1974

London Evening Standard: May 1–3, May 6, 1974

The New European: Oct 21, 2016

New York Times: Aug 1, 1966; Dec 9, 2009

Newcastle Chronicle: Aug 1, 1962
Newcastle Journal: Oct 26, 1963
News of the World: Jan 9, Feb 13, Feb 20, Feb 27, March 3, April 3, April 10, June 5, June 12, June 19, June 26, July 3, July 10, July 17, July 24, July 31, Aug 7, Aug 14, Aug 21, Aug 28, 1966; May 25, June 15, 1969; May 17, May 31, June 7, June 14, June 21, 1970; May 6, 1971; April 23, 1972; Sept 16, Sept 30, 1973; May 12, May 26, 1974; May 2, 1999
Observer: April 8, May 6, Oct 7, 1962; March 24, April 12, Oct 5, Oct 26, Nov 22, 1964; May 9, Oct 17, Oct 24, Dec 12, 1965; Jan 9, Feb 13, Feb 20, Feb 27, March 3, March 20, April 3, April 10, May 27, June 5, June 12, June 19, June 26, July 3, July 10, July 17, July 24, July 31, Aug 7, Aug 14, Aug 21, Aug 28, 1966; Feb 12, April 23, 1967; Sept 8, 1968; Aug 9, Nov 9, 1969; May 10, May 31, 1970; Jan 10, 1971; May 7, Nov 12, 1972; Oct 21, Nov 18, Nov 25, Dec 18, 1973; May 5, 1974; Aug 14, 1977; Nov 9, 1986; July 28, Aug 4, 1991; Feb 28, 1993; Jan 23, 1994; Jan 21, June 2, 1996; May 2, 1999; Feb 17, 2003; Dec 12, 2021
Reynolds News/Sunday Citizen: Jan 14, Feb 3, Oct 7, Nov 23, 1962; May 9, Dec 16, 1965; Jan 9, Feb 13, Feb 20, Feb 27, March 13, April 3, April 10, June 5, June 12, June 19, June 26, July 3, July 10, July 17, July 24, July 31, August 7, August 14, August 21, August 28, 1966
Sport: Dec 12, 1953
Sun: July 30, 1966; April 28, 1969; July 5, 1970; May 1, May 5, May 7, May 11–12, 1972; Oct 6, Oct 12, Oct 15–19, Nov 14–16, 1973; April 3, 1974; May 1–3, May 7, May 9, 1974
Sunday Express: Feb 22, March 18, April 15, April 22, April 29; May 6, Aug 5, Sept 30, Oct 7, Oct 21, 1962; Jan 9, Jan 30, Feb 13, Feb 20, Feb 27, March 3, April 3, April 10, May 8, June 2, June 5, June 12, June 19, June 26, July 3, July 10, July 17, July 24, July 31, Aug 7, Aug 14, Aug 21, Aug 28, 1966; June 17, Oct 14, Oct 21, Nov 25, Dec 2, 1973; May 12, May 19, 1974; April 9, 2006
Sunday Mirror: Oct 7, Oct 29, 1962; Dec 13, 1964; Jan 6, May 16, Aug 29, Sept 19, Oct 24, Dec 8, 1965; Jan 9, Feb 13, Feb 20, Feb 27, March 3, April 3, April 10, June 5, June 12, June 19, June 26, July 3, July 10, July 17, July 24, July 31, Aug 7, Aug 14, Aug 21, Aug 28, Sept 4, 1966; June 2, 1968; Jan 18, March 1, April 26, May 3, May 10, May 17, June 21, Dec 27, 1970; April 1, Nov 11, 1973; Feb 3, May 5, July 28, Nov 10, 1974; May 18, 1986; Aug 29, 1999
Sunday People: Jan 29, 1958; April 21, June 25, 1961; March 4, April 29, Oct 14, 1962; April 12, May 2, May 31, Sept 6, Dec 4, 1964; April 4, May 30, Oct 3, Oct 31, Nov 12, Nov 14, 1965; Jan 9, Feb 13, Feb 15, Feb 20, Feb 27, March 3, March 11, April 2, April 9, May 8, June 5, June 12, June 19, June 26, July 3, July 10, July 17, July 24, July 31, Aug 7, Aug 14, Aug 21, Aug 28, 1966; Jan 22, 1967;

May 19, May 26, 1968; Dec 7, 1969; May 30, June 7, June 14, June 21, 1970; May 12, May 19, May 26, Feb 24, 1974; May 1, 1999

Sunday Pictorial: Aug 23, 1953

Sunday Telegraph: March 15, Nov 21, 1962; March 3, May 31, June 9, Oct 27, Nov 12, 1963; Sept 20, 1964; July 31, May 15, May 22, June 5, June 6, Sept 19, Dec 8, 1965; Jan 9, Feb 13, Feb 20, Feb 27, March 3, April 3, April 10, June 5, June 12, June 19, June 26, July 3, July 10, July 17, July 24, July 31, Aug 7, Aug 14, Aug 21, Aug 28, Sept 24, Nov 25, 1966; June 2, June 9, 1970; May 16, 1976; Oct 14, 1979; May 2, 1999

Sunday Times: Feb 21, 1954; April 8, Sept 9, Nov 18, 1962; May 31, Nov 18, 1964; Jan 10, May 9, Sept 19, 1965; Jan 9, Feb 13, Feb 20, Feb 27, March 3, March 24, April 3, April 10, April 24, May 8, May 29, June 5, June 12, June 19, June 26, July 3, July 10, July 17, July 24, July 31, Aug 7, Aug 14, Aug 21, Aug 28, Nov 20, Dec 11, 1966; Aug 4, Oct 27, Dec 15, 1968; April 27, June 1, June 8, June 15, Aug 10, Oct 5, Nov 9, 1969; May 3, May 31, June 14, Oct 4, 1970; Oct 17, Nov 7, Nov 14, 1971; May 7, May 14, May 21, June 25, Nov 19, 1972; Jan 28, Feb 11, June 2, Oct 14, Oct 21, 1973; March 31, April 7, May 5, June 20, 1974; Oct 16, 1977; Oct 15, 1978; Feb 5, 1984; March 1, 1987; May 2, May 16, July 25, Nov 29, 1999; April 30, 2000; Feb 25, May 9, 2004; Sept 4, 2005; April 9, 2006; April 29, 2007; June 30, 2010; July 24, July 31, 2016

Sunderland Echo: Dec 16, 1951

Time: April 15, 1966

The Times: Feb 20, March 15, Aug 2, Aug 17, Sept 1, Oct 1, Oct 2, Oct 13, Oct 26, 1962; Feb 28, April 20, June 8, 1963; Oct 24, 1964; Aug 15, Sept 26, Oct 21, Nov 30, 1965; July 10–16, July 18–23, July 25–30, Aug 1–3, 1966; Feb 5, April 1, 1968; Feb 10, July 23, 1973; May 1, May 2, May 9, June 28, Sept 25, 1974; Jan 1, 1981; Jan 15, Feb 14, June 16, 1982; July 7, Aug 11, 1990; Oct 22, 1991; Dec 26, 1992; Feb 25, Nov 10, 1993; Dec 19, 1994; Sept 16, 1995; Dec 6, 1997; May 25, June 1, 1998; May 1, May 3, May 4, May 17, 1999; Dec 1, 2000; June 22, 2001; March 16, March 30, June 6, June 21, July 1, Sept 30, 2002; Nov 25, 2003; March 30, Sept 11, 2004; June 8, Nov 9, 2005; Jan 6, July 22, 2006; Dec 1, 2007; Oct 28, 2010; Nov 12, 2011; Nov 13, 2012; July 23, Nov 21, 2016; June 8, Sept 29, Nov 13, Dec 18, 2021

Times of India: July 31, 1966

Yorkshire Post: March 23, 1954

MAGAZINES

Charles Buchan's Football Monthly: Sept, 1961; May, June, July, Aug, Sept, Nov, 1962; Jan–Dec, 1963–9; Jan–Dec, 1971

Charles Buchan's Football Monthly's World Cup Souvenir, 1966

Christian Science Monitor: Nov 5, 1964

Country Life: July 16, 1921, Sept 7, 1935; Sept 14, 1935

Esquire: June, 2014

FA News: Jan–Dec, 1960–1974

Guardian/Observer: The Seven Deadly Sins of Football (pull-out series): May 5–22, 2009

The League: The Official Centenary Souvenir, Daily Mirror, 1988

Football League Review (renamed *League Football*): Nov 5, Dec 3, Dec 17, Dec 27, 1966; Feb 8, March 11, Aug 19, Sept 17, Sept 23, Oct 7, 1967. Other volumes (no year specified): vols 2/13, 2/33, 3/3, 3/4, 3/6, 3/18, 3/38

Jimmy Hill's Football Weekly: May 31, 1968; May 30, June 27, Aug 1, Sept 26, 1969

The Listener: Jan 20, June 30, Aug 4, Oct 27, 1966; Sept 18, 1969; May 21, 1970; Oct 25, 1973; Dec 19, 1974

Marshall Cavendish Book of Football: five volumes

Picture Post: Oct 12, 1946; Feb 24, 1951; Oct 4, 1952; Aug 29, 1953; Sept 3, 1955; March 3, Oct 15, Dec 24, 1956; Aug 15, 1966; May 13, 1971; June 10, 1982

Soccer Star: Sept–Dec (weekly), 1965; Jan–Dec (weekly), 1966–7

South China Morning Post: Feb 1, Sept 25, Nov 11, 1964; Sept 4, Sept 25, Nov 24, 1965; May 3, May 14, Aug 1, Sept 12, 1974; May 25, 1977; May 9, 1978

The Spectator: Oct 27, 1973

World Soccer: Jan–Dec, 1960–9, 1971–4; *England, '66* (special edition)

World Sports: January, 1961; May, 1963

PROGRAMMES

England v. Argentina, May 9, 1951

England v. Germany, Dec 1, 1954

Ipswich v. West Ham, April 15, 1963

The Arthur Rowe Testimonial Match, 1969

Manchester United v. Celtic (Bobby Charlton Testimonial), Sept 18, 1972

Martin Peters Testimonial, Norwich v. England, Oct 18, 1978

Ipswich Town v. Sheff Utd (Alf Ramsey Tribute), May 9, 1999

OTHER PUBLICATIONS

The Blizzard – The Football Quarterly, issue 21

England's World Cup, Daily Express *Special Publication,* 1966

World Cup, Daily Express *Special Publication,* 1970

World Cup Souvenir, A Football Monthly *Publication,* 1966

World Cup Souvenir, A Football Monthly *and* Goal *Publication*, 1970
World Soccer, winter, 2020

TV/NEWSREEL

Look at Life
Saturday Fever, 1961
The Ball at His Feet, 1961
Behind the World Cup, 1963
How to Take a Penalty, Movietone, 1954
Sportsview (partial recording), BBC, 1963
World Cup Final 1966, BBC, 1966
World Cup Final 1966, ITV, 1966
The Charlton Brothers, ITV 1969
Sir Alf Ramsey: England Soccer Manager, LWT, 1969
Big Jack's Other World, Tyne Tees, 1972
John Arlott, *Parkinson*, 1974
The World Game, ITV, 1976
Skilful Soccer, Tyne Tees, 1977
Summer of '66 (John Motson), 1986 (11-part series)
Time of Their Lives: Manchester United, Sky Sports, 2007
Sir Alf, ITV, 2002
Alfie's Boys, Sky, 2016
England v. West Germany Replay, Sky, 2016
Managing England: The Impossible Job, BBC, 2021

DVDS

Bobby: The Man, The Glory, The Legend, Matthew Lorenzo, Silvertone Films
    and Electric Shadow, 2016
Bobby Charlton: Football Legends, Demand, 2013
Boys from Brazil, narrated by John Motson, BBC, 2006
England v. Scotland 1967, Mastersound, 2004
Everton v. Sheffield Wednesday, 1966 FA Cup Final, ILC Sport, 2004
The FA Cup Finals, Pathé, 2011
Finding Jack Charlton, Noah Media Group, 2020
How England Won the World Cup: '66, Five, 2006
Match of the Day: The Best of the 60s, 70s and 80s, BBC 2004
Matthews, The Original No. 7, Imagination Factory 2017
West Ham v. Preston, FA Cup Final, 1964, BBC, 2005
World Cup Fever, 1966, Green Umbrella, 2006

VIDEOS

Reunited: The 25th Anniversary Tribute to Manchester United's Greatest Triumph, Chrysalis, 1992
They Think It's All Over . . . It Is Now, BBC, 1991

RADIO

Alf Ramsey: England Team Manager, BBC, 1970
Games That Changed Football: The 1966 World Cup Final, BBC, 1996
Desert Island Discs, Jack Charlton, BBC Radio 4, 1996
View from the Boundary, Nobby Stiles, BBC Radio 4, 1997
Jimmy Armfield's Football Legends: Jimmy Greaves, BBC Radio 4, 1997
Master Managers: Alf Ramsey, BBC Radio 5 Live, 1998
The Reunion (Geoff Hurst, George Cohen, Martin Peters), Radio 4, 2006
England Expects, BBC Radio 4, 2016
66: That Was Then, This Is Now, BBC Radio 5, 2016
Alf and Bobby, BBC Radio 5 (replay), 2018
I Was There: 1966 World Cup, BBC Radio 5 Live, 2016
Jimmy Armfield, A Football Gentleman, BBC Radio 5 Live, 2017
Captain Fantastic: Bobby Moore, BBC Radio 5 Live, 2018

LPS

World Cup 1966, Centaur Productions, 1966

INDEX

INDEX